The Global Market

Developing a Strategy to Manage Across Borders

John Quelch

Rohit Deshpande

Editors

 JOSSEY-BASS
A Wiley Imprint
www.josseybass.com

Published by Jossey-Bass
A Wiley Imprint
989 Market Street, San Francisco, CA 94103-1741   www.josseybass.com

Jossey-Bass books and products are available through most bookstores. To contact
Jossey-Bass directly call our Customer Care Department within the U.S. at 800-956-7739,
outside the U.S. at 317-572-3986 or fax 317-572-4002.

Jossey-Bass also publishes its books in a variety of electronic formats. Some content that
appears in print may not be available in electronic books.

Library of Congress Cataloging-in-Publication Data

The global market: developing a strategy to manage across borders/John Quelch, Rohit
Deshpande, editors. — 1st ed.
       p. cm. — (The Jossey-Bass business & management series)
    "A Wiley imprint."
    Includes bibliographical references and index.
    ISBN 0-7879-6857-9 (alk. paper)
    1. Export marketing—Management. 2. International business enterprises—
Marketing. 3. Globalization. I. Quelch, John A. II. Deshpande, Rohit. III. Series.
HF1416.G554   2004
658.8'4—dc22

                                                               2004003711

Printed in the United States of America
FIRST EDITION
HB Printing   10 9 8 7 6 5 4 3 2 1

The Jossey-Bass
Business & Management Series

To our friend, colleague, and mentor

*Emeritus Professor Theodore Levitt
Harvard Business School*

*Eminent marketing thought leader
for executives and academics*

Contents

Introduction

In 1983, the *Harvard Business Review* published an article entitled "The Globalization of Markets" by Harvard Business School professor Theodore Levitt. In this article, Levitt argued that consumer similarities across national boundaries outweighed the differences—that the human aspirations and emotions to which marketers responded were universal in nature. He highlighted "the one great thing all markets have in common—an overwhelming desire for dependable world standard modernity in all things at aggressively low prices."

Greater convergence of tastes among consumers around the world was both a reason for and a consequence of global marketing. In Levitt's view, the traditional decentralized multinational corporation that adapted its product offerings and its marketing programs—at considerable cost—to address the preferences of local customers was fast becoming obsolete. Instead, success would shine on the global corporation that "operates with relative constancy—at low relative cost—as if the entire world (or major regions of it) were a single entity; it sells the same things in the same way everywhere."

Levitt's observations were not motivated by the burgeoning power of American cultural icon brands such as Disney, Marlboro, or McDonald's but the rapid international advance of Japanese manufacturers such as Honda, Panasonic, and Toyota. Their innovations in manufacturing processes and production technology, and perhaps a certain naiveté about the extent of international consumer heterogeneity, resulted in long production runs of high-quality products that exploited "the economics of simplicity and standardization." These Japanese products could then be priced in international markets at levels that even the most patriotic consumers could not ignore. Twenty years on, most commentators

1

now focus on American brands such as Nike and Coca Cola as the exemplars of global standardization.

Levitt was not the first to speak of cultural convergence. As early as 1962, Marshall McLuhan coined the term *global village.* And in 1967, Jean-Jacques Servan-Schreiber published *The American Challenge,* an early complaint about American cultural imperialism. Levitt's focus, however, was on the convergence of consumer preferences being motivated by Japanese, not American, brands. His special contribution was to show how global shifts in consumer preferences stemmed from changes in production systems and demanded a shift in corporate organization structures from multinational to global. But perhaps unfairly, the black and white forcefulness with which Levitt expressed his arguments meant that the essay, in the words of Naomi Klein (2000), a contemporary critic of globalization, "instantly became the manifesto of global marketing" (p. 116).

Levitt's thesis was quickly absorbed by chief executives of large multinationals seeking good arguments to restore central headquarters control over their far-flung, decentralized empires. Aided by the international advertising agencies, they set about designing global marketing programs to reduce the independence of the barons who ran their local subsidiaries around the world. But many marketing experts did not take kindly to Levitt's arguments. Philip Kotler, for example, a leading marketing academic, complained in 1984 that Levitt was "setting marketing back. He wants to bend consumer demand to suit the product rather than vice versa." Long a proponent of market segmentation (and the tailoring of products and programs to the needs of each segment), Kotler maintained, "Many new lifestyles are emerging and new, differentiated markets are opening up. Companies need a wide range of products and a wide range of messages to the consumer, not the reverse" (Lorenz, 1984, p. 26).

The debates about what Levitt said, whether his predictions were well founded, and whether his thesis has stood the test of time were joined again at a Harvard Business School colloquium in May 2003. On the twentieth anniversary of its publication, fifty academics and practitioners from Asia, Europe, and the Americas attended the "Globalization of Markets" colloquium to share ideas about global marketing, past, present, and future.

In the remainder of this Introduction, we set the context for the fifteen colloquium papers that make up the chapters of this book. We review the forces that favor further convergence of consumer tastes around the world and those that do not.

Forces for Convergence

Levitt correctly saw technological change as a force for globalization. His focus was, however, not so much on information technology as on the new process technologies used in Japanese assembly plants to lower costs and improve product quality at the same time. Since 1983, the prodigious improvement in the productivity of computer microprocessors and an equally impressive fall in telecommunications costs have resulted in more people being able to share more information across national boundaries than ever before. The fax machine and the World Wide Web, not foreseen by Levitt, are two additional technologies that facilitate the free flow of information, unimpeded by government oversight. Satellite television enables us to sample foreign cultures, entertainment, and opinion in the comfort of our own living rooms.

The Internet is proving to be an especially important force for cross-cultural communication. Young people throughout the world can interact easily with each other through their own personal computers or those at Internet cafés and, increasingly, through mobile phones that integrate Internet access and text messaging with voice capability. Through an Internet Web site, any small company anywhere in the world with a unique product or service can inexpensively reach out to potential customers worldwide. Demand in the company's domestic market may be inadequate to justify the effort, but the business may become viable when all interested consumers worldwide can be accessed. In this way, small businesses, aided by low shipping costs from DHL or Federal Express, can become global players without having to set up complex networks of distributors in multiple countries.

Thanks to deregulation and price competition in the transportation sector, international travel has also increased dramatically, enabling people to sample and better understand different cultures. The number of passengers carried on international airline routes has trebled in the last twenty years. Travel and tourism now account for 12 percent of world gross domestic product. The results of increased tourism and increased migration are not cultural convergence toward a lowest common denominator norm but a greater appreciation of cultural diversity and an appetite for greater cultural choice in our daily lives. Cities like Amsterdam, with immigrants accounting for almost 50 percent of its population, are valuable cultural melting pots in which diversity is celebrated. As another example, an Indian dish, chicken tikka masala, is now said to be the most frequently ordered item in British restaurants.

Although tourism and migration have increased the flows of people across national boundaries, free movement of labor remains a political hot potato, even within free trade areas such as the European Community. Divergence in wage rates among neighboring countries at different stages of economic development spawns concerns about immigrants stealing the jobs of domestic workers.

Such considerations have not impeded progress toward freer trade and the free flow of capital. Almost $1 trillion worth of currencies is now traded across international boundaries each day. The value of international trade increased 1,700 percent in the second half of the twentieth century, though, interestingly, world trade as a percentage of world gross domestic product only recently returned to the 24 percent level that it stood at in 1900. Global marketing is hardly a new phenomenon. King Gillette, founder of the Gillette Company, had offices in Paris and London by 1905, within five years of opening for business in Boston, and he spoke of his vision of a "World Corporation."

The very growth of multinational corporations, which have treated the world as their oyster and used mergers and acquisitions to achieve global scale, has itself been a further force for convergence. The largest twenty-five companies in the world are now each valued at over $100 billion. In a world of 200 countries, fifty-one of the largest one hundred economies are corporations rather than nation-states. IBM generates more patents in a year than all the citizens of 139 of the world's countries. Successful multinational companies scour their worlds to identify the best new product ideas, source the labor and material inputs to make these ideas reality from wherever in the world it makes sense to do so, and focus on achieving leadership through a constant flow of "next big thing" innovations rather than through the adaptation of existing products and services to local cultures. The mind-sets of their top managements are increasingly supranational rather than wedded to the values or interests of any single nation-state. At the same time, they communicate with one voice, not just by using English as the lingua franca of global business but by sharing a common language of management and financial practices, cultivated over the past century by the leading American business schools.

Against these multinational companies, sovereign nations that might resist the forces of globalization have been largely ineffective. This is partly because the nation-state is a relatively new and fragile institution. Only four of today's nations—China, France, India, and the United Kingdom—existed in anything like their current configuration more than 250 years ago. Three-quarters of today's sovereign states did not exist fifty years ago. The 1990s put multinational companies in the driver's seat, with many emerging economies competing for corporate investment by privatizing, deregulating, and offering various economic sweeteners. Only a few countries such as China, representing vast potential consumer markets, have proved adept at managing the advances of Western multinationals to their advantage.

On the Other Hand . . .

Perhaps it was inevitable that the successful march of the global corporation during the 1990s would spawn a backlash when the economic cycle turned down, exposing the fragility of the foundations on which the promise of prosperity to the emerging economies of the world had been based. Aggravated by a softening in commodity prices and population growth rates that outpaced economic development, it became increasingly evident that with notable exceptions such as the Asian "tiger" economies of South Korea and Taiwan, the gap in per capita income between rich and poor nations had expanded rather than diminished. A comparison of Islamic countries and Organization for Economic Cooperation and Development countries shows that the average per capita income in the latter was seventeen times that in the former in 1970 but that this gap grew to twenty-seven times by 2000. Unsurprisingly, globalization and global corporations have given political leaders in emerging economies a ready scapegoat for their own failures to deliver economic progress to their citizens.

Vocal minorities in Western, notably European, countries have taken to opposing multinational, especially American, corporations. This anti-American sentiment has been more evident in Europe than elsewhere, perhaps because American multinationals during the 1990s were able to put further distance between themselves and their European rivals in almost all product categories except wireless technology and civil aircraft manufacturing. But such sentiments do not appear to spill over into substantial or sustained boycotts of American or global brands. Most consumers do not let their political views cloud their purchase decisions. As Levitt would have contended, everyone everywhere is looking for the best deal, the best price-performance ratio, and few are likely to choose second best to make a political point.

At the same time, multinational corporations have helped their cause by being adept at thinking globally and acting locally. They do so by working in conjunction with local business partners; employing local managers and workers; giving to local charities; acquiring, improving, and relaunching local brands; and adapting their global products and services to local tastes when the costs of doing so can be recouped in local pricing. In other words, by being good local citizens and setting high standards for corporate behavior that local businesses are then pressed to follow, multinational corporations are taking the sting out of potential opposition . . . and the globalization of markets marches on.

Demography and the Global Consumer

There are now 6.1 billion people in the world. The annual population growth rate is 1.2 percent. Thirty percent are under fifteen years of age, but in Germany only 15 percent are under age fifteen compared to over 45 percent in Nigeria and most African nations. Ten percent of the world's population is over sixty years of age, but in Japan, the figure is 23 percent. This will rise in Japan to 42 percent by 2050 as a result of low birthrates and improvements in health care and life expectancy. Simply put, the rich economies of North America, Europe, and Japan are accounting for a progressively lower percentage of the world's population (around only 15 percent today) yet they still command 53 percent of world gross domestic product, 62 percent of world trade, and 86 percent of world equity market capitalization.

The challenge for global marketers can be simply stated but not easily resolved. How do you allocate marketing resources between the markets of the developed world, the principal source of past success and current sales, and the markets of the emerging economies, which may represent the best long-term growth opportunities? Of course, the purchasing power of many in these emerging economies is negligible, but living there are millions of young consumers who have yet to lock in their brand preferences. All evidence suggests that younger people are less bound by cultural traditions and that higher-income, better-educated people living in the rapidly growing cities of these emerging economies are likely to be both more exposed and more receptive to new ideas. Is it the responsibility of the global marketer to figure out how to reach the mass market, or is it sufficient to skim the cream off the top of the market, targeting only the highest-income segments who can afford to pay Western prices? Alternatively, will new models of global marketing be developed by emerging market multinationals like Haier of China, a major manufacturer of domestic appliances, or Samsung of South Korea, the electronics giant that has rapidly come to be ranked as the twenty-fifth most valuable brand in the world?

Conclusion

In 1983, Levitt could not and did not foresee the fax machine or the World Wide Web, two technologies that have brought the world closer together. He could not and did not foresee the defeat of communism, the fall of the Berlin Wall, and the admission of some 3 billion additional consumers into the free market economy. But his viewpoints were prescient nevertheless. Where others saw differences—real or imagined—among the world's consumers, Levitt focused on the similarities. He understood the power of new technologies such as the personal computer and satellite television to facilitate sharing of ideas, values, and products across national boundaries. He had the optimism to believe that the good would drive out the bad. And in the corporate boardroom, his 1983 article fundamentally changed the way in which marketing was discussed. Before Levitt, the onus was invariably on managers who advocated standardized products or marketing programs to prove their case. After Levitt, the burden rested on those who argued for marketing adaptation to show how the extra expense of customization would pay out in extra profitability. Changing the way a question is asked can have a profound effect on practice. This was, perhaps, the greatest impact of Levitt's 1983 article.

PART 1

Developing the Global Mind-Set

Globalization is an accepted part of our transnational vocabulary. Evidence of this lies in part in the power of the word. It splits regions, countries, and states. To some, it is associated with the economies of scale and scope that multinational companies like Coca Cola and Sony leverage as their products become part of cultural landscapes. To others, it brings up images of rock-throwing protesters in Milan and Seattle. It is humbling to realize that twenty years ago, the concept of globalization was quite novel and that one person can take credit for making it part of our common vocabulary: Theodore Levitt.

Globalization is much more than a way of going to market. Channel strategies do not provoke violent physical protest by mobilized activists. Rather, globalization is a weltanschaung, a worldview, a mind-set. It is an ideology as well as a carefully crafted strategy to take brands across the world with a standardizable positioning and brand-level execution tone. Levitt understood this as far back as the early 1980s when he was developing "The Globalization of Markets," an article that would appear in the May-June 1983 issue of the *Harvard Business Review.* Very quickly after the publication of his provocative article, commentaries began to appear in the *New York Times, Washington Post,* the *Wall Street Journal,* and other influential publications. Academics engaged in a debate on the merits of Levitt's arguments. And the debate rages to this day. Levitt's article is required reading in business schools across the world, and it provokes much the same polarized reactions that it did twenty years ago. The question is, Why was this article so powerful and provocative when it was first published? And why does it still weigh in on our consciousness?

In Chapter One, Richard Tedlow and Rawi Abdelal approach these questions from the perspective of business history, situating their discussion within the context of five hundred or more years to understand whether globalization is a new or old phenomenon. Their surprising conclusions surface much of the essence of Levitt's deconstructed essay. It is as much about globalization as a process and a heuristic as it is about globalization as strategy. And, in fact, the former are more revealing since they suggest qualitative changes in the way managers need to look at their companies and the world today. Tedlow and Abdelal carefully distinguish between globalization and internationalization and show how Levitt was perhaps overtly polemical in his writing style but highly accurate in his depiction of what successful firms do in building global businesses.

The lens of history is used in Chapter Two as well, this time in an interview with Levitt by his colleague Stephen Greyser, who wants us to appreciate what led Levitt to write the article on globalization and whether he is surprised that it still generates controversy. In the interview, Levitt amplifies on a fundamental theme in his article—the marketing concept—and suggests that successful global firms both satisfy customer needs and standardize their product offerings. He also describes why he believes his *Harvard Business Review* article generated so much debate by offering a radically different vision of the future than most observers were willing to consider in 1983—and today as well, to some extent.

Hirotaka Takeuchi examines the implications of Levitt's arguments for one country, Japan, in Chapter Three. As he notes, Levitt used Japan and particularly Japanese corporations as exemplars of globalization in his paper. In fact, there were more mentions of Japan than the United States in his article. Yet Japan today seems anything but exemplary in the management of its economy, and very few Japanese firms are benchmarked for their global marketing strategies. Takeuchi suggests that this has happened because Japan and Japanese companies failed to learn the lessons that Levitt set out in his article and have turned their backs on active participation in the global labor, financial, and product markets. His sharply critical and incisive perspective also suggests remedies for Japan to turn around its decline.

CHAPTER 1

Theodore Levitt's "The Globalization of Markets"

An Evaluation After Two Decades

Richard S. Tedlow
Rawi Abdelal

Two decades ago, Theodore Levitt published "The Globalization of Markets" in the *Harvard Business Review*. Doing business across national borders had long been a topic of academic analysis, but Levitt's article, published in the "magazine of decision makers," was aimed separately at business managers. It hit its target.

Levitt himself was "globalized" by 1983. He was world famous for his provocative pronouncements on the new thinking and new action needed to propel business management into the new world it had to create. His articles were widely translated and anthologized, and the *Harvard Business Review* made a small fortune selling his reprints. When Levitt spoke (through the medium of the printed word), managers listened.

Teaching globalization today, it is not difficult, with the priceless benefit of hindsight, to see the flaws in Levitt's argument. In the pages that follow, we make those flaws quite clear. We do, however, believe that this article remains important not just as an artifact of its time but as a picture of the world from which managers can benefit today. It is no accident that this article is still so widely read.

In this chapter, we seek to locate globalization in the context of Levitt's oeuvre. We then offer a new way of thinking about this article, an angle of vision that we believe demonstrates its enduring usefulness.

The Marketing Message of Theodore Levitt

"And if you want biographies," Friedrich Nietzsche once wrote, "do not look for the legend 'Mr. So-and-so, and his times,' but for one whose title might be inscribed 'a fighter against his time.'" That is the role—as a "fighter against his time"—that Theodore Levitt has played during his intellectual life.

This was a role he earned the right to play. Levitt mastered "normal science" before setting off in search of new "paradigms."[1] His doctoral dissertation, "World War II Manpower Mobilization and Utilization in a Local Labor Market," was squarely in the mainstream of academic endeavor.[2] Firmly grounded in economics through his doctoral training at Ohio State, Levitt proved he could satisfy the most rigorous standards of his profession by publishing in the *American Economic Review,* the *Review of Economics and Statistics,* the *Journal of Finance,* and elsewhere.[3]

Levitt's goal, however, was always to make a difference—a big difference not only in his own discipline but in academics as a whole and indeed in society. He wanted to think creatively. It was the combination of his background in formal economics along with a jagged streak of lightning called genius that enabled him to succeed at so doing. One of Levitt's articles is entitled "Marketing Success Through Differentiation—of Anything."[4] His own greatest achievement in differentiation has been of himself.

Theodore Levitt has written numerous articles that have changed the way important people think about important matters (which was his own standard when he served as editor of the *Harvard Business Review*). Among the most noteworthy of these is "The Globalization of Markets," published in 1983.[5]

The article's argument is that new technology, which has "proletarianized" communication, transport, and travel, has created "a new commercial reality—the emergence of global markets for standardized consumer products" of a hitherto undreamed-of magnitude. The era of the "multinational corporation" was drawing to a close, Levitt asserted. The future belonged to the "global corporation." The global corporation did not cater to local differences in taste. Those differences were being overwhelmed by the ability of the global corporation to market standardized products of high quality at a cost lower than that of competitors due to "enormous economies of scale in production, distribution, marketing, and management." The global corporation was being called forth by a new era of "homogenized demand."

Levitt's claim was breathtaking in its inclusiveness. "Nothing," he declared, "is exempt." Not steel, not automobiles, not food, not clothes. Variety costs money, and the modern consumer demanded the best for less.

Levitt is a man of the world, quite aware of the conflicts that pockmark it. He makes reference to the 1979 Iranian uprising that resulted in the downfall of the shah, to the Nigerian-Biafran civil war, to life in Bahia in Brazil and in Krasnoyarsk in Siberia. But though beliefs might differ sharply from one nation or region to the next, consumption patterns were converging. The rebels in Iran were wearing "fashionable French-cut trousers and silky body shirts." In Biafra, "soldiers carrying bloodstained swords" were "listening to transistor radios while drinking Coca-Cola." The world was witnessing nothing less than the "vindication of the Model T," the basic transportation vehicle of which Henry Ford said, "It takes you there, and it brings you back."

There is no other appeal like price. People like money, and they want to spread it over as many goods as they can. What the global company understands, which the multinational does not, is the power of scarcity: "Nobody takes scarcity lying down; everybody wants more."

If "The Globalization of Markets" were the only article one had ever read about marketing, one would find its argument compelling. But in the context of its times, what Levitt was proposing was little short of a revolution in both how companies organized themselves and in how they thought about what they were doing. Levitt's argument flew in the face of hallowed principles of marketing both and what seemed to be the stark realities of the world as it was in 1983.

Consider, for example, what had come to be known during the quarter-century prior to the 1983 publication of "Globalization" as "the marketing concept." We do not mean *a* marketing concept; in fact we must italicize the article: *the* marketing concept.[6]

By 1983, this idea, so simple that it scarcely seems to deserve the label "concept," was that companies should give customers what they want. The marketing concept gained currency during the 1950s and was founded on the belief that the "problem of production" had been solved. Supply-side shortages not being in the offing, there was no need for companies to be guided by a production analogue to the marketing concept. "The sales concept," such as it was, had also fallen into disrepute in the literature. The sales concept was about pushing a product onto the consumer through sales techniques.[7] The "sales concept" was waning as early as 1941. IBM, for example, which was in the process of developing one of the greatest sales forces in history, was instructing its salespeople by that time to tell prospects that their job was not "to sell" but "to serve."[8]

Thus, we arrive at "the marketing concept." Behind the phrase lay the idea that business begins not with the factory but with the customer. Marketing was the most important of business functions because it drove everything else—or at least that was the ideal. In practice, businesses kept seeming to revert to the satisfaction of their own internal needs at the expense of customer desires. Look around, and you will find that this is true today. The promise of customer satisfaction is omnipresent. (No company promises customer dissatisfaction.) Delivering on the promise is a good deal less common.

There are two specific references to the Marketing Concept in "Globalization," and the idea is alluded to elsewhere without being labeled. Levitt treats this central idea of his discipline without much respect. Somehow, corporations had allowed themselves to fall prey to "the perverse practice of the marketing concept and the absence of any kind of marketing imagination. . . ." (p. 98). "Most executives in multinational corporations are thoughtlessly accommodating. They falsely presume that marketing means giving the customer what he says he wants rather than trying to understand exactly what he'd like."

What Levitt appears to be saying is that it is up to the company to know more about what the customer wants than the customer himself or herself does, or at least more than the customer can articulate. He uses as an illustration the failed attempt by Hoover to market its washing machine throughout western Europe. The cause of this failure was Hoover's "'proper' marketing orientation." The company conducted consumer research at a fine-grained level that revealed that customers in various countries wanted different features. The manufacturing costs of providing these features drove the price of the appliance up, and the product did not sell.

What went wrong? Two things. First, Hoover asked the wrong questions. It sought, in the type of phrase for which Levitt became famous, to learn "what features [customers] wanted in a washing machine rather than what they wanted out of life."[9]

Second, Hoover paid too much attention to what people said and too little to what was actually going on in the marketplace. Did everyone want a washing machine specifically customized to their living space? Yes. Was everyone willing to pay substantially more money for such a washing machine, thus depriving themselves of other possessions? No. "[People] preferred a low-priced automatic . . . even though [it] failed to fulfill all their expressed preferences. The supposedly meticulous and demanding German customers violated all expectations by buying the simple, low-priced Italian machines" (p. 98).

The conclusion was that a cursory examination of the Hoover story would leave one with the belief that global marketing is impossible because of the strength of national wants and needs. But what a little digging reveals is that we have seen a "distorted version" and the "perverse practice" of the marketing concept. And we have seen something else: what Levitt referred to as a "failure of nerve."

Marketers must be more than mere receptacles of information (which is sometimes poorly specified and collected). They must actively mold the markets to which they sell. If Hoover had acted in that aggressive fashion, it would have succeeded. With will and vision, global marketing could become a reality.

Levitt was well aware at that time of the appeal of low prices.[10] In recent years, Clayton Christensen of the Harvard Business School wrote *The Innovator's Dilemma*,[11] a book that became world famous and in which he asserted ideas quite similar to Levitt's. Christensen's thesis is that in their rush to give customers precisely what they want, companies customize too much, spend too much, and therefore charge too much. They thus leave themselves open to the "disruptive innovator," marketing a product that is not perfect in terms of every function and feature but is good enough and a lot less expensive. Although Christensen's book is not concerned with world trade, the basic market dynamic he sees conforms to

Levitt's. Variety is often generated by organizational dynamics internal to the firm. Customers tend to be unwilling to pay as much for that variety as marketers may like to think.

In one sense, the ideas in "The Globalization of Markets" are not surprising. For years, people had been coming to think of the world as a single unit rather than as a patchwork of nations and customers. The first armed conflict deemed a "world" war took place between 1914 and 1918 (even though it was less a global conflict than, say, the Seven Years' War of 1756 to 1763, which stretched from Canada to India). The term *global village* was coined in 1960.[12] The realization that radioactive fallout from nuclear weapons could have global consequences led to the Nuclear Test Ban Treaty of 1963,[13] and general concerns for the environment led to Earth Day in April 1970.[14] The space race, beginning with *Sputnik* in 1957 and climaxing with the moon landing in 1969, endowed human beings with a whole new perspective on "spaceship earth."

Meanwhile, a little closer to home, social critics following World War II were beginning to complain of the very homogenization that Levitt was inviting corporations to exploit. The term *Coca-Colonization* gained a certain currency during the 1940s and 1950s, suggesting the imposition of American cultural values on the world through the spread of its consumer products.[15] In 1967, the French journalist Jean-Jacques Servan-Schreiber published *The American Challenge,* in which he portrayed Europe being overrun by American capital and American business organization practices.[16] Various domestic observers as well were noting with disapproval the "global reach" of what appeared to be the inexorably growing American business firm.[17]

That said, there is another sense in which the ideas in "The Globalization of Markets" are daring. In 1983, the world was still very much a bipolar place, divided between "communist" and "democratic" nations. The cold war had heated up considerably with the Soviet invasion of Afghanistan in 1979. It was in 1983 that President Ronald Reagan called the Soviet Union the "evil empire," and this cartoon-strip phrase struck a responsive chord in much of the American public.[18] Those people living under communist regimes knew precious little of markets in the Western sense, never mind marketing.

In 1983, there were, in fact, only a handful of countries in which corporations had home offices that sold products or services outside the home country borders. North America, western Europe, and Japan fairly much exhaust the list. Firms located in these nations accounted for the overwhelming bulk of world trade, and very little of that trade was with the approximately 32 percent of the world's population living in communist countries.[19] Thus, when Levitt spoke of globalization, he was excluding a large portion of the globe as it was at that time.

Even among the democratic, capitalist countries, barriers to trade were far more daunting than they have since become. Tariffs, subsidies, orderly marketing agreements, and outright prohibitions were everywhere apparent. Markets were, and are, governed by rules. Indeed, markets cannot exist without rules.[20] The rule-making unit in 1983 (as is also predominantly true today) was neither the corporation nor some supranational body such as the World Trade Organization. It was the nation in which goods were being bought and sold, from which goods were being exported and to which imported. Levitt wrote that technology was the unstoppable force leading toward globalization, but all the technology in the world could not have opened up the Japanese home market to foreign imports in 1983.

A marketing textbook published in 1972, *Marketing: A Contemporary Analysis,* devoted only 27 of its 776 pages to international marketing. On the first of those pages, it declares: "Since this chapter is based entirely on distinctions among national markets, it is important to establish at the outset that the nation is a meaningful unit for market analysis."[21] Table 1.1, from that textbook, outlines how countries differ and the importance of those differences for marketing. Let us look at just one of the entries in this table and see what impact it might have on the globalization of marketing. The text at the bottom of the last column on the right mentions "Specific restrictions on messages."

When Polaroid introduced in the United States its camera that developed its own film, the company advertised heavily on television. The product was particularly sensitive to television advertising, which could demonstrate the seemingly miraculous phenomenon of instant photography. It was no accident that by 1960, Polaroid was selling at more than ninety times earnings as advertisements prompted excited customers to flock to retail outlets.[22] This was the essence of the "pull" strategy in marketing, and it made Polaroid the channel commander in its product category.

Table 1.1. Elements of a Marketing Program

Factors Limiting Standardization	Product Design	Pricing	Distribution	Sales Force	Advertising and Promotion; Branding and Packaging
Market characteristics					
Physical environment	Climate Product use conditions		Customer mobility	Dispersion of customers	Access to media Climate
Stage of economic and industrial development	Income levels Labor costs in relation to capital costs	Income levels	Consumer shopping patterns	Wage levels availability of manpower	Needs for convenience rather than economy Purchase quantities
Cultural factors	Custom and tradition Attitudes toward foreign goods	Attitudes toward bargaining	Consumer shopping patterns	Attitudes toward selling	Language, literacy Symbolism
Industry conditions					
Stage of product life cycle in each market	Extent of product differentiation	Elasticity of demand	Availability of outlets Desirability of private brands	Need for missionary sales effort	Awareness, experience with products
Competition	Quality levels	Local costs Prices of substitutes	Competitors' control of outlets	Competitors' sales forces	Competitive expenditures, messages
Marketing institutions					
Distributive system	Availability of outlets	Prevailing margins	Number and variety of outlets available	Number, size, dispersion of outlets	Extent of self-service
Advertising media and agencies			Ability to "force" distribution	Effectiveness of advertising, need for substitutes	Media availability, costs, overlaps
Legal restrictions	Product standards Patent laws Tariffs and taxes	Tariffs and taxes Antitrust laws Resale price maintenance	Restrictions on product lines Resale price maintenance	General employment restrictions Specific restrictions on selling	Specific restrictions on messages, costs Trademark laws

Source: Adapted from R. D. Buzzell and others, *Marketing: A Contemporary Analysis,* 2d ed. (New York: McGraw-Hill, 1972), p. 641.

Pull marketing failed in France with the same product and the same customer benefit. Why? In France, commercials were not allowed on television. That tremendous power of demonstration coming right into their living room therefore could not drive customers into stores and pull the product through the distribution system. Push marketing, with heavy reliance on the retailer, was the only alternative.[23] This one illustration could be multiplied a thousandfold.

One of the authors of *Marketing: A Contemporary Analysis,* the textbook just referred to, was Theodore Levitt. What had happened in the decade between the publication of the textbook and "The Globalization of Markets" to change his mind? A lot. The position of the United States as economic hegemon was being rapidly eroded. The oil shocks of 1973 and 1979 had exposed American vulnerability to shortages of the most basic of raw materials of what was still the auto-industrial age. The disastrous war in Vietnam and the Watergate scandal had fundamentally shaken the public's faith in government. The stagflation of the Carter administration during the late 1970s did nothing to restore that faith.

On the business scene, the decade was just as gloomy. In industry after industry, from television to tires, American firms were losing share in foreign markets as foreign-based corporations were making significant inroads in the United States. In 1980, the United States ceased being the world leader in automobile manufacture, a position that it had held since the introduction of the Model T Ford in 1908.[24] The bilateral trade deficit between Japan and the United States in this industry alone had reached previously unimaginable levels.

In this context, the moment had come for new ideas, and so the timing of "The Globalization of Markets" was perfect. Perhaps by intellectual reorientation, changes could be made in the organization and operation of business that would lead to a rebirth of growth and greatness. Perhaps the remarkable changes in technology that were taking place would enable globalization to become a reality if business executives had the courage to cast aside old ideas and adopt the new views that the future demanded.

Levitt did not hedge his bets in "Globalization." Indeed, it is the categorical nature of his expression that makes the article so easy to criticize.[25] But therein also lies its genius. As often with Levitt's work, the medium is the message. He does not offer a "ten-step program" systematically to improve the efficiency of marketing beyond the borders of the home country. Instead, he shouts, "Wake up!"

What we now propose to do is discuss the extent to which markets really have become globalized. We have read Levitt's article, and we are awake. When we look around, what do we see having happened between 1983 and today?

Two Ways to Think About Globalization

There are two ways to think about globalization—as a trend and as a heuristic—and most people do not distinguish between them.[26] We argue that they should and that if they did, they would look at the economic environment in which they make decisions in a more useful way. The first way to think about globalization is as an actual process of economic integration: the acceleration of flows of goods and capital and perhaps many other things as well. In this sense, there may be not a single globalization process but many linked processes of globalization, each of which demands an answer to the question: "The globalization of *what*?" Thus, we hear and read about the globalization of finance, of trade, of policy ideas, of culture, of almost anything else. This is perhaps the most common way people think and talk about globalization, and it is useful.

This first conception of globalization—as an evolving trend changing the world in which we live—inherently creates a certain kind of debate because there are naysayers who marshal evidence to suggest that the economic integration we have supposedly seen in the past decades is either not new, historically speaking, or, when looked at in strictly economic terms, not nearly as complete as its votaries would have us believe.

The historical question rests on whether the world economy was more globalized in the late nineteenth and early twentieth centuries, the heyday of the gold standard and British hegemony, than it is today. Some find that levels of trade and financial integration were higher (or at least as high) then as now. This historical concern with globalization rests on a particular counterfactual about the past and the future, and it is a debate encapsulated by the question, "Is globalization today really different than globalization a hundred years ago?"[27] One could push this line of thought even further back in time to the early modern world or back even further to the Phoenicians.[28] There was world trade before there were nations in the modern sense.

The economic question about globalization implies a different counterfactual: that the integration of markets for goods and capital is complete, and the evidence brought to bear on the question most often deals not only with the size of the flows but the differences in prices in national markets for goods as well. Here again the debate is not settled, but the available evidence certainly indicates that markets for goods and capital are quite far from "perfect integration," as the economist would put it.[29] In other words, the issue is whether the world's markets really function as though they are, in the words of Kenichi Ohmae, "borderless."[30] The answer is that they do not, save perhaps a few instances in Europe, Asia, or North America that did not encompass the broader perspective of the whole world.

Rivers of ink, undammed by a great many smart and well-informed scholars, have been spilled on these historical and economic debates that surround the process of globalization. We cannot resolve the debates in this chapter. Indeed, we are happy enough to conclude the following: that the markets for goods and capital across national borders are more vibrant than they were at the end of World War II (though not, perhaps, before World War I) and that there are some new aspects of the process of globalization (such as increasing intra-industry, even intrafirm trade) as well as some not-so-new aspects. One of the drivers behind all of this activity certainly was technology, but technology has been only part of the story.

Much more profound has been the revolution in politics: the ideological triumph of markets that led so many governments around the world to embrace the world economy. This revolution is not independent of technology. To some important degree, the two are intertwined. Would the Berlin Wall have fallen had there been no television or no fax machine? Television made it clear, even to the illiterate, that there was a cornucopia of consumer goods generated by market economics that communist nations knew not of. One of the hottest items that Western "subversives" smuggled (literally) into the former Soviet Union were blue jeans. This is evidence that in some form, Coca-Colonization persisted. Even such consumer goods, long taken for granted in the West, were not at all trivial to people to whom they were denied. And technology meant that knowledge of such products literally floated over the most heavily fortified of national borders on the air.[31]

One of the most important lessons derived from the study of history is not only that today's reality is different from yesterday's but that it may also be different from tomorrow's. Governments chose openness before World War I, but they chose closure after it. Governments have chosen openness again in recent years. Might some of them try to close their borders once again in the future?

Politics is fundamentally unlike technology in this respect. The steam engine, or atomic weaponry, once invented, can never be made to disappear. The genie is out of the bottle. The rules that govern trade can, by contrast, be changed by the stroke of a pen. An advantage of conceiving of globalization as a process is that it brings such thoughts to the forefront.

But what does all this mean for the business manager, Levitt's target audience? Addressing this question is a task our colleague at Harvard Business School Pankaj Ghemawat has performed admirably in the *Harvard Business Review*. Starting implicitly from the premise that the Levitt thesis is flawed, he argues that national markets are more "distant" in various ways than most managers appreciate. According to Ghemawat, national markets may be distant culturally (including religion, race, social norms, and language), administratively (including political and economic relationships), geographically, and economically (including disparities in wealth and income).[32] Moreover, Levitt's analysis does not help us to understand any of these distances. Geographical distance still limits the extent to which some markets can be penetrated with some products and services. Economic distance does so even more, since countries have not converged in their incomes during the past twenty years. Far from it. With the exception of several East Asian countries, poor countries have stayed poor, and rich countries have stayed rich.

Administrative distance is shorthand for world politics, and the politics of trade, finance, and production have unambiguously changed: the embrace of market-oriented policies by countries around the world is a defining feature of the cold war world and has been even more of the post–cold war world. This policy convergence set the stage for the economic processes in which we are interested. Without international cooperation and openness, the expansion of trade, finance, and production across national boundaries would have been impossible. Why this happened is a fascinating question, about which scholars do not agree except on one point: that it was not solely or perhaps even primarily technological change, as Levitt argues, that led to the political change that made the expansion of markets possible. Technological change played a role, as we suggested in our brief discussion of television. But although technology may have played a part in the drama of this great policy transformation, experts agree that it was a supporting actor, not the star of the show.

It is on the issue of cultural distance that Ghemawat and Levitt most clearly disagree. For Ghemawat, cultural distance is a parameter that firms should analyze and take for granted. But Levitt tells us this is changing, in part through the influence of firms. What we can see clearly is that the world of consumers did not become fully homogenized in the twenty years since Levitt wrote his article. If it were true, then the symbols of the twin towers of the World Trade Center would not have been so full of meaning for those who admired and despised them.

The events of September 11, 2001, are full of tragedy and irony with regard to the debate about the globalization of markets. Rather than homogeny, it would appear that modern products and services have generated a profound and unanticipated reaction. Groups of religious fundamentalists are using the fruits of high technology—the aircraft, the Internet, cellular telephones, and others—to attack the businesses that have created that technology and the governments under which these businesses have prospered. These antimodernists employ the most modern means to fight the modern world, which they seem to view as a godless kleptocracy. Al-Qaeda has no "homogenized" consumers.

If a prediction about trends in market integration were the only contribution of Levitt's article, then the usefulness of the concept of globalization to today's manager would be beyond questionable. Indeed, we have discovered a veritable cottage industry devoted to the task of exploring how wrong Levitt was about the trend. But if Levitt is so wrong, why would anyone still read his article? We should preface our discussion of this point by emphasizing that people do. When Harvard Business School professor Pankaj Ghemawat created the course "Globalization and Strategy," his M.B.A. students read Levitt on the first day of class, and it is still true in 2003 when Tarun Khanna teaches it. In 2002, students in Debora Spar's doctoral seminar, "The Political Economy of International Business," at Harvard Business School still read Levitt—on the first day of class. The introduction to John Quelch and Christopher Bartlett's *Global Marketing Management* has exactly one footnote: to Levitt's article.[33] This is almost twenty years later, when practically everyone is prepared to pronounce Levitt's argument wrong. One might well say that this is a puzzle that needs to be explained.

We can explain it. The reason to read Levitt is to find out not what is true about global markets but how a manager ought to begin to think about them. It is one thing to say that what Levitt argued about globalization was wrong, that what he predicted did not come true, and that the implications he derived for managers were (almost outrageously) overdrawn. It is quite another to suggest that therefore his analysis was not deeply insightful. We believe it was, and that if one treats Levitt's views on globalization as a heuristic, as an analytical lens through which to understand markets that cross national borders, then the continuing usefulness and remarkable prescience of an article that is maligned as often as it is misunderstood in the early twenty-first century becomes clear.

If one understands globalization as a heuristic, it becomes clear that there can be more than one heuristic. And this is the second perspective on globalization, shared by many other scholars, more often political scientists and sociologists than economists. Pankaj Ghemawat has translated the work of economists into English (from algebra) for managers. We want to offer just a suggestion of what might be gained by making the pertinent work of political scientists and sociologists similarly accessible.

Our View: Levitt's Globalization as a Conceptual Lens

Globalization has not always been a word, and the phrase *global markets* is a recent invention as well. There were perfectly good words to describe the markets of the world—words like *international*—and the firms that operated in international markets—like *multinational.* So why would Levitt insist on using the language of the *globe?* The answer is to indicate a qualitative change in the character of the world's markets, not a quantitative change. The world that Levitt described did not consist of more trade; it consisted of trade that was different and transformative. This is what is missing from the economists' account of globalization and from the debates about globalization as a process. From Levitt's perspective, one could not resolve the debate he sought to spark about globalization with data on world trade as a percentage of world product, or the size of capital flows across national borders, or how many countries have high ratios of exports and imports to their gross domestic product, or whether the price of an undifferentiated product was the same in Boston or Bombay. All those measures are of how internationalized the world economy is, not whether it is globalizing.

The distinction between internationalization and globalization is a deeply meaningful one and important for managers to understand. The reason is that in principle, the evidence about the size and expansion of markets could be consistent with both, since they are ways of describing the world, of interpreting the economic interdependence of societies living in different countries. We are amazed to find that the most provocative idea in Levitt's article is so systematically misunderstood. For Levitt, globalization is a concept that describes much more than just an increase in economic exchange across borders; it describes a change in the character of those exchanges, which then transforms the societies engaged in the exchange.

Thus, Levitt's central argument is that communications technology has allowed all societies to engage modernity, leading them toward the "same common goals—alleviation of life's burdens, and the expansion of discretionary time and spending power."[34] The implications for firms are his central, enduring insight: "Preferences are constantly shaped and reshaped."[35] Thus, globalization implies economic activity in the absence of national boundaries, whereas internationalization implies an increased number of transactions across the borders of nation-states, which are still very much controlled by governments that can choose, and unchoose, openness. Global corporations operate in a globalized economy, whereas multinational corporations flourish in a highly internationalized economy. Levitt insists that "the multinational and global corporation are not the same thing."[36] The multinational corporation produces goods tailored for national markets, while the global corporation produces standardized goods for all markets.

These views have, in retrospect, provided Levitt with bedfellows he may not have expected, because while not necessarily strange, they are strangers to some scholars of economics and business. We have in mind political scientists and sociologists. For the most astute students of globalization among these social scientists, the Levitt interpretation of globalization has become quite standard, although his name rarely appears in their footnotes. Perhaps his overstatement was overkill, or perhaps these scholars should be better informed of what is written in the *Harvard Business Review*. Either way, there is no getting around the fact that Levitt's views on globalization have become part of an emerging paradigm in the study of the politics of the world economy.

For political scientists and sociologists, who have developed their insights outside the radar of many managers, the distinction between globalization and internationalization as ways to understand the world is largely an elaboration of Levitt's basic insight into what economists would call the "endogeneity of preferences"—that people might change their minds about what they want depending on how they interact with others. Economic globalization is convergent and transformative, while economic internationalization is divergent and additive. Globalization is a description of a new kind of density of economic interactions among societies, while internationalization implies a reduction in national restrictions in commercial exchange. Globalization results from convergence of the preferences of consumers, who are increasingly members of a global society; internationalization results from the behavior of firms and governments in a merely international economy. Globalization is about new types of relations and new kinds of economic actors; internationalization emphasizes the behavior and attributes of traditional actors, such as multinational firms and national governments.[37]

The issue for an individual firm is to take these conceptual lenses and look at their markets through them. Is your market global or international? These are important debates to have, just as the two debates about globalization as a process are important. But answers are more elusive, since the real question is not whether the globalization heuristic is right or wrong, but whether it is useful or not—useful to understand the world, useful for marketing strategy, and useful for production strategy. One can think about the degree to which a market, or even the world economy, is internationalized. The internationalization of trade and finance has ebbed and flowed during the past 150 years, primarily in response to the conditions for political order in the world economy.[38] But whether a market is globalized, in Levitt's terms, is a matter of qualitative change.

The best tool for managers to understand their markets may be neither globalization nor internationalization. There are other ideas about how best to describe the world economy and the markets that compose it. Regionalization, for example, is another lens through which to view markets.[39] Regional integration tends to increase trade among members of a region, and perforce divert it from those outside it. And so the European Union, the North Atlantic Treaty Organization, the Association of Southeast Asian Nations, MERCOSUR, and various other regional groupings have changed the world's markets in ways that neither Levitt nor analysts of globalization can describe. To make things more complicated, the world's regionalisms are different. Each regionalism has its own logic and process, its own dominant countries, its own formal and informal political and economic ties. Managers must also therefore consider the differences between, for example, a process of European economic integration (with Germany at its center) based on formal rules and a distinctly different process of Asian economic integration (with Japan at its center) based on informal business and social networks across borders.[40] In any case, it may turn out that the regional strategy, rather than the global or the local strategy, becomes the dominant response of firms.

The central point is that each of these concepts—globalization, internationalization, and regionalization—is merely a concept, and judgment is required to apply each of them to specific situations. We believe that for many managers, the analytical lens of globalization—certainly of the extreme variety—will not significantly help them to understand their markets better or to defeat their competitors in them. John Quelch and Edward Hoff made substantially the same point just a few years after Levitt wrote his essay, arguing,

"Too often, executives view global marketing as an either/or proposition—either full standardization or local control. But when a global approach can fall anywhere on a spectrum from tight worldwide coordination on programming details to loose agreement on a product idea, why the extreme view?"[41] Levitt was right that when a global strategy works, it works astonishingly well. But we believe global strategies work, and will work, much less frequently than Levitt predicted.[42]

Concluding Reflections

In sum, we offer some reflections on the two globalizations that exist uneasily in Levitt's article—the process and the heuristic— the former about which he was mostly wrong and the latter for which his analysis is immensely useful. Levitt foresaw the power of globalization. In some ways, he overestimated its power, as we have seen. Even in France, a country that is in many ways very tightly integrated with both the European and the world economy, society has reacted against this very power and bought so many copies of a book entitled *L'Horreur économique* to make it a recent best-seller.[43] With Enron's behavior in the state of Maharahstra in mind, Indian novelist Arundhati Roy, author of *The God of Small Things*, wrote an influential antiglobalization essay that put forth a parable about Rumpelstiltskin.[44] Environmental protesters have descended on Seattle and Geneva. Governments too tend to be jealous of their autonomy from markets, as Malaysia's celebrated and infamous (depending on whom you ask) capital controls during the Asian financial crisis indicate.[45] Today we would place these reactions to globalization among the milder and less disconcerting of them.

Levitt assumed that globalization, the process of which he discerned so early on, would proceed until its ultimate completion. However, there have been many pitfalls along the way. The political and social constraints on globalization that appear more evident to us every day may not undermine the process of globalization, but they will probably prevent it from reaching an end point.

However, Levitt also underestimated the power of globalization. He wrote about nationalism as though it is a force that inherently pushes against the pressures of globalization.[46] But even some nationalisms have been transformed. Many of the nationalist movements that arose as the Soviet Union was disintegrating sought to embrace capitalism and democracy and anything else deemed by global civil society to make a state advanced, modern, and especially "European." Their idea was that if whatever came before— Soviet communism—was wrong, then its opposite must be right. Not only were we reminded about how variable nationalisms can be in their goals but how much the world really did change during the past twenty years.[47]

What constitutes globalization, in our way of thinking, is interaction that changes things rather than leaving them the same. Successful firms and the managers who run them rarely leave the world the way they found it. The same is true of the global economy, whose markets have, as Levitt predicted, been transformed by the efforts of firms to listen more deeply to consumers. Rather than taking consumers' preferences as given, as facts of lives and markets, they have treated them as outcomes themselves, with profound effect. Not all consumers have been persuaded, and not all markets transformed. Some are merely still international. Some are regional. But there are some global markets out there, and Levitt's story has rightly convinced managers to think about whether those are their markets, and if not, whether they can be made so by their efforts. If all markets were global, the world of managers would become dull. One strategy would fit them all; the relentless drive for scale and scope would dominate their thinking. In that sense, Levitt was writing about the end of business history, just as Fukuyama had written about the end of political and economic history, when a few ideas were ascendant, with nothing to challenge them.[48] Fukuyama fretted that our world at the end of history would become a boring place, as Levitt's world of globalized markets would have been for us. We are lucky that he was wrong about the outcome.

And we are lucky that he was right about the way the global markets work, through changes in preferences as firms and consumers, capitalisms and cultures, interact with one another. Globalization is transformative. The market is not what firms find; the market is what firms make of it.

Finally, we are also unlucky that Levitt was right. We now live in a world where people react negatively as well as positively to the entreaties and devices of dominant, global, and often emphatically Western firms. One other thing Levitt missed was the possibility that the globalization of markets would produce reactions against it. The various fundamentalisms of the world are frequently anti-modern, occasionally anti-Western, and sometimes strikingly violent. Some societies may have witnessed increasing homogeneity in their preferences, but others have seen increasing heterogeneity, a divergence from the direction of trade and financial integration, a withdrawal from the marketization of social life.

CHAPTER 2

"The Globalization of Markets"

A Retrospective with Theodore Levitt

Stephen A. Greyser

Ted Levitt is a legend through the impacts of his ideas on both the business and academic worlds. "Marketing Myopia" (1960), "Marketing Success Through the Differentiation of Anything," (1980), and the 1983 "The Globalization of Markets" are the best known of his two dozen *Harvard Business Review* articles. Among his numerous books are *The Marketing Imagination* and *Innovation in Marketing*.

We had hoped that Ted could join us in person to discuss the article, but this was not feasible. However, he did agree to sit down with me a short time ago and share some reflections and perspectives.

At the outset of the interview, I provide brief background on Ted's career and his influence on management thinking up to the time of the "globalization" article. We then turn to conversation. The topics and questions on which Ted comments include these: What experiences and phenomena led him to write this article? What perspective existing at that time was he trying to affect or replace? How, if at all, did he think the idea of globalization conflicted with the notion that tailoring one's offerings to groups of consumers is the most desirable marketing approach? In his view, how have changes over the past twenty years affected the core idea of globalization? Is the globalization idea affected by the growth of nationalism in many parts of the world? And is he surprised that the article still gets a lot of attention more than twenty years later?

By way of brief background, Ted Levitt came to the Harvard Business School in 1959, following an undergraduate degree from Antioch, a Ph.D. in economics from Ohio State, and several years of teaching. Almost immediately, in mid-1960, he achieved international renown with the award-winning *Harvard Business Review* (*HBR*) article "Marketing Myopia." Known to thousands of students and executives, the article asked the simple but profound and provocative question, "What business are you in?"

In 1983, with twenty *HBR* articles and six books later, the prolific Ted Levitt authored "The Globalization of Markets." He asserted in that article that well-managed companies had moved from emphasis on customizing products to offering globally standardized products. The accompanying economies of scale in production, distribution, markets, and management allowed for lower prices everywhere—and a major competitive advantage. "The globalization of markets is at hand," he wrote. "Companies that do not adapt to the new global realities will become victims of those that do," he concluded. These then controversial ideas generated a firestorm of debate.

Greyser: Ted, let me begin by asking you to roll back the years to 1983. What stimulated you to write the article originally? What events or experiences especially affected your thinking?

Levitt: For a long time before 1983, I had noted that one of the remarkable things happening was the linkage between low-priced goods, on the one hand, and fashionability, a high degree of functionality, and quality, on the other. For those companies that could do it, the result was a larger market share. I had a tendency to talk about this in terms of Woolworth's, Kresge, and other low-price retailers. Then something unusual happened. As the world moved more to high-tech products, to complex products, the world also saw suddenly a vast reduction in the price of those as well. The most obvious example was the automobile. Imports such as Toyota and VW were successful in the United States with relatively low-priced, well-performing cars. All of a sudden in this country, we were getting a high-quality, relatively low-priced automobile from a foreign company with no prior established presence here. It was contrary to expectation that low price was associated with high quality.

Greyser: So in essence what we were seeing was a global standard for the product in a technologically advanced set of categories. In addition to these consumer products, you also saw the same phenomenon on the business-to-business side, right?

Levitt: Yes. The United States imported technologically sophisticated products—milling machines, lathes, components of certain kinds of products. For these industrial products, there is a universal technical language among customers and sellers all over the world.

Greyser: If we consider your presentation of the globalization idea at the time, did you think that you were telling a story to people whose belief set was different, or did you think they just had not gotten to the observational perspective that you were advancing?

Levitt: I think it was the latter. They had grown up in a world in which companies were making things in one place and selling them in another. The most common of these were mid-European companies—in Germany, Czechoslovakia, Austria, Italy. They always exported, because local markets were not large enough to take all the output, and their costs were related to the total volume of business they could do.

Greyser: So you weren't trying to change the minds of corporate leaders?

Levitt: I didn't feel I had to change anybody's mind about anything. That was not my mission. My mission was to explain it to myself.

Greyser: Some people said then and say now that the notion of globalization runs against the grain of serving consumers in smaller groups than the largest mass. What do you say to that?

Levitt: I say yes and no. The idea of the marketing concept is to give people what they want in the places they want it at a reasonable price and so forth. That's common.

Greyser: And widely believed as the bedrock of marketing.

Levitt: That, I think, accounts for a lot of the disputation that went on regarding the article. The article did succeed in stimulating a great deal of comment. It did that by itself . . . It was just out there. The audiences were creating a big noise. The audiences were publicizing what I had said more than I was. There were newspaper articles, seminars, meetings. It became almost fashionable to talk about this. The *New York Times, Washington Post,* and the *Wall Street Journal* had feature articles about it in the course of one week. They created a lot of furor, because they emphasized the idea of globalization in contrast to multinational corporations, which tried to design their products, distribution systems, and communications for the special characteristics of certain countries and markets.

The global corporation is not that wedded to having to do that, although it may still do it. It would be in the most memorable sort of products, such as the consumer products we know about: Coke, Pepsi, McDonald's. They are not fashioned to suit the needs of certain markets. They are simply sold in those markets about the same way they are sold successfully at home. The same is true of photographic film. It comes from big manufacturers that sell all over the world, such as Fujitsu and Kodak. You see those brands everywhere.

Greyser: One of the phenomena of the early part of the twenty-first century in some places is the growth of nationalism, national pride, and the like and the allegation that global marketers are engaged in commercial imperialism. How does that affect the core idea of the globalization of markets?

Levitt: You could argue that it confirms it. It is pretty clear that in different parts of the world, we see lots of reaction and resistance to the encroaching presence and success of worldwide brands. The reason is that to some people, it looks as though it is a foreign intrusion on domestic industry and violates cultures and habits and traditional ways of doing business. This becomes converted into the notion of what you [SG] called commercial imperialism.

The octave level of reaction shows very clearly that there is a lot at stake.

Greyser: Does it change the way that the successful U.S.-based or non-U.S.-based global company should go about its business?

Levitt: It should always go about its business in a way that is responsive to the major differences from one country to another, such as the way the distribution system works, the way retailing works, or how payment systems work.

Greyser: But not the core product or service, because that's what is globalized.

Levitt: Exactly right.

Greyser: Let us take a look at those companies that you think have been the most effective in globalizing, whether in 1983 or 2003.

Levitt: A lot of them are well-known consumer goods companies, such as those in the beverage industries, fast foods, and also retailing institutions. I would cite Coke, Pepsi, and McDonald's. Also, in the cereal business, such as Kellogg. Heinz in package goods such as ketchup and soup. Fuji in film. They basically are offering the same product all over the world, but they are sensitive to the needs of distribution systems and (for food products) differences in the way people eat their products.

There are also lots of companies that are not so conspicuous—companies with generic products—such as mining firms in South Africa, copper companies in Chile, rubber firms in Malaysia, grains from different parts of the world. Those manufacturers are of necessity engaged in global activity because their local markets are too small. Those companies are almost definitionally global.

Greyser: Are you surprised that the article and ideas are still getting attention today?

Levitt: Not at all. Lots of people are in school getting assignments, whether M.B.A.s or executives in corporate seminars. They read a lot of things, and this is one of those things.

It was written in a provocative way, I admit. That is one of the reasons it still gets assigned all the time. It engages the reader in a debate. The idea reaches a new generation of students and new higher-level managers with whom the concept may resonate. The idea still gets a lot of publicity and coverage.

Greyser: Some readers of this article have said you exaggerated for effect or for some other reason. Do you have a point of view about that?

Levitt: I don't think it was exaggeration of the concept. It is presenting the concept in a provocative way that gets attention and creates contrary views, contrary arguments. When composing something, the language one uses may be more elegant, more pointed than what one would ordinarily use. One is trying to say things in a memorable way.

Greyser: Ted, you are the master of provoking useful debate through the power of your ideas, powerfully presented. We appreciate your taking the time to share your perspectives on the article.

CHAPTER 3

"The Globalization of Markets" Revisited

Japan After Twenty Years

Hirotaka Takeuchi

When Theodore Levitt wrote "The Globalization of Markets" in 1983, the entire world stood in awe of Japan's postwar economic success. Japanese companies were seen as one of the most effective world competitors back then. Levitt explained the surging success of Japanese companies in terms of their ability to incorporate superior quality and reliability into their cost structure, sell in all national markets the same kind of products sold at home or in their largest export market, and compete on the basis of appropriate value—the best combinations of price, quality, reliability, and delivery for products that are globally identical with respect to design, function, and even fashion.

Japan was depicted as a country that exemplified the globalization of markets twenty years ago. Levitt used the words *Japan* and *Japanese* twenty-four times in the article, far more than any other country mentioned. *The U.S./American* was second, being quoted fourteen times. *Japan/Japanese* was quoted almost three and

Note: I am grateful to Gary Mamoru Okamoto, Hideki Kawada, and Naoko Machimura, all at Hitotsubashi University's Graduate School of International Corporate Strategy, for their assistance in collecting data and conducting interviews for this chapter.

a half times more than *Germany/German,* four times more than *Britain/British/England,* six times more than *Italy/Italian,* eight times more than *France/French* and *Israel,* and twelve times more than *Brazil/Brazilian, Korea,* and *Sweden.* This content analysis suggests that Japan epitomized the pursuit of two ingredients considered essential by Levitt toward achieving the globalization of markets: the "unrelenting push for economy and value enhancement."

Twenty years after Levitt's article, Japan is mired in a seemingly endless slump. Real estate prices, after skyrocketing during the late 1980s, have plummeted by as much as 93.8 percent and are continuing to fall. The Nikkei stock price index, which peaked at 38,915 yen in December 1989, fell below 8,000 yen in March 2003. The unemployment rate surpassed the U.S. rate for the first time in 1999 and hit a record high 5.4 percent in 2002. The banking industry is showing few signs of recovery from its bad loans. Economic growth turned negative for the first time in postwar history in 1997, and Japan has been in a deflationary spiral since 2002.

Japan's competitiveness ranking has fallen by the wayside as well. Once ranked the number 1 nation in the world, Japan was ranked number 30 by IMD, the Swiss business school, in its 2002 World Competitiveness Ranking. It was the first year Japan was ranked below Korea and Malaysia in this ranking. Japan scored a little better in *The Global Competitiveness Report 2001–2002* (2003), published by the World Economic Forum, the organizer of the Davos Meeting in Switzerland. Its composite macro- and micro-economic rankings were number 20 and number 15, respectively, a far cry from its glory days in the late 1980s.

A myriad of articles and books have been written on why Japan has fallen from its position as the world's preeminent economic. Revisiting Levitt's article offers yet another fresh insight. Japan's fall is linked to the extent to which it has been able or unable to participate in the globalization of markets. Although Levitt's article was primarily concerned about the globalization of the product market, this chapter expands the domain to three areas—the labor market, the financial market, and the product market—and investigates the assertion that Japan has not actively participated in the globalization of all three markets.

These three markets are integral parts of a nation's business environment. The business environment that Japan faces can be understood in terms of four interrelated influences shown in Figure 3.1:

Figure 3.1. The Business Environment
of a Nation Depicted as a Diamond

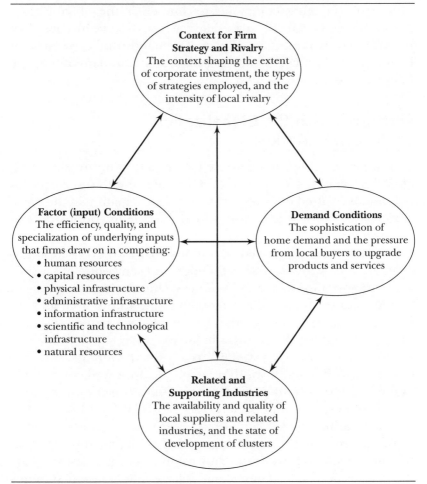

Source: Adapted from Porter and others (2002, p. 57).

(1) the context for firm strategy and rivalry, (2) the quality of factor (input) conditions, (3) the presence of locally related and supporting industries, and (4) the quality of demand conditions. These four influences are collectively called a diamond (as in baseball) by Michael Porter (1990). The labor market is included in factor (input) conditions and listed under "human resources" in the figure. The financial market is also part of factor conditions

and is listed as "capital resources." Seen from a broader context, the financial market also constitutes an important supporting industry for Japanese companies to compete in the global market and is therefore part of related and supporting industries. The product market is an integral part of demand conditions, since it is strongly influenced by how sophisticated and demanding the home market is.

Participation in the Globalization of the Labor Market

To what extent are the Japanese participating in the emerging globalization of the labor market? Our interest with respect to this question is focused on whether they are participating in the more advanced, upscale, high-value-added, knowledge-intensive, and white-collar segment of the labor market and not the low end of the market often associated with blue-collar jobs. As used in this chapter, *labor market* connotes the high-end segment often associated with jobs in software, life sciences, chip design, engineering, finance, consulting, top management, and others. We examine several indicators, starting with how eager Japanese students are to work for foreign-affiliated firms in Japan.

Among engineering students ready for the job market, only one foreign-affiliated firm, IBM Japan, has appeared consistently in the list of top twenty preferred companies to work for in Japan in selected years dating back to 1983, with DEC and Accenture each appearing once. A somewhat lower preference is exhibited by nonengineering students, with only IBM Japan appearing on the top twenty preferred company list in two of the past six years the data are available. These data indicate that Japanese students have shown almost no inclination to work for global companies in Japan, with the possible exception of IBM Japan.

A second indicator of Japanese participation in the global labor market is the number of executives working as members of the corporate board of global companies as well as members of the executive committee within leading investment banks and consulting firms in the world. Out of the top twenty companies on the Fortune 500 list, only two Japanese were listed on the board as of April 2003: Nobuyuki Idei, chairman and CEO of Sony serving on the board of General Motors, and Yoshiaki Fujimori, president and CEO of GE Asia, serving on the board of General Electric. Of the top ten investment banks in the world, only one Japanese (Masanori Mochida of Goldman Sachs) is currently a member of their executive committee. Furthermore, no Japanese are currently on the executive committee of the major consulting companies in the world.

The third indicator of whether Japan is participating in the global labor market is the number of tenured faculty members working at leading universities outside Japan. For example, we examined the situation at the Harvard Business School (HBS) as a case in point. Among the thousands of faculty members HBS has hired on the tenure track in its ninety-five-year history, only a handful of Japanese worked there as full-time faculty members. What is even more striking is the fact that only one of them, Michael Yoshino, received tenure as full professor. The situation is not much different at other Harvard University departments.

These indicators point to the conclusion that the Japanese are not advancing much in the corporate world and the academic world on a global basis. How could this be, given the heroic tales we often heard of modern samurais clad in business suits winning the market share battle in a number of important industries around the world or given the images we often have seen of young Japanese students staying up late at night to prepare for entrance exams, convinced that "four hours of sleep at night we make it, five hours of sleep we don't" in order to get ahead in life? We turn to the next section for some explanations.

Obstacles to the Globalization of the Labor Market

The reason the Japanese have not advanced far in the global labor market is that Japan's system for developing human resources, particularly its education system, has been out of sync with the rest of the world. The biggest obstacles seem to be the idiosyncrasies of the education system and that there are no world-class business schools in Japan. These obstacles put Japan at a disadvantage with respect to developing specialized input (human resources), an important element of factor (input) conditions, as we saw in Figure 3.1.

The roots of Japan's uncompetitiveness in the labor market can be traced back to its education system. We will explore its weaknesses in four fields: an outdated English language program, a deteriorating basic educational system, a weak university system, and underdeveloped business schools.

Outdated English Language Program

To be able to compete effectively in the global market, English has become a required language. It was not so critical when Japan was producing tangible products like steel, cars, motorcycles, hi-fi equipment, farm machinery, robots, microprocessors, carbon fibers, and textiles. The ability to communicate in English, however, has become critical, especially in services, which explains why India has been successful in software and entertainment and Israel in software and engineering.

The English language program in Japan is out of sync with the rest of the world due to its heavy emphasis on reading and writing skills rather than verbal skills. Nobutaka Machimura, the former minister of education, explains the historical circumstances leading to this situation as follows:

> In Japan, the English curriculum was originally established during the Meiji period in order to translate materials written in English into Japanese. Thus, the English curriculum has come to focus more on reading and writing rather than speaking and hearing since that time. The curriculum for communicating in English, on the other hand, has been largely ignored.
>
> Most of the English school teachers in Japan during the Meiji period were not required to have sufficient levels of speaking and hearing abilities. This fact has been a big obstacle for Japanese policy makers in reforming the English curriculum even though they realized the importance of communication in English. Policymakers could not discharge those school teachers who couldn't speak and understand English sufficiently. Consequently, they could not realize the change towards a curriculum that focuses more on verbal skills in English [interview, Mar. 18, 2003].

Japan is paying a huge price internationally for this unfortunate heritage. Most Japanese trained in the traditional education system are disadvantaged from getting into world-class universities, graduate schools, and companies due to their lack of proficiency in the English language. The low scores by the Japanese in two tests substantiate the English language problem. The Japanese have consistently scored low in the Test of English as a Foreign Language (TOEFL), which measures the ability of nonnative English speakers to use and understand English as it is used in university settings (Table 3.1). They also scored the lowest in the Test of English for International Communication (TOEIC), which is administered in more than four thousand corporations around the world (Table 3.2).

Deteriorating Basic Education System

In the past, Japan's basic education system was a source of praise and envy by most countries around the world, as well as a source of strength for Japan. It was anchored in high standards and served to produce a large and uniform pool of well-trained personnel. But its education system is showing signs of deterioration. For example, there is evidence that high school students are not working as hard relative to those in other member countries of the Organization for Economic and Cooperative Development (OECD), as measured by the number of hours spent on homework for language, mathematics, and science. As shown in Figure 3.2, Japan ranked last among the OECD countries surveyed in 2000.

In addition, many schools are suffering from a large and growing number of no-shows, or *toko-kyohi* (students who refuse to attend school and are absent more than thirty days in one year) in class (Figure 3.3). Partly in response to this problem, the Ministry of Education, Culture, Sports, Science and Technology (MEXT) instigated a "relaxation" (*yutori*) program at the elementary level in 2002, which in effect reduced the number of school hours by two hours per week. Some believe that this policy will worsen the deterioration problem.

Because of growing weaknesses in basic education, universities such as Tokyo University have to offer remedial courses in math, physics, and chemistry for incoming students. In a recent large-scale survey of college freshmen, for example, more than 10 percent of students in liberal arts could not solve simple calculations involving fractions (Okabe, Kose, and Nishimura, 1999).

Table 3.1. Mean TOEFL Scores for Selected Countries, 1992–2002

Rank	Country	1992–1994	1995–1996	1996–1997	1997–1998	1998–1999	1999–2000	2000–2001	2001–2002
1	Germany	588	594	594	593	617	584	592	600
2	India	575	578	579	581	583	581	575	593
3	Argentina	549	571	566	569	NA	562	574	573
4	Spain	548	560	561	566	NA	563	567	569
5	China	549	556	555	560	562	559	560	563
6	Italy	560	547	551	554	NA	558	568	562
7	Philippines	569	575	579	577	584	566	568	561
8	Malaysia	529	524	523	530	536	535	545	NA
9	France	553	557	556	557	549	557	544	549
10	Russia	546	551	552	555	541	552	545	544
11	Brazil	541	549	551	553	561	542	544	543
12	Mexico	541	551	547	551	NA	542	552	539
13	Hong Kong	510	518	520	523	524	524	531	527
14	Korea	506	518	518	522	535	533	530	533
15	Taiwan	506	509	507	508	510	515	519	523
16	Vietnam	502	505	508	511	530	530	527	522
17	Thailand	492	494	494	502	512	511	515	514
18	Japan	493	499	496	498	501	504	505	487

Source: Adapted from TOEFL [www.toefl.com].

Table 3.2. Mean TOEIC Scores
for Selected Countries, 1997–1998

Rank	Country	Total Mean	Listening Mean	Reading Mean
1	Germany	788	428	360
2	Canada	722	399	323
3	Malaysia	668	363	305
4	Switzerland	640	348	292
5	Spain	639	339	301
6	France	632	320	312
7	Italy	599	304	295
8	Brazil	570	312	258
9	Mexico	532	289	243
10	Colombia	502	289	237
11	China	502	256	246
12	Korea	480	250	230
13	Taiwan	475	257	218
14	Thailand	487	272	215
15	Japan	451	246	206

Source: Adapted from TOEIC [www.toefl.com].

Weak University System

Japan's university system is nowhere close to being competitive on a worldwide basis. According to data compiled from *The Gourman Report* (Gourman, 1997), Tokyo University, which is considered by far the best university in Japan, is only ranked ninety-ninth among the top one hundred universities in the world (see Table 3.3). Part of the problem with the Japanese university system lies with the universities themselves. They have been content to exist in a highly regulated system and have exerted little pressure on students. Most classes are large lecture sessions, where students often engage in private conversation during the lecture. Professors do not think twice about canceling class since there are almost no student evaluation systems in place (Porter, Takeuchi, and Sakakibara, 2000).

Figure 3.2. Time Spent on Homework in OECD Countries, 2000

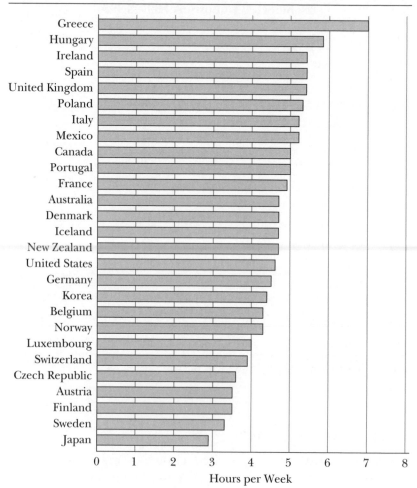

Hours per Week

Source: Adapted from OECD (2000).

**Figure 3.3. Number of *Toko-Kyohi* Students
in Elementary and Junior High Schools**

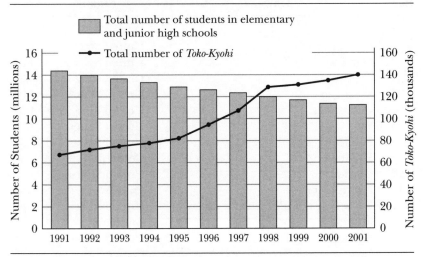

Source: Adapted from Ministry of Education, Culture, Sports, Science and Technology (2003).

In fact, when Hitotsubashi University recently decided to disclose the results of the five-point course/instructor evaluation at the undergraduate level, *Asahi Shinbum* (2003), a daily newspaper with the second largest circulation in Japan, featured the announcement in a lead article on its front page.

Part of the problem also lies with students and the companies that hire them. Many students think of their college years as four years of vacation, or "moratorium," especially in the nonengineering programs. Because of difficult entrance exams, getting into the best universities in Japan is difficult, but graduating is easy. Students have little incentive to study, since companies have relied on in-house training and have not been concerned with students' grades when hiring (Porter, Takeuchi, and Sakakibara, 2000).

In addition, Japanese universities have failed to produce enough students in important disciplines, such as computer software and biotechnology. For example, the number of Japanese college graduates who majored in biology-related subjects was 1,875 in 1996

Table 3.3. Worldwide Ranking of Universities, 1997

Rank	University	Country	Score
1	Paris	France	4.95
1	Princeton	United States	4.95
3	Harvard	United States	4.94
4	Oxford	United Kingdom	4.93
4	Michigan	United States	4.93
6	Cambridge	United Kingdom	4.92
6	Yale	United States	4.92
8	Stanford	United States	4.91
8	Heidelberg	Germany	4.91
10	Cornell	United States	4.90
10	Montpellier	France	4.90
12	University of California, Berkeley	United States	4.89
12	München	Germany	4.89
14	Chicago	United States	4.88
14	Lyon	France	4.88
16	Wisconsin	United States	4.87
17	University of California, Los Angeles	United States	4.86
17	Catholic De Lille	France	4.86
19	MIT	United States	4.85
19	Edinburgh	Scotland	4.85
21	California Institute of Technology	United States	4.84
21	Wien	Austria	4.84
23	Colombia	United States	4.83
23	Marseille	France	4.83
25	Northwestern	United States	4.82
25	Goettingen	Germany	4.82
27	Pennsylvania	United States	4.81
27	Geneve	Switzerland	4.81
29	Notre Dame	United States	4.80
29	Zurich	Switzerland	4.80
31	Duke	United States	4.79
32	Brown	United States	4.78
32	Bordeaux	France	4.78
34	Johns Hopkins	United States	4.77
34	Libre de Bruxelles	Belgium	4.77
36	Dartmouth	United States	4.76
37	Illinois	United States	4.75
37	Dijon	France	4.75
39	Minnesota	United States	4.74

Table 3.3. Worldwide Ranking of Universities, 1997, Cont'd

Rank	University	Country	Score
40	Rice	United States	4.73
40	Nancy	France	4.73
42	Carnegie Mellon	United States	4.72
43	University of California, San Diego	United States	4.71
44	Washington	United States	4.70
44	Tübingen	Germany	4.70
46	Indiana	United States	4.69
46	Erlangen, Nuremberg	Germany	4.69
48	University of North Carolina	United States	4.68
48	Grenoble	France	4.68
50	Washington State	United States	4.67
51	New York State, Buffalo	United States	4.66
52	Tufts	United States	4.65
53	Vanderbilt	United States	4.64
53	Marburg	Germany	4.64
55	Ohio State	United States	4.62
55	Rennes	France	4.62
57	Virginia	United States	4.61
57	Toulouse	France	4.61
59	University of California, Irvine	United States	4.60
59	London	United Kingdom	4.60
61	Penn. State	United States	4.59
61	Clermont-Ferrand	France	4.59
63	New York University	United States	4.58
63	Rutgers	United States	4.58
65	University of California, Davis	United States	4.57
66	Rochester	United States	4.56
67	Iowa	United States	4.55
67	Bonn	Germany	4.55
69	Georgia Tech	United States	4.54
69	Kelun	Germany	4.54
71	Michigan State	United States	4.53
72	Purdue	United States	4.52
72	Nice	France	4.52
74	Rouen	France	4.51
75	Tulane	United States	4.50
76	Frankfurt	Germany	4.49
77	University of New York, Stony Brook	United States	4.46
78	University of California, Santa Barbara	United States	4.45

Table 3.3. Worldwide Ranking of Universities, 1997, Cont'd

Rank	University	Country	Score
79	Brandeis	United States	4.44
80	U.S. Air Force Academy	United States	4.43
81	Jerusalem-Hebrew	Israel	4.42
82	Leuven Catholic	Belgium	4.40
83	Case Western Reserve	United States	4.39
84	Missouri-Columbia	United States	4.38
84	Rensselaer	United States	4.38
86	Emory	United States	4.36
86	U.S. Naval Academy	United States	4.36
86	Pittsburgh	United States	4.36
89	Kansas	United States	4.34
90	University of California, Riverside	United States	4.33
90	Münster	Germany	4.33
92	Stockholm	Sweden	4.32
93	Iowa	United States	4.30
94	Mainz	Germany	4.30
95	Wurzburg	Germany	4.28
96	Besançon	France	4.26
97	Amsterdam	Netherlands	4.24
98	Khan	France	4.22
99	Tokyo	Japan	4.21
100	Colorado	United States	4.20

Source: Adapted from Gourman (1997).

versus 62,081 in the United States (Porter, Takeuchi, and Sakak-ibara, 2000). Furthermore, Japanese universities lack strong research programs in many important fields. Their focus is in applied work rather than original sciences. As a result, Japan has won just seven Nobel Prizes (but nine if the two awards given in 2002 are included) in science in the past century (Table 3.4). This low number for Japan compares to 204 for the United States and 71 for the United Kingdom. In economics, the record is far more depressing, with no Japanese having ever won the Nobel Prize, compared to 33 for the United States and 7 for the United Kingdom (Figure 3.4).

Table 3.4. Nobel Prize Winners in Science (Physics, Chemistry, and Physiology and Medicine), 1901–2002

Country	1901–1945	1946–1990	1991–2001	Total	Physics	Chemistry	Physiology and Medicine
United States	18	141	45	204	70	51	83
United Kingdom	26	40	5	71	20	26	25
Germany	36	24	4	64	22	27	15
France	15	8	2	25	11	7	7
Sweden	6	9	1	16	4	4	8
Switzerland	6	8	1	15	4	5	6
Netherlands	8	2	3	13	8	3	2
Soviet Union/Russia	2	8	1	11	8	1	2
Austria	7	1	0	8	3	1	4
Denmark	5	3	1	9	3	1	5
Canada	2	4	2	8	2	4	2
Italy	3	4	0	7	3	1	3
Japan	0	5	2	7	3	3	1
Belgium	2	3	0	5	0	1	4
Others	6	13	2	21	5	6	10
Total	142	273	69	484	166	141	177

Source: Ministry of Education, Culture, Sports, Science and Technology (2002).

Figure 3.4. Total Number of
Nobel Prize Winners in Economics, 1919–2002

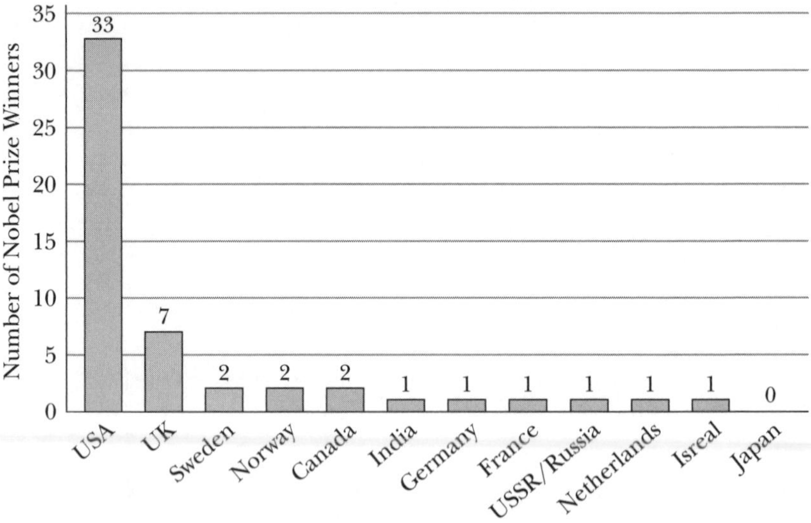

Source: Adapted from report in *Asahi Shinbun*, Nov. 30, 2002.

Lack of World-Class Business Schools

It is somewhat of a paradox that the second largest economy in the world had only one business school twenty years ago. Today, there are some thirty business schools offering M.B.A. programs in Japan, about a quarter of which are transplants of business schools from North America, Europe, and Australia. Despite the surge in the number of Japanese business schools, they have a lot of catching up to do. Not only are they uneven in quality, but most Japanese business schools have failed to produce high-quality students prepared to work for professional firms around the world. (One exception is Hitosubashi University's Graduate School of International Corporate Strategy, which placed all of its first-time graduates to professional firms and global companies in 2002.) According to *The Global Competitiveness Report, 2001–2002* (World Economic Forum, 2003), the quality of management schools in Japan was ranked forty-ninth out of seventy-five countries and regions around the world.

Part of the problem lies with how business schools are positioned in Japan. They are seen more as a continuing education program rather than as an opportunity to change or upgrade jobs. Thus, most of the so-called business schools are offered on a part-time basis or at night. Part of the problem also lies with the faculty: most do not have M.B.A.s from or experience teaching at leading business schools in the United States or Europe. In addition, there are only two business schools in Japan offering a curriculum that is taught entirely in English: Hitotsubashi's University's Graduate School of International Corporate Strategy and International University of Japan in Niigata.

Lack of world-class professional training extends beyond business schools. Japan's first law school . . . opens in 2004. Although Japan is often cited as benefiting from a less litigious approach than the Untied States, lawyers are needed in any complex economy. The shortage of lawyers can delay business transactions in Japan and pose an acute problem, especially in technical fields.

The idiosyncrasies and weaknesses of the Japanese education system have worked against producing Japanese who are equipped with the proper specialized skills necessary to participate fully in the globalization of the labor market. They have been hampered by poor communication skills in the English language; inadequate creative problem-solving capabilities; a shortage of specialized training in software, biotechnology, and other important disciplines; and lack of professional business and legal training.

A world-class education system has become increasingly important for competitiveness in an advanced industrial economy. Moving away from the tight control and micromanagement will go a long way toward rebuilding Japan's education system. Having said that, some of the recent moves on the part of the ministry are headed in the right direction. They include plans or actions to convert national government universities into independent agencies; foster competition within and across universities through the establishment of Centers of Excellence at graduate schools; establish a new legal category of professional graduate schools and bring business schools, law schools, and eventually medical schools under that umbrella; and allow national university professors in the natural sciences to launch venture companies that use technology developed at universities or national research centers. These moves can serve as the first step toward upgrading the higher education system in Japan.

Participation in the Globalization of the Financial Market

To examine to what extent Japan is participating in the globalization of the financial market, we will take a close look at the securities market, which is the more sophisticated, high-value-added, knowledge-intensive, and lucrative segment of the financial market. We will use two indicators to examine whether Japan has been able to participate in the emerging globalization of the capital market: the worldwide market share for global mergers and acquisitions (M&A) deals and the worldwide share for underwriting services.

There has been a sudden surge in the pace of M&A activities involving Japanese securities firms in recent years. Major M&A deals included Renault's investment in Nissan, GE Capital's acquisition of Japan Lease, JT's (Japan Tobacco) acquisition of RJR Nabisco's overseas cigarette business, NTT DoCoMo's investments in AT&T Wireless and KPN Mobile, NTT's acquisition of Verio, Vodafone's investment in Japan Telecom, and DaimlerChrysler's investment in Mitsubishi Motors, all of which took place after 1999. Given these activities, we would expect Japanese securities firms to be gaining significant market share for M&A deals. However, they have not been able to take advantage of this favorable environment and come out as top contenders of global M&A deals. As shown in Table 3.5, which lists the top ten market share holders for global M&A deals from 1999 to 2002, no Japanese securities firm is included in the list, a telling evidence of their uncompetitiveness.

The second indicator is a similar listing of the top ten market share holders of global equity underwriting services. Here again, with the only exception of Nomura in 2001, none of the Japanese securities firms are included as the leading underwriters of new issues (Table 3.6). As with M&A deals, they have not been able to penetrate the global underwriting services market at all. These two sets of data paint a bleak picture of where Japanese securities firms stand with respect to one of the most lucrative segments of the global financial market.

**Table 3.5. Top Ten Companies Holding the
Highest Share of Market for Global M&A Deals, 1999–2002**

Rank	1999	2000	2001	2002
1	Goldman Sachs	Goldman Sachs	Goldman Sachs	Goldman Sachs
2	MSDW	MSDW	MSDW	Citigroup/ Salomon Smith Barney
3	Merrill Lynch	Merrill Lynch	Merrill Lynch	MSDW
4	CSFB	JP Morgan	CSFB	CSFB
5	JP Morgan	CSFB	Citigroup/ Salomon Smith Barney	JP Morgan
6	Donaldson, Lufkin & Jenrette	UBS Warburg	JP Morgan	Merrill Lynch
7	Salomon Smith Barney	Salomon Smith Barney	Dresdner Kleinwort Wasserstein	Lazard Houses
8	Lehman Brothers	Rothschild	UBS Warburg	UBS Warburg
9	Lazard Houses	Lazard Houses	Lehman Brothers	Lehman Brothers
10	Warburg Dillon Read	Lehman Brothers	Lazard Houses	Rothschild

Source: Adapted from 2003 Thomson Financial report, based on announced or completed value excluding split-offs and open market repurchases.

On top of not participating as top contenders in the global securities market, Japanese securities firms seem to be retrenching from their international operations as well. Figure 3.5 shows the number of employees working in overseas offices of the three leading Japanese securities firms. In the case of Daiwa Securities, the total number of employees (including those hired locally) in their overseas offices peaked in 1997. The retrenchment of Japanese employees dispatched to foreign offices began much earlier, as the data for Nomura Securities and Nikko Securities (Nikko Solomon

Table 3.6. Top Ten Companies Holding the Highest Share of Market for Global Underwriting Services, 1999–2002

Rank	1999	2000	2001	2002
1	Goldman Sachs	MSDW	Goldman Sachs	Citigroup/ Salomon Smith Barney
2	MSDW	Goldman Sachs	MSDW	Goldman Sachs
3	Merrill Lynch	China International Capital	Citigroup/ Salomon Smith Barney	Merrill Lynch
4	CSFB	CSFB	CSFB	CSFB
5	DLJ	UBS Warburg	Merrill Lynch	MSDW
6	Salomon Smith Barney	ABN Amro	UBS Warburg	China International Capital
7	Lehman Brothers	Salomon Smith Barney	Crédit Agricole	Lehman Brothers
8	JP Morgan	Merrill Lynch	Nomura	UBS Warburg
9	Fleet Boston	Deutsche Bank	DK Wasserstein	Deutsche Bank
10	Deutsche Bank	HSBC Holdings	Société Générale	HSBC Holdings

Source: Adapted from 2003 *Investor Dealer Digest* report, based on international or global initial public offering values.

Smith Barney since 2000) suggest. Both Nomura and Nikko started to reduce the number of Japanese employees working in overseas offices in 1992.

Obstacles to the Globalization of the Financial Market

The analysis points unequivocally to one conclusion: Japanese securities firms have not been able to participate in the globalization of capital markets. This section explores why Japan has not been able to do so. The biggest obstacle seems to be the government. (This section draws on Porter, Takeuchi, and Sakakibara, 2000.)

Figure 3.5. Number of Employees of Japanese Securities Firms Working Overseas

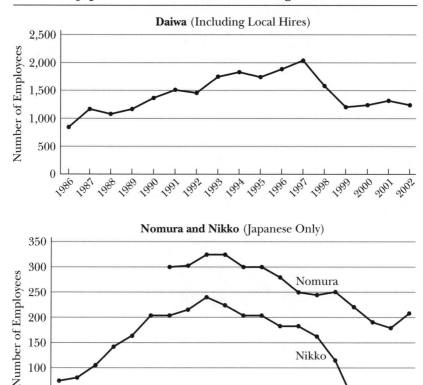

Sources: Adapted from 2003 Daiwa Securities, Nomura Securities, and Nikko Cordial Securities reports.

For years, Japan operated largely outside the international capital markets. Until 1996, when it introduced an unprecedented financial reform policy, often referred to as the "Japanese Big Bang," the Japanese government discouraged foreign companies from taking stakes in Japanese companies (see Table 3.7). In addition, foreign financial services firms were not allowed to compete effectively for funds. In the securities industry, foreign direct investment was

Table 3.7. Foreign Ownership in the Japanese Equities Market, 1980–2002

Year	Market Capitalization—Foreign (100 million yen)	Foreign Percentage
1980	21,706	3.0
1981	50,274	5.8
1982	57,416	6.4
1983	80,814	7.6
1984	137,504	8.8
1985	135.037	7.4
1986	165,448	7.0
1987	187,684	5.3
1988	177,949	4.1
1989	223,379	4.3
1990	208,102	4.2
1991	210,770	4.7
1992	196,809	6.0
1993	207,205	6.3
1994	282,966	7.7
1995	252,319	8.1
1996	409,300	10.5
1997	400,713	11.9
1998	411,309	13.4
1999	465,881	14.1
2000	859,150	18.6
2001	665,746	18.8
2002	567,334	18.3

Source: Adapted from Council of Japanese Stock Exchanges (2003).

not liberalized until 1967, branch office licenses were not granted until 1971, and membership in the Tokyo Stock Exchange was extended to only six foreign firms in 1986.

The dominant owners of Japanese companies have been Japanese banks, insurance companies, and other domestic companies that sought stable business relationships through cross-shareholdings (see Table 3.8). The government imposed stringent regulations on where they could invest. During the immediate postwar period, a series of laws were introduced to regulate the financial market, including the separation of banks and securities firms and the establishment of specialized financial institutions (such as banks for long-term loans and banks concentrating on loans to small- and medium-sized companies). These regulations were intended to allocate scarce financial resources to necessary sectors while the capital market was still undeveloped and bank loans represented the dominant form of corporate financing.

Extensive government regulations ranged from official approval requirements to so-called administrative guidance. For example, securities firms not only needed a license to operate but also Ministry of Finance (MOF) approval for decisions such as setting up new branches, pursuing mergers, and entering businesses outside traditional securities services. In addition to the formal laws and rules, MOF officials promulgated numerous guidelines, many given verbally. Thus, executives from securities firms would visit the MOF desk once or twice a day and sometimes lobby MOF bureaucrats at expensive restaurants at night.

The Japanese capital market regulations were designed to "protect" shareholders by ensuring that securities firms stayed in business. The approach has been referred to as the convoy system, in which all ships are slowed down so the slow ships (that is, the weakest firms) can maintain the pace. This was accomplished by guaranteeing profitability to the securities firms through fixed commissions. The government, through approval requirements, guidance, subsidies, and other means, inserted itself in corporate decisions instead of trusting the process of market competition to sort them out.

Inward-looking rivalry exasperated the problem. In the MOF, for example, a strong rivalry between the Banking Bureau and the Securities Bureau existed. Because each bureau tried to protect

Table 3.8. Percentage of
Cross-Shareholding in Japan, 1980–2002

Year	Percentage of Cross-Shareholding
1980	58.2
1981	57.5
1982	57.2
1983	56.5
1984	57.5
1985	59.5
1986	59.5
1987	58.9
1988	58.7
1989	58.5
1990	58.5
1991	59.5
1992	58.7
1993	58.3
1994	57.5
1995	56.9
1996	55.0
1997	53.2
1998	51.2
1999	47.5
2000	39.9
2001	37.9
2002	35.6

Source: Adapted from Council of Japanese Stock Exchanges (2003).

the territory of the firms it traditionally supervised, new products, such as floating rate notes and medium-term notes, that might blur the demarcation between banks and securities firms were never introduced. As a result, Japan became globally uncompetitive in financial services, and Japanese companies were hindered in accessing sophisticated financial products.

Japan's uncompetitiveness in financial services also influenced the behavior of Japanese citizens, who do not seem interested in pursuing sophisticated financial instruments. Savings comprised nearly 60 percent of household assets held in Japan, with a high proportion of savings held in low-risk assets such as bank deposits and postal savings. In contrast, savings account for only 11 percent of household assets held in the United States, with securities leading all financial instruments at 43 percent. As shown in Table 3.9, securities accounted for only 9.7 percent of total assets held in Japan in 1999 (Kikuchi, Nagayoshi, and Fujita, 2002).

The preponderance of evidence cited points to the government as being the biggest obstacle to the globalization of the capital market. Government policies in the past effectively worked to raise entry barriers, suppress competition, allow the weakest player to survive, discourage innovation, concentrate on the underdeveloped home market, and discourage overseas business (see Table 3.10 for an overview of government regulations in the securities industry).

Starting in the late 1990s, the Japanese government started introduced a series of measures aimed at increasing the free flow of funds across borders and making Japan a more integral member of the international community. As shown in Table 3.11, they cover a wide range of revisions involving accounting and auditing standards, corporate governance standards, legal standards, and tax standards. These revisions provide a glimmer of hope that Japan will actively participate in the globalization of the financial market in the not too distant future.

Participation in the Globalization of the Product Market

Unlike the labor market and the financial market, Japanese companies have participated actively in the globalization of the product market thus far. Japan is a world leader in a number of important

Table 3.9. Portfolio of Financial Instruments
Held by Japanese Citizens, 1980–2002

Year	Savings (million yen)	Savings (%)	Securities (%)	Insurance (%)	Pension (%)	Property (%)	Others (%)
1980	4.82	66.6	8.7	15.8	1.5	2.7	4.7
1981	5.25	64.0	9.7	15.8	1.9	3.0	5.6
1982	5.63	66.8	8.3	15.6	1.4	3.0	4.9
1983	6.06	63.7	10.2	14.4	1.5	3.1	7.1
1984	6.46	61.5	11.0	15.5	1.5	3.3	7.2
1985	6.88	58.6	11.8	15.3	1.9	3.2	9.2
1986	7.31	56.8	12.7	16.7	2.5	3.1	8.2
1987	8.21	52.3	15.6	17.5	1.8	3.2	9.6
1988	9.16	50.4	18.4	19.9	2.2	3.1	6.0
1989	10.13	48.1	18.0	18.9	1.7	3.2	10.1
1990	11.81	46.5	16.2	22.2	2.7	2.8	9.6
1991	11.65	51.1	16.0	21.2	2.1	3.0	6.6
1992	12.59	54.7	13.6	20.7	2.1	2.7	6.2
1993	13.0	50.2	14.4	20.8	3.5	2.9	8.2
1994	13.0	51.6	12.8	21.6	3.5	3.2	7.3
1995	12.9	53.8	11.3	21.9	3.9	3.2	5.9
1996	13.0	55.0	11.8	20.2	4.6	3.0	5.4
1997	13.5	56.1	10.3	21.0	4.8	2.9	4.9
1998	13.1	57.3	8.2	23.0	4.4	3.0	4.1
1999	13.7	57.2	9.7	22.2	4.8	2.9	3.2
2000	14.5	55.7	10.6	23.0	4.8	2.8	3.1
2001	14.4	58.2	9.2	22.4	4.6	2.9	2.7
2002	14.2	58.3	10.3	22.2	4.9	2.3	2.0

Note: Savings consist of private deposits and postal deposits, securities of bonds and investment trusts, insurance of life and non-life insurance, and "other" of money trusts and other financial products.

Source: Adapted from Central Council for Financial Services Information (2003).

Table 3.10. Overview of Japanese
Government Regulations in Securities Affecting Regulations

Entry	Registration system from 1948 to 1965
	Licensing system by the line of business since 1965
	Branch office licenses were not granted to foreign firms until 1971
	Tokyo Stock Exchange membership was not granted to foreign firms until 1986
Rivalry	Allocation of corporate bond underwriting shares since 1951
	Allocation of government bond underwriting shares (1965–1977)
	Approval or guidance for setting up new branches, mergers, entry to new businesses since 1965
	Fixed commission for brokerage and underwriting until mid-1980s
	Fixed pricing scheme for bond issues
	Division of work between banks and securities firms since 1948
	No "Chinese walls" to separate underwriting from brokerage until 1988
Subsidy	Emergency loans during the 1964 securities panic and the stock market crash in the 1990s
Demand	Securities purchase during the 1964 securities panic—effectively weathered the market downturn
	Lenient disclosure requirements and complicated rules for takeover bids—discouraged M&A and related businesses
	Restrictions on overseas issuance of debt securities by Japanese firms until 1973 discouraged overseas business

Source: Adapted from Porter, Takeuchi, and Sakakibara (2000, pp. 62–63).

industries. Table 3.12 lists twenty industries, ranging from industrial sewing machines to video games, in which Japan is either the world leader or the dominant competitor. Levitt saw this coming twenty years ago.

Levitt singled out Japanese companies as a role model of an effective world competitor in 1983. The most effective world competitors, according to Levitt, have to satisfy three criteria: they must

Table 3.11. Deregulation of Japanese Financial Market

Date	Description
December 1997	Lifting of ban on pure holding companies (revision of antimonopoly law)
October 1997	Streamlining of merger procedures (abolition of requirement for shareholders' meeting for mergers and simplification of procedures for creditor protection)
October 1999	Introduction of stock transfer system (system for existing companies to form a new holding company)
October 1999	Introduction of stock swap system (system for establishing wholly owned subsidiary relationship between existing companies)
April 2000	Civil Rehabilitation Law introduced (new bankruptcy law facilitating quick action)
March 2000	Accounting consolidation required (introduction of standards on real control and influence along with tax effect accounting adopted)
April 2001	Issuance of legal framework for corporate splits (system for divesting part or all of the business of a company against payment made through the assignment of shares)
June 2001	Tracking stock allowed
2001–2002	Mark-to-market accounting adopted (new rules applicable to trading securities, retirement benefit obligations, and pension assets, available for sale securities; old rule allowed cost basis or lower of cost or market
2002	Liberalization of stock options (restrictions lifted on eligibility and volume of options)
April 2002	Tax consolidation introduced

Source: Adapted from U.S. Department of State, www.state.gov.

Table 3.12. Competitive Japanese Industries

Sector	Industry	Japanese Position
Electronics	Car audio	World leader
	Facsimile machines	Dominate world production and world export share (just under 100 percent)
	Home audio equipment	World leader in the production and export of many home electronics products
	Microwave and satellite communications equipment	World leader in satellite communications products
	Semiconductors	World leader in the early 1990s
	Typewriters	World leader
	VCRs	Dominate world production and world export share (just under 100 percent)
Leisure products	Musical instruments	World leader
Machinery	Home air conditioners	World leader by the early 1980s
	Sewing machines	World leader in the production and export of industrial sewing machines
	Robotics	World leader
Materials	Carbon fiber	Share the leading position with the United States
	Continuous synthetic weaves	World leader
Optical and precision instruments	Cameras	Dominate world production and world export share (just under 80 percent)
Prepared foods	Soy sauce	World leader
Software	Video games	World leader
Transportation	Automobiles	World leader
	Forklift trucks	World leader
	Tires for trucks and buses	Share the leading position with the U.S.
	Trucks	World leader

Source: Adapted from Porter, Takeuchi, and Sakakibara (2000, p. 28).

incorporate superior quality and reliability into their cost structures, sell in all national markets the same kind of products sold at home or in their largest export market, and compete on the basis of appropriate value—the best combinations of price, quality, reliability, and delivery for products that are globally identical with respect to design, function, and even fashion.

Levitt also pointed out that the Japanese have vindicated the following theory: "If a company forces costs and prices down and pushes quality and reliability up—while maintaining reasonable concern for suitability—customers will prefer its world-standardized products." He recognized that Japan's distinction rests in "its unrelenting push for economy and value enhancement . . . [which] translates into a drive for standardization at high quality levels."

To be sure, Japanese companies are still effective world competitors, as Table 3.12 illustrates. They still adhere to Levitt's "theory" mentioned above. Why then is Japan mired in an deepening slump? Why is it trailing Korea and Malaysia in the IMD World Competitiveness Ranking? These countries were mentioned only twice and once, respectively, in "The Globalization of Markets" article, compared to twenty-four times for Japan. We will examine three assertions linked to globalization below.

Unglobal Consumers?

The first assertion is that Japanese consumers have become outright unglobal. In other words, only a limited number or percentage of Japanese consumers are buying Western brands, and these numbers have not increased much in the past twenty years. Just as the Japanese government restricted the entry of foreign securities companies into Japan, there may be restrictions toward foreign brands coming into Japan. Or, just as Japanese college graduates are showing little interest in working for foreign-affiliated companies, Japanese consumers may not be buying Western brands anymore.

To examine this assertion, we took the top fifteen brands in the world (excluding Japanese brands, italicized in Table 3.13) and investigated whether they were excluded from the Japanese market ("The Top 100 Brands," 2001). We discovered that is not the case, as all of the world's top fifty brands, shown in Table 3.13, are in one way or another present in the Japanese market. They are either being sold here or being offered as a service here.

Table 3.13. List of the World's Top Fifty Brands

Rank	Brand Name	Rank	Brand Name	Rank	Brand Name
1	Coca-Cola	21	*Honda*	41	*Canon*
2	Microsoft	22	BMW	42	Samsung
3	IBM	23	Nescafé	43	SAP
4	GE	24	Compaq	44	Pepsi
5	Nokia	25	Oracle	45	Xerox
6	Intel	26	Budweiser	46	Ikea
7	Disney	27	Kodak	47	Pizza Hut
8	Ford	28	Merck	48	Harley-Davidson
9	McDonald's	29	*Nintendo*	49	Apple
10	AT&T	30	Pfizer	50	Gucci
11	Marlboro	31	GAP	51	KFC
12	Mercedes	32	Dell	52	Reuters
13	CITI BANK	33	Goldman Sachs	53	Sun Microsystems
14	*Toyota*	34	Nike	54	Kleenex
15	Hewlett-Packard	35	Volkswagen	55	Philips
16	Cisco Systems	36	Ericsson		
17	American Express	37	Heinz		
18	Gillette	38	Louis Vuitton		
19	Merrill Lynch	39	Kellogg's		
20	*Sony*	40	MTV		

Note: The italicized entries are Japanese brands.

Source: Adapted from "The Top 100 Brands" (2001).

We then investigated whether the Japanese consumers are no longer buying the brands that used to be very popular twenty years ago. This sample included Louis Vuitton, Mercedes Benz, McDonald's, and Disney. The bar graphs in Figures 3.6 through 3.9, which depict annual sales for Louis Vuitton, Mercedes Benz, and McDonald's and the number of visitors to Tokyo Disneyland for Disney, tell us otherwise. Japanese consumers by and large are still in love with these brands.

Figure 3.6. Louis Vuitton Sales in Japan, 1981–2002

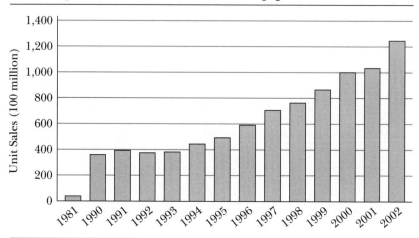

Source: Adapted from Yano Research Institute (2002).

Figure 3.7. Mercedes Benz Sales in Japan, 1983–2002

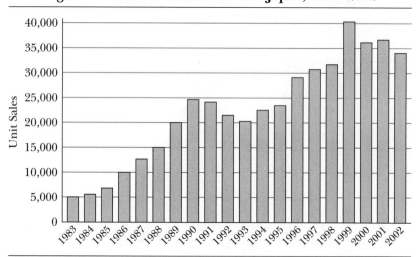

Source: Adapted from report by Daimler Chrysler Group Japan, PR Division.

Figure 3.8. McDonald's Sales, 1983–2001

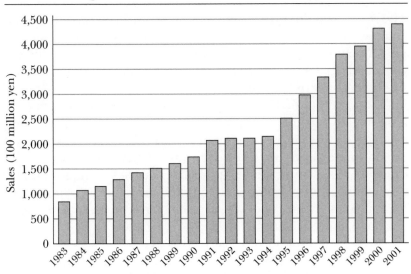

Source: Adapted from McDonald's, www.mcdonalds.com.

Figure 3.9. Visitors to Disneyland in Japan, 1983–2001

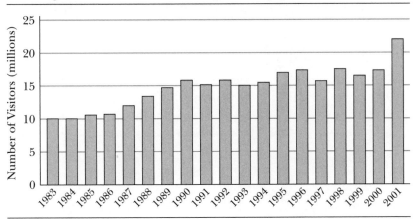

Source: Adapted from Oriental Land, www.disney.co/jp.

Two Japans

The second assertion is that there have always been two Japans: the competitive Japan, like the companies listed in Table 3.13, and the uncompetitive Japan. But what is new is the situation where the uncompetitive Japan is beginning to drag down the entire economy. The uncompetitive Japan has two segments. One is the group of internationally traded industries in which Japan has never achieved a significant world export position. Included under this heading are huge sectors such as agriculture, chemicals, consumer-packaged goods, medical products, software, and virtually all services. The other segment consists of "unglobal" industries such as retailing, wholesaling, transportation and logistics, construction, energy, and health care services, all of which are in the service sector (Porter, Takeuchi, and Sakakibara, 2000).

We found strong evidence of this assertion, especially as it relates to services. Japan has an extremely weak international position in services, as shown in Figure 3.10. When one compares the manufacturing sector with the service sector, average international

Figure 3.10. Average International Sales per Company of Japan's Manufacturing Sector versus Service Sector, 2000

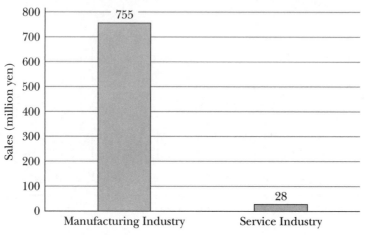

Source: Adapted from Ministry of Economy, Trade and Industry (2001).

sales per company of the service sector is small (only 3.7 percent to be exact) relative to that of the manufacturing sector.

In fact, we can find only one service industry in which Japan has been a clear-cut world leader: the video game software industry. Nintendo, Sony, and Sega dominate this industry, with Microsoft playing catch-up. To be sure, there are other pockets of international success in the service industry. Animated movies come to mind immediately, as *Spirited Away* won the Academy Award in 2003. In the music business, karaoke may be another example of international success. In educational services, an after-school supplemental education program known as Kumon has received international acclaim. It boasts of sixty-seven hundred franchised centers that teach the Kumon method of learning outside of Japan. These examples, however, constitute isolated segments within a much larger industry cluster: animated movies within the entire movie business, karaoke within music, and after-school supplemental program within education.

The Japanese weakness in services stems from a number of factors. First, the Japanese weakness in the English language is a major impediment, since international services tend to involve extensive personal communication. Second, there is a shortage of specialized talent that can deliver high-quality service in securities, engineering, or software, due largely to the weak education system. Third, a range of significant Japanese service industries (such as securities, education, and health care) are regulated by the Japanese government, making them uncompetitive in the international arena. Finally, since the standard of personal service is exceptionally high, involving large numbers of people, it does not lend itself to the "standardization at high-quality levels" that Levitt refers to, and is too costly to replicate abroad (Porter, 1990).

Anticipatory Demand versus Idiosyncratic Demand

The third assertion relates to the nature of demand in the home market. Japan has been successful in product categories where sophisticated and demanding home customers have anticipated the needs of other nations, that is, anticipatory demand. Conversely, Japan has not done well in product categories where there has been a misalignment between the idiosyncratic needs of the home customers and the needs of the global market, that is, idiosyncratic demand. In the latter, Japanese customers may be sophisticated and demanding, but their needs do not necessarily anticipate those of other nations.

Examples of Japanese anticipatory demand abound. In fax machines, the unavailability of the Japanese language typewriters and telex machines, coupled with tight office space constraints, large time differences with foreign markets, and expensive telephone charges, created a sophisticated and demanding local market. In robotics, the highly efficient operational practices of Japanese manufacturers, shortages of skilled workers, and tight plant configurations led to sophisticated home demand. In electronic keyboards, limited living space and crowded conditions created the need for products that are much smaller than pianos, can be put away after use, and can also be used with headphones to limit the noise to which others are exposed. In trucks and forklifts, a strong tendency in Japan toward overloading, poor road conditions, high energy costs, and tight space constraints created demanding home market needs. In air conditioners, small and multiple-use rooms, closely packed houses, hot and muggy summers, and high electricity charges led to stringent local needs (Porter, Takeuchi, and Sakakibara, 2000; Porter, 1990).

But more important, in all of these cases, the needs of sophisticated and demanding customers in Japan became a leading indicator of broader trends in world demand. In other words, Japanese home demand provided an early warning indicator of buyer needs that became widespread. Japanese demand for compact, light, portable, quiet, multifunctional, energy-efficient products that are affordable and reliable were sought after in other countries as well. Japanese companies that fulfilled these demand conditions gained undefended routes for foreign market entry, not only in the product categories mentioned above but also in radios, audio equipment, cameras, TV sets, motorcycles, cars, copiers, machine tools, and other consumer electronics and appliances.

Not all sophisticated and demanding needs at home, however, turn into anticipatory demand. In detergents, for example, Japanese consumers have a unique demand for light, compact detergents because they typically go shopping on foot or by bicycle almost every day and carry their groceries, in addition to living in small homes. However, Kao's premium-priced, concentrated detergent, Attack, which became instantaneously popular in Japan, has had virtually no impact in overseas markets. In plastics, Japanese consumers are highly sensitive to appearance and packaging, so manufacturers prepare thousands of grades, and supermarkets and other buyers demand shopping bags made of almost flawless high-density polyethylene; they reject bags with even tiny spots. No other country is willing to pay higher prices for flawless surfaces of shopping bags, making Japanese plastics uncompetitive overseas. In apparel, Japanese customers are extremely sensitive to fabric, texture, and stitching, have a strong attachment to designer brands, are very conscious about the latest trends, and are willing to pay some of the highest prices in the world. These demand conditions, however, are idiosyncratic to Japan and do not anticipate needs elsewhere. As a result, no Japanese manufacturer has become a dominant global player in apparel, detergents, or plastics (Porter, Takeuchi, and Sakakibara, 2000; Porter, 1990).

The conclusion to be drawn seems apparent. Sophisticated and stringent home needs benefit national competitiveness only if they anticipate needs elsewhere in the world. If they are idiosyncratic to the nation, they will undermine the competitiveness of local companies. The unglobalization of the product market takes place when there is a misalignment between Japanese home needs and the needs of the global market.

Recent examples also seem to suggest the pervasiveness of idiosyncratic demand in Japan. To lend support to this contention, we examine four Japanese mega-hit products in recent years. Two of them—a mobile phone with a camera-video function and plasma-display panel TV, a high-quality TV only one-seventh the thickness of a normal TV—are very new to the Japanese market. The other two—a car navigation system and Washlet, a warm-water bidet toilet introduced by Toto—are long-running best-sellers in Japan. Figures 3.11 and 3.12 show how Sha-mail, a mobile phone with camera marketed by J-Phone, and plasma TVs have taken off in recent months. Figure 3.13 shows how unit sales of car navigation systems increased sixfold since 1997, and Figure 3.14 shows the

Figure 3.11. Number of Sha-mail Subscribers in Japan

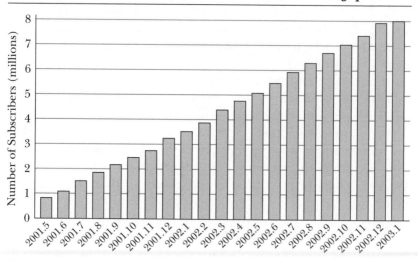

Source: Adapted from J-Phone, http://www.j-phone-tokyo.com.

Figure 3.12. Unit Sales of Plasma-Display Panel TVs in Japan

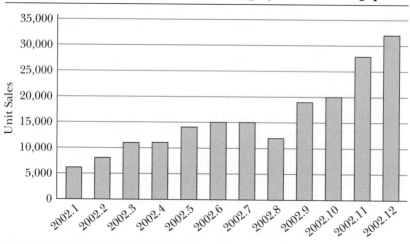

Source: Adapted from Japan Electronics and Information Technology Industries Association (2003).

Figure 3.13. Unit Sales of Car Navigation Systems in Japan

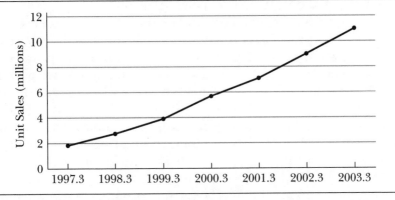

Source: Adapted from Ministry of Land Infrastructure and Transport (2003).

Figure 3.14. Penetration Rate of Washlet in Japanese Households

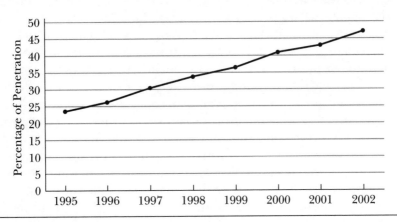

Source: Adapted from Economic and Social Research Institute, Cabinet Office (2003).

increasing penetration of Washlets within Japanese households, from 24 percent in 1995 to 47 percent in 2002.

The question we pose here is when these products will take off in other countries. It is probably too early to tell with respect to the first two products. How many American and European consumers will be willing to spend $250 to send and receive photos ($350 for video images) and e-mails over a mobile phone when a regular Motorola mobile phone costs somewhere around $40 to $50 range? Similarly, will they be willing to spend $4,000 or so for a thirty-two-inch TV with a flat, thin, and high-quality plasma display when a normal thirty-two-inch TV costs somewhere around $600? If they do, both will become further examples of anticipatory demand. If not, they will be further examples of idiosyncratic demand.

As for the remaining two Japanese mega-hit products—car navigation system and Washlet—the verdict is already out. They have not yet taken off in other countries, probably for a very simple reason: consumers in other countries are not willing to pay a premium price since they do not see the value of the added features. A car navigation system costing $2,000 or more enables Japanese drivers to automatically search the best route and avoid traffic jams. Since Japanese roads are complex, crowded, and often under construction, a car navigation system enhances value even at that price. American drivers, however, seem content to use the *Thomas Guide*, which costs $30. Washlet gives Japanese consumers a lot of comfort for $700 (the latest version costs over $2,000), such as a warm seat with adjustable temperature, a warm-water shower cleaning capability with a movable nozzle (water temperature and shower strength are adjustable), a dryer, a deodorizing feature, a water-saving function, and even automatic flushing. Most Westerners, however, have stuck with the standardized, low-cost toilet that has been around for ages.

These examples should serve as yet another reminder that the needs of Japanese consumers may be out of sync with the needs of the global market. To get back on track, Japanese companies need to go back to the basic "theory" postulated by Levitt twenty years ago, which is to make and sell "goods [and services] of the best quality and reliability at the lowest price."

Conclusion

Twenty years ago, Japan was like a canary bird that could not stop singing the favorite "twit-twit-twit-twit" tune around the world. That tune, translated into business terms, was synonymous with offering globally standardized products that are advanced, functional, reliable, and low priced. It was the formula for success for Japan, and the tune was sung over and over again in one industry after another.

Today, Japan is like a canary that has forgotten how to sing the same tune. Japan needs to start singing its favorite tune again, but with one important adjustment. This time, it has to sing the tune one octave higher, since it has to add services into the formula and now faces tougher competition from nations that have successfully emulated its formula.

To enable the canary bird to sing again, it may be best to change the environment, setting it free, letting it fly around in the open, and having it mingle with other singing birds. Similarly, for Japan to be competitive again, it needs to rebuild its business environment (the diamond) with a relentless focus on globalization. It needs to change the context for firm strategy and rivalry by eliminating government practices that limit domestic rivalry and distort the nature of competition away from forms that are valued in foreign markets. It must also upgrade the underlying inputs that firms draw on in competing (factor conditions) through the globalization of its labor market and capital market. In addition, it has to elevate the sophistication of home demand (demand conditions) by focusing on the anticipatory needs of its product market. Finally, Japan needs a strong, global financial market as its supporting industry and the formation of clusters around related industries within the financial market.

Will Japan be able to sing the globalization tune again, one octave higher this time around? Japan has demonstrated an extraordinary capacity to transform itself when it is confronted with a seemingly insurmountable challenge: examples are the devastation after World War II, the oil shock of the 1970s, and the yen shock of 1985. The bigger the challenge and adversity are, the more mobilized it becomes to undergo unmitigated change. It is with this sliver of hope that I look forward to the upcoming twenty years.

PART 2

Managing the Global Business

One of the advantages of taking a long-term perspective is that it allows us to distinguish successful from unsuccessful business practices and processes. Levitt's 1983 *Harvard Business Review* article galvanized academics and executives into polarized positions in a long-lasting conversation: the debate between standardization and localization. Stripped of the rhetoric, the debate is essentially between harvesting economies of scale by offering the same products, marketed in the same way, in as many markets as possible across the world, or of developing products to suit local needs and then marketing them with a different mix in different geographies. The principal argument for standardization is effective cost control though avoiding redundancy. And the main argument for localization is the marketing concept, starting by identifying local customer segment needs and then filling them. As we have seen in the chapters in Part One, both proponents and opponents of Levitt's thesis see it as a call for global standardization. Specifically, Levitt's use of then closely watched Japanese companies like Panasonic and Toyota as exemplars illustrates his advocacy of low price and high value through standardization as raison d'être for global success.

But what are the lessons we can learn twenty years later? Are the high-performance companies of today those that took the standardization or the localization route? And just as important, how have multinationals been organized to implement these strategies? What can we learn by studying the most successful of the global players? These are the questions taken up by the two chapters in

Part Two. Although both deal with strategy execution issues, they use different focuses: the role of customers in defining strategy and the role of collaboration and knowledge sharing in developing a sustainable competitive advantage.

In Chapter Four, Luc Wathieu, Yu Liu, and Gerald Zaltman address the standardization-localization tension head on by suggesting that both of these extreme approaches ignore how consumers really think about products and services. Their contention is that much brand meaning is co-created by consumers and companies and that in order to understand how the most effective global firms market, we need to understand how the co-creation of brand meaning and product experience works. They argue that although there are significant differences between consumers in different geographies, there is a set of identifiable human universals around which concept formulation and brand positioning can occur. This is illustrated with a case example of a successful magazine focusing on healthy lifestyles for U.S. women that was attempting to replicate that success in its launch into the Chinese market. Using this case example, they show how research based on local consumer needs can be folded into a more standardizable model of human universals. Rather than take sides in the standardization-localization debate, Wathieu, Liu and Zaltman develop a symbiotic perspective.

Morten Hansen and Nitin Nohria in Chapter Five take as a given that exploiting scale economies through standardization or taking advantage of differences in local product, labor, knowledge, and capital markets through localization may be effective in different contexts. However, they argue with the long-term viability of either approach. Since a successful business model is inevitably benchmarked and copied by competition, the gains from standardization or localization disappear over time. What then leads to sustainable global competitive advantage? Hansen and Nohria argue that it is the ability to collaborate, share knowledge, and jointly develop new ideas across business units that is the key to long-term success. They use the case example of British Petroleum (BP) to show how a historically balkanized multinational company transformed itself into a collaborative organization. In the process of describing BP and other successful firms they studied, Hansen

and Nohria identify four key barriers to collaboration (unwillingness to seek help, inability to find help, unwillingness to help, and
the inability to share knowledge) as well as three enablers of interunit collaboration (leadership and values, human resource procedures, and lateral mechanisms).

CHAPTER 4

Rooting Marketing Strategy in Human Universals

Luc Wathieu
Yu Liu
Gerald Zaltman

Global marketing strategies often follow one of two contrasting models, with each model making its own strong assumption about consumers. The localization model recommends customizing offers to fit unique local needs and wants. The globalization model, provocatively advocated by Levitt, recommends low price and product standardization, relying on product qualities that have been proved successful in the more modern economies.[1] A hybrid model sometimes called "glocal" generally tips in favor of the globalization model, allowing for only small, conveniently made changes in offerings.

Both models ignore crucial aspects of consumer behavior. In practice, both strategies, and especially localization, assume that consumers can readily and fully articulate their needs and preferences. It is then up to the firm to sense what they are and respond with an appropriate product or service offering. The fallacy here is that consumers often cannot read their own minds and often do not know what is technically feasible and therefore of potential relevance to them. This results in products being offered that are rooted in fairly superficial themes that ignore important drivers of behavior and the willingness of consumers to engage new experiences. Furthermore,

both strategies underestimate the importance of consumers' establishing a deep, personal connection with a product or service. Most
marketing strategies, and especially globalization, seem to assume
that organizations can inject a particular message into consumer
thinking. This too is a fallacy. In fact, the meaning of brands and
product experiences more generally are co-created or co-constructed
by firms and consumers, with the consumer's personal history and
sense of self being particularly important.

Localization strategies can be costly to implement, and globalization strategies may fail to create or develop demand by stressing
readily shared product features rather than shared needs. Thus the
question here is, Is there, somewhere between the extremes of
localization and globalization, an approach to global marketing
that would respect and enhance the local consumer's sense of self
while benefiting from the economic advantages of standardization?

The thesis of this chapter is that this can be achieved by rooting
marketing strategy in human universals. Beyond their superficial
benefits, consumption goods possess basic characteristics that connect them to emotional patterns and schemes of thoughts that are
almost universally shared among human beings. Research in a variety of fields concerned with human behavior (among them, neuroscience, psychology, humanities, and economics) converge to show
that individual differences emerge from basic and deeply experienced human processes that are shared by consumers in all cultural settings.[2] We propose basing product concepts in these
shared human traits and then facilitating the process by which consumers create a personal connection to the offered goods. In this
way, managers acknowledge and take advantage of the robust and
socially and culturally shared structures of thought and experience
that underlie individual preference formation. These basic or fundamental structures are not only broadly shared among otherwise
diverse consumer segments, but they are unlikely to change over
time and are thus an especially sound foundation for developing
marketing strategy.

There are three stages in the suggested strategic process:

1. *Universal positioning.* Formulate a concept and positioning
for a product not as a response to the needs of a target segment,
but rather in terms of basic emotions and feelings, or in terms of

basic archetypes and metaphors, or in relation to a basic social function or ritual. The goal here is to identify something so fundamental that it will occupy a pivotal position in people's mind all over the world. The universal positioning will generally reflect powerful, unconscious processes and outcomes that are also the raison d'être for the product or service category.

2. *Local research.* Understand how potentially different market segments, especially in local cultural settings, uniquely experience the chosen universal positioning. This requires identifying the ideas, activities, and images that are locally associated with the universal elements serving as the product's core concept.

3. *Stimulating co-creation.* Surround the universal position with just enough local associations and meanings to enable consumers to confirm their self-identify and at the same time challenge them to expand in new directions that are personally relevant. This results in personally meaningful brand stories being created by consumers that are directionally consistent with the strategic goal of the firm.

These three stages differ significantly from the usual marketing strategy process in a number of ways. They go beyond rooting products in standardized features and instead emphasize universally shared drivers of consumer behavior. They also acknowledge the need for consumers to engage in a process of personalization and create their own stories around the offered products. Moreover, they stress the importance of going beyond sensing and responding strategies and moving managers into a mode of thinking that involves anticipating consumer needs and leading consumers in directions that result in the creation of new demand. Traditional strategies of globalization and localization are most focused on harvesting demand, whereas the approach we describe permits cultivating demand as well.

The purpose of local research in this framework is not to confront local consumers with a global good and explore their reaction. Research is not about recording preferences for certain attributes or about eliciting willingness to pay for a standard offer. Research is about finding out how the local market relates to deeper ideas in relation to which a product is going to be positioned.

Co-creation does not preclude a lot of standardization. As products are positioned in terms of deep universal emotions or myths (for instance), one can obtain the paradoxical result that a greater sense of personalization is reached through greater product standardization, not through greater physical customization.

An Example

Consider the case of *Fit Magazine,* a highly successful U.S.-based magazine promoting a healthy lifestyle for active women.[3] *Fit* is planning to launch a version of the magazine in China. A survey of Chinese women in the target market has been conducted, asking them what content mix they would like to see in the magazine. Figure 4.1 contrasts their answer against the original U.S. magazine content.

These data can be used to highlight the conventional contrast between globalization and localization strategies. By supplying the China market with the (translated and mildly adapted) U.S. version, *Fit* would basically confront a mismatch of tastes. It might appeal to a certain fringe of highly Westernized consumers and hope for a trickle-down effect, but this process is unwarranted and may take a long time. By supplying consumers with what they say they want (basically, a magazine focused on beauty), success might be more immediate, but the logic that has made *Fit* so successful in the United States (an emphasis on fitness, health, and nutrition,

Figure 4.1. Chinese Women's Opinions of *Fit Magazine* Content

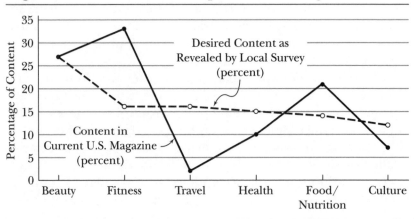

with a secondary reference to beauty) will be lost, and the adaptation will be costly, jeopardizing *Fit*'s standing as a strong competitor in that market.

What could rooting marketing strategy in human universals mean in the context of this case?

- *Universal positioning.* At the root of the magazine's success in the United States are human universals that are truly causing the U.S. customer's deep attachment to the magazine. These universals include emotions, such as the fear of being sick, the joy of feeling in control, and a fascination with beauty. The success of *Fit* is also grounded on archetypical ways of thinking, such as a quest for balance between body and mind, balance between work and leisure, and a differentiation between male and female physical activities. These emotions and metaphors no doubt can take many different shapes in different contexts, but they will always be there. *Fit* talks to women who find balance through physical activity. This is a positioning that should be universal.

- *Local research.* When exploring the connection women make between balance and physical activity, it appears that there are significant differences between China and the United States. Research on this topic through prolonged interviews and secondary sources reveals that Chinese women would view this connection as a matter of experiencing balance (for example, through pleasurable activities including badminton, tennis, and swimming that tend to take place outside and include breathing fresh air and having fun with others), while U.S. women tend to view this connection more as a matter of regaining balance (for example, through effortful individual workout routines and improved nutrition).[4] A typical sought-after outcome of physical activity is a more muscular body for U.S. women and better-looking, healthier skin for Chinese women. Although food is important in both nations in connection with a balanced and healthy life, Chinese women are not inclined to view changes in traditional food habits as contributing to the linkage between balance and physical activity.

- *Stimulating co-creation.* It transpires from the survey results that Chinese consumers do not readily desire a product as contrasted and focused as *Fit Magazine*. However, balance between body and mind and the connection between balance and physical activity can be used as universal roots on which to develop a highly valued press product. Local research indicates that the U.S. emphasis on nutrition should be reduced and replaced by some emphasis on beauty, which reinforces both fitness and health constructs in the Chinese frame of mind. Besides this basic adaptation, there are other minor ingredients that need adaptation, but research reveals that a mix of local and Western elements is viewed as more exciting than the sole use of local symbols and ideas.

Foundations: Human Universals and the Self

The claim that global strategies should start by choosing a universal positioning is inspired and justified by converging research identifying a number of profound and seemingly universal traits in the human way of approaching the world. Cataloguing human universals is beyond the scope of this chapter, but it is useful to understand the broad categories in which they fall.

Emotions and Feelings

Recent research in psychology, motivated by findings in neuroscience, has emphasized that emotions play a central role in human thinking, often underappreciated because it is mostly unconscious. Emotions are now viewed as biologically determined, complex, and stereotyped patterns of chemical and neural responses to stimuli. These patterns form the inherited core of our avoidance-approach behavior. Feelings are more inwardly directed images engendered on the basis of emotional responses. Reason, in this framework best outlined by Damasio,[5] appears as an effort to devise plans of response and to manage a consistent self beyond the here and now, but it is unclear that reason can (or is even meant to) supersede emotions.[6]

Damasio speaks about six universal emotions: happiness, sadness, fear, anger, surprise, and disgust. These emotions are like primary colors, and most products can be seen as resting on a cocktail of emotions. For instance, a sequence of fear and happiness is at the core of most memorable entertainment products: a crispy chocolate bar offers a combination of happiness and surprise. Then there are secondary or social emotions: embarrassment, jealousy, guilt, or pride, which are emotions based on the observation and perception of our own behavior.

The old idea that the conscious assessment of a product's benefits precedes or supersedes affective evaluation is misleading. The conventional marketing approach of treating awareness separately from liking is also highly questionable. Sometimes we view emotional appeals as surface ingredients that managers can decide to use or not use. This is also misleading, as emotions are our basic way of perceiving the world. The most successful marketers know that every detail of the marketing mix, even price, has the potential to produce a persistent emotional response.

A strong connection to basic emotions is at the root of the subjective value created by large industries (ranging from games, to insurance, to entertainment). The resulting products touch everyone and lend themselves well to relationships. They usually carry a high potential of internalization, as they tend to be central to the set of things consumers will call theirs and treat as building blocks of their identity.

Archetypes and Deep Metaphors

When consumers attempt to make sense of their feelings and seek to determine what to do, they use mental models that allow them to give meaning to their environment and to conceive a role for themselves. The mind supplements missing information with elements that are consistent with mental models and schemes. For instance, if someone has been hurt, someone must be guilty of some wrongdoing.

All societies share many archetypical roles such as the hero, the villain, and the wizard. Such archetypes appear in stories such as Little Red Riding Hood that have universal appeal and constitute a basic meaning even though the images and other details expressing universal archetypes may differ.

Archetypes have been classified in a number of ways.[7] Mark and Pearson highlight the fact that the use of archetypes in marketing, offering shared structures that consumers and firms dynamically animate with relevant stories, can help marketers transcend the somewhat unfortunate stereotyping that often results from conventional positioning strategies.[8] According to these authors, managers should actively discover which archetype their brand is living out. This process transcends conventional positioning: instead of putting brands in a well-defined and well-controlled box targeted at certain people, universal positioning relying on archetypes can direct marketing campaigns that are naturally inclusive and transnational.

While archetypes mostly refer to roles or situations that can be built into stories, deep metaphors refer to robust and widespread ways of expressing one thought in terms of another. The Zaltman metaphor elicitation technique is a research process that seeks to isolate deep metaphors as they apply to specific topics or products. Balance between body and mind is a metaphor that will prove useful in both the United States and in China to express the idea of fitness. Games, wars, human qualities, growing plants, fluid mechanics, and body movements are some of the most widespread sources of metaphors that people use to express their thoughts vividly. The purpose of metaphors is to convey meaning in a way that people are almost certainly relating to. The spontaneous process of using metaphors consists in stepping back and using a shared experience to describe something. Thus, metaphors are core elements of effective universal positioning.

Shared Cultural Traits

While emotions relate to embodied patterns of response and archetypes (and metaphors) relate to shared ways of thinking, there is a third source of human universals. It has been argued recently, mostly by Brown, that a number (larger than usually assumed) of cultural traits and social activities and arrangements are largely shared among humans.[9] Research on cultural systems has spent much of its energy focusing on particular differences across cultures, but Brown insists that many codes, norms, and social practices (such as those related to cults or parenting) are universally shared. For example, social elements related to stages of life (as simple as who is teaching children to walk and talk and read) tend to be central to all human experience and are a fertile source of inspiration for universal positioning.

Building the Self

The idea that global products imposed from outside should be replaced by universally positioned products opening up to local co-creation is based on a long tradition that consistently emphasizes the construction of self in response to events and experiences that find their primary source in our body or in basic social structure. Freud understood that people spend energy trying to define their self over time, reconciling states of mind and the pressures of the environment, in a generally consistent and productive fashion. Psychologists heavily inspired by the findings of neuroscience, such as Damasio, LeDoux, and Wilson, call consciousness the locus of an autobiographical self, a kind of second-order process that helps us guide our actions.[10] Memory plays an essential role in this self-building activity.[11]

The existence of a desire to co-create[12] is central to another body of work that consistently suggests that a certain amount of exercised control, challenge, and stimulation, besides causing pleasure and acknowledging personal skills,[13] is critical for sustainable product adoption, as these elements will lead to the product's being registered as an authentic extension of the self.

Conclusion

Marketers should start any effort by digging below superficial attributes and benefits in search of an important and universally human terrain where consumers can grow in their own terms but in a direction strategically set by the firm.

This approach implies a new viewpoint on the potential of standardization. Beyond returns to scale, standardization (grounded in human universals and challenging consumers to a process of internalization) can harvest returns to mental depth in the form of broad demand. The process we advocate allows someone to call a product his while not feeling impoverished or threatened when someone else is calling the same product hers.

This approach also clarifies the role of market research by insisting that its primary goal should be to explore personal connections with the universal positioning themes. This logic may resonate more naturally with managers in certain industries (such as entertainment or toys). However, we believe that this logic should be central to any sustainable marketing effort.

CHAPTER 5

Organizing Multinational Companies for Collaborative Advantage

Morten T. Hansen
Nitin Nohria

Traditionally, many multinational corporations (MNCs) could compete successfully by exploiting scale and scope economies or by arbitraging imperfections in the world's goods, labor, knowledge, and capital markets. But these advantages have tended to erode over time. In most industries, MNCs no longer compete primarily with national companies. Rather, they go head to head with a handful of other giants that tend to be comparable in size, international resource access, and worldwide market position. Against such global competitors, it is hard to sustain an advantage based on economies of scale and scope. Consider the oil industry. The industry is dominated by a handful of global players such as Exxon-Mobil, BP, Shell, and Chevron-Texaco. They each have a global scale in exploration, refining, and distribution operations, leaving little room for gaining competitive advantage based on economies of scale. Similarly, they each have brands that are more or less equally well recognized the world over, reducing opportunities for competitive advantages based on economies of scope. This situation of relative parity among MNCs when it comes to economies of scale and scope can be observed in most industries: consumer electronics, information technology, pharmaceuticals, banking, professional services, and even retailing.

Under these circumstances, what can be a source of competitive advantage? Our premise in this chapter is that the ability to collaborate, including sharing knowledge and jointly developing new ideas among units, is one organizational capability that will increasingly be the basis of an MNC's competitive advantage. MNCs that can stimulate and support collaboration will be better able to take full advantage of their dispersed resources and capabilities in subsidiaries and divisions across the globe. Collaboration can be a source of competitive advantage because it does not occur automatically, even within the boundaries of the same organization. Indeed, there are several barriers that impede collaboration within complex multiunit organizations like MNCs. Overcoming these barriers requires distinct organizing capabilities that cannot be easily imitated. As a result, some MNCs can be much better than others at building a collaborative organization, and therein lies the potential for competitive advantage.

This chapter unpacks the premise of a collaborative advantage in the context of MNCs and presents a framework that links managerial action, barriers to interunit collaboration, and value creation in MNCs. To set this premise in context, it is useful to start with a brief review of how the organization of MNCs has historically evolved.

A Brief History of the MNC Organization

Vernon's life cycle model is widely thought to explain the early evolution of modern MNCs.[1] After developing and then exhausting the home market for its innovative products, a firm would expand abroad, first through export and later, once the market had developed sufficiently, through production facilities abroad. In time, the firm would attempt to supply all its markets through local or geographically proximate subsidiaries. Eventually, when the product matured and became fully standardized, the firm would concentrate production in the lowest-cost location and even export the product back to the home country. This process of exploiting markets and shifting resources through the product life cycle led to the development of MNCs—firms with markets and assets in multiple countries.

In this early evolutionary phase, the key structural decision confronting these firms was the organization of their expanding international operations. Stoppard and Wells proposed a popular stages model as a way to think about the structural evolution of MNCs during this phase.[2] They suggested that during the early stages of foreign expansion, when foreign sales and product diversity were limited, MNCs managed their international operations through an international division. Subsequently, firms that expanded foreign sales without increasing product diversity typically adopted the area divisional structure. In contrast, firms that expanded by increasing product diversity adopted the worldwide product divisional structure. Finally, when both foreign sales and foreign product diversity were high, firms adopted the global matrix structure.

The focus on different structural archetypes was in keeping with the issues most germane to the early period of the MNC's development.[3] But once MNCs spawned a significant number of subsidiaries, each a quasi-autonomous organization, the focus shifted to the structure of the headquarters-subsidiary relationship. Born out of the legitimate fear that due to their remote location and host country pressures, subsidiaries might simply pursue their own local interests, the paramount issue was that of control: how the parent organization or headquarters could properly govern its various national subsidiaries.[4]

Managers and scholars devoted a considerable amount of energy to questions arising from this focus on headquarters-subsidiary relations.[5] Specifically, what are the various mechanisms by which subsidiaries may be controlled? They concluded that there were a large number of formal and informal mechanisms by which subsidiaries could be governed. Given these choices, it was argued, the structure of each headquarters-subsidiary relationship should be differentiated to fit its contextual circumstances.[6]

The literature on headquarters-subsidiary relations reflected a headquarters bias. The structure of interactions and linkages across subsidiaries was neglected. Each subsidiary was treated as being independent of the other, and any connection was through a hub-and-spoke arrangement, with the MNC's headquarters at the center.

The rise of global competition revealed the limitations of the hub-and-spoke model. In a pair of seminal articles on the nature of global competition and its implications for multinational organizations, Kogut pointed out that as a result of increasing international technological and economic parity, rapidly improving transportation and communication technologies, and converging consumer tastes, the key to global competition was recognizing the strategic interdependence among the MNC's markets and subsidiaries.[7] The distinctive feature of competition was now the MNC's ability to leverage its globally dispersed value-adding capabilities. For instance, a firm could respond to exchange rate changes by shifting sourcing to locations with a cost advantage. Alternatively, it could subsidize its competitive battles in one market with profits earned in another. These strategic choices required a great deal of operational flexibility, which meant paying more attention to exactly how each subsidiary was structured and connected to the others. Indeed, subsidiaries needed to be considered as parts of a global value-added chain.

Following Kogut, a substantial literature developed to describe the distinctive character of global competition and to explain its implications for the organization of the MNC.[8] Its theme was that global competition required simultaneous attention to multiple strategic drivers, including pressures for global integration and local responsiveness.[9] For example, global integration opens up the potential for economies of scale and scope that a company must exploit to maximize efficiency. And the need for local responsiveness implies that the MNC must remain sensitive to the differences across the various countries in which it operates. To respond to these strategic drivers, MNCs now had to organize themselves more as a "heterarchy,"[10] a "multifocal organization,"[11] or a "transnational corporation."[12] In short, they had to abandon the hub-and-spoke concept and become more like an integrated network.[13] This meant paying greater attention to the nodes of the network—the divisions and subsidiaries—and the linkages among them.

The integrated network model focused attention on two organization design parameters. The first was the geographical configuration of the firm's value chain: where production and research and development (R&D) facilities should be located and how much marketing should be done globally versus in locally in each market, for example. These value chain configuration choices were critical to ensure that the firm was best able to exploit economies of scale, scope, and learning. The second design parameter was the mechanisms that would facilitate coordination across this now increasingly dispersed and interdependent value chain.[14]

We believe the competitive advantage that could be obtained by such configuration and coordination choices has eroded during the past twenty years. As we briefly discussed using the example of the oil industry, most multinational oil companies now have similarly distributed value chains that make them equally capable of exploiting economies of scale and scope based on the configuration of widely dispersed assets such as oil fields, refineries, pipelines, gas stations, various logistics and transportation systems, and a company-wide brand. Having built a globally dispersed value chain, the real advantage that MNCs must now exploit are the gains from cross-unit collaboration within this integrated network model.

To concretely grasp the notion of collaboration in a multinational company, consider the case of BP, one of the largest companies in Europe with operations in more than one hundred countries worldwide.[15] Over the past decade, senior executives of this oil and gas giant have transformed the company from a collection of individual fiefdoms in the form of independent business units into a vast collaborative organization; as a result, they have cut costs, improved efficiency, and increased revenues based on lateral collaborative behaviors across units. A number of cross-unit interactions were put in place to foster collaboration across business units and country operations. Executives changed the resource allocation process so that a group of peers—business unit heads who run similar businesses—became responsible for the capital expenditure allocation of that group, effectively forcing the peers to work together to optimize the allocations for the group rather than each individual. They also developed "peer assist" and "peer challenge" processes, whereby managers and engineers in a business unit receive help from other units, including technical expertise and advice on how to solve difficult problems. Engineers in a typical business unit spend about 5 percent of their time on peer assists in other units. Frequent rotation of managers across units and country operations has created a set of interpersonal relations across units that facilitate search for help and knowledge transfers. BP also developed several electronic knowledge management systems and used videoconferencing technology to support the peer assists. The promotion and reward systems were changed as well. Managers receive a 360-degree review that includes reviews from peers; managers who do not collaborate effectively across the organization suffer when they are being considered for promotion. In addition, 30 to 50 percent of bonuses for senior managers are contingent on the performance of the firm as a whole. Naturally, BP executives continue to change these practices as the company evolves, but the fundamental idea of creating additional value through interunit collaboration remains at the center of the company's organizational model.

A Framework for Understanding Collaboration in MNCs

If interunit collaboration appears to be so beneficial for BP and some other companies, why is it not more prevalent in contemporary MNCs? One important reason is that collaboration is difficult to achieve. The concept of collaboration is also poorly understood, leading to an incomplete understanding of the antecedents and consequences of interunit collaboration. In our research efforts, we have tried to unpack the concept, as illustrated in Figure 5.1. According to this framework, collaboration can be conceptualized in a parsimonious way as a set of management levers that reduce four barriers to collaboration, which in turn lead to several types of value creation. In essence, interunit collaboration represents a

**Figure 5.1. Framework for Creating Value
Through Interunit Collaboration in a Multinational Company**

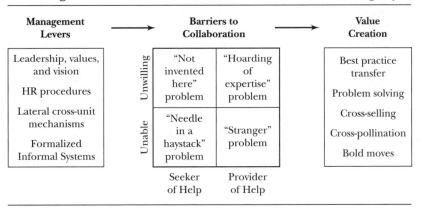

set of individual interactions that take place across the organization—a lateral way of conducting work across discrete business units and country operations. We discuss each aspect of this framework, starting with value creation from collaboration in MNCs.

Value Creation from Interunit Collaboration

A company should collaborate across units only if by doing so it can reap economic benefits. The potential varies by company: a company with many related businesses or country subsidiaries stands to benefit more than a loose conglomerate of businesses, for instance. Our research shows five main benefits, ranging from exploiting efficiencies to engaging in exploratory actions: cost savings through the transfer of best practice from other units in the company, improved quality of decisions by obtaining advice from colleagues resident in other subsidiaries, revenue enhancements through sharing of expertise and products across subsidiaries, innovation through combination and cross-pollination of ideas among units, and enhanced capacity for collective actions involving dispersed units. While MNCs in the past realized economies of scope principally by using physical assets, such as distribution systems, and exploiting a company-wide brand, these new economic values are principally derived from the exploitation and recombination of the firm's intellectual capital, a process that to a large extent requires lateral collaborative behaviors to be realized.[16]

At BP, there are numerous examples of these benefits (see Figure 5.2 for examples of these five benefits at BP). For example, a business unit head in the United States sought to improve the inventory turns of service stations and used the peer group to obtain best practice from operations in the United Kingdom and the Netherlands, leading to a 20 percent decrease in working capital for the U.S. service stations. Another unit head was faced with a difficult decision of ordering oil tankers and used a peer assist to receive input from six people in other units who had particular expertise to help make a better decision. In another case, during the development of an acetic acid plant in western China, more than seventy-five people from various units in BP flew to China to assist the core project team, enabling BP to finish the project on time and to realize revenues from the plant earlier than planned.

Figure 5.2. Examples of Five Types of Value Creation from Interunit Collaboration at BP Amoco

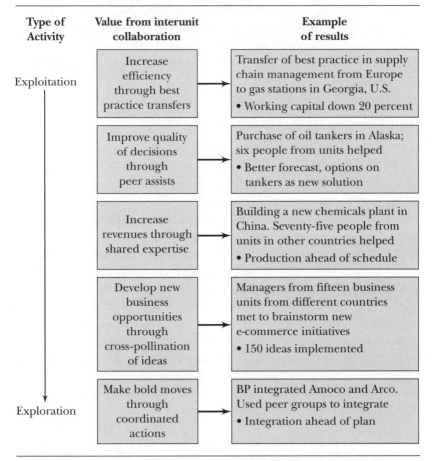

Type of Activity	Value from interunit collaboration	Example of results
Exploitation	Increase efficiency through best practice transfers	Transfer of best practice in supply chain management from Europe to gas stations in Georgia, U.S. • Working capital down 20 percent
	Improve quality of decisions through peer assists	Purchase of oil tankers in Alaska; six people from units helped • Better forecast, options on tankers as new solution
	Increase revenues through shared expertise	Building a new chemicals plant in China. Seventy-five people from units in other countries helped • Production ahead of schedule
	Develop new business opportunities through cross-pollination of ideas	Managers from fifteen business units from different countries met to brainstorm new e-commerce initiatives • 150 ideas implemented
Exploration	Make bold moves through coordinated actions	BP integrated Amoco and Arco. Used peer groups to integrate • Integration ahead of plan

Source: Adapted from M. T. Hansen and B. von Oetinger, "Introducing T-Shaped Managers: Knowledge Management's Next Generation," *Harvard Business Review* 79 (2001): 107.

The company was also able to take collective action and effectively integrate two large acquisitions. According to Nick Butler, BP's group vice president for policy development, "We would not have been able to complete the mergers with Amoco and Arco success-fully without the collaborative structure, because we were able to bring the new people into an environment where people were already working together."[17]

Four Barriers to Interunit Collaboration

To realize this value creation potential, employees in an MNC need to be able to collaborate effectively across business units and coun-try subsidiaries, but such collaboration appears not to occur by itself. This is curious, especially because recent social science re-search on basic drivers of human action suggests that cooperation may be a natural human state.[18] From this viewpoint, collaboration in MNCs may not occur because the organization, for whatever rea-sons, has erected barriers that prevent individuals from engaging in collaborative activities that they might otherwise have under-taken. The first task therefore is to understand what these barriers may be and what causes them. According to our research, the main reasons for a lack of interunit collaboration can be grouped into four barriers (see Figure 5.1).[19] Preliminary results from a survey that we conducted of managers in 107 companies suggest that all four barriers are prevalent in MNCs, although there was a great deal of variance among the companies surveyed.

Unwillingness to Seek Input and Learn from Others

Employees may not want to seek input and learn from others. This motivational problem may have several causes. Employees may believe they cannot learn anything from others or there may be a prevailing norm that one ought to fix one's problems by oneself. The formal and informal reward system may enable more credit for heroic individual efforts than for collaborative efforts. In addi-tion, people in a subsidiary may have developed an inward-looking orientation, focusing their time and energy on activities inside their focal subsidiary. As social psychologists have found, there is a tendency in some groups to develop in-group and out-group biases, where group members systematically overvalue group members and undervalue nonmembers.[20] Such in-group biases can develop when group members spend considerable time interacting with other members of the group, restricting the inflow of new viewpoints and differences and reinforcing commonly held beliefs.[21] As a result, they become prone to the "not-invented here" syndrome, which refers to the bias in a group of employees of valuing their own skills, knowledge, and inventions more than those of others and henceforth rejecting ideas, knowledge, and inventions developed outside their own group.[22]

To illustrate, consider an experience in Hewlett-Packard's European operations a few years ago. Executives had created a new internal benchmarking system that compared the time to process computer orders across factories in various countries. Although this system revealed several underperforming country operations relative to other high-performing ones, the managers with worse processing times were not willing to contact and visit the best performers, in part because they did not believe that others could teach them useful practices and that their problems were unique (which they were not). Only when senior managers intervened did the necessary collaboration across country operations take place.

There are several management levers that can be used to attenuate this problem. BP uses peer pressure to make sure people seek input and learn from others.[23] Senior executives keep a close eye on the extent to which a business unit manager asks for peer assists and will intervene if the manager seeks too little. A peer challenge is an even more direct form: peers, not superiors, will go directly to a business unit, challenge it, and lend support to help it improve in areas in which it is underperforming. Another fundamental lever is to recruit employees who have a natural inclination to ask for help. When in trouble, they have the confidence to seek help instead of keeping problems to themselves. An international chain of upmarket restaurants in the United States, whose management philosophy is to instill collaborative behaviors among its staff, does this deliberately. In interviewing prospective staff, they ask the person, "What obstacles have you faced in a previous job that prevented you from doing a quality job, and how did you overcome these obstacles?" The desirable answer should include asking for help and communicating the problem to others, and not trying to be a hero and fix it alone.

Inability to Seek and Find Expertise

Even when employees are willing to seek help in other business units or country subsidiaries, they may not be able to find it or search efficiently so that the benefits of the help they may receive justify the search costs incurred.[24] In large and dispersed MNCs, this "needle-in-a-haystack" problem can become a significant barrier to collaboration: somewhere in the company, someone often knows the answer to a problem, but it is nearly impossible to connect the person who has the expertise with the person who needs it.

Databases and electronic search engines serve a useful role here, including the role of serving as electronic yellow pages. In most management consulting companies, for instance, consultants upload sanitized documents containing their finished work into databases, which are then subsequently accessed by other consultants across the globe who review prior work and contact the consultants who did it.[25] Another way to help people find expertise is to create transparent benchmarking systems. Ispat International, one of the largest steel companies in the world, has a system that performs costing at the plant level and compares the various plants around the world. Managers can compare all their operating units in the world on a range of dimensions, use this information to spot deviations from best practice in the company, and then contact the best-performing plant in certain areas. For example, a manager who used the system found that his furnace maintenance costs were higher than in other plants, prompting him to contact the most cost-efficient plants in this area.

However, technology has its limits. Expert directories become out of date and do not fully capture what each person knows. More important, they do not allow for creative combinations of ideas and individuals. Companies may therefore need to cultivate connectors, that is, people who know where experts and ideas reside and who can connect people who do not know each other but can benefit from helping each other and recombine their skills to develop new products and services. Connectors play a vital role in creating a "small world," providing short-cuts that reduce the degrees of separation between any two people.[26] They tend to be long-tenured employees who have worked in many areas in the company and hence have an extensive personal network.

Consider how a manager in GlaxoSmithKline created substantial value for his company by connecting two country managers who did not know each other. A few years ago, an area director located in Singapore received a telephone call from the company's managing director in the Philippines, who was looking for new product opportunities that could be introduced in his country. Acting on a hunch that there might be an opportunity in India, the area director set up a meeting with the managing director in Bombay. During his visit, the managing director from the Philippines saw that the Indian product developers were developing line extensions in the area of antituberculosis medication, a field that was not emphasized by the company worldwide but is highly relevant in developing countries. The visit to the lab sparked a joint effort between the teams in India and Philippines, resulting in a modified anti-TB medication for the Philippines and several other line extensions for the Philippine market. The area director, acting as a connector, ignited cross-pollination by connecting people who otherwise would have remained disconnected. Employees who are connectors are in fact entrepreneurs within a large company. They see opportunities for new value creation based on the combination of talent, ideas, and expertise from different units.

Unwillingness to Help

Employees may be willing to seek input and able to find someone who can help, but other employees will not share what they know and make the effort to assist others, leading to a hoarding-of-expertise problem. While a potential helper could refuse outright, a more subtle lack of motivation occurs when the helper drags his or her feet and only reluctantly shares the knowledge or parts of it.[27] Paradoxically, the emphasis on performance management over the past decade has fueled this problem: by pressuring each manager and employee to perform in his or her job, people have become overfocused on delivering their work and underfocused on helping others—they do not have the time to do so or do not care because all they are asked to do is to deliver their own numbers. While this focus on individual performance is clearly important, executives also need to create a counterbalancing force by developing incentives to help others and cultivating a shared identity among employees in the company.

Another reason for a lack of motivation to help others concerns the extent of intersubsidiary competition in a MNC.[28] A subsidiary may be in competition with another subsidiary to the extent that both subsidiaries sell products to the same external markets and seek to develop the same types of technologies. In such a situation, one subsidiary's product development efforts may constrain the opportunities of a competing subsidiary to the extent that new products and technologies crowd out the available market and technology opportunity set for the competing subsidiary. Employees in a subsidiary may therefore be reluctant to help a competing subsidiary because there is a perceived negative consequence of helping.

Unwillingness to help is a significant problem in many investment banks, where bankers chase their own opportunities without properly assisting others. To combat this tendency, John Mack, when he took over Morgan Stanley in the early 1990s, set out to create a more collaborative culture and changed the promotion criteria.[29] "Lone stars"—those who delivered great results but did not assist others—would not be promoted. Bankers needed to demonstrate both individual performance and contributions to others to attain the coveted position of managing director, the level at which bankers reap the most rewards. To measure this, executives put in place a 360-degree review procedure where peers and subordinates were asked to evaluate a person's contributions beyond his or her department. As a result, individuals started to cooperate and assist each other on a much different scale than they had before. Tom DeLong, chief development officer for the firm at the time, reflected on one of the consequences of the performance evaluation process at Morgan Stanley: "Operating Committee members who normally did not share the important knowledge of their divisions realized that at the end of the year, they would be evaluating one another. All of a sudden, they began to share more information knowing the consequences at year-end for their evaluations if they didn't." This system also helped break down some of the barriers to collaboration across geographical boundaries. Bankers from Europe, Asia, and the United States were now more willing to collaborate with each other to serve global clients collectively rather than following their tradition of chasing the local business of such clients in each country.

Inability to Work Together and Transfer Knowledge

Finally, even if two or more employees are willing to work together, they may not be able to do so effectively because they do not know each other and do not know how to work together. This "stranger" problem is worse in some situations. Specifically, research has demonstrated that the tacitness of the knowledge to be transferred across subsidiaries and business units affects the ability of employees to effectively incorporate knowledge from others into their work.[30] This problem may also occur when the knowledge is viewed as being context or culture specific.[31] When the knowledge to be transferred is easy to explain, as when it is explicit or general, employees in a helping subsidiary should have few problems conveying and transferring the content to employees in other subsidiaries. When the knowledge is tacit or specific, however, the helping subsidiary will find it more difficult to explain the content and nuances of the knowledge to others who may find it difficult to understand, thereby making the tasks of modifying and incorporating the knowledge into their own local conditions difficult. Because of these difficulties, transferring tacit or specific knowledge is likely to be more cumbersome, take longer, and thus be more costly than transferring explicit or general knowledge.

As research has shown, however, the difficulty of transferring tacit or specific knowledge can be alleviated to some extent if the two parties to a transfer know each other well and have learned to work together.[32] When the two parties have developed a strong relation, with frequent and professionally close interactions, they have likely developed a shared communication frame where each party has come to understand how the other party uses subtle phrases and ways of explaining difficult concepts. In the absence of such relations, strangers are likely to find it difficult to work together effectively. For example, in a study that one of us undertook of time-to-market performance of new product development projects in a global high-tech company, results revealed that project engineers who worked with engineers from other divisions or subsidiaries took 20 to 30 percent longer to complete their projects when there were no established close personal relations between them.[33] The reason was that engineers found it hard to articulate, understand, and absorb complex technologies that were transferred between organizational units in situations where the engineers had not learned to work together beforehand. They thus had to learn to cooperate during the project, which slowed them down even though they were highly motivated to cooperate.

To alleviate this "stranger" problem, executives can work to establish relations between employees from different subsidiaries.

Such relationships need to be developed before specific collaborative events, so that employees know each other before they start to collaborate on a specific project or problem. Without this level of preparedness, employees would have to get to know one another as they work on a specific project, increasing the risk that they would be slowed down. In addition, training sessions on teamwork and coaching of people as they try to work together are useful mechanisms for reducing this barrier to collaboration.

In summary, the four barriers reduce the extent to which an MNC will be able to reap the five values from collaboration that are depicted in Figure 5.1. In the survey we conducted with 107 managers in multinational companies, there was a strong negative association between their perceived levels of the four barriers present in their company and the perceived levels of benefits from the five lateral sources of value—the higher the barriers, the lower the five types of value creation. Although based on managers' subjective assessment of benefits, these data suggest that senior executives who are able to reduce these four barriers in their company reap economic benefits from interunit collaboration.

Management Levers to Reduce Barriers to Interunit Collaboration

The overarching framework suggests that leaders of multinational companies can deploy a set of levers to reduce the four barriers to interunit collaboration. Based on a factor analysis of our survey data, potential management levers that can reduce any of the barriers fall into three broad categories:[34] leadership values, and vision. The last category can be divided into formalized cross-unit mechanisms, informal cross-unit networks, and information systems (see Exhibit 5.1 for a listing of specific survey items that fall into each category).

An important insight from our research is that different management levers affect the four barriers to collaboration differently (see Table 5.1 for a summary of statistical results confirming this). Reducing each barrier thus requires a different set of management levers. For example, developing an electronic knowledge management system will not help if the problems are that employees

Exhibit 5.1. Survey Items for Each Category of Management and Organization Levers

Value/Leadership Levers

The company has a clear *shared vision and a set of objectives* that unify the various units in the company.

The company's *leadership team* is very good at signaling and communicating the need to work together and be a unified company.

The company has a clearly articulated *shared value* of teamwork and cooperation to which many people in our company adhere.

The members of the company's *leadership team* demonstrate a willingness and ability to cooperate among themselves.

Human Resource Levers

The company's *compensation system* significantly rewards people who proactively *ask for help* and seek to learn from others in the company.

The company's *promotion system* makes sure that employees who do not want to *ask for help* and seek to learn are *not* given senior positions in the company.

The company's *recruitment* procedures effectively screen out job candidates who try to *solve problems alone* and do not want input from others.

The company's *compensation system* significantly rewards people *who help others* outside their area of responsibility in the company.

The company's *promotion system* makes sure that "lone stars" *who do not help others* are *not* given senior positions in the company.

The company's *recruitment* procedures effectively screen out job candidates *who do not want to help others* outside their area of responsibility in the company.

Lateral Cross-Unit Mechanisms

Lateral formalized levers

The company has cross-unit and cross-functional *committees* that make people willing and able to work together and coordinate activities effectively.

The company has cross-unit and cross-functional *business processes* (for example, strategic planning, budgeting, and product release scheduling processes) that effectively enable people to work together and coordinate activities.

Exhibit 5.1. Survey Items for Each Category of Management and Organization Levers, Cont'd

Lateral informal network levers

The company has well-developed *peer networks, communities of practice, practice groups, or subject matter expert groups* that effectively enable people from different places in the company to find the expertise and help they need.

The company has an adequate number of individuals who function as *"people connectors,"* who effectively help people find experts.

Information systems levers

The company has *electronic knowledge management systems* that effectively enable people to find the information and documentation they need.

The company has an *information system* that effectively enables similar units (for example, plants, stores, country sales offices) to easily benchmark their performances against each other and use that information to find and transfer best practices in the company.

Note: Respondents were asked to rate the extent to which they agreed or disagreed with each statement, on a scale from 0 (strongly disagree) to 100 (strongly agree).

will not seek help or will hoard what they know. Likewise, making employees' promotion opportunities contingent on the extent to which they seek input from others will not help if the problem is that people cannot find experts.

Leadership and Values Lever

The leadership and values levers reduce unwillingness to seek and provide help. That is, as leaders signal the importance of collaboration, demonstrate the importance of collaboration by collaborating among themselves, and articulate shared values around teamwork, employees in an organization are more likely to be motivated to seek and provide help. However, the leadership and values levers do not affect the ability to find help and work together. This makes intuitive sense: a leader who preaches collaboration may motivate the troops but will not by those words alone help them locate experts and enable employees to work well together. Thus, leadership behaviors

**Table 5.1. Summary of Regression Results Analyzing
the Effect of Each Management Lever Category on
Each Barrier to Interunit Collaboration**

	Leadership and Values	Human Resource Procedures	Lateral Mechanisms
Unwillingness to seek help	↓	↓	NS
Inability to seek and find help	NS	NS	↓
Unwillingness to help	↓	↓	NS
Inability to work together and transfer knowledge	NS	NS	↓

Note: N = 107 managers responded to a survey on collaboration in multinational companies. A down-pointing arrow denotes a negative significant effect, such that an increase in the level of the management lever reduces the barrier. NS denotes a nonsignificant effect. For example, an increase in the leadership and value score reduced the unwillingness to seek help but had a nonsignificant effect on the inability to seek and find help.

and the articulation of shared values are perhaps necessary but not sufficient conditions for effective collaboration to occur in MNCs.

Human Resource Procedures

Recruitment and promotion criteria also reduce the two unwillingness barriers, as do compensation criteria based on demonstration of collaborative behaviors. By selecting job candidates who have an inclination to seek and provide help, an organization over time will be populated with people who are motivated to seek and provide help. Making demonstrated collaborative behaviors a criterion for promotion to senior positions in a company ensures that the top team will, over time, be composed of leaders who exhibit collaborative behaviors. In addition, having such a selection criterion sends a powerful signal to employees vying for leadership position; those who do not have the inclination to collaborate are likely to leave a company to the extent that this selection criterion is enforced consistently. Finally, compensating employees based on their collaborative behaviors is also a useful lever, albeit a difficult one to implement. It requires a fair process for collecting data on who is seeking and providing help.

Lateral Cross-Unit Mechanisms

If the problem is the inability to find help, then the most effective levers tend to be the development of informal networks of experts to be used by others in the organization when searching for expertise, the cultivation of connectors, the development of electronic yellow pages that list experts in certain areas, and the development of benchmark systems that allow employees to identify best practice in the company.

If the problem is the inability to work together, then another set of levers needs to used, such as the development of organizational processes that structure regularly occurring interactions and thereby provide a forum for people to get to know each other and develop personal bonds that facilitate sharing. The peer groups at BP provided such forums.

In summary, while leadership behaviors, shared values, and human resource procedures (recruiting, promotion, and compensation criteria) primarily reduce motivational barriers such as the unwillingness to seek help and give help, the lateral mechanisms reduce search and transfer barriers such as the inability to find help and work together. The implication for executives of MNCs is that multiple management levers are required to foster collaboration across business units and country subsidiaries. Putting in a benchmarking system or revamping the incentive system are likely to be partial solutions.

The appropriate intervention for executives therefore is first to understand what the specific barriers are in a MNC. Our data show that companies have widely different problems: although all four barriers may be high in some MNCs, others have only one or two of these barriers. It is therefore paramount to diagnose which barriers cause a problem. For example, if the problem is an inability to find help in a large and dispersed MNC, an appropriate intervention would be to put in a knowledge management system or benchmarking system—but not a new incentive plan promoting collaboration. In contrast, if the problem is a widespread not-invented-here syndrome, changing the HR procedures may be appropriate, but a new knowledge management system is unlikely to have any effect in this situation.

Potential Downsides of Collaboration

Collaboration can create substantial value, but it also has a downside that executives need to manage. One pitfall of collaboration is that it can easily be overdone. Prompted by collaboration initiatives, employees may begin to participate in all kinds of meetings without getting anything done, quickly leading to ineffective collaboration that undermines overall performance. For example, in the early days of developing collaborative behaviors in BP, employees started to form an unforeseen number of cross-unit networks.[35] An audit within the oil exploration business alone identified several hundred of these networks, such as the helicopter utilization network. According to John Leggate, who ran several business units during that time, "People always had a good reason to meet . . . but increasingly we found that people were flying around the world and simply sharing ideas without always having a strong focus on the bottom line." Executives had to reduce the number of networks and limit interunit meetings to those focusing on results.

Management levers to create a collaborative organization must be counterbalanced with performance management of each individual and business unit, including a clear specification of who is responsible for what. It is this balance that has made BP perform: each manager has a clear individual performance contract that is coupled with clear expectations for participating across the organization. These managers have a T-shaped role: while their primary responsibility is typically to deliver results for their own individual business unit or country subsidiary (the vertical part of the T), their other responsibility is to seek help and help (the horizontal part of the T).[36] This dual role is undoubtedly difficult to carry out well and is a source of stress. Effective T-shaped managers whom we have interviewed tend to be good at prioritizing, excellent at delegating to subordinates, and extremely hard working. These are attributes of any good manager, but they are especially important in MNCs that demand that their business unit and country subsidiaries managers are T-shaped in their values and capabilities.

Conclusion

We end by reiterating our main premise that collaboration provides a relatively untapped opportunity for multinational organizations to gain a competitive advantage in a world in which advantages based on traditional economies of scale and scope are rapidly diminishing. Although human beings have a natural instinct to bond, countervailing forces can create barriers to collaboration. These barriers can be overcome by using a variety of organizational levers that are hard to implement and not easily imitated. MNCs that successfully implement these organizational levers and foster greater levels of collaboration relative to their competitors can enjoy a durable source of competitive advantage.

Our emphasis on collaboration also has consequences for how we envision the purpose of any corporation and the reason for its existence. In the standard economic argument, firms arise when markets fail.[37] In consonance with this view, market failures in the exchange of goods, people, and knowledge across geographical boundaries have long occupied center stage in economic theories of the multinational enterprise.[38] When global markets were relatively underdeveloped and prone to failure, this view had a legitimate cachet. But now that global markets have become much more developed and relatively more efficient, it is time to remember an equally long-standing alternate conception of why firms exist.[39] In this view, firms exist because they enable human beings to achieve collaboratively what they could not achieve alone. If we accept this as the true purpose of any organization, the main focus of our attention should be on how to foster collaboration within organizations.

PART 3

Managing Global Products

Nowhere is the tension between proponents of global standardization versus local adaptation more poignant than in the area of
product development. Levitt's 1983 article was titled "The Globalization of Markets," and since he taught in the marketing area, we
might expect that his arguments were based on a demand-side, customer-centric logic: give the customer what the customer wants.
Yet critics of Levitt's article take issue with the fact that his arguments were primarily supply side and scale economies related. In
fact, the situation is more complicated. The beauty of Levitt's article, as noted in the Introduction to this book, is that he carefully
integrated both a demand-side and a supply-side perspective.
Although his examples were those of companies (mostly Japanese)
that marketed consumer products that were enthusiastically received, Levitt was arguing for a low-price, value-based approach
grounded in lowering costs through product rationalization. Once
again we have the benefit of hindsight to look at successes and failures of companies that have attempted such an approach.

The two chapters in Part Three use high-visibility case examples
to discuss what a focus on global standardization has achieved. The
industries are very different—satellite television and automobiles—
but the lessons learned are remarkably similar.

In Chapter Six, Pankaj Ghemawat uses a case study of STAR in
Asian satellite TV. His historical overview describes STAR's initial targeting of the top 5 percent of Asian TV consumers, which allowed
for a standardizable product of largely Western programming in

English. Very quickly, however, STAR was forced to abandon this approach and move toward localizing programming content with local regional languages. STAR's miscues are revealing, all the more so because of the key lessons learned. Ghemawat builds an economic model based on the STAR TV case example and then elaborates on why the anticipated convergence of consumer tastes did not occur. He points to three specific antistandardization factors: cultural (especially linguistic) differences between countries (the "home bias"), administrative and political differences between countries, and infrastructural differences (such as differences in the sophistication of TV ratings systems in the STAR TV case).

Nick Scheele in Chapter Seven provides learnings from his own company, Ford, where he has had a long career and where he is the chief executive officer. He suggests that the automobile industry is a prime candidate for global standardization because of the capital intensity, worldwide overcapacity of 30 percent, which motivates efficiencies from product standardization, global competitors, liberalized trade, and some degree of customer convergence. Yet surprisingly, Ford has almost no globally standardized products. Scheele's explanation for this counterintuitive fact is similar to Ghemawat's analysis. He points to significant disparities between countries in terms of geography, environmental conditions, government regulations, and customer needs. He concludes by saying that Ford is only "selectively globalized," a condition that Ghemawat refers to as "semiglobalization."

CHAPTER 6

Global Standardization versus Localization
A Case Study and a Model
Pankaj Ghemawat

Gone are accustomed differences in national or regional preference. . . . The global corporation operates with resolute constancy—at low relative cost—as if the entire world (or major regions of it) were a single entity: it sells the same things in the same way everywhere.
THEODORE LEVITT, *The Globalization of Markets*

Today, nearly every industry has a significant global segment in which customers prefer products or services that are much more global than they are local. . . . The global segment is increasing in size in nearly all cases.
GEORGE YIP, *Global Strategy in the Twenty-First Century*

Clearly, many prominent international marketers believe that globally standardized products are increasing their share of total demand in most product categories from levels that are already significant, if they have not already taken them over. Many people whom one might describe as antimarketers share this belief: thus, in *No Logo*, Naomi Klein (2000, p. 129) writes that "market-driven globalization doesn't want diversity; quite the opposite. Its enemies are national habits, local brands, and distinctive regional tastes." This chapter scrutinizes this hypothesis of global product standardization.

Antecedents

Levitt's argument about the global standardization of products has triggered considerable debate. Although some prominent scholars have come to agree with Levitt, others have disagreed vociferously. Their counterarguments—that consumers are not really becoming that similar, that most product markets are still segmented to a significant extent at national boundaries, that certain kinds of brand equity lack the heritage or meaning to be transferable across such boundaries, and so on—were identified some time ago and will not be elaborated here (see, instead, Douglas and Wind, 1987). What is worth emphasizing here is that systematic evidence about this debate is still sparse.

One relevant strand of empirical research originated with Vern Terpstra's study (1967) of U.S. marketing in what was then the European Common Market and was followed up by Jean Boddewyn and various coauthors (see Boddewyn, Soehl, and Picard, 1986, for a description). The Boddewyn-led surveys, in particular, found a substantial increase in product standardization for consumer nondurables (although falling well short of complete standardization), a smaller increase for consumer durables, and a substantial decrease for industrial goods between 1973 and 1983. But sample sizes were small and the data dated (ending in 1983, the year in which "The Globalization of Markets" was published). Somewhat more recent but narrower studies (for example, of international advertising by Kanso, 1992) seem to suggest that standardization has, if anything, decreased since the earlier period.

A second, more elaborated strand of empirical research has sought to identify and investigate alternate customer rationales for global standardization. Batra and others (2000) has offered a useful classification of consumer rationales for global brands that can mostly be reinterpreted more broadly as applying to global products. Global brands may be preferred not only because (1) they cater to homogenizing tastes or preferences, as emphasized by Levitt but, alternately, because (2) they convey higher quality, defined broadly to include expertise, authority, credibility, and so on, (3) they enjoy higher prestige and status in the minds of many customers because of their foreign origins, or (4) they satisfy customers' cravings to become part of a global community. Rationale 2 can be traced back to Robert Buzzell's argument (1968) that a global image can be a powerful way of increasing sales but has been framed more recently as the idea that a global brand is likely to be viewed by consumers as possessing a special "high-quality" credibility because of the signal supplied by its broad acceptance (Kapferer, 1997) and might therefore be able to tap into increasing-returns-to-scale dynamics. Rationale 3 is rooted in the idea, elaborated by cultural anthropologists, that national elites might desire to demonstrate competence with regard to foreign cultures—a display that the masses might then try to emulate—to communicate nonprovincial tastes or cultural mastery and to build self-identity (Hannerz, 1990). One way of demonstrating such competence is by consuming foreign brands, a favorable foreign-origin effect thought likely to be strongest for First World brands in Third World product markets. Finally, rationale 4 resembles rationale 3 in having been elaborated by cultural anthropologists (for example, Appadurai, 1990), but operates at the level of a multicultural or even acultural global community rather than being focused on particular foreign countries of origin.

These alternate customer rationales for global brands receive some support from recent empirical research, particularly a body of work by Batra and coauthors (for example, Batra and others, 2000, and Steenkamp, Batra, and Alden, 2000), with quality-signaling effects, rationale 2 seeming to be the most strongly supported. Attempts have been made as well to test some of the contingencies related to product category, customer type, and geography that might be expected to determine whether global brands actually are preferred over local brands. But the findings and even some of the predictions in this regard (for example, the prospects for global brands in durables versus nondurables) are equivocal. In addition, a complementary perspective is provided by work concerning the conditions under which local brands are likely to thrive, which places comparatively more emphasis on early-mover entrenchment and comparatively less on (other) sources of advantage or disadvantage (for example, Kapferer, 2000). All in all, this work suggests that there might be more momentum behind global standardization on the demand side than suggested by Levitt's focus on customer rationale 1, which has attracted particular debate. But it does not address whether global standardization has actually been increasing over time.

A third, emerging strand of empirical research has focused on the business or supply-side rationale for global standardization: the economies of simplicity and standardization adverted to by Levitt in "The Globalization of Markets." Work in this vein recognizes that businesses that are themselves globalizing might spur global standardization in consumer products as well as in business products and services. For instance, the spread of retailers across borders has made integrated global account management as important a challenge as global brand development and maintenance in many fast-moving consumer good categories. Thus, Henkel recently reported that euro accounts represent one-half of its turnover and that these accounts, rather than end consumers, supply the major motive for its attempts to standardize across key European markets (Morwind and Schroiff, 2000). The incidence of global account management, in particular, does appear to have increased over time (for example, Montgomery, Yip, and Villalonga, 1999; Arnold, Birkinshaw, and Toulan, 2000). But such work focuses on motives and mechanisms for standardization rather than on levels of standardization achieved over time.[1]

Taken together, these two more recent strands of research do not so much supply definitive answers to the specific question of whether global standardization is increasing as highlight the importance of integrating supply-side and demand-side effects in addressing that question. This, arguably, is the most enduring contribution of Levitt's "Globalization of Markets" article: it correctly flagged both types of effects as jointly determining market outcomes in terms of standardization versus customization. But the sort of cross-functional analytical approach integrating the supply and demand sides that Levitt effectively called for has generally been passed up in pursuit of narrower problems. The case example presented in the next section underscores the importance of such analytical integration and helps suggest a simple theoretical structure for achieving it.

The Case of STAR TV

Given the dearth of systematic evidence that specifically addresses the global standardization hypothesis, this chapter takes a more inductive tack: it looks at an interesting sector, focuses on a particularly interesting company within it, and then uses a simple theoretical model to generalize from the specifics of the case study. The case study not only constitutes a counterexample to the global standardization hypothesis but also supplies guidance for building a theoretical model and employing it to perform comparative static analyses that highlight a range of barriers to global standardization.

More specifically, this chapter looks within the media sector at television broadcasting. This sector is quite concentrated globally and has become more so in recent years, to the point that there has been recent agitation by antiglobalization activists against "media monoculture." Media and especially television are also supposed, as a result of the work of cultural anthropologists such as Appadurai (1990), to play a direct role in promoting further globalization through customer homogenization. On the supply side, electronic content, in particular, is subject to strong economies of global scale given its nonrival nature: its provision to one set of customers does not affect the ability to make it available to others. In terms of distribution, satellite television itself is often cited as a key driver of globalization given its ability to stretch broadcast content across geographies (versus conventional over-the-air terrestrial broadcasting). And since satellite broadcasting is a new industry, would-be global competitors have not had to confront entrenched local players. For all these reasons, we might assess a higher-than-average likelihood of penetration of this market by globally standardized offerings.

Within satellite broadcasting, the focal company, STAR TV, is a particularly interesting organization on which to focus in the context of the global standardization hypothesis (see Ghemawat 2000a, 2000b, for additional details). STAR was founded in 1991 by Li Ka-Shing and his Hong Kong–based Hutchison Whampoa group as an English-language broadcaster of mainly Western fare that targeted the top 5 percent of Asia's socioeconomic pyramid. STAR's launch strategy assumed that this regional segment was economically advanced enough to demand higher-quality television entertainment than what was then available, that it shared tastes that could be satisfied at least in part by Western programming, and that it was of interest as a group to regional advertisers. Thus, STAR's original strategy was highly standardized across the Asian countries in its footprint and was predicated on the globalization and regionalization of businesses (potential advertisers), as well as the homogenization of viewers' preferences.

In 1993, News Corporation, controlled by Rupert Murdoch, acquired a 64 percent interest in STAR TV for $525 million. Two years later, it bought out the rest of Hutchison Whampoa's interest for $300 million. This large investment was justified on the basis of perceived supply-side, as well as the original demand-side, reasons for standardization. News Corporation hoped to use STAR to arbitrage the million-plus hours of programming it already owned, particularly the Twentieth Century Fox movie and television program library and BSkyB sports and news programming, in the Asian market. Thus, analysts described News Corporation's purchase of STAR as "paying for global distribution of [its] product" ("Murdoch Bets on Channels' Star Potential," 1993, p. 20). It was envisioned that this strategy would cut the cost of programming for STAR to the bare minimum associated with copying tapes and broadcasting them.

But over time, STAR ended up transforming itself under News Corporation's ownership from a standardized pan-Asian platform to a series of platforms around the region, each targeted at a specific geography and aimed at a much broader swath of the local population.[2] The share of Western programs in STAR's broadcasts shrank as they were replaced at first with versions dubbed into local languages and later, in order to keep up with local productions whose quality and availability was improving greatly, with locally produced content. By 2001, CEO James Murdoch described STAR as "a series of local [national] businesses largely independent from each other," offering more than thirty channels of programming in eight languages, and also as "a mass market player."[3] Table 6.1 provides details and indicates that localization was particularly evident in STAR's two largest markets, China (which had 220 million TV households in 1994) and India (which had 46 million), which had been targeted as the principal growth drivers from the time that News Corporation had taken the company over.

In the course of buying and repositioning STAR, News Corporation invested what company officials characterized as a nominal total of $1.8 to $2 billion in the venture, or about $4 billion in present value terms, before it finally hit operating break-even in the first quarter of 2002.[4] James Murdoch indicated that this invest-

Table 6.1. STAR TV's Principal Channels in 2001

	India[a]	Greater China[b]	Rest of Asia[c]
Local languages	STAR Plus	Phoenix Chinese	VIVA Cinema
	STAR Gold	Phoenix Movies	(Tagalog)
	STAR Sports[d]	Phoenix InfoNews	[V] Korea[d]
	ESPN[d]	STAR Chinese	[V] Thailand
	Channel [V][d]	STAR Mandarin Movies	
	STAR News[d]	STAR Sports[d]	
	National Geographic[d]	ESPN[d]	
	Adventure One[d]	Channel [V][d]	
	Vijay	King Kong Wei Shi	
		National Geographic[d]	
English	STAR Movies	STAR World	STAR Movies
	STAR World	STAR Movies International	STAR Sports
			ESPN
			STAR World
			[V] International

[a]Hindi/Tamil. [b]Chinese. [c]Other. [d]Contains some programming in English.

ment was significantly higher than had been originally contemplated and reflected, to a significant extent, STAR's switch to a more localized strategy that required substantial country-specific programming investments after its initial choice of a regionally standardized strategy proved untenable because of strong, if initially latent, cultural preferences for local programming. He also reckoned that given those preferences, STAR could not have become financially viable if it had persisted with its initial strategy.

Others agreed that STAR had indeed switched the core elements of its strategy, but argued that the company's performance and prospects had suffered from an unduly slow pace of localization.[5] In particular, delays in, or confusion about, localization seem to have led to disadvantages over longer time horizons associated in part with letting competitors seize the initiative. In India, for example, News Corporation struck an early deal with Zee, the leading provider of Hindi-language programming, that restricted STAR's involvement in parallel efforts. While Zee quickly grew into the leading competitor in the Indian market, STAR was unable to unwind this contractual restriction on its activities in Hindi until the year 2000, squandering some of its early-mover advantage.[6]

Whatever one's assessment of how quickly STAR switched strategies, it clearly seems to constitute a counterexample to the global (or in this case, regional) standardization hypothesis. More broadly, it seems representative of the experience in TV broadcasting around the world in two important respects. First, cross-sectional data from a number of different sources on imported TV programs' share of total programming in thirty-one countries in Europe, Asia (not including China and India), and South America suggest a strong home bias toward local as opposed to imported content in all but very small markets, particularly in Asia (see Figure 6.1).[7] This pattern should have been of particular interest to STAR given the importance of China and India to its business plan and the fact that the European and Asian data were available when it was initially deciding whether to standardize content. But according to current and former STAR employees, there was no analysis of this sort until several years after News Corporation took over the company.

Second, in intertemporal as opposed to cross-sectional terms, STAR's trajectory anticipates what became, within a decade, the common wisdom about the evolution of the shares of local versus imported TV programming. Thus, according to a recent survey of television in the *Economist*, "When TV first takes off in any country, and there is only a fledgling production industry, cheap imports from America tend to fill the airwaves. With time, however . . . the share of locally made programmes grows" (Pedder, 2002, p. 12). And in the words of Peter Chernin, president and chief operating officer of News Corporation, cited in the same survey, "In almost every TV market in the world, local product has been growing in the past five years, at the expense of American."

Can one predict theoretically why the share of foreign TV programming varies the way it does in Figure 6.1? And what do various dynamics imply about predicted changes in this share over time? The development of a simple microeconomic model of the

Figure 6.1. Foreign Penetration and Domestic Market Size in TV Programming

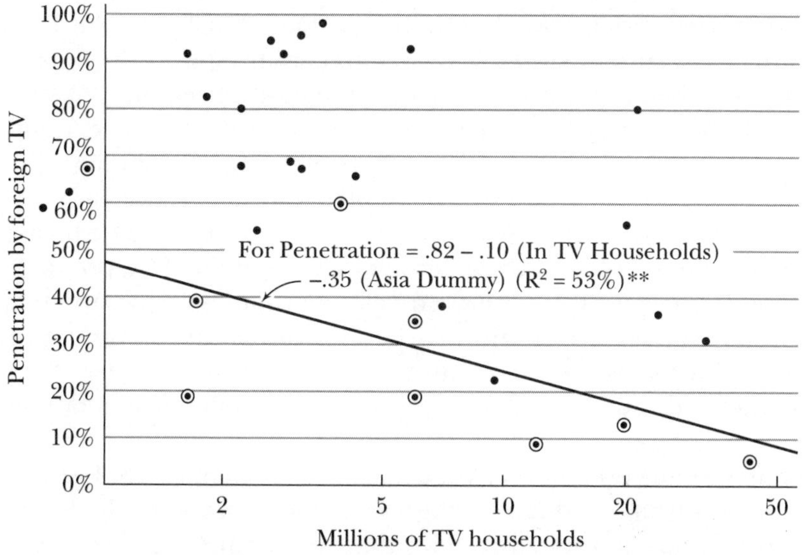

Note: Points represent individual countries; circled points are Asian countries (not including China or India). The line was drawn with ASIAN DUMMY set equal to 1; coefficients on both independent variables are significant at the 1 percent level.

Sources: Data for Asian countries for 1989 from Waterman and Rogers (1994), for European countries for 1990 from Biltereyst (1992), and for Latin American countries for 1996 from Chmielewski-Falkenheim (2000).

competition between globally standardized and locally customized varieties, stimulated in large part by the STAR case, will help answer both questions. The next section builds a simple model that is integrative in this sense; the following section elaborates some of its dynamic properties.

A Microeconomic Model

The model developed in this section and the next draws on Ghemawat and Spence (1986) but keys off the setting described in the previous section, generalizes certain parametric assumptions in

Ghemawat and Spence, and extends the analyses undertaken. The basic theoretical mechanism driving the model can be illustrated simply in terms of Figure 6.1. The most obvious reason that locally customized varieties might fare better than globally standardized varieties in larger markets is related to country-specific fixed costs of customization that are incurred with customized but not standardized offerings: larger markets are more likely to be able to support these country-specific fixed costs than smaller markets. This characterization of costs seems consistent with both the emphasis in STAR's initial strategy on minimizing country-specific investments and, more broadly, with the observation that U.S. programming for television (which dominates world exports) is sold into foreign markets for tenths of a percentage point of production costs to perhaps a few percentage points in the case of very large markets, according to *Variety* magazine. As a result, the cost of original programming tends to be several times as high as imported programming even in very large markets (for example, in Europe) and hundreds of times as high in smaller markets. To a first approximation, then, assuming that zero country-specific fixed costs are entailed in supplying the globally standardized (as opposed to locally customized) product seems reasonable.

The model developed in this section focuses on the competition between locally customized producers that incur country-specific fixed costs and a globally standardized producer that supplies an "outside" product and does not incur such costs. In order to support a simple examination of intermodal competition, intramodal competition is suppressed: it is assumed that there is one globally standardized producer and, potentially, one locally customized producer per country. Note that it would be simple to allow for multiple locally customized producers per country and, for that matter, multiple globally standardized producers as long as one is prepared to assume that the form of production that is most efficient, in a broad sense, in each country wins out there. However, a full-fledged treatment of intramodal competition that allows for the possibility of strategic interactions leading to outcomes that are inefficient in this sense is beyond the scope of this chapter.

Competition between these two modes of production is assumed to unfold in two stages. In the first stage, potential local producers (one per country) decide whether to enter their respective country markets. In the second stage, the global producer, whose existence is taken as given, and the local producers that have entered and whose identity is common knowledge simultaneously announce prices, that is, engage in Bertrand competition. It is provisionally assumed that customers' preferences are homogeneous within countries and that the global producer is allowed to price-discriminate across countries, which seems to be consistent with both the STAR case and, more generally, the pricing of U.S. exports of TV programs.

This one-sided formalization of what was, in the case of STAR, a two-sided market (two groups of customers, advertisers and viewers, the former caring about consumption by the latter) can be justified at least in the context of the initial strategy of free-to-air broadcasting.[8] Note that this strategy, although not necessarily appropriate, depended on advertisers for revenues and therefore boiled the relevant primitives down to advertisers' willingness to pay for viewership without requiring separate tracking of viewers' willingness to pay as a second revenue source. In terms of other extensions to the formalization, intranational heterogeneity is incorporated into the analysis, and the implications of constraints on price discrimination are then examined.

It is also worth highlighting one respect in which the model deliberately generalizes the conditions that characterized the case study. Instead of assuming that locally customized varieties are always preferred to globally standardized ones (or vice versa), the theoretical setup is flexible enough to let customer preferences tilt in either direction to encompass product categories in which globally standardized varieties are preferred as well as ones in which locally customized varieties are preferred (for example, TV programming). One of the strengths of this modeling effort is that all the conclusions derived here apply to both sorts of situations unless explicitly noted otherwise. By implication, we do not have to await resolution of the broad debate about whether globally standardized or locally customized products are preferred in general in order to make some headway. This is useful since the wait seems a long one.

It is time to be more specific in laying out the structure of the theoretical model, starting with the demand side. Suppose that there are n customer segments, each internally homogeneous, in the world. For simplicity, assume a one-to-one match between customer segments and countries such that all N_i customers in country i share common preferences with each other but not with customers in any other country.[9] Demand is taken to be price inelastic: each customer buys a given quantity, normalized to be one unit, of either the global variety or the relevant local one.[10] Denote the gross benefit (that is, the value of the product, gross of the price paid for it) that a representative customer in country i derives from the relevant local variety as u_i and from the global variety as $u_i - t_i$. Rational choice implies that customers in country i will purchase the globally standardized product in preference to the locally customized one if and only if

$$p_{iG} < p_I - t_i, \qquad (6.1)$$

where p_{iG} is the price of the globally standardized product in country i and p_i is the price of the relevant locally customized product.

The t_i term is worth elaborating. In the context of the STAR case, t_i was probably positive—that is, entailed penalties in terms of willingness to pay for the globally standardized product—across most values of i given the apparent preference for local programming over compromise "outside" programming. In addition to heterogeneity in tastes, reasons for positive t_i include various sorts of (extra) costs associated with cross-border economic activity—transportation costs; transaction costs associated with information, search, and communication; translation costs, tariffs; and so on—that are intermediate to the "manufacturer" and the end user and are tacked on to the base price by the time the product is sold. Such costs drive (differently sized) wedges between prices paid by end users and prices received by manufacturers, calling into question inferences about the latter (which are of primary interest in the present context) based on information about the former. So for t_i to be negative requires more than vertical differentiation or extra willingness to pay for the globally standardized product: it requires the pass-through of a higher price realization to the global producer after typically higher transportation and distribution costs, tariffs, or even risks are netted out of the premiums that customers are assumed to be willing to pay for the global product over the local one. Empirical evidence from the trade literature indicates that some of these cost elements, such as the extra costs and risks of cross-border operation, continue to be very significant (for example, Rousslang and To, 1993; Anderson and Marcouiller, 1999). Thus, in empirical assessments of whether t_i is positive or negative, it is advisable to focus on the net price available to producers rather than the total price paid by end users. Having said all that, the conclusions concerning (static) market characteristics and demand and cost dynamics that follow are generally robust to whether the t_i is positive or negative.

That completes the demand side setup. On the supply side, the model focuses on intermodal rather than intramodal competition. It posits, potentially, a different local competitor in each country that, because it has chosen to customize its product, cannot serve countries other than the one it has targeted. If a locally customized producer were to enter and supply country i, its total costs would be

$$TC_i = F_i + c_i N_i, \tag{6.2}$$

where F_i is a fixed, country-specific cost and c_i is its constant marginal cost. The corresponding terms for the globally standardized producer are F_G and c_G. Note that F_G pertains to global fixed costs rather than to country-specific fixed costs, which, by definition, are not incurred under strategies of maximal standardization. The assumption that the fixed costs are exogenous to the model reflects the sense that investments in building up News Corporation's million-plus hours of programming were mostly made with an eye to existing (non-Asian) markets before the company purchased STAR TV: in fact, a reasonable approximation in the context of STAR might be to set these fixed costs to zero, although no specific value of this sort is assumed in what follows. The invariance of the globally standardized producer's marginal cost, c_G, across countries, while inessential, is a simplification suggested by Levitt's characterization of the global corporation as one that "operates with resolute constancy—at low relative cost—as if the entire world (or major regions of it) were a single entity: it sells the same things in the same way everywhere."

Assuming the existence and operation of the globally standardized producer, it will incur the fixed costs F_G no matter what;

as a result, only the c_G term is relevant to its calculations about whether to beat out a local competitor that has elected to enter a particular market. Given the (provisional) assumption that it can price-discriminate perfectly, it is in the global producer's interest to beat out a local competitor that has entered and is charging price p_i if and only if

$$c_G < p_I - t_i. \tag{6.3}$$

Given equation 6.2, the minimal price that the locally customized competitor in country i can charge without losing money is $F_i/N_i + c_i$. Substituting this term for pi in inequality 6.3, the globally standardized product will take over country markets for which

$$c_G < \frac{F_i}{N_i} + c_i - t_i, \tag{6.4}$$

with locally customized products accounting for the remainder. Note that the right-hand side of inequality 6.4 is the average cost of the local producer if it supplies its entire national market minus any advantages (possibly negative) that it enjoys in terms of net price realizations. This suggests defining a "globalization index" for each country i of the form

$$G_i \equiv \frac{F_i}{N_i} + c_i - t_i. \tag{6.5}$$

If the global producer charges a price less than or equal to G_i, the locally customized producer in country i will drop out. Consequently, if country j has a higher globalization index than country k, then locally customized production is less likely to prove viable in j than in k. If locally customized producers do survive in both countries, the one in country j will post lower margins.

Examination of equation 6.5 confirms that locally customized producers are more likely to survive (and to earn high margins) in large countries with exotic tastes that can be catered to relatively cheaply.[11] In contrast, small countries whose tastes are close to cosmopolitan yet still expensive to satisfy strictly will tend to purchase the global product.[12] Note the affinity with the pattern depicted in Figure 6.1 and with the finding that at least in the European sub-sample, linguistic autonomy, as well as size, reduced the penetration of national markets by foreign programming (Biltereyst, 1992).

Market Dynamics and Global Standardization

The preceding predictions about global product market configurations at equilibrium, while interesting in and of themselves, are rendered even more interesting by the possibility of using them to track the links, positive or negative, between market dynamics and global standardization. The particulars of the STAR case suggest analyzing a number of different market dynamics, most of which can be overlaid on the simple theoretical structure specified in the previous section. It is convenient to group them into demand dynamics, cost dynamics, and convergence dynamics.

Demand Dynamics

The most obvious change in demand experienced by STAR during the 1990s consisted of rapid demand growth. STAR reached 11 million households in January 1993, before News Corporation acquired control; by January 1994, its reach had exploded to 42 million households, and by January 2000, it had expanded further to 95 million households. Rapid demand growth, especially early on, has been cited as one of the reasons STAR had to switch strategies from regional standardization to local customization. The question of broader interest, though, is whether this effect is a general one—whether demand growth should generally be expected to reduce the viability of standardized products relative to customized ones. Addressing this question requires turning from the case study to the model.

Scalar demand growth is most easily injected into the model by assuming that aggregate demand increases in all countries. This will lower the average cost of producing the country-centered varieties, shifting the G_i schedule downward. Because the global producer's marginal cost, c_G, stays put, increasing demand reduces the range of countries in which the globally standardized product wins out. Although this effect might come as a surprise, it can be explained relatively intuitively. As country markets expand, the importance of scale economies effectively decreases, as does the local producers' fitness disadvantage from their inability to spread their fixed costs across country borders.

A second aspect of demand dynamics that was bound up with rapid growth but had a nonscalar component concerned the broadening of demand beyond the elite that STAR originally targeted (Asia's top 5 percent) to the mass market. Since an important part of the rationale for focusing on the elite was that it was likely to have relatively cosmopolitan tastes, the broadening to cater to mass market viewers might have tipped country markets to locally customized products to a greater extent than would be expected as a result of the market size effect alone. This intuition can be confirmed by extending the model developed in the previous section to allow for within-country heterogeneity of demand.

Specifically, assume that the N_i customers in country i are divided between n_i elite customers and $N_i - n_i$ mass market customers and that initially only the elite customers are in the market. An elite customer's gross benefit from the relevant locally customized product (if offered) is u_i^E and from the globally standardized product $u_i^E - t_i^E$. The locally customized product secures country i if and only if

$$c_G > \frac{F_i}{n_i} + c_i - t_i^E. \tag{6.6}$$

Now let the mass market customers ($N_i - n_i$ in country i) enter the market as well, each experiencing gross benefits of u_i^M from the local product and $u_i^M - t_i^M$ from the global product. Assume a single product per competitor, a single price per product across the two segments within a country, and tipping toward a single mode of production at the level of an individual country. The local producer in country i will then be able to secure both segments, the elite and the mass market, if and only if

$$c_G > \frac{F_i}{N_i} + c_i - \frac{n_i t_i^E + (N_i - n_i) t_i^M}{N_i}. \tag{6.7}$$

Compared to condition 6.6, condition 6.7 embodies two distinct effects: a market size effect hurts global standardization, and a market mix effect tilts in the same direction if $t_i^M > t_i^E$ (that is, if the elite segment is more cosmopolitan than the mass market). Also note that if the mass market segment is as cosmopolitan as the elite segment or, by continuity, even slightly more cosmopolitan, that will not suffice to overturn the market size effect. So both the demand dynamics discussed in this subsection—scalar demand growth and the broadening of demand beyond the elite to the masses—are capable of reducing the equilibrium level of global standardization over time.

Cost Dynamics

On the cost side, the single most notable change that affected Asian satellite TV during the 1990s, particularly the second half of the decade, was the sharp decline in broadcasting costs per channel associated with the oversupply of transponders and the development of digital compression that allowed more channels to be squeezed onto the same bandwidth.[13] Should the failure of global standardization in the STAR case be read as having occurred in spite of, or because of, such cost reductions? (Cost increases could be discussed in symmetric fashion.)

The model forces useful precision in answering this question. Consider how its workings are affected by reductions in the costs of the globally standardized product and all locally customized products. The effects turn out to depend on the degree to which fixed rather than marginal costs are affected. Equal cost reductions that affect only marginal costs do not matter, for reasons that should be obvious from inequality 6.4; however, asymmetric reductions in marginal costs favor the mode of production whose marginal costs fall more. The impact of reductions in fixed costs is quite different. Then globalization indexes decrease, but the global producer's marginal costs do not, reducing the equilibrium degree of global standardization. The intuition, as in the case of increases in market size discussed in the previous section, is that reductions in the effective importance of scale economies hurt global standardization.

Returning to the case of STAR, whether the (predictable) cost reductions that it experienced over time should have been expected to hamper its pursuit of standardization depends on the cost components affected. As far as marginal operating costs are concerned, one could argue that there was greater room for reductions in locally customized competitors' costs given that the marginal production and distribution costs for a global (or regional) competitor were already so low. Such asymmetric reductions, were they to materialize, would hurt global standardization. And reductions in fixed costs, evident in the STAR case in the form of declining broadcast costs per channel, also hurt global standardization.

This analysis of the impact of changes in marginal and fixed costs can be melded by looking at the impact of changes in scale sensitivity in the relative proportion of fixed costs and marginal costs in total costs. In tracing the effects of such changes, it is important to guard against altering the values of other parameters. Note that at the initial equilibrium, the outputs of the global and country-centered producers are uniquely determined. Hold each producer's average cost at its original level of output constant, but shift the technology so that fixed costs account for an increased fraction of average costs. What is the relationship between the degree of global standardization at the new equilibrium and at the old one? The technology shift does not, by definition, affect globalization indexes at all, but it does decrease the global producer's marginal cost, c_G, favoring increased global standardization. Once again, fixed costs are strategic because the global competitor and its local rivals have implicitly chosen to cover them in two different ways (internationally versus intranationally). Note that decreases in scale sensitivity can be dealt with symmetrically. Thus, in the case of STAR, it was probably the combination of the increasing number of channels per market and the decreasing fixed costs per channel that hurt standardization.

Of course, the question of whether scale sensitivity is actually increasing or decreasing in a general sense is as yet unanswered. Some contend that we are moving toward a winner-take-all, increasing-returns economy, which would presumably help global standardization. Others argue that mass customization and, more broadly, sense-and-respond technology are fundamentally restructuring the trade-offs between scope and variety in a way that permits more of the latter at no extra cost (Pine, 1992). But agreement in this regard is not required to draw a simple conclusion: distinguishing more sharply between different types of cost reductions, or increases, can help sharpen predictions about how cost dynamics are likely, if at all, to affect the relative viability of globally standardized versus locally customized varieties.

A final dynamic that might also be described as cost related concerns the relative timing of entry. Note that the order of moves can affect market outcomes only if the moves involve irreversible commitments (Shapiro, 1989; Ghemawat, 1991). Such commitments are most naturally associated with the fixed costs in the original model, F_G and F_i, reinterpreted as one-time costs of entry that are sunk once they are incurred and that enable production at the applicable marginal costs (which continue to be incurred in the short run on an ongoing basis rather than just once in the long run). It is simple to confirm that if the global producer enters first, the set of countries that it serves at equilibrium will, as in the original model, continue to be given by condition 6.4. Things are different, however, if locally customized producers have entered first. The condition for the global producer to find it profitable to displace them, given that their entry costs are already sunk, is now given by

$$c_G < c_i - t_i, \tag{6.8}$$

which is more stringent than condition 6.4. Whether local producers move first matters because, unlike the global producer, they make commitments to particular country markets. The broader implication is that given such commitment opportunities, global standardization is less likely in "old" industries with entrenched local competitors than in "new" industries in which key competitors are global from the outset.

The effect of reductions in marginal costs on the equilibrium degree of global standardization depends on whether the globally standardized or locally customized varieties experience greater absolute cost reductions as a result. But reductions in fixed costs or decreases in scale sensitivity (in the sense defined above) unambiguously hurt global standardization. So does the ability of locally customized producers to make preemptive sunk-cost commitments to particular country markets.

Convergence Dynamics

A third set of dynamics concerns what might broadly be called convergence: the process whereby countries might be coming to look more like each other along certain dimensions over time. Whether countries actually are converging is a large question that cannot be addressed here. What can be pointed out, however, is that even if convergence along particular dimensions is taking place, predictions that this will induce increases in global standardization are subject to several qualifications. To see this, one has to distinguish several different convergence dynamics and analyze them one by one in the context of the model.

The most obvious kind of convergence, stressed by Levitt among others, involves homogenization of tastes. In the model, convergence in tastes can be expressed in terms of reductions, toward zero, of the absolute values of the t_i parameters. If t_i is initially positive (so that locally customized products are preferred), it is easy to check that their tending toward zero *does* increase the equilibrium level of global standardization by increasing globalization indexes while leaving the global producer's marginal costs unchanged. Less obviously, though, if t_i is initially negative, as is often actually assumed by global marketers about the current environment, declines in their absolute values can be seen as declines in favorable lead country or foreignness effects that can lead to decreases rather than increases in global standardization.[14] So whether the globally standardized or locally customized product is initially preferred does matter in the context of this dynamic, in contrast to the others that have been examined thus far.

A second kind of convergence entails countries starting to look alike in ways that extend beyond similarity in tastes to include the other components of the globalization index specified in equation 6.5. Note that as countries converge in this sense, globalization indexes tend toward equality across them. With identical globalization indexes across countries, the globally standardized producer succeeds either everywhere or nowhere. In other words, if countries' globalization indexes are sufficiently alike, they are likely to be subject to a domino effect: either the global producer or the country-centered producers will tend to win out across the board. Which of these two possible outcomes obtains will depend on the specifics of the parameterization of the situation.

A third possible kind of convergence concerns the prices of the globally standardized product across countries. Mechanisms that have been cited as drivers of convergence along this dimension include Internet-related declines in search costs (Quelch, 2000) and the insistence on global pricing by globalizing customers such as retail chains (Narayandas, Quelch, and Swartz, 2000). Again, without offering any independent evidence that such convergence is generally taking place, it is possible to look at its implications. Compare the original model, in which perfect price discrimination by the global producer across countries is possible, with the polar situation in which there are no price discrimination possibilities of this sort: the global producer has to charge the same price across all the countries that it serves. This iso-pricing constraint does not affect globalization indexes or, therefore, the ordering of countries by fitness of local players relative to the global one. But it does mean that the global producer will refrain from penetrating some of the marginal countries that satisfy condition 6.4 because the price reductions required to penetrate them result in inframarginal losses that more than offset the gains to be had from additional business at the margin. As a result, convergence in the prices of the globally standardized product across countries is predicted, other things being equal, to reduce its equilibrium degree of penetration.

Summing up, the predicted effects of convergence on global standardization vary across different kinds of convergence dynamics. The effects of convergence of tastes vary with whether locally customized or globally standardized products are (initially) intrinsically preferred. The effects of convergence of globalization indexes more broadly depend on the parameterization of the problem, although at the limit, we can predict an extreme outcome in which the globally standardized product either wins out across the board or nowhere at all. Finally, the convergence of prices of the globally standardized product across countries hurts the equilibrium degree of global product standardization.

It is also useful at this point to look back across the analysis that has been performed so far. Substantively, it suggests that the global standardization hypothesis has much less momentum than it is sometimes said to possess. And methodologically, it illustrates the usefulness of specifying some sort of theoretical structure, if only a simple one, when working through such issues; intuition alone would probably be inadequate.

Discussion

The simple model of global standardization versus local customization presented and analyzed here could be extended and
elaborated in a number of obvious ways. A particularly high priority would be to unbundle horizontal and vertical differentiation
and look at the effects of endogenous sunk-cost investments in the
latter on market outcomes. The possibility that investments in raising willingness to pay can sustain or raise concentration even in a
growing market is highlighted in models that Sutton (1991, 1998)
develops and applies to manufacturing industries, but that also
seem applicable to the cultural sector, especially in the case of the
global film industry, which is worth discussing briefly.

Although the U.S. share of fiction programming for TV is
shrinking, it (principally Hollywood) continues to dominate the
film industry worldwide. By some estimates, it accounts for close
to 80 percent of worldwide film-related revenues, up substantially
since the 1960s (Gabler, 2003). Hollywood's dominance in revenue
terms seems to involve taking a product that was already far more
expensive to make than other cultural products such as TV programming and music recordings and further escalating investment
levels to create films that are more entertaining, visible, and potentially global in their appeal as well as costing much more, on average, than films made elsewhere. (Hollywood was arguably the
natural candidate to escalate because of its access to the largest
home market in the world, the privileged role of English as a language of wider communication, its highly commercial orientation,
and its earlier exposure to threats from television.) Such escalation
applies to the costs of talent and marketing as well, but is particularly evident on the production side in categories such as action
films. Such films, with their expensive scenes of adventure and
mayhem, constitute a category in which U.S. dominance is particularly pronounced. Similar escalation of endogenous sunk costs is
not as evident in TV programming over the period of the STAR
case, partly because of the cost-cutting pressures felt by traditional
networks facing new, more cost-effective competitors, both direct
(for example, News Corporation's Fox TV in the United States and
Sky TV in Britain) and indirect (for example, cable in the United
States). In fact, the emergence of TV seems to have reinforced the

process of concentration in the film industry by drastically shrinking the traditional market for films: movie tickets sold reportedly declined by more than one-half between 1946 and 1956 in the United States and by about three-quarters, mostly between the mid-1960s and the mid-1980s, in a number of other major markets (Cowen, 2002).

The film example suggests that extending the model presented in this chapter to allow for endogenous sunk costs would be highly useful. So too would a generalization of the demand side to allow local varieties, not just a standardized "outside" product, to compete across borders: cross-border competition from within countries is essential to modeling possibilities such as large home markets helping to make varieties from those countries more viable global (not just local) competitors.

Specific extensions to the model such as the incorporation of endogenous sunk costs and attention to the variation in cross-border competitors' home bases do not, however, exhaust the STAR case. It also offers broader insights about the country-level influences on and the firm-level content of cross-border strategy. The rest of this section focuses on two types of insights that emerge. First, I argue that STAR's missteps serve as a reminder of the importance in international business strategy of thinking broadly about the differences or distance between countries: along the cultural, administrative, political, institutional and economic dimensions, as well as the geographical one. Then I discuss some of what has worked for STAR and use this to argue for broader consideration of strategies that fall, in some sense, between the extremes of local customization and global standardization (including but not limited to adaptation).

Differences Across Countries

Starting in the 1980s, satellite television started to arouse great interest in Li Ka-Shing, Rupert Murdoch, and many others because of its potential to dissolve constraints on the geographical reach of terrestrial broadcasting, portrayed as the death of geographical distance in one formulation advanced in the late 1990s. Fascination with the death of geographical distance seems to be the most plausible explanation of the otherwise puzzling failure, early in STAR TV's history, to pay adequate attention to other categories of differences or distance between countries that clearly remained significant.

Cultural differences, particularly linguistic ones, constitute one underemphasized category. In the context of TV programming, the home bias evident in Figure 6.1 has already been discussed. A prominent component, although not the only one, consists of local preferences for local language programming. Yet in initially positioning STAR as an English language broadcaster, its ethnically Chinese founders managed, at least in their own minds, to overcome this fact. Possible missteps in this regard after News Corporation acquired control included the handling of negotiations with Zee TV in India, originally STAR's partner there and later its most bitter competitor, which delayed STAR's entry into Hindi language programming while allowing Zee its independence, and the relatively slow pace of localization efforts even after it became clear that local language programming was the way to go. For example, STAR News finally dropped English in March 2003 in favor of an exclusive focus on Hindi, after which its share of viewers reportedly increased from 7 to 30 percent in four months (Pedder, 2003).

Linguistic and other cultural effects might be less salient in most other products or services, but they continue to be large on average. For instance, fitting trade data to "gravity models" suggests that a common language should be expected to lead to 40 percent more trade on average between a country pair than would occur in the absence of this cultural tie (Ghemawat and Mallick, 2003). Effects this large cannot sensibly be neglected, but often they are.

A second underemphasized category of differences concerns administrative and political differences across countries. Media, particularly TV broadcasting, are salient politically because of their potential to affect public opinion and therefore remain subject, around the world, to extensive state control through licensing, regulation, ownership, and even censorship (Djankov, McLiesh, Nenova, and Shleifer, 2001). Thus, even in the relatively free-wheeling United States, the purchase of local television stations required News Corporation's Rupert Murdoch, formerly Australian, to become a U.S. citizen.[15] In much more tightly controlled Asian contexts, particularly China (STAR's key market), foreign firms could expect to be scrutinized closely, making circumspect handling of political issues a precondition for commercial success. Early on, however, the strategy of News Corporation and STAR did not seem to pay much more attention to political issues than did the model. Perhaps the most glaring political misstep was Rupert Murdoch's public pronouncement, after gaining control of STAR, that satellite television was "an unambiguous threat to totalitarian regimes everywhere" because it permitted people to bypass government-controlled news sources.[16] Unsurprisingly, the Chinese government retaliated by enacting a ban on the reception of foreign satellite TV services. Although News Corporation has since made strenuous attempts to rebuild its relationships with the Chinese government, its progress has generally been regarded as limited. And mainland China remains extremely important because it still accounts for more than half of the households that can receive STAR.

More broadly, administrative and political differences or their converse, commonalities, are enormously important in general as well as in the STAR case. Thus, gravity modeling indicates that a common membership in a regional trading bloc should be expected to increase bilateral trade by about 50 percent on average, a common currency by more than 100 percent, and a colony-colonizer relationship (mostly in the past) by nearly 200 percent, after controls are implemented for a number of other factors, including common language and geographical distance (for example, Ghemawat and Mallick, 2003).

A final category of differences that seems to have mattered more than expected in the case of STAR is the economic one. Whereas parent News Corporation's previous broadcasting experience mostly involved advanced (and English-speaking) markets, STAR TV was squarely targeted at emerging markets (its ambit deliberately excluded Japan, where News Corporation's television interests were separately organized and operated). In addition to implying lower per capita incomes for viewers, which STAR's business model tried to overcome by targeting Asia's top 5 percent, there were two apparently underappreciated corollaries related to the difficulties of deriving revenues from advertising given the poor level of development of Asian ratings systems and from subscription service given the dearth of billing, collection, and subscriber management systems (as well as environments in which the enforceability of agreements with cable operators was often weak). While progress has been made on both fronts, the difficulties created by the dearth of specialized infrastructure (or intermediaries) have been substantial.

Having catalogued the range of differences, it is worth making two additional comments about them. First, although industry context obviously has a profound impact on how much a specific type of difference matters in a particular context, industry-level analysis might itself be too aggregated a frame: disaggregation down to the level of individual products or product types may be required. For example, focusing on just cultural differences, industry sources propose a hierarchy of TV program globalizability (in decreasing order): nature films, action and animation, drama, sit-coms, sports, weather, and news (although there are global niches even for news). For many purposes, it is more useful to think about cultural differences at this disaggregated level instead of at the level of TV programming in general.

Second, it is worth adding that the barriers or effective distance between countries can increase over time instead of necessarily decreasing (as assumed by Levitt, among others). Thus, STAR's recent success in Hindi language news broadcasting seems to have provided some of the impetus for a new Indian rule, lobbied for by STAR's chief local rival, Zee TV, that limits foreign ownership of TV news outlets to 26 percent. As of July 2003, disputes about the way in which STAR had spread equity in its editorial firm among six apparently friendly Indian investors to comply with this rule meant that STAR News had to obtain permission on a week-to-week basis from the Indian government to uplink news content from India while it sought to secure a ten-year license ("Murdoch's Twinkler," 2003).

To attempt a broad summary, the question of why countries differ—the key supplement, in an international context, to the fundamental strategic question of why firms differ—must be thought through in all its multidimensionality in a way attuned to the specifics of the industry being considered. A simple framework for doing so is proposed by Ghemawat (2001) under the rubric of CAGE to denote cultural, administrative, geographic, and economic differences across countries (all the metadimensions discussed above; also see Ghemawat and Mallick, 2003).

Strategy Alternatives

The litany of missteps notwithstanding, STAR has enjoyed some notable successes, and these provide clues about the content of cross-border strategies that fall between the extremes of complete localization and complete standardization. These alternatives include but are not limited to traditional notions of adaptation.

As of mid-2003, STAR's leadership position in the Indian market was considered the jewel in its portfolio: STAR Plus, its Hindi language entertainment channel, had forty-five of the top fifty programs and 56 million viewers versus 33 million for Zee TV, its leading Indian-owned rival, and STAR News had come from behind to build up an even slightly larger lead over Zee's news channel after completing the switch to Hindi earlier in the year ("Murdoch's Twinkler," 2003). At one level, these successes can simply be seen as the natural consequences of an adaptation, local language programming, that was the obvious thing to attempt in the industry context being considered. But at another level, the STAR case suggests that to treat adaptation of a particular type as the one and only alternative to the strategies of complete localization and complete standardization is to underestimate the richness of the strategist's choice set.

For one thing, even within the very narrow category of linguistic adaptation, one can imagine a range of responses to home language bias that have potentially different performance implications: local language dubbing, voice overs, subtitles, on-air promotions and teasers, and local hosts and commentators as well as the (local) production of local language programming. Global broadcasters within the same local market can vary substantially in their choices from the menu of options listed above.[17] So the choice of what types of adaptation to pursue is a nontrivial one, even if one thinks of adaptation relatively narrowly.

Second, it is often possible and even essential to envision more innovative responses to the challenges of adaptation than are summoned up by the stock image of taking an existing product or service and tinkering with it to achieve better fit with a local market. Thus, STAR's recent success in India reflects, as much as anything else, the effects of one dominant show, *Kaun Banega Crorepati?* (KBC).[18] KBC first aired in July 2000. In less than two months, STAR's viewership over its entire weekly lineup jumped from 1.6

television rating points to 8.2. In addition to KBC's own unprecedented ratings, it had huge positive spillovers because of aggressive promotion of STAR's other shows, as well as halo and inertial effects: ratings for STAR's other shows on the four nights each week that KBC was aired went up by 380 percent and for its shows on other nights by 320 percent.

The show that sparked this turnaround is the Hindi-language version of *Who Wants to Be a Millionaire?* a concept STAR licensed from the British production house of Celador. STAR used the same basic set, music, and rules in KBC as in the original but decided that the participants, questions, and marketing had to be adapted to local conditions. In particular, it hired a leading Hindi-language film actor as host and took him and other talent to the United Kingdom to see the British version of the show being taped, on the basis of which the actor developed key catchphrases that might work in Hindi. Heavy investments were made in marketing as well, which ensured that the debut of the show was a major event in Hindi language broadcasting. Although the success of KBC inspired direct imitation, none of these efforts fared very well, including erstwhile local leader Zee TV's attempt to increase the prize dollars from about $225,000 to about $2.25 million. Any foreign or local competitor could have licensed the show from Celador for the Hindi language market, as James Murdoch, CEO of STAR TV noted: "We all go to the same fairs."[19] But STAR's specific knowledge of local viewers' preferences combined with its and News Corporation's production expertise (which included other game shows) to give it an advantage at identifying and investing in what was, in many respects, more an attempt at innovation—or at least recombination of elements of the parent business model with some of the new possibilities implicit in the local environment—than adaptation, conventionally construed.

Third, the case of STAR's parent, News Corporation, suggests another strategy for creating value through cross-border operation that is clearly distinct from the ones considered so far: arbitrage. News Corporation is, among other things, a widely cited example of tax arbitrage. While taxes were not an issue in the first few years of the new millennium given large write-downs, through the 1990s News Corporation paid income taxes at an average rate of less than 10 percent, compared to statutory tax rates of 30 to 36 percent in the three main countries in which it operated (Britain,

America, and Australia) and actual rates close to that range for major competitors such as Disney. Given the profit pressures on News Corporation—net margins consistently less than 10 percent of sales in the second half of the 1990s and an asset-to-sales ratio that ballooned to three-to-one—these tax savings may have been critical to its attempts to generate economic value. The tax savings were largely achieved by organizing operations as holding companies in tax havens: thus, STAR TV was incorporated in the British Virgin Islands. Overall, News Corporation had approximately one hundred subsidiaries incorporated in jurisdictions with minimal corporate taxes or financial disclosure requirements. The intangibility of its informational assets facilitated the movement of profits to low-tax jurisdictions. As one accounting authority put it, "There's absolutely no reason why a piece of paper, which is the right to show something, couldn't sit anywhere, so it could be sitting in the Cayman Islands."[20] As this example indicates, cross-border arbitrage keys off the differences rather than the similarities across countries.

These examples start to suggest the richness of the strategic alternatives to the extremes of complete localization and complete standardization. Note that the additional alternatives are of interest in situations in which national markets are neither completely segmented (which would dictate complete localization) nor completely integrated (which would dictate standardization), an intermediate level of cross-border integration that I refer to as semiglobalization. Ghemawat (2003b) provides a review of the evidence on the cross-border integration of markets that leads to a diagnosis of semiglobalization and some insights into appropriate strategies. In addition, Ghemawat (2003a) elaborates on the arbitrage strategy, in particular, using the CAGE framework for thinking about the differences between countries that have already been cited. Further exploration of strategies for semiglobalization would seem to be at least as high a priority as continued wrangling over whether standardization is better or worse than localization.

Conclusion

The case of STAR TV provides a counterexample to the global standardization hypothesis in a context, satellite television, that might make proponents of global standardization take notice since the medium is often supposed to be highly globalized or globalizing. It also supplies guidance about how to build a simple microeconomic model of the competition between globally standardized and locally customized products and the comparative static analyses to be performed with such a model.

The conclusions from the modeling effort are worth resummarizing. Demand growth, the broadening of demand beyond the elite to the masses, and reductions in fixed costs or scale sensitivity on the supply side are all capable of reducing the equilibrium level of global standardization, as is the ability of local producers to precommit costs to particular markets. The effects of the convergence of tastes and of globalization indexes depend on what things are converging from or toward, although at least in the former case, it is possible to add that narrowing taste differences are likely to increase global standardization if taste differences initially favored local producers and to decrease global standardization if the reverse were true. Convergence of the price of the globally standardized product across countries does, however, unequivocally reduce the global product's degree of penetration in equilibrium.

Overall, the theoretical analysis, of which Table 6.2 supplies a partial summary, suggests that Levitt's "The Globalization of Markets" was almost certainly too extreme in the emphasis that it placed on global product standardization. Levitt's more enduring contribution seems to be that he correctly flagged demand-side preferences and supply-side economies of simplicity and standardization as the joint determinants of standardization versus customization in market outcomes. In that sense, this chapter has built directly on Levitt's pioneering insight, although it has done so using a simple formal model, since pure intuitions about such complex phenomena seem capable of going astray.

Looking beyond the model, the case study also calls attention to the multidimensionality of the differences across countries and the need to think explicitly about strategies for semiglobalization, strategies for the midrange in which the barriers between countries are neither so large as to effectively isolate them (which would imply a strategy of localization) nor so negligible as to effectively integrate them (which would imply a strategy of standardization).

Table 6.2. Barriers to Global Standardization Summarized

Country Attributes	Demand Dynamics	Cost Dynamics	Convergence Dynamics
Large countries	Demand growth	Reductions in fixed costs/ scale sensitivity	Convergence of tastes if initial $t_i > 0$; divergence of tastes if initial $t_i < 0$
Exotic tastes but low cost to serve	Mass market penetration (if mass market customers are less cosmopolitan)	Precommitment possibilities (local producers)	Convergence of prices of global product

CHAPTER 7

It's a Small World After All . . . or Is It?

The State of Globalization in the Worldwide Automotive Industry

Nick Scheele

When you consider the term *globalization* in a broad sense, it certainly is a topic with immediate meaning in this time we are in. Geopolitical tensions have had the entire world on edge. And now war and its aftermath will certainly engage most of the world either directly or through the global repercussions.

Supply and cost issues for vital commodities like oil are concerns around the globe. Investment money flows across national borders at the click of a mouse. And economic activity, or inactivity, in one region increasingly has an impact on other regions.

Even the term itself—*globalization*—has tremendous emotional force, becoming for some a rallying cry to protest what they believe is the negative and growing influence of global institutions and corporations.

Obviously, *globalization* is an expression, and a phenomenon, that has numerous meanings in numerous circumstances. I suspect that even inside the narrower framework of the globalization of markets, there are probably different definitions of what constitutes globalization, just as there are differing views on what constitutes globalization, whether we are a global industry, and where the trend is headed.

Many factors push us to examine globalization and anything promising better economy of scale and more efficient product development. First and foremost is the incredible capital intensity of the auto industry. It takes staggering sums of money to be in this business. Ford Motor Company's yearly material and services costs are $60 billion in North America and $30 billion in Europe and elsewhere. Its capital expenditures run about $7 billion annually. And it spends billions on top of that to develop and stay abreast of new technology.

The drive for efficiency, including product commonization, is made all the more urgent by worldwide overcapacity of somewhere around 30 percent, as well as explosive growth in Asia. Before we leave this decade, the Asian auto industry outside of Japan will grow by more than 50 percent and will rival or surpass each of Europe and North America in volume. You can't be a global player and not be there.

Competition on a scale I would not have imagined twenty years ago is another factor. And as this industry ties itself ever closer to the customer, the customer has an ever larger voice in its direction. As a result, auto companies are racing to introduce new and differentiated products at an incredible pace.

Ford is introducing sixty-five new Ford, Lincoln, and Mercury products in North America over five years; forty-five new products over five years in Europe; thirty-five new products globally in its premium brands; and a host of new products in the next several years at Mazda and in both its Asia-Pacific and South America operations.

Liberalized trade is another trend that prompts Ford to look for globalization opportunities, as does progress in technology. For instance, advancements in computer-aided design and manufacturing have removed a lot of past geographical restraints.

Today, we do not necessarily need design, engineering, and production expertise all colocated in a target market. In fact, we can have an engineer in Dunton, England, and an engineer in Dearborn, Michigan looking at the same three-dimensional image simultaneously, with either of them making changes in real time.

Finally, there is also a certain amount of customer convergence in the world. Some of this convergence is driven by economic growth and increasing affluence. Much of it is driven by the rapid increase in nearly instantaneous communication. The Internet, for example, can introduce consumers in any part of the world with the products and product features that any other consumers are choosing. And Ford knows the impact of this from firsthand experience. In developing countries especially, it is often confronted with consumers whose tastes and demands are leapfrogging their market's current products because they have seen something else they like on the Internet.

Where does all this put us in terms of globalization in the auto industry? Let me begin to answer that question with a history that illustrates my viewpoint.

One hundred years ago, after much trial and tribulation and preceded by years of uncertainty as to the eventual outcome, Henry Ford and his original partners signed the papers of incorporation for his eponymous company. Five years after that, having run through nineteen earlier iterations, as well as letters of the alphabet, the Model T debuted.

It was a remarkable machine for its time, and it fulfilled Henry Ford's dream and promise to provide an automobile for the masses. Ted Levitt mentions the Model T in his *Harvard Business Review* article. The vehicle was highly standardized, with superior craftsmanship, high reliability, and low cost—the key characteristics that Levitt identified as driving global product acceptance.

In fact, Henry referred to the Model T as his "universal car." And while at first reflection you might consider the Model T to be only a microcosm of Levitt's proposition, vehicle sales were not limited to the United States. The Model T sold briskly in Europe and in lands as diverse as Thailand, Ethiopia, and Barbados. Henry's "universal car" was a global car.

Now jump ahead about seventy-five years. Levitt publishes his landmark article, and I am working in the United States as a purchasing manager, assigned to Ford Motor Company's global small car product program: the compact-sized Escort.

While Henry Ford may have considered it absolutely and completely natural that one product sell around the world, we had certainly moved a considerable distance from that point by the 1980s. The Escort program was our first attempt to move back in the direction of a global product offering and was originally planned as a totally common vehicle in both the United States and Europe. But when the Escort launched in the United States in the early 1980s, it shared with its European sibling exactly one common part: the radiator cap. And even that one part was changed within six months of launch.

There were certainly reasons in that era that argued for having a common vehicle in both the major markets of Europe and the United States. For one thing, the oil shocks of the 1970s had reinforced the need for a small, fuel-efficient entry in this country. And a deep recession in the early 1980s made product costs and strategies for more efficient development a huge factor.

But there were strong currents pushing against commonality. In the first place, the perspective was entirely different from one market to the other; in other words, the Escort was mass-market, middle-class, family transportation in Europe. In the United States, it was economical transportation. And this had an impact on design and development decisions, as well as feature and material selection.

It was a good idea, and the benefits were expected to be considerable. But in practice, in the real-world execution of the plan, the idea was whittled away piece by piece, decision by decision, as regional market thinking and issues overwhelmed corporate-level strategy.

Today, we are more than twenty years beyond that first modern attempt to build a global car, and a number of broad factors push us to seek more product commonization. Yet I still cannot say that Ford is a globalized company or industry, at least not if applying a strict definition.

Ford is certainly a global company and a global industry in that it exists virtually everywhere. It has a number of processes and best practices in the business (in the area of quality, for example) that have been globalized; that is, they have been standardized from one region to the next. Some components and some vehicle systems lend themselves to global development and deployment.

But in that criterion that I would rank as most important—and the criterion that I believe Levitt would consider the ultimate measure—Ford is not global. I am referring, of course, to the total and end product itself and to the quality of having a truly standardized product line across the globe.

This is not to say that Ford has not made strides in that direction. Let me offer another example: the Ford Focus, which replaced the Escort program and debuted in Europe in 1999 and in North America in 2000.

The story with Focus is significantly different from its predecessor and the one common part. The European version and the North American version of Focus are about 65 percent common. Someone not in the business who looked at the vehicles side by side would probably have difficulty distinguishing between them. Still, it is not a global car. A number of factors drove some key differences, including a disparity in geography and environmental conditions, government regulations, and customer preferences.

When I look at the auto industry in total, and at Ford as a good representative example, my conclusion is that we are only selectively globalized: in some products, components, and processes. But in total, and especially in most of the high-volume, mass-market heart of the business, the auto simply is not there.

Barriers to Wide-Ranging Globalization

The single biggest barrier to globalization, despite the recent run-up in prices, is the relatively cheap cost of motor fuel in the United States. There is a tremendous disparity between the United States and basically the rest of the world, and it creates an accompanying disparity in some of the most fundamental of vehicle characteristics: size and power.

The best-selling vehicle in the United States is the Ford F-Series pickup truck. You will not see too many of them in, say, Italy. But in Italy, you will see quite a few Fiat Seicentos, with horsepower most Americans would say is more appropriate for a midsize street motorcycle.

The F-Series and Seicento are examples at the margins. Nevertheless, it is pervasively true that most vehicle classes in the United States are not viable products in many other parts of the world, and certainly not in volume. Even within the same product, fuel price differences can push major vehicle differences. Basically 100 percent of Ford's Land Rover Discovery is sold with a 4.6 liter V-8 engine in the United States. But in Europe, 95 percent of the Discovery SUVs are sold with a 2.5 liter turbo diesel. The differences in vehicle size and in power plant between the United States and most of the rest of the world are going to continue as long as fuel prices remain relatively low here.

A second factor that often works against common product is government regulation and policy. There can be substantial differences in safety and emissions regulations across regions and even among national markets.

In safety, it is not a question of providing more or less that drives product differences. Ford is committed to effective as well as affordable safety in every market where it sells cars and trucks. It is more a question of the nature of a given safety requirement. Crash testing provides an example. The basic frontal crash test that must be passed in Europe or Japan is different from the basic test in the United States. Different dynamics come into play, and different systems are emphasized. The result is that body structures and bracing strategies can be significantly different.

There are times when, given current circumstances, different requirements are appropriate. Side impact requirements, for instance, are also different in the United States than in Europe and Japan. The disparities in vehicle size as well as traffic patterns and conditions warrant different crash philosophies and strategies in this case. But overall, we at Ford would prefer to see more convergence in regulations, which would drive more product commonization rather than product differentiation.

There are other differences to contend with too: in geography, climate, infrastructure, cultural diversity, temperature swings, travel distances, road character, towing patterns, work habits, leisure activities. . . , and more. All of these can vary widely from one region to another. Some of them may push large product differences and some may small differences. Some may be noticeable to the customer, and some may not. But all of them do interfere with the ability to produce truly global product lines.

A last barrier is customer preferences. Although they are converging in many respects, they still drive a lot of product differences as well.

While the love of cup holders is often offered as the quintessentially American product feature, there are other differences in taste that compel large differences in the vehicle. Vehicle size is a major differentiator between North America and basically the rest of the world. In Japan, possibly even more so than in Europe, small size and high fuel efficiency are key attributes for most of the market.

Ride quality, which influences many underside components and systems, can be a significant difference between Europe and many other parts of the world. Many European drivers like a tighter, stiffer feel that others might find harsh and uncomfortable.

Plastic, in both the interior compartment and for body panels, is much more readily accepted in North America than Europe. And diesel engines, virtually nonexistent in U.S. and Japanese passenger cars, are nearly 40 percent of the Western European market.

Areas of Progress in Global Products

With all these limiting factors to contend with, where have we at Ford enjoyed any success at commonizing the product? Around the world, there are only a couple of products where there is at least some demand in every market: small cars . . . (I use the term here to mean basically what an American would consider small—a car like Ford Focus) and compact pickup trucks.

With small cars, Ford is rolling out a product that will be much more ambitious than the common Ford Focus that closed out the previous decade. This product will include more than a dozen distinct vehicles and be spread over three brands at the start: Ford Brand in Europe, Volvo, and Mazda. Ford has shown a couple of these cars publicly already and is launching the first vehicles in the line.

Shared architecture, systems, and components in non-customer-sensitive areas will result in a range of commonality of about 40 to 65 percent. But to the customer, the vehicles will be unique, and their individual brand character will be preserved.

Ford is going to great lengths in this search for efficiency to understand and appreciate what parts of a vehicle communicate brand and what parts are transparent to the customer. And it is finding those undifferentiated hard points that can be common across product lines. All this is absolutely essential if commonality is going to work.

In compact trucks, Ford sells a product in about a hundred markets around the world—about sixty being Ford-branded products and forty being Mazda. As recently as about ten years ago, it could not have sold a similar product across the main regions of the world. There were still too many barriers and too much customer divergence.

Today Ford can sell a compact truck with substantial commonality in small truck markets as diverse as Europe, Japan, and Thailand. The consumers in these markets have moved a lot closer in their tastes and requirements over the past decade. It will, however, be some time before there is one small pickup that suits the entire global market.

Outside of small cars and compact trucks, perhaps the next best example of global success is in luxury brands. Although there may not be large demand in every market around the globe, there is demand in all the key regions. And in these cases, what is sold—basically, with some exceptions—is the same product across all of those regions.

With premium vehicles and globalization, I still make something of a fine distinction. I do not really consider Jaguar a global car. It is an English car sold globally. Mercedes is a German car sold globally. Ferrari is an Italian car sold globally.

At Ford, where globalization may apply more is in how it treats its luxury and premium brands as a collection. Ford has assembled Jaguar, Land Rover, Volvo, and Aston Martin into the Premier Automotive Group (PAG). Lincoln, certainly a luxury marque, is grouped with other North American brands for synergy.

Inside PAG, Ford looks for opportunities to commonize certain product components or systems. For example, it is going to use one six-speed automatic transmission in all of PAG's midsized vehicles. By doing this, it is shifting from individual volumes (in some cases of as few as 40,000 units) to a joint volume of more than 300,000. The savings will be substantial.

But it has to take these actions very carefully. It may be nowhere more important to preserve brand character than in luxury vehicles. Their distinctiveness and exclusivity are among the main reasons people buy them, so employing commonality across premium brands is especially delicate.

The six-speed automatic transmission is an illustration. By using a common transmission, Ford did not decrease value in any product. In fact, it increased value. Joint sourcing allows each brand to have a premium component, and one that is likely better than most of the brands could have afforded individually. And

Ford is able to tailor the transmission to fit the driving characteristics of each brand.

Regional Strategies for Commonization

There are a number of things Ford is doing on a regional basis that support the objectives of efficiency, competitive advantage, and customer responsiveness.

Commonality within a region is a key strategy to push cost savings and better quality. In both Europe and North America, as well as its other regions, Ford is moving toward fewer platforms and more product from each platform.

In North America, it has announced plans for a midsize sedan, with the underlying architecture of the product ultimately resulting in up to ten different vehicles and 800,000 units of volume across several brands—about 20 percent of the entire North American volume.

Overall, the objective is a 25 percent reduction in platforms by the end of this decade, without a negative impact on the massive new product plan in place for this region. To help meet that goal, it is supporting the initiative in some of its key processes. For example, it has realigned its North American product development organization. It will be focused more on platform families, which will allow more common and flexible vehicle architectures. In addition to being more efficient, the change is expected to help improve vehicle quality and reduce development times.

Another big regional process change is flexible manufacturing. This is basically a manufacturing system that allows rapid and less expensive changeover inside a plant so that more types of vehicles can be built at the same location. It allows Ford to meet shifting consumer demand much more effectively and efficiently. Much of its European production capacity is already operating under flexible manufacturing. And by the end of the decade, about 75 percent of its North American facilities will be flexible.

Ford 2000: Lessons and Direction

In the 1990s, Ford developed Ford 2000, a globalization initiative to combine its regions into one global operation. One analyst said that it was, in a sense, the largest business merger in history. Certainly, it was huge, and it was bold. For many people at Ford, the duplication between the two major regions offered too large a target to ignore. And theoretically, eliminating the overlap in design costs, engineering, and administration would yield cost savings that were intoxicating to think about.

There were, however, some disadvantages and some very important lessons learned. One of those lessons was that there still are differences among consumers across separate regions that must be accommodated. Another lesson was that centralized control can be taken too far. In Ford's zeal for the efficiency of a global operation, it lost some of the financial and operational discipline that local management had been able to provide. It also lost some of the direct contact with the market and the consumer that is imperative anymore for success in this business.

Nevertheless, in many respects, Ford 2000 did work. It could not have produced that 65 percent common Focus for Europe and North America without Ford 2000. And much of what it is attempting to implement today, globally or regionally, is based on ideas, experience, and philosophies that came out of Ford 2000.

It has preserved much of the good from that chapter in its history, updated it for today's marketplace and competitive realities, and is incorporating the product of that thinking into some of its most important strategies today and plans for tomorrow.

Future of the Industry and Globalization

Just what tomorrow will bring is something we cannot know with precision, but we at Ford have an idea of what we think the future holds and how we are proceeding.

The first thing to know is that competition will only increase. In 1992, there were 52 product actions ranging from minor to major among automakers operating in this market. In 2002, there were 184 product actions, including a number in segments that did not even exist a decade earlier. That is the template for the future and for every significant region on the globe.

Emerging markets and a worldwide growth of the middle class are trends with huge impact on the industry as well. Urbanization is giving more and more people higher levels of disposable income. In China, average family income has tripled in twenty years.

Income growth is also being fostered by the rapid rise of women in the labor force, a trend particularly true in South America.

China is worth singling out. Over the next ten years, China could account for anywhere from a quarter to a third of all global auto industry growth. About 300 million people in China have reached the purchasing power threshold that generally supports a consumer auto market.

In the short term, most people look at China, and rightfully, as a huge opportunity for new sales and potentially as a low-cost sourcing base. But there are a couple of longer-term issues that the industry would be well advised to consider. For instance, how is it going to affect the industry when a well-developed China accounts for 20 or 25 percent of global consumers? How is it going to influence global consumer trends in the auto industry? And will it help or hinder the drive for more product commonization? What about energy requirements to power what will eventually be a huge vehicle fleet? Could balance-of-trade issues cause the Chinese to look at alternative energy sources? With no huge investment yet in any fixed infrastructure, China could more easily than most other nations look at simply leapfrogging to a future technology. And that too could have a profound impact on how the global automakers operate in China and elsewhere.

Technology, with or without China's influence, is another of the developments influencing Ford's future. Electronics will continue to drive advancements and added content, certainly in the areas of safety and environment. And there will also continue to be big changes in communications, information systems, and computer-type interfaces. This will likely offer a lot of opportunity for commonization at the component and systems level.

All of these trends are going to ensure that immense demands on finite resources will only keep growing. And they will lead to strategies for efficiency, meeting customer expectations, and smarter product development vital to Ford's survival. It could push more industry consolidation, maybe de facto in the form of increasing alliances. But it also will continue to make product commonization a key strategic tool.

Over time, there will be more globalization of markets in the auto industry. We will continue to see regional markets and consumer tastes converge. Still, many of the hurdles are going to remain for a long time yet. So Ford will globalize where possible, but a strong regional focus is going to remain an important part of its thinking.

It will take a mixture of global and regional strategies to drive efficiency and meet the constantly growing demands of customers on a worldwide basis. Those automakers best able to strike the proper balance, while also connecting with customers ever more personally, will be the automakers enjoying the most long-term success.

PART 4

Managing Global Brands

Interest in global brands is fueled by annual rankings of the most valuable brands in the world, published by *Business Week* and based on methodology developed by the Interbrand management consultancy. The ten most valuable brands for 2003, based on estimates of future worldwide cash flows, are, in order, Coca Cola, Microsoft, IBM, GE, Intel, Nokia, Disney, McDonald's, Marlboro, and Mercedes. All of these brands dominate their domestic markets and enjoy strong sales in all regions of the world. The brands are positioned in the same way around the world, addressing a common set of customer benefits. They are tightly focused: Disney means family entertainment; Sony means consumer electronics. Only GE could be accused of spreading itself too thin across multiple lines of business. And, significantly, in every case except that of Marlboro, the brand name is the company name. The benefits of concentrating resources behind a single brand name worldwide are increasingly evident: only the most powerful global brands can, for example, afford to sponsor World Cup soccer or the Olympics. Such options are not open to the likes of Procter & Gamble, Unilever, and Henkel. Although these companies are effective marketers, none of their brands appears in the top ten list because resources are not concentrated on the corporate umbrella name.

In many product categories, the global brand leaders took advantage during the 1990s of the opening up of formerly closed economies to put ever more distance between themselves and the competition. Consumers in these markets wanted to enjoy the forbidden fruit of Western brands to which they previously could not gain access. The very globalness of these brands was in itself a source of added value. Many consumers continue to view a brand's global reach as an assurance of quality. Global brands are presumed to be on the cutting edge, constantly innovating. Other consumers, particularly in emerging markets, see consumption of global brands as enhancing their social status or enabling them to be, however fleetingly, citizens of the world. A Coke or a Big Mac are to many the affordable luxury that enables them to connect with the world at large.

Many multinationals have seen their brand portfolios develop incrementally over time through a combination of organic growth and acquisitions. The results are not always neat and clean. The same product may be marketed under different brand names in different country markets, or the same brand may be on offer worldwide but the product formula may be varied according to local market tastes. In Chapter Eight, Hans-Willi Schroiff and David Arnold draw on examples from the European laundry detergents category to distinguish between product formula and functionality and brand meaning. They discuss, using a four-cell contingency model, the circumstances under which it makes sense for managers to standardize or customize either product attributes or virtual brand attributes.

In Chapter Nine, Douglas Holt, John Quelch, and Earl Taylor examine the degree to which consumer perceptions of globalness influence their brand choices. The results of a twelve-country study show elements of globalness consistently explaining over 60 percent of the variance. The authors find that the degree to which a global brand is or is not perceived to be imbued with American values has little significance in driving brand choices, even in Muslim countries.

These findings mitigate the widespread concerns about American cultural imperialism through cultural icon brands like Disney and Coca Cola. True, higher percentages of global market shares are today concentrated in the hands of global American brands. Eight of the top ten brands on Interbrand's list are American. So are sixty-two of the top one hundred, even though the United States accounts for only 28 percent of gross domestic product. However, in many categories, the successful global brands are stealing share from other global brands, and local brands continue to flourish, aided by their responsiveness to local tastes and by the desire of many consumers to support the home team. Often these local brands have been acquired and their product quality enhanced by Western multinationals that recognize the value of offering simultaneously a portfolio of global and local brands to appeal to different consumer segments.

As companies increasingly realize the value of their brands, managers want to know more about how to nurture and develop these assets. Developing either a single worldwide approach or a different marketing program for each country is equally impractical. So is a panregional approach, particularly in a region like Asia with huge disparities of wealth from Cambodia to Japan. Increasingly, multinationals are clustering their country markets according to a combination of category development (per capita consumption of the product category) and brand market share. The relevant marketing objectives (such as secure trial, build the category, or defend share) vary, but countries can be clustered into groups depending on their category and brand development positions, and cross-learning can usefully be encouraged across countries (from whatever geographical region) that share similar challenges.

CHAPTER 8

Strategies for Managing Brand and Product in International Markets

Hans-Willi Schroiff
David J. Arnold

In the twenty years since Levitt's seminal article on globalized markets, sweeping changes in technology, information, and regulation have transformed the way in which many companies address their international markets, as he predicted. There is one domain of the global marketplace, however, in which it is far from clear that a globalization process has occurred: the consumer. Although it is clear that in some instances consumers perceive value in a globally present and consistent brand or product, in the majority of decision situations, the globalism or localism of the offer is evidently of little or no importance.

Without globalization at the consumer level, what we have are globalized industries but not necessarily globalized markets. Indeed, the vision of globalized markets that Levitt so powerfully articulated was not a consumer-driven one. Globalization is clearly defined as a process fueled by corporate push for economies of scale and control rather than by consumer pull for global brands and products. Consumers are described as the beneficiaries rather than the instigators of globalization, their compliance assumed on the grounds that they will accept superior product propositions, in line with microeconomic models of utility maximization in decision making:

A powerful new force now drives the world towards a single converging commonality, and that force is technology. . . . The result
is a new commercial reality—the emergence of global markets for
standardized consumer products on a previously unimagined scale of
magnitude. Corporations geared to this new reality benefit from
enormous *economies of scale* in production, distribution, marketing
and management. By translating these benefits into *reduced world
prices,* they can decimate competitors that still live in the disabling
grip of old assumptions about how the world works. Gone are
accustomed differences in national or regional preference. . . .
Ancient differences in national tastes or modes of doing business
disappear. The *commonality of preferences* leads inescapably to the
standardization of products, manufacturing, and the institutions
of trade and commerce [Levitt, 1983, pp. 92–102, italics added].

The focus of the debate on market globalization has now
shifted from product standardization to brand standardization.
This is important because it turns Levitt's vision upside down.
While the corporations that own and develop product technology
have indeed pursued technological convergence in the way he
envisioned, this has not proved to be a sufficient condition for the
globalization of markets. Rather, many now view consumer acceptance, or lack of it, as the bottleneck in this change process. Cause
and effect are thus reversed, in that consumer pull is posited as the
necessary condition for globalization, and only when that condition is satisfied will standardized product offerings find a market.
According to one recent commentator, consumers are moving in
the opposite direction, their fragmenting tastes provoking a "backlash" against global and particularly American brands, leading to
the conclusion that Levitt's thesis was "just plain wrong" (Tomkins,
2003, p. 19).

This issue has been pushed onto a wider political stage by the
antiglobalization movement that emerged in the 1990s. The focus
is on brand because this is seen as the vehicle through which consumer pull will be expressed. As marketing academia has come to
recognize in the past thirty years, consumers have a more complex
relationship with the products they buy than the utility maximization paradigm that Levitt seems to assume, and to varying extents
they are expressing themselves through their brand choices. In
other words, a global market for standardized products is possible

only in a world of standardized consumers. For those opposed to brand globalization, therefore, it is the values and culture of individuals, regions, and countries that would have to make way for standardized offerings.

To the antiglobalization lobby, the perceived unfolding of Levitt's doomsday scenario is a prime motivation for opposition to the spread of brands across the globe. To brand marketing executives within multinational companies, however, it is the resilience of local variations in taste that dominates their decision making, representing an ongoing challenge to any attempt to reap global economies of scale and control in marketing. Indeed, many multinationals, in consumer markets in particular, are adding local brands to their portfolio as eagerly as they are investing in global power brands. Nevertheless, there is a sea change occurring in this field two or more decades after Levitt made his bold predictions, but it is not driven by technology in the manner he forecast. Instead, internationalization at the intermediate level in the market system, especially in retail distribution and media, is offering the prospect of a future global distribution system in which brand owners are pulled toward global branding strategies by their customers (as opposed to their retailers). This only exacerbates the underlying dilemma, however: if consumer tastes remain variable around the world, does a global branding policy risk alienating the company's brands from its customer base? This is the core challenge of international marketing: companies are growing more global in their presence and their degree of integration, but consumers retain varying levels of local orientation in their tastes and demands.

Managing the Branded Product in International Markets

The question of whether an international company should pursue a policy of global branding—whether it should seek globally consistent brand names, identities, and positions—encapsulates perfectly the core dilemma of international marketing. On the one hand, brands work because of their consistency and omnipresence, offering customers a short-cut in the purchase decision by a promise of reliability and familiarity. Standardization is therefore at the heart of branding, and consistency in execution is a keystone of effective brand management. It is also true, of course, that it is more efficient for companies to manage a single brand worldwide than a portfolio of different brands, both in terms of economies in marketing expenditure and also in terms of managerial control and accountability. These two factors suggest that brands should seek wide presence and a uniform identity on a global scale.

On the other hand, it is also true that brands work because of the resonance of meaning and identity they offer to customers at a deep, sometimes emotional or subconscious level. Indeed, many trends in the wider field of marketing are enabling marketing companies to get ever closer to their customers, and even in some cases customize their offering or messages to individuals. Rare is the company for which a central element of marketing strategy in the twenty-first century is not to get closer to customers and build a database of individual customer identities. Until people are the same around the globe, therefore, we might expect brands to succeed when they reflect local and even individual taste and culture.

Increasingly, thinking on international marketing is moving away from the either-or approach (that is, either global or local) toward what might be termed a both-and approach (that is, seeking to capture the benefits of both global integration and local responsiveness). In managing brands internationally, such a contingency framework, and the managerial flexibility that flows from it, can be enhanced by disaggregating an offer into the brand and product offerings. Our approach is based on the concept of a branded product: we clearly differentiate between the functional contributions of a product and the more emotional persuasive elements of a brand. This differentiation is key to our understanding of the global branding issue.

The treatment of brand and product as independent decision fields goes against the conventional wisdom in brand-oriented industries. Marketing executives in consumer packaged goods companies are trained to regard the branded offer as a holistic unity in which all elements must be closely aligned to create a compelling proposition. The differentiation of the offer, according to this wisdom, comes only from the synergy of all elements, including both product and brand name and identity, which together form a positioning in the consumer's mind. The complexity of such propositions is what makes flexibility in heterogeneous international markets such a challenge. Moreover, it is clear that in some categories, there is considerable variation along both brand and product dimensions. This is noticeably true in the laundry detergents sector, the basis for the research behind this chapter. Under the same brand name, for example, powders are sold with inert green flecks in the Netherlands but inert blue flecks in Italy; products are offered as powders, liquid, capsules, or gels; and fragrances and cleaning ingredients are varied by country to meet differences in demand. Conversely, the same product is offered under different brand names in different countries. A most striking example is the fact that Persil, the leading brand name of the German company Henkel, was awarded to Unilever in France and the United Kingdom as part of the reparations after World War II; in France, therefore, Persil is a different product from that offered under the same brand name in all bordering countries, while Henkel markets as Le Chat the same range of products it offers under the Persil brand name in neighboring Germany.

We begin the development of our framework, therefore, by clarifying the understanding of product and brand.

Products

Products come to life in the manufacturer's lab and are owned entirely by the producer. They are faceless aggregates of ingredients. In terms of the detergents category, products are a combination of mechanics, chemicals, and other tangible factors such as fragrance and color, mixed to perform in a certain way that is more or less required or appreciated by their users. Their characteristics can be altered deliberately by their producer.

Brands

Brands come to life in consumers' minds: they are meaningful aggregates of associations, meaning, perceptions, and all other intangibles. Brands have a face that helps them to be recognized by a person who then immediately associates certain characteristics with this person-like entity. Brands as intangibles are thus owned jointly by the producer and the user. A change on the one side does not necessarily entail that the change is also followed on the other side. For example, if the consumer chooses to ignore that the brand personality as expressed in advertisements has changed (in order to maintain his cognitive consistency), all efforts on the manufacturer's side might be in vain. Consumers in fact elaborate on what they know and feel about brands, actively modifying and changing the designated set of associations that companies have in mind regarding their brand. A brand is therefore a dialectical relationship, or contract, with either side having veto power over any changes.

Together, these two elements constitute the branded product, thus clearly emphasizing that the brand part is only one component and should not be mistaken as also comprising the product part. Why not simply call it a brand? We believe that the classical notion of a brand included an inseparable combination of a product base and a brand frame around it. Thus, the base of the offer was a functional product with the brand added on as a presentational enhancement. In fact, the two can be managed quite separately. Coca-Cola is a good example. Originally exported widely in its original American formulation, it has now evolved to the point where its ingredient mix is adjusted by region to cater to differences in taste in areas such as sweetness, while the (largely American) brand attributes have remained unaltered for the most part. As a branded product approach, it appears to be managed following the regional adaptation strategy, which we elaborate on later in this chapter.

The Elements of the Branded Product

The branded product is viewed as an array of so-called persuasive elements that together make up the value proposition to the consumer. A persuasive element is simply any element that contributes to the total value perception from the consumer's point of view, whether this element is a tangible or intangible asset. For laundry detergents, for example, the amount and the characteristics of cleaning agents like tensides will obviously matter, as will the color of the powder and its speckles, alternative product forms such as liquid or gels, the brand name, the producer, and so on. The elements need to be carefully orchestrated to create a consistent offer to the consumer. The brand plays a major role here: it helps to provide an overall frame of reference for the multitude of sensory perceptions and mental elaborations that are taking place when a contact with a branded product is established.

Figure 8.1 schematically describes the branded offer as a hierarchical set of related persuasive elements. From "real" bottom (chemical ingredients) to "virtual" top (corporate endorser), we find a carefully tuned architecture that seeks to provide psychological synapses between the various parts (for example, capitalizing on the consumer insight that a fine fabric detergent should have rose-colored speckles in it). The more of these connecting synapses between the different value layers of the branded offer, the better. In this hypothetical detergent example, besides the characteristics of the chemical formula (for example, aimed more at stain removal or aimed more at fiber protection), other persuasive elements matter to consumers. The application form—powder, liquid, tablet, pouch, pearls, or something else—provides clear signals to generate

Figure 8.1. Hierarchy of Persuasive Elements of the Branded Product: Detergent Example

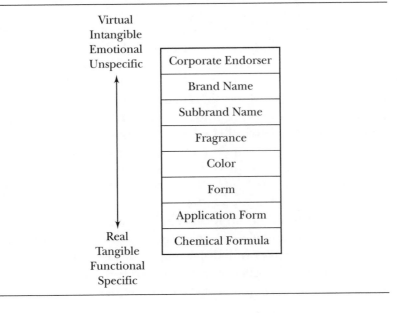

implicit expectations about the product performance spectrum and its quality. Other aesthetics like form, color, and fragrance do the same. Fragrance is already on the edge to more emotional and intangible persuasive elements.

Our concept entails that the branded offer is owned jointly by the producer and the consumer. The more we move to the virtual top of the hierarchy, the more we must be aware that these parts are not in the package or on the shelf but reside in the mind of the consumer, who actively changes or maintains her or his idea about the total value concept of a branded product. The producer may choose to exchange, add to, or remove parts of the lower end of the hierarchy without even asking the consumer, but changing parts of the jointly owned modules against the consumers' consent represents a cruel violation of the contract that is the branded offer.

The producer and the consumer should have the same mental representations regarding particularly the virtual top elements of the hierarchy of persuasive elements. Corporations spend huge amounts of money on image studies or associative maps in order to understand how their communication efforts influence consumers' mental models about the branded offer (particularly its brand part). Understanding the brand in its functions as a psychological carrier system is of vital importance. The worst thing that may occur is a severe discrepancy between the mental models on the corporate and on the consumer side.

The example in Figure 8.2 refers to the perception of the corporate endorser Henkel for two major Henkel brands in Germany: the detergent brand Persil and the hair styling brand Taft. Although both brands are under the Henkel roof, the persuasive contribution of the overall Henkel endorser is very different. While Persil as the mother brand of a big detergent brand family benefits considerably from the overall Henkel endorser, the situation looks very different for Taft. Henkel plays only a minor role in the branded product hierarchy of Taft. What really matters for consumers besides the brand itself is the persuasive contribution of Schwarzkopf, a Henkel cosmetics company in Germany with a long independent heritage of hairdressing expertise. So the consumer actively modifies branded product hierarchies and places emphasis on different layers than the corporation does.

**Figure 8.2. Different Roles of the Corporate
Endorser Henkel for Two Major Henkel Brands in Germany**

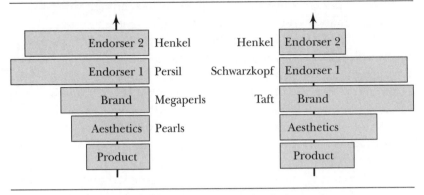

Source: Adapted from Henkel Corporate Image Study, internal company document, 2003.

If we now extrapolate from the situation in one country, we must conclude that different branded product hierarchies can result in different geographies. For example, Heineken is one of the premium imported beers in the United States, it is a mainstream brand in the Netherlands, and it is almost not visible in Germany. In any specific purchase situation, we subscribe to the traditional view of a branded offer: that it is a holistic proposition based on a synergistic alignment of all persuasive elements. From the perspective of managing a brand across a portfolio of heterogeneous markets, however, we believe that the requisite flexibility can be better managed within the framework of an adaptive approach to configuring product and brand elements. This offers the opportunity for market-driven adaptation, while allowing for a degree of harmony (rather than standardization) that will provide a platform for building brands with international equity.

An Example: The Fairy Tale

In order to illustrate our thoughts with an actual example, we have chosen the case of a dishwashing detergent in Germany. (We thank Raimund Wildner from the Gesellschaft für Konsumforschung for this example.) The brand Fairy was supported strongly by Procter & Gamble (P&G) for years and gained a healthy market share of around 12 percent. Figure 8.3 shows the percentage value shares of the German market by quarters for 2000–2001.

In the second half of 2000, the brand was renamed Dawn, P&G's international dishwashing brand. As far as we know, there was no basic change in the product itself; the only change was regarding the name of the branded offer. It is assumed that this change was part of P&G's well-publicized moves at the time toward consolidation of its portfolio into a smaller group of better-supported global power brands. Although the brand switch was backed up by huge media investments to inform consumers of the name change and gain their acceptance, the market share losses were striking: by the end of 2001, the Dawn market share fell to less than half of the Fairy share at the beginning of 2000. Without even considering the supplemental marketing costs involved in supporting the name change and focusing on only top-line revenue losses, we estimate the loss in turnover for 2001 at around 16 million deutsche marks (or approximately 8 million euros or U.S. dollars). Similar outcomes were observed at this time in Austria, where P&G's attempt to rebrand its local detergent brand Dash with the name of its international power brand Bold. Within two years of these changes

Figure 8.3. Fairy Value Market Shares in Germany: Quarterly Periods, 2000–2001

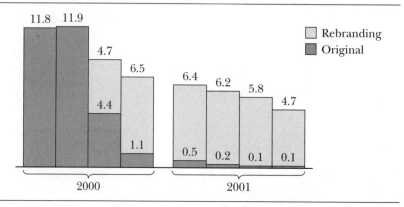

Source: Adapted by the authors from market research data purchased by International Research Division, Henkel KgaA, internal company documents.

being made, both decisions were reversed, and the original brand names, Fairy and Dash, were reintroduced.

What had happened? Obviously Fairy represented a known and trusted brand personality with its consumer franchise in Germany; the virtual entity Fairy had become an essential persuasive element on the consumer side, particularly with its users. Then the producer decided to withdraw this persuasive element for a chemical product in a one-sided manner. The consumer reaction was clear and quick: although the product remained entirely the same, its consumers decided to turn their back on it. The psychological bond in the form of the brand was broken; the unspoken agreement symbolized by the brand was violated and obviously could not be restored, even after P&G reinstalled the old Fairy name.

Interestingly, the rebranding of Fairy into Dawn did not take place in the United Kingdom, where the dishwashing detergent Fairy has a long history and a particularly strong heritage in the market, although with a main benefit that is not focused on grease cutting, as it is positioned in most other markets. Perhaps it was thought that the brand name could be changed easily in markets (like Germany) in which the underlying product proposition was fairly similar to that of Dash (that is, "cuts grease").

The Need for Flexibility in Managing Branded Products in International Markets

Marketing managers are confronted with an ever-lasting dilemma: on the one side, they are forced to deeply penetrate their market down to its last consumer at all costs; on the other side, they are required to minimize costs (again, at all costs), the obvious route to which is by selling the same product to every consumer to achieve economies of scale (one of the few laws of business, although not necessarily of marketing). As the Fairy example suggests, the only flaw in this make-and-sell ideology is the consumer. Our experiences in the European detergents and toiletries markets lead to three basic conclusions:

- A *brand* is not the same brand everywhere (in consumers' minds).
- A *product* is not the same product everywhere.
- A *consumer* is not the same consumer everywhere.

Taking these three statements for granted, the foundations of a global branding approach (same product under identical brand name everywhere) quickly fall apart. The basic assumptions have not materialized to the present day—that global consumers' needs, desires, and attitudes merge and can be satisfied by identical products put to market under identical brand labels. In the language of the branded product thinking, the dilemma is that the hierarchy of persuasive elements and their relative weight diverges sharply between the people in the boardroom putting products on imaginary shelves and the people in the supermarket taking them off the real shelves. There is frequently little agreement between the corporate mind-set and the consumers' mind-set. Global branding—the policy of satisfying universal needs and wants by universal branded products—can be successful only if there is a large overlap between the hierarchy of persuasive elements as envisaged by corporations and by consumers.

A Framework for Managing Global Branding Decisions

What are the consequences of our observations for global branding decisions? A first consequence would be a strict separation of the brand and the product in order to look separately at the various elements that govern the more functional persuasive elements and the more virtual elements. Depending on the product group, one may arrive at different cut-off points. But the essential principle remains the same: in contrast to traditional marketing thinking, we strongly believe that in international marketing, the product and the brand parts have to be managed separately.

So let us imagine that we fold the hierarchy described in Figure 8.1 at a certain cut-off point and create two orthogonal dimensions: a product dimension and a brand dimension. Now let us introduce another feature to each of these two dimensions: a low and a high degree of international standardization. Thus, product standardization between countries may be high or the product may be locally adapted or customized, and the same applies to the branding decision set. This leads to the simple four-quadrant matrix shown in Figure 8.4 and four generic strategies that are briefly summarized here and described in more detail in the following pages:

**Figure 8.4. Different Levels of Standardization of
Product and Brand Parts and Respective Strategic Options**

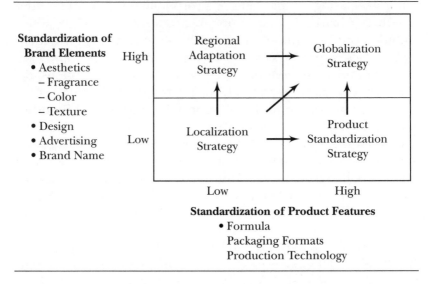

**Standardization of
Brand Elements**
 • Aesthetics
  – Fragrance
  – Color
  – Texture
 • Design
 • Advertising
 • Brand Name

High   Regional
         Adaptation   Globalization
         Strategy   Strategy

Low   Localization   Product
         Strategy   Standardization
                             Strategy

Low   High

Standardization of Product Features
 • Formula
  Packaging Formats
  Production Technology

• *Localization strategy.* This is a common situation for corporations with broad local portfolios characterized by a high level of
complexity due to low standardization of the product and the
brand part. Thus, each market has its own name and advertising,
for example, and each product part has it own formula, fragrance,
color, and other characteristics.

• *Globalization strategy.* This is the exact opposite of the localization strategy. The same product is marketed everywhere under
the same brand name, with high to complete standardization of
brand and product elements.

• *Regional adaptation strategy.* This strategy is characterized
by a limited number of global brands; however, the features of the
product part (for example, the sugar content in soft drinks) may
vary according to local and regional specifics.

• *Product standardization strategy.* This strategy removes complexity from the product part by international harmonization wher-
ever possible. The standardized (global) product part is then
marketed under different (local) brand names, maintaining the
established bond of the brand to the consumer.

The four strategic directions can be dealt with in a flexible way. In the figure, we have used arrows to indicate several migration paths depending on the status of a corporate portfolio of branded products. Clearly, an international corporation launching a new branded product will follow a globalization strategy, since it can achieve economies of scale and reduced managerial complexity free from the constraint of ingrained consumer perceptions. For the more common situation of existing branded products, a common scenario for a multilocal corporation with global branding intentions might be to examine the possibilities of a direct path toward global branding (that is, move directly from a localization strategy toward a globalization strategy) or two indirect routes (by either a regional adaptation strategy or a product standardization strategy). It is also conceivable that a corporation follows different strategies at the same time, depending again on the type of products (for example, food versus electronic appliances) and the type and number of geographies in which the firm participates.

A further factor to consider is the state of maturity of the individual brands at a given time. Although the brand is marketed in different countries and regions, this should not lead to the conclusion that its franchises with consumers are identical.

Branding Strategies in International Markets

In this section, we take a more in-depth look at the characteristics and the implications of the various strategies.

Localization Strategy

The localization strategy (different brands, different products) is designed for brands with a strong local heritage and products with a very specific ingredient of known local origin, mainly addressing a specific local consumer need. In Europe, many organizations are currently facing a vast portfolio of local brands as a consequence of a series of acquisitions in the past two decades. Industry mergers have created graveyards for once-trusted and established brands that had to be killed in the postmerger search for financial synergies. A good example for a localization strategy is the Spanish toiletry brand La Toja, which uses salt from hot springs at La Toja island as an active ingredient. Both product and brand form a credible entity and respond to the established needs of the Spanish toiletry market, commanding a reasonable and stable market share in Spain.

Globalization Strategy

The globalization (same brand, same product) strategy still seems the most desirable strategy to follow, since it entails the highly desired financial advantages that corporations seek as they grow large. Product would be manufactured in huge quantities and put to market under the same brand name everywhere; production complexity and marketing costs would go down to a minimum, and managerial complexity would be significantly reduced. In practice, however, this strategy can be successfully implemented only when all persuasive elements of the branded product have been carefully aligned and agreed with consumers around the globe. Only once a company is secure in the knowledge (acquired via international market research) that it is addressing a universal need with a universal product under a universally accepted psychological carrier system in the form of a commonly understood brand can it feel relaxed that the marketing effort will be a profit pillar and not a profit killer. Such a situation is rare, but occurs most frequently in the case of a launch of a new branded product.

Regional Adaptation Strategy

The regional adaptation strategy (same brand, different products) is another interesting alternative. Here the same brand appears under different product frames. Although this may sound odd to marketing strategists (Why produce different products when you already have a global brand?), it makes a lot of sense to consider this strategy. The strategy is designed for scenarios where the brand part already stands for trust and confidence in consumers' minds, yet due to different consumer habits or different needs, it seems indispensable to provide different product characteristics. Let us also look at some examples here. Washing dishes is done differently in different countries in Europe: the German user does it in hot standing water and the Spanish user under running cold water.

It seems clear even to chemical laypersons that these different conditions must be met with different chemical ingredients. So if a global brand is positioned as the ultimate product against burned-in grease, it must meet this functional expectation under all kinds of different usage situations. As another example, Asian hair has different structure and different shades compared to Caucasian hair. A coloration product promising ultimate gray coverage must take these different hair structures into account in its formula. Again, different products may result, even under the same brand. The only requirement is to match the respective functional expectations on the user side in order to achieve stable sales.

Product Standardization Strategy

The product standardization strategy (same product, different brands) respects the local heritage and character established by brands over time, yet avoids the complexity that is normally associated with maintaining a huge local brand portfolio by standardizing product. Economies of scale are achieved by harmonizing as many product features as possible and producing the harmonized product in international batch production facilities. The degree of international standardization can even reach to advertising content and shared advertising executions. The only difference in the end might be the brand name and the company endorser.

A good example is the Henkel strategy for value-for-money brands, also known as the Fox brands. A number of local brands across Europe, the Middle East, and North Africa share a large portion of common persuasive elements, including product and a brand endorser of a cartoon fox character. The fox, a symbol of self-interested wisdom in all these cultures, emphasizes the value-for-money proposition that these brands stand for. Nevertheless, Henkel has kept the local and trusted brand names to ensure broad consumer penetration.

Conclusion

We have suggested ways of dealing with the apparent global branding dilemma by separating brand and product decisions. In particular, we advocate flexibility in establishing the cut-off point at which the company trades off the economic benefits of standardization against the market benefits of localization. The frame for this trade-off decision is the hierarchy of persuasive elements in the branded offer, from functional and tangible product characteristics to intangible psychological brand images. The branded product hierarchy includes product elements that can easily be altered and brand elements where changes must be done with caution and only with the consent of the consumer as the co-owner. We reiterate that this framework is intended to help understand how to manage brand across countries rather than explain individual purchase choices by consumers.

Managing the brand-product continuum in this way leads to the four basic strategies described. We regard them as viable alternatives in order to find an acceptable compromise between the mutually exclusive objectives to reach maximum consumer penetration and still have attractive economies of scale. The various strategies help us to make "a dovetail joint": on the product side, we harvest the required economies of scale, and on the brand side, we ensure that we achieve maximum consumer penetration using a balanced portfolio of global and local brands.

CHAPTER 9

Managing the Global Brand

A Typology of Consumer Perceptions

Douglas B. Holt
John A. Quelch
Earl L. Taylor

The decades-old debate concerning whether to build global brands seems finally to be moving toward equilibrium—to a world in which there are two different kinds of brands that play very different roles. At the product level, while companies continue to push for standardization when economics dictate, the primary decision rule now is to optimize customer value as defined by local market conditions. As brand competition has heated up, the particularities of national cultures have become ever more important. Brands fail to respond at their peril.

The opposite is true for the world's leading corporate brands. As the largest companies now wrap around the globe, the globalization of their corporate brands has become a fait accompli. Such companies now operate in most countries, using the same corporate brand marks, and hold dominant market shares in many categories. For these brands, the question is no longer whether to globalize but how to manage the global brand.

Managers understand well the many advantages that global branding brings to the firm in terms of production and marketing efficiencies and also in easing administrative burdens. And they readily acknowledge that global brands seem to have extraordinary market power. Once a brand expands its reach around the globe, it achieves favored perceptions that are greater than the sum of its national parts. But while this is an intuitively attractive story to tell about the evolution of the corporate brands that populate the one hundred most valuable brands listed on Interbrand's Global Brand Scorecard, we have little idea how global brands work.

Understanding is limited because the global branding debate, driven by a focus on product brands rather than corporate brands, has focused largely on the question of standardization: Shall the brand speak with the same voice around the world? Or must it tailor its interactions with consumers to heed differences in culture and competition? What this formulation leaves out is the impact of the brand's globalness on how the brand is valued. Global brands are not just more standardized than nonglobal ones. Rather, consumers understand them as global, and these understandings shape brand preferences.

This study draws on cultural theories of globalization to explore the extent to which consumers' inferences about the globalness of a brand influence their brand preferences. We used the cultural anthropology literature to isolate five dimensions of globalness that we hypothesized would have an impact on brand preference. Then we used qualitative research to explore these dimensions in considerable detail, paying attention to how people discuss global brands in their everyday talk and how they use this discourse to make judgments about brand value. Finally, we used these preliminary investigations to structure a survey fielded in twelve countries that examined seventeen leading global brands in six distinct product categories.

In the survey, we found that four of the five dimensions had a significant impact. The importance of the four dimensions holds up strongly across all twelve countries, though with some interesting country differences. We also investigated whether there were important segments with respect to global brands. We found striking differences. Our analysis revealed seven segments, present in all twelve countries, that are defined by the relative importance of the various globalness dimensions in shaping preference.

The Global Brand Debate

In his seminal article, "The Globalization of Markets," Ted Levitt (1983) argued that two mechanisms—one supply side and one demand side—would together lead to standardized products competing around the globe. Levitt argued that the costs to deliver products to international markets were declining rapidly due to revolutionary transformations in the supply chain. Organizational theorists (for example, Bartlett and Ghoshal, 1998) have expanded on these arguments, documenting the emergence of the transnational organization, which increasingly require global presence not only for scale efficiencies but also to develop competencies in innovation that accrue from the scope of such enterprises.

Levitt also posited a change in demand: the national structuring of consumer tastes was breaking down as media and labor routinely crossed national boundaries and international air travel became "proletarianized." In marketing, this part of Levitt's argument is frequently misinterpreted as an argument for the homogenization of preference. Rather, Levitt argued that national markets will recede, and in their place global segments will form. Target segments may be mass or niche, but, whichever they are, the segment will be global (a sliver of every country) rather than national. He insisted on the fading relevance of national market boundaries to the extent that the overall value for money of the offering of a standardized product designed to meet the needs of a global segment will easily overcome remaining national differences in tastes.

Levitt's arguments set off a debate to determine whether consumer preferences were similar enough to allow standardizing market offerings across countries. Levitt's arguments were critiqued as antimarketing because he did not consider the brand—that is, the product as understood from consumers' perspectives, particularly its intangible properties. Critics used this limitation as rhetorical ballast to argue for the continued need to tailor brands at the national level.

As business evidence has accumulated, it has become clear that no rule of thumb is possible. There are many global brands, many local brands, and many brands that seem to fall somewhere in between depending on the branding dimension that is considered.

Every so-called global brand tailors its marketing program to some degree to account for the exigencies of local markets. The optimal solution depends on idiosyncratic factors concerning consumer tastes, competitive dynamics, and market infrastructure. To manage these contingencies, Quelch and Hoff (1986) provide a decision framework to derive the appropriate global-regional-national strategy across the marketing mix.

In our view, Levitt's arguments make good sense for corporate and flagship brands but are often less appropriate for the other product brands that these companies offer. Interestingly, Levitt's critics who were so concerned with branding never really engaged Levitt's thesis in branding terms. If, as Levitt argues, global products are able to deliver higher quality at a given price, then these products should develop a reputation for doing so. That is, their globalness should become an important asset of the brand. While seemingly concerned with global branding, the global-local debate has overlooked the possibility that the globalness of a brand may in fact be used by consumers to ascribe value or lack thereof. Rather than ask whether global brands can get away with standardizing, instead we ask, What do the perceived global characteristics of a brand contribute to (or detract from) the brand's value?

Academics are just beginning to consider the idea that globalness is a dimension of brand value. The first academic study on the topic, by Steenkamp, Batra, and Alden (2003), examines how perceptions of a brand's globalness affect whether global brands are favored over local brands. They examine two global dimensions (quality and prestige) in two countries (the United States and South Korea) across four product categories. Their structural equation model of attitudinal measures indicates that both of these globalness dimensions have a positive impact. In a working paper, Johansson and Ronkainen (2003) are seeking to dimensionalize what they call the global brand's "esteem," based on perceived quality, country of origin, and other factors. Our study is somewhat different from these two pioneering studies in the following manner:

- We offer a cultural framework—the *global brand* as a cultural category in global discourse—to conceptualize the rise of the global brand.

- We are interested specifically in global corporate brands.
- We aim to develop a comprehensive typology of the dimensions of the global brand (so we begin with detailed qualitative work to specify these dimensions).
- We are interested in how global corporate brands compete with each other (rather than global-local competition).
- We want to understand how the dimensions of globalness affect brand preferences in a competitive choice situation rather than investigate attitudes.

To understand how global brands are understood and valued, we need to conceive of the issue in cultural terms. Culture is created and maintained in large part through communications (what cultural theorists like to call discourses). While cultural discourses circulated primarily at the national level for the past 150 years or so, helping to constitute national cultures (Anderson, 1983), a number of discourses have become global. The primary impact of the rise of global media, the mobility of labor, and the growth of international tourism is that many of the discourses that brands inhabit and help to circulate have become shared across the world.

These dramatic increases in transnational connections between people through the circulation of labor and media and products have led to what anthropologist Ulf Hannerz (1992) calls a culture of common differences. National cultures still play a powerful role to be sure. But everyone now participates in a global conversation (which gets inflected through the prism of the nation). People make sense of the world and form their identities in relation to Hollywood films and Bollywood, CNN reports as well as Al-Jazeera, MTV and Japanese cartoons, Coke ads and Sufi music. People now understand their lives, at least in part, in close proximity to the (usually mediated) cultures of other nationalities around the globe. In particular, due to the dominance of American entertainment worldwide, people are forced to come to terms with their lives in relation to an American way of life. There is no necessary homogeneity in this process. In fact, such a complex field of differences tends to promote fragmentation and creolization of identities (Hannerz, 1992).

One of the most potent new cultural categories in this worldwide discourse is the global brand. Global brands are understood by people worldwide as the marketing face of the world's most powerful companies. People have come to understand these brands through a wide variety of experiences: as consumers; through films, books, and even music; through news reports and advertising; and in discussions with friends. People around the world are increasingly reflexive about the role of global brands in their lives. Now that the largest multinational companies are more economically powerful than many nations and with a rising global coalition seeking to counter their influence, the global brand has become entrenched as a core cultural category. People now regard global brands as a class and attribute particular qualities to them. These attributions have a significant and distinctive impact on the brand.

Global Brand Research

To investigate the global brand as a cultural category, we conducted a three-stage research project. First, we developed hypotheses about the global brand discourse, informed by the cultural anthropology literature as described above. We identified five dimensions that consumers across many countries used to evaluate global brands: International Success, Global Status Symbol, Best-in-Class, Social Responsibility, and American Values. We then investigated these dimensions in considerable detail, drawing on findings from the 2002 Research International Observer (RIO), a global qualitative study involving fifteen hundred focus group participants in forty-one countries. We used these qualitative results to refine the dimensions and develop survey measures that accurately captured each dimension. Finally, we fielded a global survey with eighteen hundred respondents in twelve countries. (See the methods appendix at the end of the chapter for a comprehensive description of the research design and methods used.)

For the survey, we selected seventeen major global brands—all but one from Interbrand's top 100 list—to analyze. We picked three top competitors from each of six different product categories so that we could set up realistic competitive choices among global brands. We asked survey respondents to evaluate each brand using twenty specific measures of the brand's globalness, which together make up the five dimensions.

We also asked consumers, in a different section of the survey, to indicate their relative preference for each of the three brands— for instance, between Adidas, Reebok, and Nike. This task was repeated for each of the six product categories. When we used respondents' evaluations of the brand's globalness to predict which brand they most preferred, we found that the five dimensions explained an impressive 6 percent of the variance in their choices. Surprisingly, however, we found that one of the dimensions that is important in the global discourse, American Values, does not have a significant influence on brand preferences.

International Success: The global brand acts as a quality signal because it is perceived to be successful across many competitive national markets.

At the center of Levitt's argument was the idea that globally standardized products could deliver better value, higher functionality, and better reliability for a given price. If so, global brands should develop quality perceptions based on their success in delivering such value across many national markets. In our RIO focus groups, we found that people often associated global brands with better manufacture and more innovative products than local or regional companies. Global companies are perceived to have extraordinary resources that allow them to develop the breakthrough technologies to compete effectively in fierce international markets. Thus, their very ubiquity acts as a signal of quality:

"I like [global] brands because usually they offer more quality and better guarantees than other products." (Spain)

"[Global brands] must be very good in order to sustain a global presence. Some local brands are good too, but they don't have the ambition to venture into other countries. They are not as successful." (Hong Kong)

"The more people who buy a brand, . . . the better quality it is." (Russia)

"International brands are well known and the best quality. They are expensive, but the price is reasonable when you think of the quality." (Thailand)

"When you think of an international brand, you already assume it has better quality." (United Kingdom)

"They [global brands] are very dynamic, always upgrading themselves." (India)

"They [global brands] are more exciting because they come up with new products all the time, whereas you know what you will get with the local ones." (Australia)

"[Global brands are] brands that don't need to call attention to themselves—you know they're good." (Belgium)

In the survey, we found that quality attributions inferred from the brand's international success had by far the most powerful impact on brand choice, explaining 34 percent of the variance.

Global Status Symbol: The global brand conveys status on a global scale.

Global brands exude power and success. Our focus groups revealed that global brands are preferred because they are associated with powerful and successful people in other countries. To use them is to feel part of a global elite. If you are in South Africa, it matters what successful upper-middle-class people in the United States and France consume:

"International brands are more prestigious than local brands, which sometimes give the impression of being second-rate brands." (Belgium)

"Global brands make us feel citizens of the world, and we fear their leaving because they somehow give us an identity." (Argentina)

"Global brands make you feel part of something bigger and give you a sense of belonging." (New Zealand)

"Local brands show what we are; global brands show what we want to be." (Costa Rica)

"If you buy something because Americans use it, you feel at their same level." (Mexico)

"You appear to be of the same class when you use global brands." (Nigeria)

In the survey, we found that these global status attributions predicted about 12 percent of the variance in preference.

Best-in-Class: The global brand acts as a quality signal if it is a leading brand exported from a country with particular expertise.

Consumers worldwide make attributions about global companies that are understood as leaders in sophisticated home markets. Brands that are the best-in-class from nations that are known to specialize in the product category are viewed as highly desirable:

"I link clothing with Italy. I don't know why." (South Africa)

"I grew up with the thought that you don't buy American cars, but you buy German cars." (South Africa)

"If it is electronics, I will go for Japanese products because they are the best, but for clothing I prefer American labels and British made." (Nigeria)

"In technology, Japan is the leader. The best perfumes are French. Italian silver is really good. American clothes have better quality. Colombian leather is excellent." (Panama)

"Japanese products remind me of technology, innovation, discipline." (Turkey)

"German cars are very reliable. They are produced by employing the highest technology." (Turkey)

"With Italian things, it is very stylish and more sophisticated, better quality. Less is more, not as loud as everything American, which has to be bigger and better." (Australia)

In our survey, we find that about 10 percent of the brand preference variance is explained by such best-in-class quality attributions.

Social Responsibility: The global brand is expected to be socially responsible.

Over the past fifteen years, the idea that brands should not only deliver customer value but also address the broader demands of society has become an explosive and often divisive aspect of the global brand. As infamous cases filled the airwaves—Nestlé's infant formula sales in Africa, Union Carbide's Bhopal explosion, the *Exxon Valdez* spill, Shell's *Brett Spar* sinking and popular protests at its production facilities in Nigeria, and Nike's so-called sweatshop factories in Asia—consumers worldwide have come to see global brands as carrying a special responsibility to take on social issues that were once viewed as externalities of the market.

In our focus groups, we found that consumers worldwide think global brands can have a dramatic influence on the quality of life and on the future of the planet, for good or for bad. On the one hand, global brands are viewed as engines of economic development, raising standards of living and modernizing economies as they bring better jobs and diffusing new technologies. On the other hand, some people fear that global brands, in their quest for higher profits and market dominance, can harm consumers, workers, and the environment. Some people therefore view claims to promote social welfare and corporate social responsibility as a smokescreen:

"I still haven't forgiven Shell for what they [did] with that oil rig." (Germany)

"If an issue affects my health in an immediate way such as I will get sick or lose hair right after consuming it, I will care." (Hong Kong)

"McDonald's pays back locally, but it is their duty. They are making so much money, they should be giving back." (Australia)

While social responsibility is relevant to all brands, the issue has become particularly crucial for global brands because they are so powerful. People do not expect the local brand of petrol to tackle global warming, but they increasingly expect Shell and Exxon-Mobil to do so. They do not expect the local fashion brand to deal with worker rights in less developed countries, but they increasingly expect Nike and Polo to do so. We find that social responsibility explains about 8 percent of variance in global brand preference.

American Values: American values have little influence on the global brand.

One of the most pervasive ideas in the media for many years has been that global brands have sold the American dream to other countries. Since French attacks on American cultural imperialism in the 1960s, the idea that American mass culture is running roughshod over the indigenous cultures of nations and ethnic groups throughout the world has gripped the global media. Alternatively, the modernization counterargument suggests that peoples around the world want to partake of the American dream, and brands such as Coke, Levi, and Nike are the ambassadors that provide access to it. Many of our focus group participants readily discussed the "Americanness" of global brands:

"[American brands are] an imperialistic threat that undermines French cultural specificity." (France)

"They [the United States] want to impose 'their way' on everybody." (Germany)

"I hate the country [the United States], but I love their products." (South Africa)

"I used to go on anti-American rallies when I was still a student, but I never thought about the brand of clothes or shoes I wore!" (Philippines)

"We are not concerned how America governs their country, . . . we look for quality in their products." (India)

"Politics is politics. . . . The important thing is that the clothes we wear are nice. That's all that matters." (Indonesia)

However, our survey results indicate that a global brand's association with American values has only a negligible impact on brand preference. What is interesting here is that when we asked respondents directly about the importance of American values, positive or negative, they told us that they were important. But when we used statistical techniques to measure indirectly how much their evaluations of a brand shifted depending on whether it championed American values, we found little influence. The rhetoric, in this case, seems to be much more heated than the economic reality.

Product Category Differences

We expected to find significant differences in the relative importance of the global dimensions across product categories. For example, we expected that the social responsibility would be particularly important in petrol and athletic wear since nongovernmental organization activities have particularly focused on these brands. And we expected that quality attributions due to international success and best-in-class would be particularly important for cell phones and food, less so for petrol and soft drinks, because perceived risk is higher in these categories. Although we did find some aggregate category differences, they were small, muffled by idiosyncratic differences that varied from country to country. Although there was no systematic pattern across all twelve countries, we did find significant differences within each country that appear to be driven by the particulars of the country's consumer market and competitive set.

For example, if we look at the dairy products category, the global dimensions are significantly less important across the board in the United Kingdom. Our interpretation is that in the United Kingdom, dairy products are a core part of the country's cuisine and national heritage, and so consumers are less impressed by what global companies can provide. In addition, there are many powerful local brands that compete fiercely to win share in a sophisticated marketplace. Alternatively, in South Africa and Brazil, countries in which dairy is not as developed in the national cuisine, the perceived quality and status value of Nestlé, Dannon, and Kraft were particularly strong in predicting brand preferences relative to other countries.

We found this type of idiosyncratic difference in each country. For instance, global brand dimensions have less power in Brazil for athletic brands, which we attribute to the fact that these brands rely so heavily on Brazilian soccer to forge their global identities that Brazilians consider them their own.

Country Differences

The relative importance of the globalness dimensions varies significantly across countries. As a first cut, we explored whether typical country differences—East versus West and developed versus less developed countries—structure these differences. For instance, we hypothesized that global status would be more important in the less developed countries (LDCs). What we found instead is a more complicated story in which economic power, religion, politics, size of national markets, and other factors influence the result.

The United States is the least influenced by global drivers, followed by the United Kingdom. This result is not surprising. Because of the dominance of U.S. companies in world markets as well as the huge domestic market and perhaps a certain ethnocentrism, Americans do not generally view the tastes of other countries as signals.

At the other end of the spectrum were the Muslim countries. The most surprising result of the country comparisons is that in the midst of the buildup to the Iraq War, respondents in Muslim countries—Indonesia, Turkey, and Egypt—were significantly more influenced (favorably) by the globalness dimensions than all of the other countries in the sample. We can only speculate why this is so. In LDCs, we interviewed people from the top 50 percent of the country in terms of socioeconomic class. These were people who are familiar with global brands, live in urban areas, watch television, and have enough money to buy at least some of the brands. In the Muslim countries, this population is made up of the most Westernized, most secular part of the population. The fact that these countries all have strong fundamentalist religious movements among the majority poor perhaps causes this class to value global brands as the most ubiquitous and powerful markers of the way of life they value and hope for their countries to follow.

We were somewhat surprised to find that India, Brazil, and South Africa are relatively less persuaded by the globalness of brands. Once again, without follow-up research to explore the cultural understandings that informed their answers, we can only speculate why the results came out this way. We can speculate that the result was driven by strong anticolonial national cultures and also large domestic markets with strong local manufacturers in the case of India and Brazil.

Overall, the country differences, while statistically significant, are negligible in terms of managerial implications. That we did not find stark differences in the importance of globalness across countries supports the idea that these brands are understood within a global discourse. However, it does not follow that people around the globe share a uniform view of global brands. We conducted another analysis in which we looked for global consumer segments in order to explore whether there are important differences within countries.

Global Segments

To explore whether distinctive segments exist with respect to global brands, we conducted latent class segmentation analyses on all eighteen hundred respondents, sorting them according to similarities in how the five global dimensions shaped their preferences across all of the seventeen brands. The results are striking. Rather than variances that ranged to plus or minus 10 percent at the maximum for country comparisons, we find dramatic differences in the relative importance of the globalness dimensions. Several dimensions were even negatively correlated with preferences for some segments. The most informative statistical solution yields seven distinctive segments that form around differing cultural understandings of global brands. (In a related article, we have reduced these clusters to four segments, a scheme that gives up some of the statistical information in the data but yields a more useful segmentation scheme for managers. Holt, Quelch, and Taylor, 2003.)

- Global climbers. The largest segment (23.3 percent) consists of a group that is extremely conscious of and attracted to brands that exude global status. These people also place higher emphasis on citizenship qualities and are unimpressed by brands that are tied to countries with strong reputations for quality of specific products. Differences between countries are not significant: all have 20 to 25 percent of the population who are global climbers.
- Civic libertarians. A second large segment (21.5 percent) consists of people who place heavy emphasis on social responsibility and also are one of the two segments for which American values become barely significant. Conversely, they make negative attributions to brands they perceive as reflecting global status and are not impressed by brands that are produced in countries reputed to excel in the product category. No significant country differences were evident in this segment either.

- Multinational fans. The third largest segment (15.5 percent) is characterized by an unquestioned admiration for how global companies do business and what they represent. This segment ranks highest on the influence of reputation and global status on brand preference and also very high on best-in-class. However, they also reject brands they perceive to embody American values. Multinational companies are great, but they should be truly global in nature rather than selling the values of the United States. We found no significant country differences for this segment.

- Antiglobalists. The fourth largest segment (13.1 percent) approximates the antiglobalization movement. They are firmly against brands that express American values, and they are also deeply cynical about the ethics of corporations that own global brands. They are even more against brands as global status symbols than the libertarian citizens are. They have only a slight positive preference for brands based on their global quality. We find significantly more antiglobalists in the United Kingdom and China and significantly fewer in Egypt and South Africa.

- Global citizens. The fifth largest segment (10.1 percent) values social responsibility significantly more than average. The United States and the United Kingdom have significantly more global citizens and Brazil, China, and Indonesia significantly fewer.

- Global agnostics. Agnostics (7.6 percent) are people who evaluate global brands without using the global dimensions as important heuristics. They evaluate global brands as they would any other brand. We find very high percentages of agnostics in the United States and South Africa and very low percentages in Japan, Indonesia, China, and Turkey.

- Pro-West. Pro-West consumers (7.6 percent) are highly positive in the extent to which they are influenced by best-in-class perceptions, and they also view American values positively. They are significantly more influenced by global status and citizenship than average and relatively less influenced by international success. Indonesia and China have significantly more pro-West consumers than do other countries.

The segmentation analysis provides strong evidence that while global brands are now an important cultural category, there is considerable fragmentation in points of view within this global conversation. The quality signaled by the international success of a global brand is the only robust finding, holding up for 80 percent of the sample. The influence of the other three significant dimensions varies dramatically across segments. For about 45 percent of the sample, global status is a powerful driver of brand value, while for 40 percent it is negligible. Best-in-class attributions are very important for 23 percent and negligible or negative for 65 percent. Social responsibility is very important for 63 percent of the sample and negligible or negative for 36 percent.

Conclusions

Since Levitt's manifesto appeared twenty years ago, the world's largest companies have organized globally, coordinating their activities across most of the world's markets. Along the way, they have aggressively expanded the global reach of their corporate brands, even as they have become more sensitized in recent years to crafting their product brands to attend to local market conditions. But what actually does this globalization accomplish from consumers' points of view? Upon achieving this global reach, how should global brand owners manage these brands? While global brands have become the Goliaths of the marketplace, managers have yet to adopt brand policies crafted to address the particular global characteristics of their brands.

This chapter reports the first empirical study detailing the dimensions of the global brand and specifying the extent to which these dimensions influence brand preference. We find that consumers worldwide form preferences for global brands based on four ideas that are prominent in today's global media discourse: international success, global status, social responsibility, and best-in-class. We also find that while global brands are frequently associated with American values in discourse, these attributions seem to have little influence on brand preferences.

Managing the global brand requires understanding how the brand stacks up on these dimensions compared to competition, identifying opportunities to enhance these global perceptions, and shoring up weaknesses. Our segmentation scheme provides global brand owners with specific guidance on how to target such customers.

Our findings also document the size of the antiglobalist movement as an economic force. We find that fully 13 percent of our sample forms preferences against globalness characteristics. And these consumers live not only in Europe. They are just as prevalent in developing countries. Global brand owners must take heed to address the concerns of this group or risk losing a substantial fraction of their market.

Finally, we find that the influence of social responsibility on brand choice has become widespread. Corporate social responsibility (CSR) is no longer simply a stakeholder issue. It is becoming a front-and-center consumer issue as well. And CSR concerns are no longer confined to Europe. Many CSR efforts today focus on impressing consumers and other stakeholders in the richest countries. But our results indicate that corporate responsibility is just as important in the major emerging markets like China, India, and Brazil. Consumers around the world hold global brands particularly responsible for addressing social issues that the company can have an impact on. Most do not begrudge global companies their power, but with power comes increased responsibilities.

Methods Appendix

Our report draws on two global research studies. The Research International Observer (RIO) 2002 global qualitative study was conducted by Research International Qualitatif during the second half of 2002. Over fifteen hundred young urban consumers (ages twenty to thirty-five) participated in focus groups held in forty-one countries around the world representing various regions, cultures, and levels of economic development. Some countries conducted additional groups with social activists.

Second, we fielded a quantitative survey in twelve countries that also varied widely in terms of stage of economic development, geographical region, religious heritage, political history, colonial influences, and so on:

United States	United Kingdom	India	China
France	Poland	Japan	South Africa
Brazil	Indonesia	Egypt	Turkey

We investigated six product categories and offered respondents three competing global brands within each category. In choosing these categories, our priorities were categories in which at least three global brands competed and diversity in product type (durables versus FMCG, technology versus craft versus extraction). We selected brands that are among the most powerful and widely marketed in the world. We used the 2002 Interbrand Global Brand Scorecard as the selection source (almost 90 percent of the Interbrand 100 are global corporate brands rather than product brands). We relaxed this assumption in only two instances. For athletic wear, Reebok was not among the top one hundred brands. And in soft drinks, the most powerful third brand after Coke and Pepsi was typically a local brand, so we included the most powerful local brand in each country survey.

We submitted twenty possible product categories to Research International field managers in the twelve countries. We wanted to identify the product categories for which all three brands had a broad global presence and competed effectively against each other in many markets. All of the brands we tested had strong franchises across all twelve countries, with only a handful of exceptions. Based on this feedback, we culled the categories and brands to the following:

Category	*Brands*
Soft drinks	Coke, Pepsi, local brand
Cell phones	Nokia, Motorola, Samsung
Automobiles	Mercedes, Ford, Toyota
Athletic wear	Nike, Reebok, Adidas
Petrol	BP, Shell, Exxon-Mobil
Dairy/Packaged	Dannon, Nestlé, Kraft

We wanted to find out, first, the extent to which consumers' evaluations of global brands could be captured by the five hypothesized dimensions of globalness. And, further, we wanted to explore whether consumers use these dimensions to make brand choices. We developed multiple measures for the five dimensions and pretested these measures in the United States and Great Britain.

The pretest results yielded good psychometric properties for all five factors and allowed us to reproduce these dimensions using a reduced set of twenty individual measures. We fielded the survey in the other ten countries using these twenty measures. The psychometrics remained solid in the remaining ten countries, giving us confidence that the five constructs are stable and robust (see Table 9.1).

In addition to the attitudinal questions, we asked each respondent to reveal his or her brand preferences in each category by asking them to divide eleven points among the three brands. We treat this brand preference measure as the dependent variable and use the five factors as independent variables to predict preference.

We completed 150 interviews in each country, for a total sample of eighteen hundred respondents. We adopted a split-sample design in order to keep the questionnaire length down to approximately twenty minutes. This meant that each respondent evaluated brands in three categories, and so about seventy-five respondents per country evaluated each category. The analysis consisted of deriving importance weights for each of the five global dimensions by modeling the extent to which each factor explained brand preferences. We then examined how these importance weights varied by country, category, segment, and so on.

This international survey was fielded in February and March 2003. Participants consisted of a broad mix of consumers in each country, selected randomly between the ages of eighteen and seventy-five. No quotas were set, and a random sample of occupations, household revenues, gender, and ages was achieved. In developed countries, the sample approximates the country's population in terms of demographics, while in developing countries, the sample is predominantly from the top half (that is, nonpeasant) of the population in terms of socioeconomic status.

The survey was administered in both Web and paper-and-pencil interviewing (PAPI) formats. On the Web, each participant saw three randomly selected categories (for example, soft drinks, autos, and dairy/packaged). On PAPI, the categories were varied across six versions of the questionnaire (Table 9.2). The goal, either Web or PAPI, was to have seventy-five completed interviews per category.

We used a dual methodology, with Web interviewing in France, the United States, and the United Kingdom (via WPP's Lightspeed

Table 9.1. Dimensions of Globalness (Factors)

Dimension	Attributes	Factor Coefficient
International Success (alpha = .93)	As a global producer, it is able to make the best-quality products. (Q4)	0.80
	Must be a good-quality product because people all over the world buy it. (Q2)	0.80
	Has best-quality products because it is a winner in global competition. (Q1)	0.78
	As a global company, it must lead the market in innovation. (Q3)	0.78
	As a global company, it must deliver great service. (Q5)	0.75
Global Status Symbol (alpha = .91)	Used by powerful people around the world. (Q11)	0.75
	People I admire in other countries use this product. (Q10)	0.74
	Used around the world by the kind of people I respect. (Q12)	0.72
	Used by successful people around the world. (Q9)	0.69
Best-in-Class (alpha = .86)	I associate this brand with a particular country. (Q8)	0.79
	From a country with a rich tradition for producing [product]. (Q7)	0.69
	From a country known for the quality of its [product]. (Q6)	0.65
Social Responsibility (alpha = .91)	Cares about the environment. (Q16)	0.78
	Cares about the safety and health of me and my family. (Q19)	0.77
	Has high ethical standards. (Q17)	0.74
	Treats its employees well. (Q18)	0.73
	Acts like a good neighbor in my country. (Q20)	0.72
American Values (alpha = .93)	Embodies the American dream. (Q14)	0.88
	Is all about what America stands for. (Q15)	0.88
	Represents American values. (Q13)	0.87

Table 9.2. Six Versions of the Survey Instrument

	Completes	First Category	Second Category	Third Category
Version 1	25	Automobile	Athletic wear	Cell phones
Version 2	25	Athletic wear	Cell phones	Dairy/packaged
Version 3	25	Cell phones	Dairy/packaged	Petrol
Version 4	25	Dairy/packaged	Petrol	Soft drinks
Version 5	25	Petrol	Soft drinks	Automobile
Version 6	25	Soft drinks	Automobile	Athletic wear

Research Web panel) and interviewing in all other countries conducted face-to-face with Research International interviewers in major cities in each country. Web interviewing was conducted in the United States and the United Kingdom as the most time-efficient way in which to conduct the pilot study. Research in France was also conducted on the Web because the Lightspeed panel had broad enough participation to represent the entire country fairly.

The basic matrix for analysis was preference among the three brands within each category across each of the countries. Initial comparisons based on aggregate summaries of all these 208 brand-category-country combinations were not considered flexible enough, so both hierarchical Bayes and latent class regression models were built to allow for individual respondent-brand estimates. Both approaches attempt to "borrow" information from similar respondents to provide individual estimates of traditionally aggregate data, in this case linear regression beta coefficients. Hierarchical Bayes techniques use the Bayes theorem to develop a hierarchical framework to simulate draws from the relevant distributions to estimate the model. Latent class models use an expectation-maximization algorithm approach to simultaneously estimate the regression model and draw classes or groups that fit the model differently.

Both models used the actual normalized factor scores for the five global dimensions: International Success, Best-in-Class, Global Status Symbol, Social Responsibility, and American Values. This procedure eliminates multicollinearity issues associated with the weighted averages but does require a normalized interpretation.

For this reason, the brand preference scores were also normalized to a mean of 0 with a standard deviation of 1 (the same as the factor scores).

Because of the lack of replication at the respondent-brand level, the hierarchical Bayes regression model has very little variability from the overall model averages and is not suitable for comparisons on the level required for respondent and brand analyses. Latent class modeling proved a more useful approach. Latent class models from six to sixteen classes were fit with an eight-class solution fitting best (based on minimum BIC). (A residual class representing 1.3 percent of respondents was discarded, resulting in the seven substantive classes discussed above.) Each class's beta estimates were then multiplied by their latent class probabilities to create a unique set of beta coefficients for each respondent and brand. While this approach does minimize the absolute differences found in the latent class beta coefficients, it is not as homogeneous around the overall averages as the hierarchical Bayes approach and it allows respondent and brand ratings to be combined in any way desired.

These individual beta estimates were then compared by country, category, country-category, and category-country using the Kramer-Tukey ANOVA comparison test at the 90 percent significance level. Because of the sample sizes, the results are slightly more sensitive than initial correlation-based comparisons, although the absolute differences are much smaller.

Our five global dimensions explain nearly 70 percent of the variance in global brand preferences. While further precision on the importance of these global attributions awaits studies that measure these global drivers in conjunction with other dimensions of the brand, we can say conclusively that consumers' perceptions of a global brand's globalness have a powerful impact on the brand's value.

PART 5

Managing Global Services

Prior to the 1980s, decentralized multinationals purchased marketing services including advertising from local suppliers. In some cases, the suppliers of these services were subsidiaries, affiliates, or agents of an American or European agency. However, the quality of any agency's global network was highly variable. As a result, country general managers of multinational client companies with profit and loss responsibility cherry-picked the best marketing services suppliers to meet their local needs. The marketing services industry was local and highly fragmented.

As the forces of globalization motivated consolidation through mergers and acquisitions in many industries, so the structure of the marketing services industry began to change. Increasingly, chief executives of major multinational companies identified a wasteful duplication of effort and an unproductive not-invented-here syndrome in their country organizations. They sought to rein in their far-flung empires, reduce the power of their country barons in favor of worldwide product business units, and encourage internal learning across national boundaries.

Marketing services were enlisted to fulfill this mission. In 1983, top management at British Airways worked with the Saatchi & Saatchi agency to develop a global advertising campaign that would be shown in all markets throughout the world. An unprecedented 1 million pounds sterling was spent to create a single ninety-second blockbuster television advertisement. Many British Airways country managers, comfortable in their cosy relationships with local suppliers, complained that the ad was culturally insensitive or otherwise

203

unsuitable for their markets. Their behavior reflected Levitt's contention that country managers invariably magnified local differences either because they had "gone native" or in order to protect their jobs. The campaign was implemented in a blaze of favorable and free publicity, and to reinforce their influence and media buying power, British Airways consolidated all its advertising worldwide with Saatchi & Saatchi. Levitt joined its board of directors, and the agency scrambled to improve its worldwide network to deliver a consistent quality of service to its new global client.

An international airline was a rather obvious candidate for a global advertising campaign. Could the concept of global advertising implemented through a single agency be extended to the business-to-business arena? The answer came in 1994 when IBM consolidated its $500 million of annual advertising expenditures with the Ogilvy & Mather agency. The new CEO of IBM, Lou Gerstner, used the centralization of advertising oversight to signal a new approach to his decentralized network of overseas subsidiaries. Ogilvy & Mather put its best people on the IBM account, resigned from competitive business, and benefited greatly in new business wins from the publicity around IBM's vote of confidence in the agency.

Martin Sorrell lived through both of these events. He was finance director of the Saatchi & Saatchi agency in 1983 and left a couple of years later to establish WPP Group plc, which subsequently acquired the J. Walter Thompson, Ogilvy & Mather, and Young & Rubicam agencies, among many others. In 2003, London-based WPP Group was the second largest marketing services company in the world, after Omnicom Inc. of the United States. WPP is a financial holding company in an industry where conflict-of-interest rules still require Chinese walls if agencies in the same group are to serve competing clients in the same category. As a result, holding companies such as WPP and Omnicom are frequently challenged by investors to demonstrate that their value as consolidated enterprises is greater than their break-up value.

Has global consolidation of the marketing services sector created or destroyed value? The large holding companies are able to achieve lower media costs for their clients through consolidated buying power. Sorrell points out in Chapter Ten that there are few barriers to entry in the marketing services business, that the industry remains highly fragmented in every country of the world, and that new creative boutiques open every day. Silk and Berndt explore in Chapter Eleven the extent of size and scope-related economies (in terms of the mix of services and markets served) in the industry. They find some evidence of efficiencies resulting from the joint production of advertising and other marketing services and the joint production of services (such as advertising copy) for both domestic and international markets. This is good news for the global holding companies like WPP and Omnicom that find themselves frequently under margin pressure from their savvy, price-sensitive, and demanding global clients.

CHAPTER 10

The Globalization of Marketing Services

Martin Sorrell

Did markets in fact go global as Levitt so confidently predicted in his article twenty years ago? If so, to what extent? Is the trend now toward increased globalization or in retreat from it? And where can we expect to be, in respect of global markets, twenty years from today?

Whatever the consensus that may or may not emerge, Levitt's 1983 article takes its place among the classic works of marketing literature. There cannot be many others that have taken such a lasting hold on the imagination of business people worldwide—and on their strategy and decision making.

I remember vividly the impact that Levitt's article had on me when I first read it back in May 1983. I immediately took it to Maurice Saatchi, one of the founders of the Saatchi & Saatchi advertising agency, and he agreed that this was an extraordinarily important pointer to the future and an important means of agency differentiation.

We immediately ordered five hundred or so reprints to be sent to clients. And it was no coincidence that Saatchi & Saatchi subsequently devoted itself to becoming a global agency, using global advertising to market what we now identify as global brands.

One example of that vision was the agency's "Manhattan" television commercial for British Airways that used some impressive special effects to show the entire island of Manhattan flying into Heathrow. It was dubbed into twenty languages and shown in thirty-five countries around the globe. And this was before world-wide markets were as open as they are now, when one-third of the world's population lived within the closed society of communist regimes.

What was it that grabbed so many peoples' imagination at that time about Levitt's ideas? For me, it began with the essential simplicity of his proposition. Two unstoppable trends—the convergence of consumer desires and the compelling cost advantages of standardized products—were fast converging. When they came together, Levitt declared, nothing would be the same again.

In a world community, homogenized by proliferating mass transport and communications, the multinational company with its vision of multiple customized markets was obsolete. The global company, however, offering standardized high quality at aggressively low prices to uniformly receptive markets shorn of their cultural preferences, was, by contrast, absolute.

And in case we were left in any doubt about the irrevocable advance of this revolution, Levitt assured us that "no one is exempt and nothing can stop the process." The question is, Was he right? Here I offer my response.

Back in 1983, while it is true that some forward-looking companies were beginning to take their brands international, most advertising agencies were still handling their clients largely on an office-by-office or, at best, a national basis. The real move toward global account management did not begin until the late 1980s and into the 1990s.

One watershed event for my company, Ogilvy, occurred in 1994, when IBM parted company with over forty different agencies and consolidated its $500 million account at Ogilvy. Here at last was a client that recognized that its strength and viability resided in its global scale—indeed, that global was its only option. The advertising the agency developed—"Solutions for a Small Planet," articulated a proposition that rang true across the world.

Many of our other clients were in one sense going global at that time. In the mid-1990s, Unilever resolved to redouble efforts to leverage its brands, principally by investing in the stronger ones and expanding their reach. Dove soap and Pond's lotion are two of their great global brands with universally understood propositions.

But an interesting point begins to emerge here. Both Dove and Pond's are also, and equally, local brands. Their global brand positioning has always been expressed in local terms. Most of their users anywhere in the world think of them as their own national brands.

To take just one other example, the same is true of Nestlé. It's the biggest seller of bottled water in the world, but consumers would not know or care about that. Instead we call for Perrier, San Pellegrino, Poland Spring, or one of dozens of other nationally or regionally established Nestlé brands. These, then, are hardly the single standardized products that Levitt hailed as the inevitable future of globalized markets.

In the late 1980s and into the 1990s, as political and economic barriers tumbled, there is no doubt that Levitt was looking increasingly right. McDonald's opened in Moscow, Coca Cola flooded across newly open frontiers, and MTV became a shared experience for young people from Rome to St. Petersburg.

Two other factors came into play. Regional trading blocs, including the European Community and the North American Free Trade Agreement, began to dismantle trade barriers. Later in the 1990s came the Internet, hugely accelerating global familiarity with products and services of every kind and pushing the standardization of their offering, brand, and price worldwide—but interestingly, increasingly customizing communication.

Levitt had not foreseen any of this. Nonetheless, global trade over the period 1980 to 2000 just about tripled.[1]

So far so good, some might argue, for the Levitt view. But I am not among them.

As I see it, Levitt's argument has proved too black and white over time. This is largely because he looked at the globalization of products as a supply-side, rather than a demand-side, phenomenon. In short, he neglected the consumer. To quote him directly from the famous article:

> It [the global competitor] will never assume that the customer is a King who knows his own wishes. . . .
>   There is only one significant respect in which a company's activities around the world are important, and this is in what it

produces and how it sells. Everything else derives from, and is subsidiary to, these activities. . . .

Instead of adapting to superficial and even entrenched differences within and between nations, it [the global competitor] will
seek sensibly to force suitably standardised products and practices
on the entire globe.

The fact is that people do not now, nor will they any time soon,
buy the same product in the same way in different markets around
the world. There always were, still are, and I am convinced will continue to be substantial and enduring differences in what and how
consumers consume.

This it seems to me is Levitt's principal oversight: he assumed
that the cost and quality advantages of product standardization
would impress themselves on peoples and cultures everywhere,
sweeping aside their desire for variety and choice. But we consumers are not so easily coerced. So January 1, 1993, the inauguration
date for the European single market, did not see the birth of a uniform "Euro-consumer." Quite the opposite occurred.

Just consider Welsh and Scottish devolution, the Catalans, the
Basques, the Canadian separatists—even in Iraq, the Shiites, the Sun-
nis, and the Kurds. In all cases, consumers are more interesting for
their differences than their similarities.

What we actually witnessed was that as people win greater freedom and prosperity, they quite naturally begin to demand more
variety and choice in the things they purchase. And more and
more of them have the money to pay for it.

For evidence, I need look no further than WPP. We are responsible for the brand images of many corporate and product brands
around the world. Yet these truly international products and services, which range from soft drinks and fast food to computer hardware and software, account for only about 10 to 15 percent of our
revenues. And even in these categories, there may be significant differences in the purchasing decision from one market to another.

What is more, as people exercise ever more choice over their
purchasing decisions, the cultural distinctions between their buying habits are likely to grow ever more pronounced. Contrary to
Levitt, the consumer is in control. Companies that intend to succeed in international business must understand this simple fact.

No more than 15 percent of our business at WPP is truly global, in the Levitt sense of employing the same marketing methods throughout the world. The rest of our business is by definition local—that is, where our clients must offer brands with more local appeal and also structure themselves to manage their businesses if not on a country basis, then on a regional one. The local touch is essential. Such companies are equally decentralized and continuing country management.

WPP is doing the same. We are all listening more closely to our local business partners, learning how to tailor products, services, and marketing communications to local conditions. Global brand owners are balancing authority over product development and marketing spending with local managers, and they are replacing expatriate executives with locally hired executives. At the same time, we are experimenting with global client or brand coordinators and WPP country managers.

Look around, and you will see the results. After being a one-product company for nearly a century, Coca Cola now has some two hundred local brands, and the number is growing. Unilever India has set up the autonomous Wheel organization to market quality low-price local brands to the mass market. Unilever also has developed a rural marketing sales force in India. McDonald's varies its menus to appeal to local tastes as well as investing in local food retailing chains. MTV programming reflects a strictly local view of what's cool.

Coca Cola, McDonald's, MTV, IBM, Disney, American Express. Brand names like these raise the inevitable suspicion: Is what has been going on not globalization but, when it comes down to it, plain Americanization?

Although Levitt was inspired as much by Toyota and Panasonic as by any U.S. cultural icon, it remains true that American multinationals rode the wave of the American triumph over Soviet communism fourteen years ago. As scores of new markets opened their borders, it was U.S. companies that had the virtually unlimited capital and resources to finance rapid global expansion.

In this, they were abetted by the eagerness of local consumers to taste the forbidden fruits of Marlboro, the Whopper, Levis, and other luxuries hitherto dreamed about but never experienced. By the year 2000, sixty-two of the world's one hundred most valuable brands were American.[2] To their owners, local adaptation must have seemed an irrelevance.

As we all know, this has laid the United States open to charges of cultural or commercial imperialism (or both)—the sort of thing that gets the French very upset and encourages them to ban Americanisms in their advertising language. Antiglobalization protesters, always vocal, are becoming increasingly organized and articulate. Some are successfully using entrepreneurial business methods to counter American hegemony.

Early in 2003, it was reported that Mecca-Cola, a new soft drink with Islamic investment behind it and a self-declared stance against "American imperialism and Zionism," had taken orders for 16 million 1.5 liter bottles.[3] Farousz, a nonfermented, hence nonalcoholic, drink in Egypt has gained an 18 percent market share in a short period of time due to its attraction to Muslim consumers. The war in Iraq and its aftermath have done nothing to change this situation and may have deepened the issue.

Clearly there is an opportunity for companies to enhance their corporate social responsibility and ethical behavior to counter the antiglobalization movement. Such measures in any case promote customer satisfaction, loyalty, and profits. But equally, we must stand our ground against extremist overstatements and reassert the truth that no brand is ever likely to overturn a culture single-handedly.

However, we at WPP believe the very best response to accusations of imperialism is to point out, as we have done in the past, that any company that intends to build a global brand or business must dominate the American market. This market accounts for nearly half the volume in most sectors—and some 40 to 45 percent in the advertising and marketing services industry.

We know the reasons: the scale and homogeneity of the U.S. market as a whole, the size and efficiency of its capital markets, and its overwhelming technological domination. In fact, I am hard pressed to recollect any sector where the Americans do not have a lead except, perhaps, third-generation telephony and, given the prices paid by license holders, perhaps this was a mixed blessing.

At WPP, our top forty clients represent 40 percent of revenues. Twenty-seven of those forty are based in the United States. That is why we run our operations mainly out of New York.

Commercial reality, then, not imperialist conspiracy, is what lies behind the Americanization of the markets. But in any case, American hegemony may change soon enough. In the temporary absence of a countervailing power, China is the obvious candidate. Greater China, with its 1.3 billion population and huge commitment to infrastructure investments over the coming five years, is already WPP's fifth largest market.

If we think the Athens Olympic Games in 2004 will stimulate the economy, just stand by for the 2008 Beijing Olympics. The Chinese government has already effectively committed itself to some $45 billion of infrastructure and investment around the games. In addition, the mayor of Shanghai has committed a further $3 billion around the Shanghai 2010 Expo.

Indeed, Asia-Pacific as a whole may well come to predominate. After all, by 2014 two-thirds of the world's citizens will live there. Western companies that want to continue expanding will have to come to terms with marketing products and services in the region. At the same time, companies in these and other emerging markets are likely to take advantage of anti-American sentiment to launch their own competing global brands. It may be that the Iraq war marks the high point of American hegemony as the twin forces of Chinese development and Muslim population growth become increasingly important.

There are almost 1.5 billion Muslims today or about 26 percent of the world's population. By 2014, Muslims will account for over 30 percent of the projected world's population. This will make it increasingly important for the West to make an attempt to understand the Muslim mind. To date, we have assumed that their goals, values, and ideas are broadly the same as ours. It looks increasingly as though they are very different, and we had better make a sincere and serious attempt to understand exactly how and why.

In what other ways will the globalization of markets—however we interpret its effects on the last decades—influence the future of management and marketing practice?

We are going to have to rethink brand management. Population trends will mean less homogeneity across markets. Companies and their marketing focus will therefore become more localized, which will probably call for more, rather than less, emphasis on national management, national approaches, and national customs. Refocusing on the local will help correct the situation if, as I believe, the global pendulum may have swung too far. There are interesting examples of regional management and local strategies being developed. For example, in Italy, Banca Intesa is pursuing a local, or Italian, regional strategy instead of banging heads with Citigroup, HSBC, or American Express.

But we must also recognize that disparate peoples do indeed have a shared body of tastes, emotions, and aspirations, which we ignore at our peril. That is a simple matter of human psychology. Shrewdly—or mischievously—Levitt noted in his article that country managers had an obvious incentive to talk up local differences: the justification of their position and salary.

So while some commentators characterize the evolution of international marketing strategy over the past two decades as progressing from "think global, act global" to "think global, act local" right through to "think local, act local," we would differ. Depending on the company, product, and brand concerned, any one of these prescriptions might be right.

One further challenge that we at WPP are also aware of facing is that of transferring and applying ideas and talent around the world so as best to help our clients manage their brands. In this respect, globalization is far less about leveraging economies of scale than it is about leveraging economies of expertise or knowledge. It is about taking global advantage by sharing knowledge instead of reinventing the wheel in every different market.

To return to Levitt's "The Globalization of Markets," the more I consider it, the more I believe that our discomfort with some parts of it is rooted in a very curious omission.

Twenty-eight years earlier, the *Harvard Business Review* had published Gardner and Levy's "The Product and the Brand," the first authoritative analysis of the nature of brands and why the words *brand* and *product* should never be used interchangeably.[4] "The Product and the Brand" began a revolution in consumer understanding that continues to this day. David Ogilvy, then running a relatively fledgling agency, found its arguments compelling—not least because they conformed to his own instinctive views—and embraced them wholeheartedly. Even today, the Ogilvy agency's mission statement owes much to Gardner and Levy's early insights into the nature of brands and how they differ from mere products.

Yet twenty-eight years on, Levitt made no reference to the earlier article and made no attempt to draw a useful distinction between the meaning of the two words. Indeed, the word *product* must be used a hundred times in the Levitt article, while the word *brand* barely figures. Either Levitt believes the words are synonymous or chose to ignore the crucial distinction between the two.

The difference, as we all know today, is this. A product is a product is a product: the identical object as it leaves the factory gates, of uniform specification and susceptible to objective, universal measurement. A brand is a subjective thing: it is the experience of a product as encountered by any given individual. And that experience not only can, but invariably will, differ from user to user.

Consider two Boeing 747 planes: identical products. Both bear British Airways livery: identical design. Routes, prices, and onboard services: also identical. Then two businessmen board these two planes: one is British and one Japanese. And their brand experiences simply cannot be identical: for one, the experience is an experience of home; for the other, it is one of relative unfamiliarity. And if the two 747s were from JAL rather than British Airways, their experiences would be equally diverse, though their responses would be neatly reversed.

Even if the food, the price, and the decor are identical, the experience of eating at a McDonald's for someone with a weekly disposable income of five hundred dollars will be totally different from that of someone with a weekly disposable income of fifty dollars.

Even in 1983, for consumer goods companies to fail to distinguish between the nature of a product and the nature of a brand was a certain recipe for insensitive marketing. I believe that if Levitt had preached the opportunity for, and desirability of, many more identical products across the globe—but had at the same time recognized that identical products can play hugely divergent roles in different people's lives—his contribution to marketing literature and marketing effectiveness would have been even more immeasurably greater.

I conclude with a few words about how we view one of the most recent phenomena in our industry: the development of the so-called superagencies.

When Levitt's article appeared, the ad agency was a very different organization from what it is now. At that time, a client would walk into an agency and find multiple departments with a wide range of different services, such as creative, planning, production, public relations, research, media investment management, branding, and more, all under one roof. For example, J. Walter Thompson in Berkeley

Square, London, in the 1950s had a creative department, an account handling department, a planning department, a production department, a public relations agency, a research company, even an operations research department.

That is no longer the case. Extensive consolidation has occurred among both the global agencies and the holding or parent companies. We are down to a Big Three, arguably a Big Four, and there are different operating philosophies.

But increasingly the discussion of providing global communications services has moved to the "superagency" level of holding or parent companies. These, rather than the agencies themselves, are the repositories of communications services, which are housed in specialized operating companies carved out of traditional agency networks that have seen their offerings refined and sharpened, their economics redefined as stand-alone businesses. The former full-service agencies were unbundled by clients because they believed they would receive the unbundled services at lower cost. In addition, many "specialists" inside the full-service agencies believed that their specialisms were undervalued. For example, the media planners and buyers felt they were second-class citizens— underresourced and underpaid in comparison with their creative department colleagues.

By amassing disciplines and making them cost-effective and best in class, the superagencies are well placed to offer precisely what clients now demand: creativity first and foremost, much improved coordination, and at the lowest possible price.

Note that this does not imply a single global message for a client or brand. On the contrary. While the superagency takes a role in helping companies manage their brands on a transnational basis, the messaging and the tactics of the various advertising and marketing disciplines are locally focused through the specialized service cells.

Success in the coming years will depend on sustaining and refining the superagency concept, and on managing and transferring knowledge and talent out to the transnational service providers for local deployment.

CHAPTER 11

Cost Economies in the Global Advertising and Marketing Services Business

Alvin J. Silk
Ernst R. Berndt

The globalization and diversification of advertising agencies that have taken place over the past two decades represent a major structural change in the organization of the advertising and marketing services business. Ted Levitt's influence on both thought and practice in this field is well recognized in advertising agency history. His prized "Globalization of Markets" essay (Levitt, 1983) played a direct role in stimulating the international expansion of both U.S. and overseas agencies.

Note: For assistance in obtaining data, we thank Barbara Esty, David Doft, and Lauren Rich Fine and their staffs at Baker Library, CIBC, and Merrill Lynch, respectively. We are also indebted to Masako Egawa and Yumi Sudo at Harvard Business School's Japan Research Office, Tokyo, for their help in collecting data. The encouragement and advice of John Quelch is gratefully acknowledged, as is the support of the Division of Research, Harvard Business School. A special note of thanks is due to members of the Harvard/MIT Advertising Agency Research Seminar for valuable discussions, especially Charles King, Tuba Ustuner, and Andrew von Nordenflycht. The usual disclaimer applies.

We dedicate this chapter to the memory of Diane D. Wilson.

The 1983 annual report of Foote, Cone, & Belding featured a short article entitled, "Global Markets, Global Advertisers, Global Agencies—The Wave of the Future." That essay foresaw advertising embarking on a new era: "A powerful new challenge and opportunity faces advertisers and advertising agencies—with results even more profound than the great transformation for which Albert Lasker, the founder of modern advertising, is justifiably credited." The author was none other than Theodore Levitt. He went on to become very much involved in the agency business, not at Foote, Cone, & Belding, but rather at Saatchi & Saatchi in London. In his account of the growth of the Saatchi & Saatchi, Ivan Fallon (1989) describes how Maurice Saatchi viewed Levitt as his "private philosopher" (p. 187). Levitt served on the board of that agency for several years. After having contributed to the rise of Saatchi & Saatchi, he also had a hand in its notorious demise, becoming, according to one industry observer, "Saatchi's most vocal critic on the board" (Goldman, 1997). He later served on the board of Cordiant after it separated from Saatchi & Saatchi. Levitt's 1983 paper sparked a substantial literature debating the merits of standardized versus localized advertising campaigns.[1] However, there has been surprisingly little empirical study of the economics of firms engaged in the production of global advertising and marketing services required to plan and execute such campaigns.

This chapter addresses that void. How important are scale and scope economies in the global advertising and marketing services business? Much of the rationale underlying the growth strategies of these organizations emphasizes size-related advantages (Elliot, 2002). At the same time, whether global firms possess a sustainable competitive advantage over smaller, regional players is the subject of an ongoing debate within the industry (Anholt, 2000). Several waves of mergers and acquisitions have fueled concerns about the rising concentration level in the industry (Kim, 1995). The holding company model employed by global firms has also recently come under renewed scrutiny (Cardona, 2002b; Khermouch, 2003). For all these reasons, the issue of size-related economies in this industry is one deserving empirical analysis. To the best of our knowledge, this is the first econometric study of such cost economies.

We treat holding companies as multiproduct firms and estimate a translog model of firm costs applying three-stage least squares to a time series of annual data for an unbalanced panel consisting of the eight leading global advertising and marketing services firms. Collectively, this group of holding companies accounted for more than 90 percent of the estimated total revenue earned in 2001 by the one hundred largest firms in this industry.

Our results can be briefly summarized. We demonstrate that a firm's costs are affected by its size, scope (mix of services offered and markets served), and the interaction of the latter two dimensions of firm scope. The presence of the interaction effect supports a major but controversial element of holding company strategy: that coordination economies are available from the delivery of integrated advertising and marketing services globally. Using the parameter estimates for the translog cost function, we then investigate the extent to which overall scale economies and diseconomies and product-specific scale and scope economies and diseconomies are available to firms in this industry. Our estimates indicate that the industry's long-run cost function is subject to very slight economies of scale. Growth obtained by extending either the breadth of services offered or market coverage is accompanied by diseconomies of scale, a result we show not to be inconsistent with the existence of overall or global economies of scale. These findings do not point to any substantial level of potential scale economies that remains to be exploited by the largest firms in this industry. Such findings are to be expected in a highly competitive industry with relatively low fixed costs.

Small scope economies involving cost savings of 1 to 2 percent are realized through diversification of either lines of business or market coverage. The institutional constraint arising from the long-standing industry norm that prohibits an agency from serving competing accounts that Silk and Berndt (1995) hypothesized to limit the growth and diversification potential of traditional full-service advertising agencies appears to have been obviated by the holding company form of organization.

The Global Advertising and Marketing Services Business

We begin this section with a brief review of the historical research on the internationalization of the advertising and marketing services industry. Following that, we discuss the dominant organizational form that the industry has adopted in pursuit of growth and globalization: the holding company.

Globalization of Advertising and Marketing Services

The beginning of the internationalization of the advertising and marketing services industry dates back at least as far as 1899 when J. Walter Thompson opened an office in London (West, 1987). In 1927, Thompson became General Motors' "export agency" and embarked on a rapid international expansion. In the late 1920s and early 1930s, Thompson opened thirty-four branch offices in Europe, the Middle East, South Africa, India, Australia, and South America (Merron, 1999). Thompson was not GM's domestic agency, and its appointment on the export account lasted only five years. Interestingly, Merron (1999, p. 469) observed, "The key to the branch offices' survival was that they aggressively pursued local clients." Weinstein (1974) traced the international expansion of fifteen U.S. agencies over the period 1915 through 1971 and found that the rate at which agencies opened offices in countries for the first time almost quadrupled over the period 1960 through 1971.

Comparatively little appears to have been written about the international expansion of Asian or European agencies. A notable exception is West's insightful (1988) study of multinational competition in the British advertising agency business over the period 1936 through 1987. West's analysis identified two distinct phases of development. The first, beginning in the interwar period and lasting until the late 1970s, is characterized as the "Americanization of British advertising." The share of total advertising billings in the United Kingdom held by U.S. multinational agencies grew from 13 percent in 1936, peaking at 42 percent in 1970. Unlike the United States, the agency business in Britain has long been a highly concentrated industry. The billings share of the ten largest agencies was 70 percent in 1936 and reached 82 percent in 1970. The pioneering U.S. agencies in the United Kingdom were greenfield entrants following the multinational growth path of their U.S.-based clients. Reciprocal alliances between American and British agencies became commonplace in the interwar period. Later in the post–World War II period, West shows that acquisitions became important, noting that between 1957 and 1967, U.S. agencies purchased thirty-two British agencies.

The second phase of West's historical analysis covers the comeback of the British. The share of U.K. billings held by U.S. multinational agencies fell from a high of 42 percent in 1970 to 34 percent in 1980 and 22 percent in 1987. The major developments in this period were the aggressive growth and stunning success, at home and abroad, of two London-based firms: first, Saatchi & Saatchi (beginning in the late 1970s), and then WPP in the late 1980s. West (1988) contrasts the advantage exploited by the British in their domestic comeback and international expansion with that of the earlier American penetration of the high end of the U.K. market:

> The advantage accruing to British advertising agencies in the changing trends in foreign direct investment flows in the 1980s was different from that previously held by the Americans. It provided access to capital, rather than to the patronage of large advertisers. Throughout the entire period, British agencies have never been able to exploit the indigenous British-based MNE advertiser in the same way that U.S. agencies have used American MNEs [p. 487].

West argues that Saatchi & Saatchi's domestic success inspired confidence within the British financial community, giving advertising agencies improved access to capital and permitting them to grow by means of acquisitions: "The new ease in raising capital facilitated the spectacular entrance of British multinational advertising agencies into the American domestic market from 1982 onward" (p. 499). That advance was marked by two highly publicized deals: Saatchi & Saatchi's acquisition of New York–based Ted Bates Worldwide in May 1986 and WPP's takeover of J. Walter Thompson in June 1987.

The Holding Company Concept

The world's largest advertising and marketing services firms are all public holding companies that own (partially or outright) numerous operating companies offering a wide variety of related or competing services to clients. To varying degrees, the parent organization performs a coordinating role and supplies subsidiary organizations with support programs, systems, and resources. However, as the chief financial officer of a leading firm in this industry was recently quoted as saying, "There is no single model for a successful holding company. Their success depends on how they perform their functions, whether as a hands-off financial entity or a structure to help networks work together" (Cardona, 2002b).

The pioneering global advertising and marketing services holding company is the Interpublic Group of Companies. Marion Harper, who served as its chairman and CEO throughout the 1960s, is widely acknowledged to have been the architect of this organizational innovation. Harper saw adherence to the industry's longstanding norm that an agency not serve competitors in the same category of business as a major impediment to achieving the twin goals of growth and diversification (American Association of Advertising Agencies, 1979). He proposed the holding company concept as a means of circumventing that stricture. His biographer and colleague reported Harper as having said, "I don't see why it shouldn't be possible for us to own more than one agency and serve competing accounts, as long as we keep the two agencies completely separate" (Johnson, 1982, p. 96). Despite initial resistance from clients and criticism from competitors, Harper eventually prevailed, and the holding company concept gained acceptance and spread.

Silk and Berndt (1995) analyzed the industry norm on conflict policy as an institutional mobility barrier (in the sense of Caves and Porter, 1977) that induces individual agencies to grow by diversifying their lines of service offerings rather than by expanding existing ones. A second institutional factor identified by Silk and Berndt (1995) as affecting agency growth and diversification strategies of advertising agencies was the industry practice of agencies bundling creative and media services, a strategy encouraged by the fact that it is customary for clients to advertise simultaneously in several media. Based on these two considerations, Silk and Berndt (1995, p. 439) advanced the hypothesis of "excessive" diversification: "The joint presence of media bundling on the demand side and conflict policy on the supply side constitute institutional constraints that induce firms to diversify more extensively than might otherwise be cost justified." Consistent with this hypothesis, in a cross-sectional analysis of 1987 data for 401 U.S. advertising agencies, Silk and Berndt (1995) found that media-specific scope economies were negatively related to agency size.

Silk and Berndt's analysis and empirical study (1995) were conducted at the level of individual advertising agencies rather than that of holding companies. Two important structural changes have occurred since 1987, the year of the data Silk and Berndt used. First, over the past two decades, there has been a growing tendency for advertising agencies to unbundle their services as multiproduct clients have sought to gain bargaining power with media suppliers by consolidating media buying for their brands in organizations specializing in media planning and buying (Horsky, 2002). Second, all of the major holding companies have established media planning and buying units that are available to perform these functions for clients of the networks of agencies controlled by the holding companies (Mandese, 2002). Thus, it may be that these changes have allowed holding companies to obviate the disadvantage of excessive diversification Silk and Berndt (1995) argued as being present at the level of individual agencies in 1987.

Holding company management faces an ongoing challenge to achieve a balance between policies that favor centralization in ways that may improve coordination and profitability versus those that allow decentralization in order to foster creativity and maintain credibility with clients as to the independence of individual organizations. For example, Omnicom has the reputation for granting considerable autonomy to its operating divisions (Elliot, 2002). WPP is one of the organizations studied by Raynor and Bower (2001) in their research on how strategic integration is accomplished in contemporary diversified companies facing dynamic and uncertain environments. They observe that WPP has been successful in building a strategically flexible organization by pursuing different degrees of relatedness among the operating divisions, some being closely linked and others less so. (See Bower and Hout, 2001, for details.)

Based on *Advertising Age*'s estimates of holding companies' worldwide gross incomes, the annual nominal growth rate of the world's ten largest holding companies averaged almost 13 percent over the twelve year period 1990 through 2001. This growth is almost three times greater than the growth rate of worldwide expenditures for advertising and marketing services that averaged only 45 percent over the same time period.[2]

Scale and scope economies figure prominently in the reports of investment analysts who follow this industry closely, especially with respect to how cost economies relate to the basic elements of firm strategy (growth, globalization, diversification) and industry consolidation. Among the major industry trends emphasized by Doft, Ammon, and Gawrelski (2002) are client demand for integrated marketing services and cross-national consistency in brand communications, as well as interest in consolidating the multiplicity of accounts with fewer service suppliers. Fine and others (2003) point out that the growth rate and margins of marketing services tend to be greater than those for advertising-related services. However, they see size-related improvements in margins as being difficult to realize, in part because of client cost consciousness and bargaining power. Diversification with respect to both lines of service offered and markets served may also affect the sensitivity of holding companies' performance to the business cycle. However, Fine and others (2003) note that diversification can serve not only to dampen downturns but may also limit speed of recoveries.

Against this background, we move on to a discussion of the modeling framework and analytical methods used in our empirical study.

Econometric Model and Method

We begin this section with the specification of the cost function employed in the empirical analysis. Definitions of the measures of scale and scope economies reported later are then presented along with expressions for estimating them in terms of the variables and parameters of the translog cost function. Detailed derivations are given in appendix A at the end of the chapter.

Model Specification

We employ a translog (transcendental logarithmic) model to represent a firm's total variable costs of producing its output of services. Widely used in empirical econometrics, the translog model is a flexible functional form that can be used to capture a variety of size-related cost phenomena arising from the operations of multiproduct firms, including, in particular, scale and scope effects (Berndt, 1991; Paul, 1999). The translog cost function for firm i $(i = 1, \ldots, k)$ may be written as follows:

$$\ln TVC_i = \ln \alpha_i + \beta_1 \ln Y_i + \tfrac{1}{2} \beta_2 (\ln Y_i)^2 + \gamma M_{id} + \delta P_{ia} + \theta M_{id}P_{ia} \qquad (11.1)$$

where TVC_i is the total variable cost, Y_i is a measure of the scale of total output, M_{id} is the share of the firm's output (Y) produced for the U.S. market rather than for the overseas markets, $(1 - M_{id})$, $M_{id} \leq 1$ and P_{ia} is the share of the firm's total output consisting of advertising services rather than of other marketing services, $(1 - P_a)$, $P_{ai} \leq 1$, where α_i, β_1, β_2, γ, δ, and θ are parameters to be estimated.

Now the firm's average variable cost (AVC_i) is given by:

$$\ln AVC_i = \ln (TVC_i/Y_i) = \ln TVC_i - \ln Y_i$$

$$= \ln \alpha_i + (\beta_1 - 1) \ln Y_i + \tfrac{1}{2} \beta_2 (\ln Y_i)^2 + \gamma M_{id} + \delta P_{ia} + \theta M_{id}P_{ia} \qquad (11.2)$$

This specification of the translog cost model allows for the possibility of both scale and scope effects. Depending on the signs and magnitudes of the scale parameters, β_1 and β_2, the AVC function may be either everywhere decreasing or U-shaped in Y.

The two potentially important sources of scope effects discussed are represented in the translog cost function. The first arises from how a firm's total output is distributed across the regional markets it serves. We attempt to capture this effect by treating the global market as a dichotomy, consisting of a domestic (U.S.) segment and a composite overseas market. These account for M_{id} and $(1 - M_{id})$ of the firm's total output, respectively.

The other dimension of scope relates to the composition of the firm's output with respect to its lines of business or products or services. We treat a firm's output as consisting of either "advertising" or "other marketing" services, representing P_{ia} and $(1 - P_{ia})$, respectively, of its total output. Note that the definitions treat these two dimensions of the firm's scope as completely separate from one another.

The final term of equation 11.2 is the cross-product of the shares of firm output accounted for by the domestic (U.S.) market (M_{id}) and advertising services (P_{ia}), respectively. This interaction term allows for the two dimensions of scope to affect costs jointly as well as separately. A negative sign on the coefficient for this interaction term would be consistent with the view that firms may realize a cost-reducing benefit through their pursuit of a key feature of their business strategies: providing global clients with "one stop shopping" for a broad array of advertising and marketing services (Lawrence, 2000). Economies of coordination may be achieved through exploiting synergies in delivering a variety of services to a geographically dispersed client base that are not available when operations are more specialized and localized. Alternatively, firms may incur additional coordination costs in providing global clients with an array of services that are absent in more specialized and localized operations. Even when economies of coordination are available, they may be bargained away in negotiating compensation and service levels with clients (Fine and others, 2003). Such conditions would suggest that "one-stop shopping" could raise costs and lead to a positively signed coefficient for the interaction term. Thus, a priori, it is not clear whether the expected sign for the coefficient of the cross-product of the share terms for the two dimensions of scope should be positive or negative.

We now turn to defining explicit measures of scale and scope effects.

Scale Economies

In traditional economic theory, the firm produces a single product, and in such cases returns to scale are measured by the inverse of the elasticity of total cost with respect to output: the percentage change in total cost associated with a 1 percent increase in output (Pindyck and Rubinfield, 1995). The returns-to-scale measure is also equal to the ratio of average cost to marginal cost.

In the case of a multiproduct or multiservice firm, the notion of average cost is not well defined since the mix of outputs may change with overall size. To circumvent this problem, returns to scale are defined in terms of the effects on total cost when all the service outputs are increased proportionately, that is, holding the mix of service outputs constant. This concept is referred to as *global* or *ray returns to scale* (Bailey and Friedlander, 1982) and in the present context is defined as:

$$\text{RRS}_i = (\text{TVC}_i/Y_i) / (\partial \text{TVC}_i/\partial Y_i), \text{ evaluated at } M_{id} = M^*_{id}, P_{ia} = P^*_{ia} \qquad (11.3)$$

For our translog cost model, equation 11.1, it is readily shown that:

$$\partial \ln \text{TVC}_i / \partial \ln Y_i = (\partial \text{TVC}_i / \partial Y_i)\ (Y_i / \text{TVC}_i) \qquad (11.4)$$

$$= \beta_1 + \beta_2 \ln Y_i$$

Rearranging terms, we obtain:

$$\text{RRS}_i = 1/(\beta_1 + \beta_2 \ln Y_i) \qquad (11.5)$$

When there are economies of scale, total cost (*TVC*) increases less than proportionately with output (*Y*), marginal cost ($\partial TVC / \partial Y$) is less than average cost (*TVC/Y*), both of which are declining in *Y*, and *RRS* is greater than one. When there are diseconomies of scale, marginal cost exceeds average cost, and *RRS* is less than one.

Another measure of scale economies that is particularly useful for the multiproduct or multiservice firms is that of *product-specific scale economies* (Bailey and Friedlander, 1982). In the present context, one may view a firm as producing two types of outputs: advertising-related services (denoted by the subscript *a*) and other marketing services (*m*). We assume that the mix of domestic (U.S.) and overseas volume is the same for both types of services and equal to the share, M_{id}, and $(1 - M_{id})$, respectively, so that the composition of the firm's total volume in terms of markets served is unchanged.

$SCL(MS)_i$, is then defined as the ratio of average incremental cost, AIC_{im}, to the marginal cost, MC_{im} of producing other marketing services (*m*), in addition to advertising (*a*):

$$\text{SCL(MS)}_i = \text{AIC}_{im} / \text{MC}_{im}, \qquad (11.6)$$

where average incremental cost (AIC_{im}) is defined as the incremental cost of adding other marketing services to a firm previously producing only advertising-related services,

$$\text{AIC}_{im} = [\text{TVC}(Y_i) - \text{TVC}(Y_{ia})]/Y_{im}, \qquad (11.7)$$

with $Y_i = Y_{ia} + Y_{im}$,

and where $TVC(Y_i)$ is the total variable cost of producing both advertising and other marketing services as defined above by equation 11.1. $TVC(Y_{ia})$ is the total variable cost of producing only advertising-related services (with $Y_{ia} = P_{ia} Y_i$) and $Y_{im} = (1 - P_{ia}) Y_i$ is output of other marketing services. MC_{im} is marginal cost is defined as $\partial TVC(Y_i) / \partial Y_{im}$.

For the multiproduct cost function, equation 11.1, $SCL(MS)_i$ turns out to be (see appendix A for details of the derivation):

$$SCL(MS)_i = \frac{[\exp\{\ln \alpha_i + \beta_1 \ln Y_i + \tfrac{1}{2} \beta_2 (\ln Y_i)^2 + \gamma M_{id} + \delta P_{ia} + \theta M_{id}P_{ia}\} - \exp\{\ln \alpha_i + \beta_1 \ln (P_{ia} Y_i) + \tfrac{1}{2} \beta_2 (\ln P_{ia} Y_i)^2 + (\gamma + \theta)M_{id} + \delta\}]}{[\{\beta_1 + \beta_2 \ln Y_i\}\exp\{\ln \alpha_i + \beta_1 \ln Y_i + \tfrac{1}{2} \beta_2 (\ln Y_i)^2 + \gamma M_{di} + \delta P_i + \theta M_{di}P_{ia}\}]}$$

(11.8)

The above analysis may be viewed as assessing the scale economies associated with adding "other marketing services" to the firm's existing offering of advertising-related services. Such an analysis is meaningful in that it reflects the growth path of our sample of firms. Historically, these firms were initially full-service advertising agencies and over time expanded their operations to include other marketing services.

In our scale economy calculations, we assume that the mix of U.S. and overseas volume is the same for both types of services and equal to that for the firm's total output, as given by M_{id}. Note that for a dichotomous scope variable, the sign of its coefficient in the cost model, equation 11.1) and expression 11.8 for product-specific scale economies are both sensitive to the manner in which the dichotomous scope variable is defined, that, P_{ia} versus $(1 - P_{ia})$ and M_{id} versus $(1 - M_{id})$.

It is also of interest to assess the scale economies associated with becoming global by adding the volume sold in the overseas market $([1 - M_{id}] Y_i)$ to that for the domestic (U.S.) market ($M_{id} Y_i$). For these calculations, we assume that the mix of advertising and marketing services is the same for both the domestic (U.S.) and overseas markets and equal to the share of the firm's total output of advertising and marketing services, as given by P_{ia} and $(1 - P_{ia})$, respectively.

We define a product-specific index of scale economies, $SCL(OV)_i$ associated with extending operations from the domestic (U.S.) market (d) to the overseas market (denoted by the subscript o). $SCL(OV)_i$ is the ratio of average incremental cost, AIC_{io}, to the marginal cost, MC_{io} of producing the volume sold in the overseas market (o) in addition to that being sold in the domestic market (d):

$$SCL(OV)_i = AIC_{io}/MC_{io}, \qquad (11.9)$$

where average incremental cost (AIC_{io}) is defined as the incremental cost associated with producing for the overseas market incurred by a firm previously producing only for the domestic (U.S.) market:

$$AIC_{io} = [TVC(Y_i) - TVC(Y_{id})]/Y_{io}, \qquad (11.10)$$

$$\text{with } Y_i = Y_{id} + Y_{io},$$

where $TVC(Y_i)$ is the total variable cost of producing the volumes sold in both the domestic (U.S.) and overseas markets as defined by equation 11.1. In this context, $TVC(Y_{id})$ is the total variable cost of producing only the volume sold in domestic (U.S.) market ($Y_{id} = M_{id} Y_i$) and $Y_{io} = (1 - M_{id}) Y_i$ is the output sold overseas. MC_{io} is marginal cost and is defined as $\partial TVC(Y_i)/\partial Y_{io}$.

For the multiproduct cost function, equation 11.1, SCL_{io} may be shown to be (see appendix A for details of the derivation):

$$SCL(OV)_i = \frac{[\exp\{\ln \alpha_i + \beta_1 \ln Y_i + \frac{1}{2}\beta_2 (\ln Y_i)^2 + \gamma M_{id} + \delta P_{ia} + \theta M_{id}P_{ia}\} - \exp\{\ln \alpha_i + \beta_1 \ln (M_{id} Y_i) + \frac{1}{2}\beta_2 (\ln M_{id} Y_i)^2 + (\delta + \theta)P_{ia} + \gamma\}]}{[\{\beta_1 + \beta_2 \ln Y_i\}\exp\{\ln \alpha_i + \beta_1 \ln Y_i + \frac{1}{2}\beta_2 (\ln Y_i)^2 + \gamma M_{id} + \delta P_{ia} + \theta M_{id}P_{ia}\}]} \qquad (11.11)$$

Note that $SCL(MS)_i$ and $SCL(OV)_i$ may differ because in general, $TVC(Y_{ia}) \neq TVC(Y_{id})$. The manner in which both AIC_{io} and MC_{io} are defined above assumes that a firm expands operations from its home base in the United States to serve the overseas market. As will become apparent, this assumption is consistent with the operational definition of the scope variable for markets served as the share of output arising from U.S. operations used later in the estimation of the cost model (equation 11.1). Analysis of product-specific scale economies associated with expansion from a home base in the United States to the overseas market conforms to the history of four of our sample of eight firms that follows (Grey, Interpublic, Omnicom, and WPP). However, the historical growth paths of the other four firms were different. In the cases of the other four firms in our sample (Cordiant, Dentsu, Havas, and Publicis), their operations were initially in overseas markets and later expanded to the U.S. Hence for the latter firms, $SCL(OV)_i$ as defined in equations 11.9 and 11.11, does not have an historically meaningful and comparative interpretation. For this reason, we report estimates of $SCL(OV)_i$ only for the former four firms (Grey, Interpublic, Omnicom, and WPP).

Scope Economies

Scope economies arise when cost savings are realized from producing multiple services or from serving multiple markets rather than splitting up the firm into separate smaller entities, each producing just one service and serving a single market. (See Bailey and Friedlander, 1982, for a detailed discussion of the distinction between scale and scope economies in a multiproduct firm, as well as references to the literature.)

To measure the degree to which there are scope economies in the case at hand, we estimate the percentage of the total variable cost of production that is saved when the advertising-related and other marketing services are produced jointly by the same firm rather than produced by two stand-alone firms. As in the case of scale economies, we consider two alternative ways of splitting production: according to either service mix (advertising-related versus other marketing services) or market served (United States versus overseas).

Consider first cost savings that arise from joint rather than stand-alone production of different lines of business, that is, components of the service mix. For that split, returns to scope ($RSPLB_i$) or the percentage cost savings realized from joint versus individual production is:

$$RSP(LB)_i = [TVC(Y_{ia}) + TVC(Y_{im}) - TVC(Y_i)]/TVC(Y_i) \qquad (11.12)$$

When economies of scope are present, the joint cost, $TVC(Y_i)$, is less than the sum of the individual costs, $TVC(Y_{ia}) + TVC(Y_{im})$, and $RSP(LB_i)$ is greater than zero. If the joint cost exceeds the sum of the stand-alone costs, $RSP(LB_i)$ is negative and there are diseconomies of scope.

For the multiproduct cost function, equation 11.1, it can be shown that (see appendix A for details):

$$RSP(LB)_i = \frac{[\exp\{\ln \alpha_i + \beta_1 \ln P_{ai} Y_i + \tfrac{1}{2}\beta_2 (\ln P_{ai} Y_i)^2 + (\gamma + \theta) M_{id} + \delta\}] + [\exp\{\ln \alpha_i + \beta_1 \ln (1 - P_{ia}) Y_i + \tfrac{1}{2}\beta_2 (\ln (1 - P_{ia}) Y_i)^2 + \gamma M_{id}\}]}{[\exp\{\ln \alpha_i + \beta_1 \ln Y_i + \tfrac{1}{2}\beta_2 (\ln Y_i)^2 + \gamma M_{id} + \delta P_{ia} + \theta M_{id}P_{ia}\}]} - 1$$

(11.13)

For the alternative stand-alone split based on market served, returns to scope, $RSP(GL)_i$, the percentage cost savings gained from joint versus stand-alone production is:

$$RSP(GL)_i = [TVC(Y_{id}) = TVC(Y_{io}) - TVC(Y_i)]/ TVC(Y_i)]$$ (11.14)

where $[TVC(Y_{id} + TVC(Y_{io})]$ is the sum of the costs of producing the volumes sold in the domestic (U.S.) and overseas markets (Y_{id} and Y_{io}, respectively), and $TVC(Y_i)$ is the total cost of producing these outputs jointly. As is shown in appendix A, for the multiproduct cost function, equation 11.1, $RSP(GL)_i$ turns out to be:

$$RSP(GL)_i = \frac{[\exp\{\ln \alpha_i + \beta_1 \ln M_{id} Y_i + \tfrac{1}{2}\beta_2 (\ln M_{id} Y_i)^2 + \gamma + (\delta + \theta) P_{ia}] + [\exp\{\ln \alpha_i + \beta_1 \ln (1 - M_{id}) Y_i + \tfrac{1}{2}\beta_2 (\ln (1 - M_{id}) Y_i)^2 + \delta P_{ia}]}{[\exp\{\ln \alpha_i + \beta_1 \ln Y_i + \tfrac{1}{2}\beta_2 (\ln Y_i)^2 + \gamma M_{id} + \delta P_{ia} + \theta M_{id}P_{ia}\}]} - 1$$

(11.15)

Note that $RSP(MS)_i$ and $RSP(GL)_i$ may differ because in general, $[TVC(Y_{id}) + TVC(Y_{io})] \neq TVC(Y_{ia}) + TVC(Y_{im})$. We also note in passing that in the case of two products, the measures of global and product-specific scope economies are numerically equivalent.

Estimation Procedure

The database available for estimation is an unbalanced panel consisting of a cross section of eight global advertising and marketing service firms with a maximum of thirteen time series observations per firm. For estimation purposes it is convenient to work with equation 11.2. To capture the diversity among these firms, we allow α_i in equation 11.2 to vary cross-sectionally, and thus we treat them as fixed effects. The parameters for the scale and scope variables are assumed to be equal across the eight firms. Adding a normally distributed disturbance term to equation 11.2, our estimation equation becomes:

$$\ln AVC_{it} = \ln \alpha_i + (\beta_1 - 1)\ln Y_{it} + \tfrac{1}{2}\beta_2 (\ln Y_{it})^2 + \gamma M_{idt} + \delta P_{iat} + \theta M_{idt} P_{iat} + u_{it}$$

$$i = 1,\ldots,8;\, t = 1989,\ldots 2001. \tag{11.16}$$

The scale, scope, and interaction explanatory variables are likely to be jointly determined, along with average variable costs. To accommodate this endogeneity, we use two types of instruments, each one correlated with the scale, scope, and interaction variables but not with the random disturbance term in the cost equation. The first instrument is common to all eight firms and is defined as the growth rate of real worldwide gross domestic product (GDP), lagged one year. A second set of instruments varies by firm. The firm-specific variables are the book value of shareholder equity, long-term debt, and tax payments, as well as the cross-product of shareholder equity and taxes. Each of these instruments is expressed in constant U.S. dollars, following the convention of using average daily and end-of-the year exchange rates for income statement and balance sheet items, respectively.

Below we report econometric results allowing the scale, scope, and interaction variables to be endogenous using instrumental variable methods. In the light of the fact that the firms in our cross section regularly compete directly with one another, contemporaneous correlations in the residuals across firms can be expected. Each firm is therefore treated as a separate equation, in the context of a system of equations framework. Parameter estimates are obtained via three-stage least squares (3SLS) that allows for both heteroskedasticity and contemporaneous correlation in the residuals. Assuming the vector of disturbances across the eight firms is multivariate normal, then the parameter estimates for equation 11.16 are consistent and asymptotically efficient. (See Schmidt, 1975, and Wooldridge, 2002, for further details.) The estimation was executed using EViews 4.0 (2000).

Database and Econometric Results

This section begins with a description of the essential features of the database employed here: the panel of firms included and the set of measures used in estimating the cost model. We then discuss the resulting parameters estimates.

Cross Section of Global Advertising and Marketing Services Firms

Our cross section of firms consists of the eight largest global advertising and marketing services firms, according to *Advertising Age*'s (AA) size rankings of the world's leading "ad organizations" for 2001 (Endicott, 2002). Table 11.1 lists the firms alphabetically along with their worldwide gross incomes for 2001 (as presented in their annual reports) and the length of times series for which data were available for use in the analysis.

The absence of publicly available data precluded extending the sample to include additional firms or earlier time periods. For six of the eight firms, thirteen annual observations were available. Only four years of data were available for Cordiant, which was not formed until late 1997, following a de-merger from Saatchi & Saatchi. Reports covering ten years of Havas's history as a public company were obtained. Thus, the maximum number of observations available for estimation purposes was ninety-two. Missing data for certain variables reduced that number of observations available for the econometric analyses undertaken to eighty-three.

Collectively, these eight firms accounted for 93.9 percent of the combined 2001 gross income of the world's 100 largest ad organization identified by AA.[3] Although these eight firms dominate the industry's size structure, they differ considerably in scale: a pair of firms (Cordiant and Grey) had gross incomes in 2001 of $0.9 to $1.2 billion, three midrange firms (Dentsu, Havas, and Publicis) earned gross incomes of $2.2 to $ 2.7 billion, and three "giants" had gross incomes of $6 to $7 billion.

Table 11.1. Cross Section of Firms

Firm	Headquarters	Time Series — Period	Number of Years	2001 World Gross Income (Millions in Current U.S. Dollars)
Cordiant Communications Group plc[a]	London	1998–2001	4	$871.26
Dentsu	Tokyo	1989–2001	13	2,417.7[b]
Grey Global Group Inc.	New York	1989–2001	13	1,217.0
Havas Advertising[c]	Levallois-Perret	1992–2001	10	2,241.4
Interpublic Group	New York	1989–2001	13	6,726.8
Omnicom Communications Group Inc.	New York	1989–2001	13	6,889.4
Publicis Groupe SA	Paris	1989–2001	13	2,718.9
WPP Group plc	London	1989–2001	13	5,791.7
Total				$28,874.1

Note: For non-U.S. firms, conversion to U.S. dollars of gross income reported in other currencies were made at the daily average exchange rates for 2001.

[a]Cordiant was taken over by WPP on August 1, 2003.

[b]For the fiscal year ending March 31, 2002.

[c]Data for 1991–1992 are for Europ RSCG, which became Havas Advertising in 1995.

Source: Annual reports.

Definitions of Variables

Table 11.2 lists the measures used to operationalize the variables in our translog cost model 11.1. Firm annual reports were the primary sources of our data. Worldwide gross income (WGI), consisting of commissions and fees paid by clients, has long been recognized as the preferred measure of firm size in the advertising and marketing services industry (Paster, 1981).[4]

Total variable costs (*TVC*) are operating expenses and consist primarily of employee salaries and benefits, plus office expenses.

Table 11.2. Variable Definitions and Data Sources

Abbreviation	Definition
WGI_{it}	Worldwide gross income from commission and fees for agency i in year t in millions of constant U.S. dollars, $i = 1, \ldots, 8$; $t = 1989, \ldots, 2001$.
$LWGI_{it}$	Natural logarithm of WGI_{it}.
TVC_{it}	Total variable operating costs in millions of constant U.S. dollars
AVC_{it}	Average variable operating costs, calculated as TVC_{it} / WGI_{it}.
$LAVC_{it}$	Natural logarithm of AVC_{it}.
ADS_{it}	Share of WGI_{it} accounted for advertising-related services. The share contributed by other marketing services is $(1 - ADS_{it})$.
USS_{it}	Share of WGI_{it} accounted for output sold in the U.S. market. The share for the overseas market is $(1 - USS_{it})$.
$XAUS_{it}$	Interaction term, $XAUS_{it} = ADS_{it} \times USS_{it}$.

Note: Annual reports for each of the firms were sources for the income and cost data used to compute the set of variables listed above. For non-U.S. firms, variables reported in foreign currencies were converted to U.S. dollars following the accounting convention of making the conversion of income and costs at the average daily exchange rate for each year. Quantities of current U.S. dollars were transformed into constant U.S. dollars using the GDP implicit price deflator. In cases where data for ADS and USS were not included in the annual reports, estimates found in the reports of financial analysts or in the annual issues of *Advertising Age*'s Agency Report were used, where such data were available.

Depreciation and amortization charges were excluded in an effort to reduce interfirm and or cross-national differences in accounting methods and standards. Average variable cost (*AVC*) was computed as the ratio of total variable costs to gross income (*TVC/WGI*). Note that $(1 - AVC)$ is equal to the firm's gross margin, a measure routinely monitored and discussed by firm management and industry analysts.

Two dimensions of firm scope, corresponding to markets served and line of services offered, respectively, were treated separately from one another. Each was measured as a dichotomous share of total firm gross income, that is, share from the U.S. market (*USS* versus the overseas market, $(1 - USS)$) and share from advertising-related services (*ADS* versus other marketing services, such as promotion, public relations, and research, $(1 - ADS)$). Finally, the cross-product term, $XAUS = ADS \times USS$, was created as an interaction term for the two dimensions of scope.

Systematic measurement error arising from interfirm or cross-national differences in accounting methods and standards was mitigated by applying consistent definitions of variables across firms and time. When comparing the quality of our measures, we judge the advertising share, *ADS*, as the most problematic due to the absence of detail and consistency in reporting the decomposition of gross revenue by lines of services. Both interfirm differences and intrafirm variability were apparent. Furthermore, this was the one variable that was most likely to be missing from the firm annual reports, particularly in the early phase of our time series. In the interests of preserving degrees of freedom, estimates from external sources were used, as noted in Table 11.2. To the extent that measurement errors are firm specific and fixed over time, we capture them by specifying a fixed effect intercept for each firm.

Finally, we attempt to control for any remaining sources of systematic error by treating the intercept term in equation 11.2 as a firm fixed effect, thereby allowing the unobserved firm intercept term to be arbitrarily correlated with the explanatory variables (Wooldridge, 2002).

Table 11.3 presents summary descriptive statistics for the database. The wide variation present in the scale and scope variables is evident from the diverse values of the median, max, and min. Intercorrelations among the variables used in average cost model are shown in the lower panel of the table. Not unexpectedly, $LWGI_{it}$ and $(LWGI_{it})^2$ are virtually perfectly collinear ($r = 0.9989$). The market scope variable, USS_{it}, and scope interaction term, $XAUS_{it}$, are also highly intercorrelated ($r = 0.9137$).

Parameter Estimates

Table 11.4 presents the three-stage least-square estimates of the twelve parameters (eight coefficients for the firm fixed effects and four coefficients for the scale variable, two scope variables and their interaction) obtained using the eighty-three observations from the unbalanced panel available for estimation of the average variable

Table 11.3. Summary of Statistics
for Revenue and Cost Variables ($n = 83$)

Variable	Mean	SD	Median	Max	Min
AVC_{it}	0.8491	0.0384	0.8478	0.9271	0.7489
WGI_{it}	1,932.928	1,381.857	1,598.954	6,296.295	484.664
ADS_{it}	0.7200	0.1340	0.7200	0.9471	0.3900
USS_{it}	0.3251	0.1854	0.3985	0.6383	0.0102
$XAUS_{it}$	0.2179	0.1271	0.2306	0.4482	0.0073
$LAVC_{it}$	−0.1664	0.0468	−0.1651	−0.0757	−0.2892
$LWGI_{it}$	7.3415	0.6728	7.3771	8.7477	6.1835

Correlation Matrix ($n = 83$)

	$LAVC_{it}$	$LWGI_{it}$	$(LWGI_{it})^2$	USS_{it}	ADS_{it}	$XAUS_{it}$
$LAVC_{it}$	1.0000					
$LWGI_{it}$	−0.2439	1.0000				
$(LWGI_{it})^2$	−0.2437	0.9989	1.0000			
USS_{it}	0.4289	0.3948	0.4002	1.0000		
ADS_{it}	−0.0840	−0.5275	−0.5390	−0.4024	1.0000	
$XAUS_{it}$	0.4623	0.1312	0.1327	0.9137	−0.0145	1.0000

cost model 11.2. The dependent variable of equation 11.2 is the natural logarithm of average variable cost (LAVC). Note that since it is expressed relative to revenues, this log-transformed variable is less than zero, reflecting the fact that average variable cost is always less than one.

Referring to column 1 of Table 11.4, we see that the estimate of the coefficient for scale variable, $(\beta_1 - 1)$, has the expected negative sign but is less than its estimated standard error. The coefficient for the quadratic scale term $(\beta_2/2)$ is also negative and less than its standard error. The negative sign of $\beta_2/2$ implies that over the considerable range of scale represented in our panel data, AVC is everywhere decreasing with increases in scale. A Wald test (Eviews, 2000) indicated that the null hypothesis that $(\beta_2/2) = 0$ is not be rejected

Table 11.4. Three-Stage Least-Square Parameter Estimates for Alternative Specifications of Log Average Cost Model ($n = 83$)

Variable	Parameter	Dependent Variable: $LAVC_{it}$	
		Parameter Estimate (Ratio of Parameter Estimate to Asymptotic Standard Error)	
		(1)	**(2)**
$LWGI_{it}$	$(\beta_i - 1)$	−0.008517 (0.247)	−0.024713 (4.698)
$(LWGI_{it})^2$	$\beta_2/2$	−0.000705 (0.307)	
USS_{it}	γ	0.579196 (5.710)	0.662785 (6.406)
ADS_{it}	δ	0.324241 (6.196)	0.363235 (6.715)
$XAUS_i$	θ	−0.636157 (4.501)	−0.763902 (5.297)
Firm-specific intercept	$\ln \alpha_i$		
$i = 1$		−0.327982 (2.394)	−0.278684 (7.742)
$i = 2$		−0.382490 (2.677)	−0.332183 (8.538)
$i = 3$		−0.305785 (2.220)	−0.250309 (7.364)
$i = 4$		−0.328578 (2.376)	−0.276019 (8.793)
$i = 5$		−0.387107 (2.807)	−0.327275 (9.434)
$i = 6$		−0.358471 (2.574)	−0.302363 (9.124)
$i = 7$		−0.355101 (2.574)	−0.305281 (9.512)
$i = 8$		−0.292106 (2.095)	−0.235310 (7.146)

($p = 0.7589$). However, another Wald test indicated that the null hypothesis of constant returns [($\beta_i - 1) = 0$, ($\beta_2/2) = 0$] can be decisively rejected ($p < 0.0001$).

The coefficient estimates for the scope variables (γ and δ, respectively) in the full model (column 1 of Table 11.4) are both positive (and statistically highly significant), indicating that *AVC* increases as the share of gross income contributed by either U.S. operations or advertising-related services rises. The former effect is almost 80 percent greater than the latter. However, what is especially noteworthy is that the coefficient for the interaction of the two scope variables (θ) has a negative sign and is more than four times greater than its standard error. If the effects of the two scope variables were independent of one another, we would expect the estimate of θ to be zero. That does not appear to hold for these data, and indeed, the interaction effect of the two scope variables on total costs appears to be in the opposite direction from that of their individual effects. This result is consistent with the view that firms may realize cost economies through the joint production of both advertising and marketing services. Apparently, the coordination economies accompanying the pursuit of the strategy of one-stop shopping are not completely bargained away in negotiations with client about compensation and service levels. The coefficients for the fixed firm effects are in all cases at least twice their standard errors.

Given the collinearity of linear (*LWGI*) and quadratic terms (($LWGI)^2$) of the scale variable noted earlier, we omitted the latter and reestimated the model with only the linear term included. The results are shown in column 2 of Table 11.4. It is immediately apparent that signs of all of the coefficients remain unchanged, but the magnitude and precision of the estimates have increased considerably. The coefficient on *LWGI* increases markedly in absolute magnitude by a factor of more than thirty and is now more than four times its estimated standard error. The coefficients for the two scope variables, *USS* and *ADS*, each increase in magnitude by about 10 percent, and the precision of these estimates also improves modestly. The coefficient for the interaction of the two scope variables remains negative but increases in absolute magnitude by about 20 percent. The precision of this estimate also increases modestly. In this simpler specification, the estimates of all eight coefficients for the fixed firm effects decrease algebraically, but their precision increases dramatically, the estimates now all being at least seven times their estimated standard errors.

With three-stage least squares, the usual goodness-of-fit statistics such as adjusted R^2 are not well defined. As an alternative summary indicator of fit, we regressed the fitted values of $LACR$ on their observed values using the parameter estimates reported in column 2 of Table 11.4. This yields a value of R^2 equal to .657. We conclude that dropping the quadratic scale term from equation 11.2 results in an adequate specification of the behavior of average variable costs here. Based on the parameter estimates from column 2 of Table 11.4, we now proceed to investigate scale and scope effects.

Estimates of Scale and Scope Economies

Scale Economies

Here we present empirical estimates for the cost economy indexes already developed: the measures of scale economies and then the measures of scope economies.

We have already discussed the concept of global or ray returns to scale (RRS) as one possible measure of size-related economies. (See equation 11.3 for the definition.) RRS is the ratio of average variable cost to marginal cost for the firm's total gross income, holding fixed its mix of outputs which we have operationalized in terms of shares of gross income contributed by different markets and lines of services.

As noted above, in our preferred model specification $\beta_2 = 0$ and hence the expression for RRS, equation 11.5, simplifies to:

$$RRS = AVC/MC = 1/\beta_1. \qquad (11.5a)$$

From Table 11.4, we have $(\hat{\beta}_1 - 1) = -0.0247$ and hence $\hat{\beta}_1 = 0.9753$. Substituting the estimate for $\hat{\beta}_1$ in equation 11.5a), we find RRS = 1.0253.

Note that RRS is not firm-specific. If we interpret our results as representing a point on the long-run average cost curve (Pindyck and Rubinfield, 1995) for a typical firm in the advertising and marketing services industry, then given that RRS is slightly greater than one, we may infer that firms in this industry are operating on a long–run cost curve that is subject to very slight economies of scale. It also bears noting that the alternative hypotheses of constant returns to scale ($\beta_1 = 1$ and hence $RRS = 1$) was decisively rejected by a Wald test ($p < 0.0001$).

We also computed the indices of product-specific scale economies defined already as the returns to scale associated with two alternative strategies for expanding a firm's scale: (1) extending its line of business from advertising to marketing service, $SCL(MS)_i$ and (2) extending the markets it serves from the domestic to overseas, $SCL(OV)_i$. Recall that each is defined as the ratio of average incremental cost to marginal cost for the additional volume gained by extending the firm's service mix or market reach. Firm-specific values of both indices were computed for each year using the parameter estimates for our preferred model (with $\beta_2 = 0$) in equations 11.8 and 11.11. The results are summarized in columns 1 and 2 of Table 11.5.

Across all eight firms and time period for which data were available, diseconomies of scale prevailed for extending lines of business from advertising to marketing services. As may be seen in column 1 of Table 11.5, the mean and median for this index were both less than one: 0.282 and 0.239, respectively, for $SCL(MS)_i$. The range of values for the 83 observations of this index was from 0.052 (MIN) to 0.609 (MAX). For each of the eight firms, a separate Wald test was performed of the null hypothesis that returns to scale were constant ($AIC = MC$ and $SCL = 1$). For all eight firms, the null hypothesis of constant returns was strongly rejected ($p < 0.0001$).

In the cases of the four firms where the extension of markets served from the United States to overseas could be validly assessed, diseconomies of scale were also uniformly observed for all time periods for which data were available. The mean and median for this scale index ($SCL(OV)$, column 2 of Table 11.5) were again both less than one (0.492 and 0.501, respectively), as were the extreme observed values (MIN = 0.333) and (MAX = 0.654). Here again, Wald tests indicated that the null hypothesis of constant returns was strongly rejected ($p < 0.0001$) for all (four) firms.

Whereas our estimates indicated global scale economies ($RRS = 1.053$), product-specific diseconomies of scale for both extension of lines of business and expansion of markets served. None of the

Table 11.5. Summary Statistics for
Estimates of Scale and Scope Economies

	Returns to Scale: AIC/MC		Scope Economies: % Cost Savings from Joint Production over Stand-Alone Production for:	
	(1) Extending Lines of Business from Advertising to Marketing Services, $SCL(MS)_i$	(2) Extending Markets Served from United States to Overseas, $SCL(OV)_i$	(3) Advertising and Marketing Services, $RSP(LB)_i$	(4) United States and Overseas Markets, $RSP(GL)_i$
Mean	0.282	0.492	1.709	1.733
SD	0.146	0.073	0.521	0.920
Median	0.239	0.501	1.713	1.777
Max	0.609	0.654	3.755	3.688
Min	0.052	0.333	0.518	0.152
Number of observations	83	44	83	83
Number of firms	8	4	8	8

calculated values of either SCLMS or SCLOV summarized in Table 11.5 exceeded unity. To see why global scale economies are consistent with product-specific scale diseconomies in this context, consider equation 11.8 for $SCL(MS)_i$ which, with $\beta_2 = 0$, may readily be shown to simplify to:

$$SCL(MS) = \frac{[TVC(Y_i) - TVC\,Y_{ia})}{TVS(Yi)} \; \frac{1}{\beta 1} \qquad (11.8A)$$

The first term on the right-hand side of equation 11.8a is the estimated incremental total cost of producing marketing services separately as a proportion of the total costs of jointly producing both advertising and marketing services. The second term in the equation is the index of global scale economies, equation 11.5, ray returns to scale ($RRS = 1/\beta_1$). Since our estimate of $\beta_1 = 0.975$, product-specific diseconomies will obtain unless the incremental total cost of producing the addition to the line of business as a proportion of the total cost of producing both lines of services is equal to or greater than $\beta_1 = 0.975$. Inasmuch as the maximum value of marketing service's share of firm gross income in our sample was 0.610, it is not surprising that the latter condition does not hold here for the addition of market services. Hence, we find that the latter strategy is accompanied by diseconomies of scale ($SCL(MS)_i < 1$). A similar analysis accounts for why extending market coverage overseas was also found to involve diseconomies of scale ($SCL(OV)_i < 1$). The maximum value of the overseas market's share of firm total gross income for the four firms included in our analysis of $SCL(OV)$ was 0.640.

To gain insight into the sources of variation in the magnitude of scale diseconomies across firms and times, we regressed the scale indices on the four scale, scope, and scope interaction variables affecting the scale indices, as indicated by equations 11.8 and 11.11. Given that these expressions indicate that the relationship between the product-specific scale indices and the measures of scale and scope variables is nonlinear, linear and quadratic terms were included in the regressions for the three scale and scope variables. The results are summarized in columns 1 and 2 of Table B.1 in appendix B, where the standard partial regression coefficients are shown for the set of explanatory variables. The estimated standard partial regression coefficients measure the change in a scale index as a fraction of its standard deviation associated with a change of one standard deviation in the explanatory variables (Ezekiel and Fox, 1959). The regressions are intended to serve only as a means of describing how scale economies covary with measures that reflect the size and composition of a firm's output. Below we highlight the key features of the relationships with firm size and the scope variable relevant to each type of product-specific scale economy. Details for the full set of covariates are given in columns 1 and 2 of Table B.1. In interpreting these results, the reader should be mindful of our basic finding that diseconomies of scale prevailed across all firms and over all time periods for both $SCL(MS)$ and $SCL(OV)$.

Consider first the results pertaining to variation in scale diseconomies relating to firms' broadening their lines of business to include marketing services as well as advertising-related ones. The relationship between $SCL(MS)$ and the firm size (WGI = worldwide gross income in constant dollars) was found to be nonmonotonic (concave from below) with $SCL(MS)$ increasing over a small range of values of firm size: from WGI' MIN of \$484.7 million to a gross income level of \$767.7 million, which is well below WGI's median value of \$1599.0 million. The range from MIN to the inflexion point encompassed almost 28 percent of our sample of eighty-three observations. Beyond the inflexion point, $SCL(MS)$ declined with further increases in size for the remaining 62 percent of observations. Not unexpectedly, $SCL(MS)$ decreases at a slightly decreasing rate (convex from below) as advertising service's share of firm gross income (ADS) increases over the entire range of observations.

Turning to the variability in the diseconomies of scale associated with extending coverage from the United States to overseas markets, we find that SCL(OV) bears no reliable relationship with firm size. While the sample of relevant observations ($n = 44$) here was restricted to only four of the eight firms, it nonetheless encompassed a wide range of values of the firm size variable (WGI; MIN = \$603.1 million, MAX = \$6,296.3 million). As is to be expected, $SCL(OV)$ decreases at a slightly decreasing rate (convex from below) with increases in the U.S. share of firm gross income (USS) over the range of available observations.

Scope Economies

The possible advantages accruing to a firm with a broad product line rather than a narrow one, or cost advantages arising from serving the global market rather than just the U.S. market, may be assessed by estimating returns to scope. As defined in equations 11.12 and 11.14, our index of scope economies represents the percentage cost savings realized from the joint production of some mix of services (or for a combination of markets) over the costs of producing the services separately (or for the markets separately). In the case of two products (or markets), global and product-specific scope economies are identical.

Substituting the parameter estimates for our preferred model (with $\beta_2 = 0$) into equations 11.13 and 11.15, we calculated for all firms and time periods scope economy indices that estimate the percentage savings for joint production as compared to stand-alone production of (a) advertising-related and other marketing services ($RSP(LB)_i$) and U.S. and overseas markets ($RSP(GL)_i$). The results are summarized in columns 4 and 5 of Table 11.5.

It is immediately apparent from Table 11.5 that economies of scope were realized by all firms in all time periods from joint as opposed to separate production for both diversification strategies. The cost savings were small but uniformly positive. The median savings for either expanding the line of services offered or extending the scope of markets served was less than 2 percent, with the variation in savings distributed over a limited range of less than 1 percent to under 4 percent. For the case of the joint production of advertising and marketing services, the estimated cost savings was less than 1 percent for only about 6 percent of the sample observations. Realization of only minimal cost savings was more frequent for the joint production of services for the U.S. and overseas markets; the estimated cost savings was less than 1 percent for 19 percent of the sample observations. However, the null hypotheses that the joint costs equal the sum of the stand-alone costs ($RSP(LB) = 0$ or $RSP(GL) = 0$) was strongly rejected ($p < 0.0001$) for all eight firms for both indices of scope economies.

As with the indices of scale economies, we analyzed variation in the magnitude of scope economies by regressing each of the indices of scope economies on the four scale, scope, and scope interaction variables. Here we limit the discussion to focus on relations involving the size and relevant scope variable. Detailed results for the full set of covariates are presented in columns 3 and 4 of Table B.1.

The estimated relationship between scope economies associated with joint production of advertising and marketing services and firm size was found to be J-shaped (convex from below) with the minimum level of $RSP(LB)$ occurring when firm size was \$813.4 million. Thus $RSP(LB)$ fell as firm size increased for almost a quarter of the sample observations and then increased over the subsequent range of observations, which accounted for the remaining three-quarters of the sample observations.

The estimated relationship between $SCL(LB)$ and the share of firm revenue arising from advertising services (ADS) was concave (from below). However, over the range of observations of $RSP(LB)$ contained in the sample, $RSP(LB)$ decreased monotonically as advertising share increased. That relationship is consistent with the expectation that as firms add marketing services to their prior line of advertising services, savings from the joint production of both increase with increases in the share of firm revenue realized from marketing services since the latter share equals $(1 - ADS)$.

In the case of the other dimension of scope $(RSP(GL)$, the form of the relationship between firm size and savings from producing for both the U.S. and overseas markets jointly rather than separately was found to be J-shaped (convex from below), similar to the manner in which $RSP(LB)$ and firm size were found to be related. $RSP(GL)$ declined as size increased when gross income was $1,462.4 million or less (which accounted for about 42 percent of the observations) and then increased as firm size increased beyond that level for the remaining 58 percent of the sample observations. For at least a majority of our sample of observations, both $RSP(LB)$ and $RSP(GL)$ increased as firm size increased. Thus, in contrast to Silk and Berndt's (1995) results for individual advertising agencies, we find no evidence of any tendency for large holding companies to overdiversify. To the contrary, at low levels of firm size, scope economies appear to decrease with increases in firm size, and hence small firms may be underdiversified in the sense that greater scope economies could be realized were they able to achieve gross incomes above the inflexion point in J-shaped relationship between size and scope economies.

Contrary to expectations, the parameter estimates for the relevant standardized partial regression coefficients indicated that $RSP(GL)$ increased (rather than decreased) monotonically as share of firm revenue from U.S. operations (USS) increased (convex from below). This counterintuitive result may be accounted for by the presence of an influential cluster of observations for firms based outside the United States with extremely small shares of their gross income coming from U.S. operations, especially in the early years of the time series. When that set of observations was removed, the expected negative relationship between $RSP(GL)$ and USS emerged.

Implications of Findings

We next further interpret our main findings with respect to scale and scope economies, noting some limitations surrounding the results reported here. We then consider what the estimates of cost economics found in this study imply about the competitive advantage of holding companies over the traditional form of organization in this industry (that of the independent full-service agency), and changes in the size, structure, and organization of the industry.

Scale and Scope Economies

Our results suggest that the industry's long-run cost function is subject to very slight economies of scale. We also find that modest diseconomies of scale accompanied the broadening of lines of business (from advertising to marketing services) or market coverage (from the United States to overseas). Product-specific scale diseconomies were shown to be consistent with overall or global scale economies in this context, given the limited level of global scale economies available and the composition of firm income with respect to lines of business and markets served. Taken together, these findings do not point to any substantial level of potential scale economies that remains to be exploited by the largest firms in this industry. Such findings are to be expected in a highly competitive industry with relatively low fixed costs.

However, two cautions should be noted. First, recall that the parameter estimate for the quadratic term in our cost model turned out to be nonsignificant. Hence, we have been unable to learn much about the shape of the long-run cost curve or how firms might be arrayed along it. Second, we have not attempted to model the adjustment processes surrounding mergers and acquisitions, and that omission may have clouded our results. In particular, the adjustment costs associated with digesting mergers and acquisitions could manifest themselves in our empirical analyses as diseconomies of scale. (See Johnson and Simon, 1970, for a provocative but now dated study of advertising agency mergers and acquisitions.)

Our estimates of scope economies indicate that a small cost advantage, typically only 1 to 2 percent, is realized through the joint rather than separate production of advertising and market-ing services and for the domestic and overseas markets. Obviously, this is a crude partitioning of the global market, and a more finely grained decomposition would be preferable, especially one that separated the overseas market into European and Asian compo-nents. A more detailed disaggregation of firm revenue shares with respect to both lines of business and markets served would allow the scope and interaction variables to be defined and measured in terms of specific combinations of services and markets. These issues are deserving of further research.

We also note the possible threats to the validity of statistical con-clusions posed by currencies fluctuations, cross-national differences in accounting standards, and intrafirm and interfirm differences in accounting methods. The adequacy of our estimates of firm fixed effects as controls for those factors remains to be assessed.

The Advantage of the Holding Company Form of Organization

In earlier studies, we investigated the role of scale and scope econ-omies in the domestic operations of U.S. agencies (Schamalensee, Silk, and Bojanek, 1983; Silk and Berndt 1993, 1995). Using a proxy for average cost (employees per dollar of gross income) in a cross-sectional analysis of four hundred agencies, Silk and Berndt (1993) found that both scale and particularly scope economies (measured by shares of output in different advertising media) were highly significant in the operations of U.S. agencies. They esti-mated the minimum efficient size of a domestic agency to be $3 $4 million of gross income in 1987 dollars ($6 to $8 million in 2001 dollars). Of the approximately 10,000 firms comprising the indus-try in 1987, 200 to 250 had domestic gross incomes at that level or larger and therefore had output levels and media mixes sufficient to take full advantage of all the size-related efficiencies seemingly available at that time.

The 2001 worldwide gross income of the smallest of the eight holding companies included in this study (Cordiant) was more than a hundred times greater than the estimate of minimum effi-cient size of a domestic agency; the largest in our study (Omni-com) was almost eight hundred times greater. The overwhelming difference in scale raises the question: What, exactly, are the advantages of the holding company structure not available in a single agency structure?

Fine and others (2003) suggest that the answer lies in cost economies and the ability to cope with the constraints imposed by the account conflicts. Our results are consistent with such advantages in the sense that we find that holding companies appear to be operating in the vicinity of a point on the long-run cost curve subject to scale economies, albeit quite modest ones, and are generally diversified to an extent that permits realization of positive scope economies, again of quite limited magnitude. Furthermore, our analyses of how variability in scope economies is related to firm size indicated that holding companies are not subject to the excessive diversification that Silk and Berndt (1995) found in their study of individual advertising agencies and that they attributed to the constraints on growth imposed by conflict policy and the bundling of services. Thus, the holding company appears to be a form of organization that circumvents the institutional constraints that restricted the growth and diversification opportunities of the traditional full service advertising agency.

Holding companies are publicly owned enterprises, and no explicit attention has been given to that condition in the present study. Research underway by von Nordenflycht (2003) emphasizes the advantages of holding companies with respect to access to capital markets and the ability to exploit size as a proxy for capabilities. Interestingly, he finds no relationship between public versus private agency ownership and winning awards for creativity.

Organization of the Advertising and Marketing Services Industry

Historically, the U.S. advertising agency business has been characterized as a classic example of an industry with minimal barriers to entry, low fixed costs, and geographically dispersed demand (roughly 40 to 45 per cent of total U.S. advertising expenditures are accounted for by local, as opposed to national advertisers. Silk and Berndt (1995) argued that the structure of demand and costs in the U.S. advertising agency business conforms to the conditions MacDonald and Slivinski (1989) showed were required for an industry to sustain an equilibrium with diversified firms. A highly diverse and unconcentrated size structure has long persisted in the U.S. advertising agency industry, and over time, it has become more geographically dispersed (King, Silk, and Kettelhohn, 2003). That size structure has enabled holding companies to cherry-pick from a large and varied pool of midsized and small U.S.-based agencies (and human capital) in making hundreds of acquisitions over the past several decades.

More than a decade and a half ago, Sheth (1986) predicted that three global firms would eventually dominate the industry.[5] Silk and King (2003) found that the concentration level in the U.S. advertising agency business, as traditionally defined, rose during the 1990s, although not to the extent that has sometimes been suggested. Their estimates indicate that the major advertising agency brands controlled by the eight largest holding companies represented about a quarter of the total gross income earned from traditional advertising-related services in 2001 by all U.S. agencies. How the industry structure in other countries that represent smaller regional and local markets has been affected by globalization and diversification awaits further study. The shifts in client demand toward more global and diversified advertising and marketing services has, of course, also raised barriers to entry and fixed costs for suppliers of those services. The nature of the industry equilibrium that can be sustained under these altered conditions is also an important topic for further research.

Conclusion

This chapter has reported an econometric analysis of cost economies experienced by holding companies operating in the global advertising and marketing services business. Treating holding companies as multiproduct firms, we estimated a translog model of costs. A firm's total variable costs are affected by its scale, scope of its lines of business and market coverage, and the interaction of the latter two dimensions of scope. Our results indicate that the long-run cost function for firms in the global advertising and marketing services business is subject to very slight scale economies. Growth in volume obtained through either extending the lines of business to include marketing services in addition to advertising services or expanding market coverage overseas from the United States were subject to modest levels of product-specific diseconomies of scale. These findings do not point to any substantial level of potential scale economies that remains to be exploited by the largest firms in this industry. Such findings are to be expected in a highly competitive industry with relatively low fixed costs.

Small scope economies amounting to a few percentage points of cost savings accompany diversification through both extending lines of business and expanding market coverage. While small in percentage terms, in an industry where firms strive to achieve operating margins of 15 percent and where income and costs are measured in billions, these economies (diseconomies) clearly matter. The institutional constraints, especially adherence to the industry norm of an agency not serving competing accounts, that limited the potential of traditional full service advertising agencies for growth and diversification appear to have been obviated by the holding company form of organization.

APPENDIX A: DERIVATION OF INDICES OF SCALE AND SCOPE EFFECTS

Product-Specific Scale Economies

Advertising and Marketing Services as Separate Products

Given that a firm is producing advertising-related services, we wish to measure the scale economies (or diseconomies) associated with adding other marketing services to its service mix. Following Bailey and Friedlander (1982), we may define the returns to scale for this case as:

$$\text{SCL(MS)}_i = \text{AIC}_{im}/\text{MC}_{im} \qquad (A11.1)$$

where AIC_{im} is the average incremental cost of producing the quantity Y_{im} of marketing services in addition to its output of advertising-related services, Y_{ia}.

$$\text{AIC}_{im} = [\text{TVC}(Y_i) - \text{TVC}(Y_{ia})]/Y_{im}, \qquad (A11.2)$$

where:

$$Y_{im} = (1 - P_{ia})Y_i \qquad (A11.3)$$

The numerator of the right-hand side of equation A11.2 is the difference between the total costs of producing both products jointly, $TVC(Y_i)$, and the total cost of producing the advertising services separately, $TVC(Y_i)$. For our translog cost model, equation 11.1, $TVC(Y_i)$ is:

$$TVC(Y_i) = \exp(\ln \alpha_i + \beta_1 \ln Y_i + \tfrac{1}{2}\beta_2 (\ln Y_i)^2 + \gamma M_{id} + \delta P_{ia} + \theta M_{id}P_{ia}) \quad (A11.4)$$

Now if advertising services were produced separately, the volume of such services would remain unchanged ($Y_{ia} = P_{ia} Y_i$), but would now account for all of the output ($P_a = 1$). We assume that the composition of the advertising services volume in terms of mix of production for the U.S. and overseas markets remains the same as for the firm as a whole, as given by the share, M_{id} and $(1 - M_{id})$, respectively. Substituting in equation A11.4, we obtain:

$$TVC(Y_{ia}) = \exp(\ln \alpha_i + \beta_1 \ln P_{ia}Y_i + \tfrac{1}{2}\beta_2 (\ln P_{ia}Y_i)^2 + (\gamma + \theta) M_{id} + \delta) \quad (A11.5)$$

The denominator in equation A11.1 is the marginal cost defined as:

$$MC_{im} = \partial\, TVC(Y_i)/\partial\, Y_{im} \qquad (A11.6)$$

Using equation A11.4 and taking the partial derivative of $TVC(Y_i)$ with respect to Y_{im}, we obtain:

$$MC_{im} = [\{\beta_1 + \beta_2 \ln Y_i\}\exp\{\ln \alpha_i + \beta_1 \ln Y_i + \tfrac{1}{2}\beta_2 (\ln Y_i)^2 + \gamma M_{id} + \delta P_{ia}$$
$$+ \theta M_{id}P_{ia}\}]/(1 - P_{ia})Y_i \qquad (A11.7)$$

Substituting equations A11.3, A11.4, and A11.5 in A11.2 for Y_{im}, $TVC(Y_i)$, and $TVC(Y_{ia})$, respectively, and dividing by equation A11.7 in A11.1, we get:

$$SCL(MS)_i = \frac{[\exp\{\ln \alpha_i + \beta_1 \ln Y_i + \tfrac{1}{2}\beta_2 (\ln Y_i)^2 + \gamma M_{id} + \delta P_{ia} + \theta M_{id} P_{ia}\} - \exp\{\ln \alpha_i + \beta_1 \ln (P_{ia} Y_i) + \tfrac{1}{2}\beta_2 (\ln P_{ia} Y_i)^2 + (\gamma + \theta)M_{id} + \delta\}]}{[\{\beta_1 + \beta_2 \ln Y_i\}\exp\{\ln \alpha_i + \beta_1 \ln Y_i + \tfrac{1}{2}\beta_2 (\ln Y_i)^2 + \gamma M_{id} + \delta P_{ia} + \theta M_{id} P_{ia}\}]}$$

$$(A11.8)$$

Markets Served as Separate Products

The product-specific index of scale economies, SCL_{io}, associated with extending operations from the U.S. market (d) to the overseas market (o) is defined as SCL_{io}, the ratio of average incremental cost, AIC_{io}, to the marginal cost, MC_{io} of producing the volume sold in the overseas market (o) in addition to that sold in the U.S. market (d):

$$SCL(OV)_i = AIC_{io}/MC_{io}, \qquad (A11.9)$$

AIC_{io} is defined as the incremental cost of adding volume sold in the overseas market to the costs incurred by a firm previously producing only for the U.S. market:

$$AIC_{io} = [TVC(Y_i) - TVC(Y_{id})]/Y_{io}, \qquad (A11.10)$$

where:

$$Y_{io} = (1 - M_{id})Y_i \qquad (A11.11)$$

$TVC(Y_i)$ is the total variable cost of producing the volume sold in both the domestic and overseas markets and is given by (equation A11.4.

$TVC(Y_{id})$ is the total variable cost of producing only the volume sold in the U.S. market ($Y_{id} = M_{id} Y_i$) and $Y_{io} = (1 - M_{id}) Y_i$ is output sold overseas. MC_{io} is marginal cost and defined as $\partial TVC(Y_i)/\partial Y_{io}$. If output for the overseas market were produced separately, the quantity required for that segment would remain unchanged ($Y_{ia} = P_{ia} Y_i$), but would now account for all of the output ($P_a = 1$). We assume that the composition of the advertising services volume in terms of mix of production of advertising and marketing services remains the same as before for the firm as a whole, as given by the share, M_{id} and ($1 - M_{id}$), respectively. Substituting in equation A11.4, we obtain:

$$TVC(Y_{id}) = \exp\{\ln \alpha_i + \beta_1 \ln (M_{id} Y_i) + \tfrac{1}{2} \beta_2 (\ln M_{id} Y_i)^2 + (\delta + \theta)P_{ia} + \gamma\}$$
$$(A11.12)$$

The denominator in equation A11.1 is the marginal cost defined as:

$$MC_{io} = \partial\, TVC(Y_i)/\partial\, Y_{io} \qquad (A11.13)$$

Using equation A11.4 and taking the partial derivative of $TVC(Y_i)$ with respect to Y_{io} we obtain:

$$MC_{io} = [\{\beta_1 + \beta_2 \ln Y_i\} \exp\{\ln \alpha_i + \beta_1 \ln Y_i + \tfrac{1}{2} \beta_2 (\ln Y_i)^2 + \gamma M_{id} + \delta P_{ia}$$

$$+ \theta M_{id} P_{ia}\}] / (1 - M_{id}) Y_i \qquad (A11.14)$$

Substituting equations A11.11, A11.4, and A11.12 in A11.10 for Y_{io}, $TVC(Y_i)$, and $TVC(Y_{io})$, respectively, and dividing by equation A11.14 in equation A11.9, we get:

$$SCL(OV)_i = \frac{\begin{aligned}&[\exp\{\ln \alpha_i + \beta_1 \ln Y_i + \tfrac{1}{2} \beta_2 (\ln Y_i)^2 + \gamma M_{di} + \delta P_{ia} + \theta M_{id} P_{ia}\} \\ &- \exp\{\ln \alpha_i + \beta_1 \ln (M_{id} Y_i) + \tfrac{1}{2} \beta_2 (\ln M_{id} Y_i)^2 + (\delta + \theta) P_{ia} + \gamma\}]\end{aligned}}{\begin{aligned}&[\{\beta_1 + \beta_2 \ln Y_i\} \exp\{\ln \alpha_i + \beta_1 \ln Y_i + \tfrac{1}{2} \beta_2 (\ln Y_i)^2 + \gamma M_{id} + \delta P \\ &+ \theta M_{id} P_{ia}\}]\end{aligned}}$$

$$\qquad (A11.15)$$

Global Scope Economies

Advertising and Marketing Services as Separate Products

We wish to measure the cost savings (or dissavings) that may arise when the two lines of business (advertising versus marketing services) that constitute the firm's service mix are produced jointly in the same organization rather than separately in separate organizations, each producing a different lines of business. For this case, returns to scope ($RSPLB_i$) or the percentage cost savings realized from joint versus individual production is:

$$RSP(LB)_i = [TVC(Y_{ia}) + TVC(Y_{im}) - TVC(Y_i)] / TVC(Y_i) \qquad (A11.16)$$

where $TVC(Y_{ia})$ and $TVC(Y_{im})$ are the costs of producing advertising (denoted by the subscript a) and marketing services separately (m), respectively, and $TVC(Y_i)$ is the cost of producing those services jointly.

If advertising services were produced separately, then the volume of such services would remain unchanged ($Y_{ia} = P_{ia} Y_i$) but that volume would account for all of the output of the specialized organization ($P_{ia} = 1$). We assume that the volume of both the specialized organizations with respect to the shares of output produced for the United States and overseas markets remain the same as for the firm under joint production: M_{id} and $(1 - M_{id})$, respectively.

Applying these assumptions to our translog cost model, equation 11.1, we find the total variable cost of producing advertising services separately to be:

$$TVC(Y_{ia}) = \exp\{\ln \alpha_i + \beta_1 \ln P_{ia} Y_i + \tfrac{1}{2} \beta_2 (\ln P_{ia} Y_i)^2 + (\gamma + \theta) M_{id} + \delta\}$$

(A11.17)

Next we derive the total variable cost of producing marketing services separately, $TVC(Y_{im})$. The volume of that output is $Y_{im} = (1 - M_{ia})$, but $P_{ia} = 0$, since only marketing services are produced. Inserting these assumptions into the translog cost model, equation 11.1, we find:

$$TVC(Y_{im}) = \exp\{\ln \alpha_i + \beta_1 \ln (1 - P_{ia})Y_i + \tfrac{1}{2} \beta_2 (\ln (1 - P_{ia})Y_i)^2 + \gamma M_{id}\}$$

(A11.18)

As before, the total variable cost of joint production, $TVC(Y_i)$, is given by equation A11.4.

Substituting equations A11.17, A11.18, and A11.4 in A11.16 for $TVC(Y_{ia})$, $TVC(Y_{im})$, and $TVC(Y_i)$, respectively, we get:

$$RSP(LB)_i = \frac{\begin{array}{l}[\exp\{\ln \alpha_i + \beta_1 \ln P_{ai} Y_i + \tfrac{1}{2} \beta_2 (\ln P_{ai} Y_i)^2 + (\gamma + \theta) M_{id} + \delta\}] \\[6pt] + [\exp\{\ln \alpha_i + \beta_1 \ln (1 - P_{ia}) Y_i + \tfrac{1}{2} \beta_2 (\ln (1 - P_{ia}) Y_i)^2 + \gamma M_{id}\}]\end{array}}{[\exp\{\ln \alpha_i + \beta_1 \ln Y_i + \tfrac{1}{2} \beta_2 (\ln Y_i)^2 + \gamma M_{id} + \delta P_{ia} + \theta M_{ii} P_{ia}\}]} - 1$$

(A11.19)

Markets Served as Separate Products

For the alternative split based on market served, returns to scope, $RSPMS_i$, the percentage cost savings gained from joint versus separate production is:

$$RSP(MS)_i = [TVC(Y_{id}) + TVC(Y_{io}) - TVC(Y_i)] / TVC(Y_i)]$$

(A11.20)

Following similar reasoning to that discussed above with reference to the costs of split production of advertising and marketing services, we obtain the following expressions for the total variable costs of separating production for the U.S. and overseas markets, $TVC(Y_{id})$ and $TVC(Y_{io})$, respectively:

$$TVC(Y_{id}) = \exp\{\ln \alpha_i + \beta_1 \ln M_{id} Y_i + \tfrac{1}{2} \beta_2 (\ln M_{id} Y_i)^2 + \gamma + (\delta + \theta) P_{ia}\}$$
$$(A11.21)$$

$$TVC(Y_{io}) = \exp\{\ln \alpha_i + \beta_1 \ln (1 - M_{id})Y_i + \tfrac{1}{2} \beta_2 (\ln (1 - M_{id})Y_i)^2 + \delta P_{ia}\}$$
$$(A11.22)$$

Substituting equations A11.21, A11.22, and A11.) for $TVC(Y_{id})$, $TVC(Y_{io})$, and $TVC(Y_i)$, respectively, in equation A11.20, we obtain:

$$RSP(GL)_i = \frac{[\exp\{\ln \alpha_i + \beta_1 \ln M_{id} Y_i + \tfrac{1}{2} \beta_2 (\ln M_{id} Y_i)^2 + \gamma + (\delta + \theta) P_{ia}\}] + [\exp\{\ln \alpha_i + \beta_1 \ln (1 - M_{id}) Y_i + \tfrac{1}{2} \beta_2 (\ln (1 - M_{id})Y_i)^2 + \delta P_{ia}\}]}{[\exp\{\ln \alpha_i + \beta_1 \ln Y_i + \tfrac{1}{2} \beta_2 (\ln Y_i)^2 + \gamma M_{id} + \delta P_{ia} + \theta M_{id}P_{ia}\}]} - 1$$
$$(A11.23)$$

APPENDIX B: STANDARDIZED REGRESSIONS RELATING SCALE AND SCOPE INDICES TO FIRM VARIABLES

Each of the four product-specific indices of scale and scope economies summarized in Table 11.5 were separately regressed on the four size, share, and share interaction variables affecting the indices, as given by equations 11.8, 11.11, 11.13, and 11.15, which define the indices. Inasmuch as those expressions suggest that the relationships are nonlinear, we included both linear and quadratic terms in the regressions for the three size and share variables. To facilitate comparisons across the regressions, all dependent and explanatory variables were scaled in units of the sample values of their standard deviations. Table B11.1 presents the set of estimated standard partial regression coefficients for each regression. Standard partial regression coefficients measure the change in a scale index, expressed as a proportion of the sample value of its standard deviation, associated with a change of one standard deviation in an explanatory variable (Ezekiel and Fox, 1959). Given the panel structure of our data, parameter estimates were obtained by treating each of the four equations as a set of seemingly unrelated regressions (SUR), one per firm. The intercept term was allowed to vary across firms (and treated as fixed effects) while the coefficients for the explanatory variables were assumed to be equal across firms. In the interests of conserving space, estimates of the intercept terms are not shown.

Table 11B.1. Standardized Regressions for Scale and Scope Indices

	Dependent Variable			
	Returns to Scale: AIC/MC		Scope Economies: Percentage Cost Savings from Joint Production over Stand-Alone Production for:	
	(1) Extending Lines of Business from Advertising to Marketing Services, $SCL(MS)_{it}$	(2) Extending Markets Served from United States to Overseas, $SCL(OV)_{it}$	(3) Advertising and Marketing Services, $RSP(LB)_{it}$	(4) United States and Overseas Markets, $RSP(GL)_{it}$
Explanatory Variable	Standardized Regression Coefficients (Ratio of Coefficient to Standard Error)			
$LWGI_{it}$	0.139 (9.847)	−0.033 (1.486)	−1.442 (2.266)	−0.791 (2.810)
$(LWGI_{it})^2$	−0.155 (10.273)	0.038 (1.550)	1.594 (2.386)	0.804 (2.604)
ADS_{it}	−0.857 (116.409)	0.503 (34.989)	0.872 (3.054)	−1.754 (12.969)
$(ADS_{it})^2$	0.091 (15.923)	−0.125 (12.026)	−2.184 (8.812)	1.268 (10.814)
USS_{it}	0.605 (45.922)	−0.978 (76.485)	−4.005 (8.697)	1.323 (5.182)
$(USS_{it})^2$	−0.019 (5.177)	0.120 (12.449)	1.086 (9.799)	0.994 (15.332)
$XAUS_{it}$	−0.355 (33.118)	0.037 (4.435)	2.165 (5.853)	0.268 (1.310)
Number of observations	83	44	83	83
Number of firms	8	4	8	8
Adjusted R^2	0.999	0.999	0.712	0.890
Standard error of estimate	0.011	0.005	0.536	0.331

PART 6

Managing Global Supply and Distribution

The globalization of supply chains in the past decade has been driven by three principal forces. First, reductions in tariff and nontariff barriers to international trade have led companies to seek out new markets for their goods and services and also to source their inputs internationally as well. In particular, the admission of China to the World Trade Organization has helped to transform China into a factory to the world in short order. Second, competitive price pressures have forced companies to source overseas to retain share against competitors that have lowered their cost structures by doing so. Sooner or later, the need for survival dominates patriotism and forces production offshore. Third, increasing sophistication and falling costs in data processing and information technology enable companies to track product being manufactured, either internally or by subcontractors, at geographically dispersed locations.

Ananth Raman and Noel Watson in Chapter Twelve document these influences and consider the special challenges that global supply chain managers, like global marketers, face when they go beyond their national boundaries. These challenges include longer and uncertain lead times (a particular challenge for fashion-sensitive merchandise), currency fluctuations, variations in the cultural norms and regulations affecting negotiations, contract terms and compliance, and higher capital costs that discourage small manufacturers in emerging markets from holding inventories. These challenges have spawned supply chain coordinators like Hong Kong–based Li and Fung that can transfer knowledge, build trust, and inject low-cost capital into the supply chains they manage.

While Raman and Watson focus on product supply chains, it is important to note the rapid increase in overseas sourcing of services such as call center response lines, software development, and even the preparation of standard legal documents. With services now accounting for 62 percent of the world economy compared to 38 percent some forty years ago, outsourcing of service activities to highly educated but lower-paid workers in emerging economies such as India and China is sure to continue apace.

The history of the retailing industry is replete with examples of domestically successful brands that have failed internationally. True, flagship stores carrying the merchandise of a single luxury designer brand such as Gucci or Armani are to be found on the Ginza, Fifth Avenue, and comparable streets in the world's leading cities. Some tightly focused apparel chains with broader appeal, such as Benetton and Zara, have enjoyed success. But until recently, domestically successful mass merchandisers, especially of soft goods (for example, Britain's Marks & Spencer), have repeatedly failed to take their retail concepts international. This failure is variously attributed to different consumer tastes in different countries, a lack of distinctiveness in the merchandise on offer compared to that of existing local retailers, the complexities of remaining price competitive while sourcing both locally and globally, and constraints on the availability of prime real estate locations. As a consequence, many retailers that have conquered their domestic markets decide to grow by investing in existing overseas retailers without attempting to change the name on the door.

One exception to the rule is Carrefour of France, which has exported its hypermarket format to multiple emerging economies successfully. Carrefour's success stems from several factors. First, its stores are enormous and therefore not easy for local entrepreneurs to imitate. Second, the stores sell well-known brands of hard goods on which prices can be compared easily and which require little cultural adaptation (compared to, say, food and apparel). Third, they turn their inventories faster than they pay their receivables. Fourth, they have developed processes to source efficiently locally as well as globally, thereby keeping costs down and becoming good local citizens. But for all the concerns global suppliers voice about being forced by Carrefour to negotiate global or regional pricing contracts, fewer than 5 percent of Carrefour sales are of global brands.

David Bell, Rajiv Lal, and Walter Salmon examine the market entry strategies of Carrefour, Wal-Mart of the United States, and Ahold of the Netherlands, with particular focus on Latin America. They analyze the appropriate mode of market entry (greenfield investment, joint venture, or acquisition) contingent on whether the country is developed or developing and contingent on whether the perceived need for customization is high or low. Carrefour's cumulative experience in international markets enables it to confidently decentralize many merchandise assortment decisions to local managers; the consumer sees a locally adapted selection under a global brand umbrella and at the same time benefits from Carrefour's backroom expertise in procurement, quality controls, information technology, and financial management. The same might be said of McDonald's (which is not addressed in the chapter), which adapts its menus and restaurant designs around the world and at the same time leverages its expertise in the procurement of beef and potatoes (it is the biggest buyer of both worldwide).

But the equivocal success to date of Wal-Mart in international markets highlights the challenges any domestically dominant company faces when it ventures abroad: how to achieve efficiency without the scale of the domestic operation and, more broadly, how to play the unaccustomed role of humble newcomer. It remains to be seen whether Wal-Mart will be able to achieve its ambitious worldwide vision of "lowering the cost of living for everyone everywhere."

CHAPTER 12

Managing Global Supply Chains

Ananth Raman
Noel Watson

Managers with responsibility for supply chain operations are thinking globally for three reasons.[1] First, in recent years, they have encountered opportunities to expand their markets into countries in which they previously had not sold their products or services and to source products and services from suppliers in countries in which they had not done so previously. Second, the availability of newer, more powerful information technologies has empowered decision makers to manage globally dispersed operations more effectively. Third, the global strategies of dominant firms are influencing, and in some cases determining, the global approaches and operations of their supply chain partners.

Geographical expansion of markets and more economical and effective sourcing opportunities with overseas suppliers can afford firms opportunities for gaining competitive advantage or catching up with competitors. Decreasing tariffs, including those as a result of trade agreements such as the General Agreement on Tariffs and Trade and the North American Free Trade Agreement, increase the potential of foreign growth or supply opportunities. Improvements in transportation, communication, and information technology increase the awareness along with the potential of foreign growth or supply opportunities. Thus, firms are being forced to adopt either an ad hoc global approach or, if they are already serious participants in the global economy, a more sophisticated approach to how they will participate in the global economy. Managers of supply chain operations are being called on to support this approach.

Managers previously lacked the tools to do better than to make decisions that were locally optimal. Advances in information technology have made it feasible to render visible demand and operating conditions in distant parts of supply chains, in close to real time, for managers to exploit this information to make globally optimal decisions. In other words, supply chain management is becoming more global because managers now have the information and decision tools to optimize their supply chains globally.

Dominant supply chain partners with global strategies concerning potential and existing partners are also exerting pressure on supply chain managers and their firms to consider their global approaches carefully. Raman and Rao (1997) note that in the electronics industry, many original equipment manufacturers now want to source from the same distributor in all of the countries in which they operate and that this preference for single global contracts has forced some distributors to go global. Large food retailers such as Royal Ahold, which owns and operates supermarket chains in many countries, also expect suppliers of consumer goods to tender similar contracts in different countries. Supply chain managers are thinking globally about their operations because the operations have become an important feature of how their firms are perceived by their already global (supply chain) partners.

Supporting evidence for these arguments is offered in this chapter, and certain industry-specific issues that some supply chain managers need to consider are discussed. We trace, for example, the growing volume of imports for many products, with particular emphasis on the increasing importance of Chinese manufacturing, noting that not only products but also services are being outsourced to firms in developing countries. We further observe that in many product categories, manufacturing, even of a single product, is being outsourced to supplier firms in more than one country.

Figure 12.1a and 12.1b summarize imports (in dollars and as a percentage of U.S. sales) for a number of products in five categories from 1997 to 2001. Figure 12.1b shows that imports, as a percentage of U.S. sales, are very high for categories such as footwear (94 percent in 2001), consumer electronics (77 percent in 2001),

Figure 12.1 U.S. Imports, 1997–2001

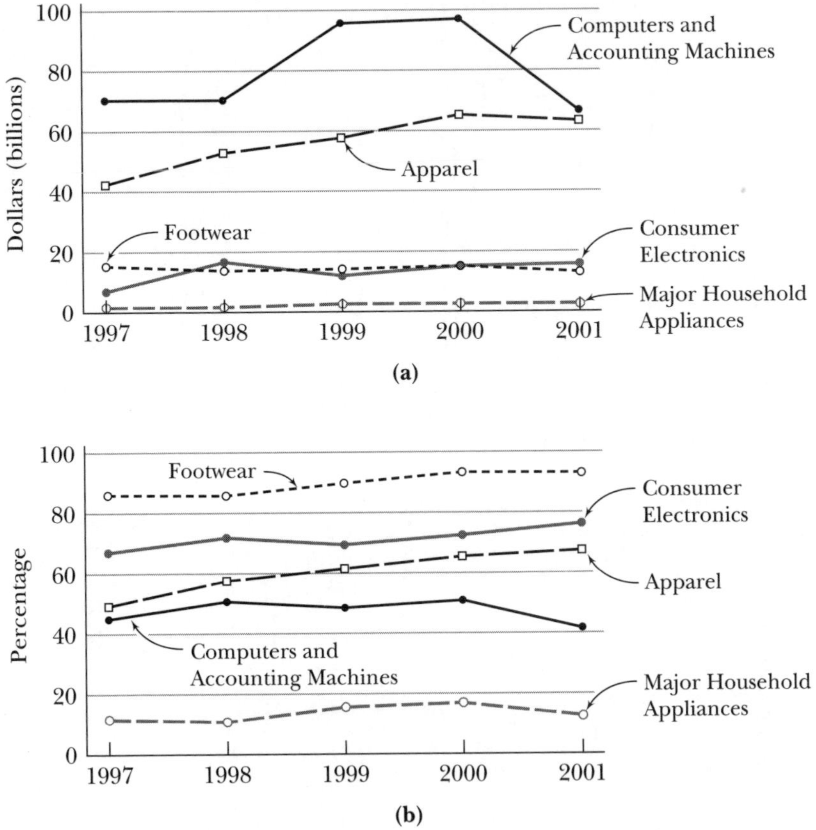

(a)

(b)

Source: Adapted from U.S. Department of Commerce data, 2002.

and apparel (64 percent in 2001). Growth in the share of imports is apparent for all five categories up to 2000, with the share for only computers and household appliances decreasing in 2001.

In many product categories, China is the source of much of the growth in imports of manufactured goods to the United States. Figure 12.2 traces China's percentage of total U.S. imports in a number of product categories. In umbrellas and artificial flowers, for example, Chinese firms accounted for more than 80 percent of U.S. imports in 2001. In footwear, in which European firms are

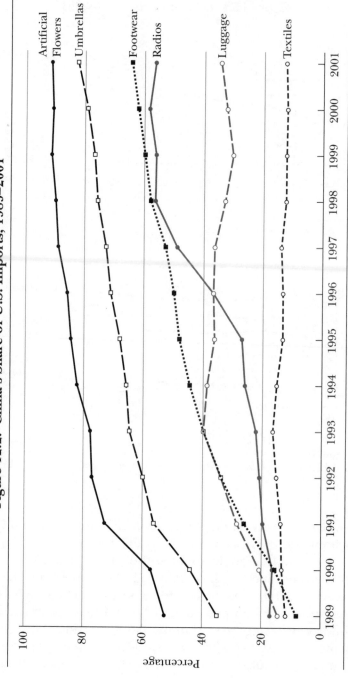

Figure 12.2. China's Share of U.S. Imports, 1989–2001

Source: Adapted from U.S. International Trade Commission data, 2002.

often competitive at higher prices, Chinese firms accounted for more than 60 percent of U.S. imports in 2001, up from approximately 9 percent in 1989.[2] Textiles is an interesting exception to the pattern of growth in Chinese exports to the United States, China's share of U.S. imports has remained flat, at around 13 percent. Unlike other product categories, textiles are governed by the Multi-Fiber Agreement that has constrained (through quotas) China's ability to increase its textile exports to the United States (Yoffie and Austin, 1983). Subsequent to the phase-out of this agreement starting in 2005, we might see rapid growth in textile exports from China.

We also seem to be observing more examples of supply chains that span multiple countries, with different stages of production often occurring in different countries. Consider the following example from the pharmaceutical industry of a representative flow for penicillins and cephalosporins. The bulk precursors (fermented raw materials) originate in Syracuse, New York, and are shipped to Latina, Italy, where they are transformed into crude, intermediate, and finished bulk materials. The finished bulk materials are shipped to finishing plants in Italy, Puerto Rico, Turkey, and Egypt that transform the material into the finished product (pills). The finished product might be packaged and labeled at the finishing plant or by the pharmaceutical firm or third-party manufacturers and shipped to global markets. Another interesting aspect of this supply chain is that the products are sometimes financially tolled (on paper, the goods travel through a certain location for tax benefit reasons) from Italy to Puerto Rico through a tax haven such as Ireland, even as they are physically shipped to directly to Puerto Rico.

Supply chains for even such relatively simple products as apparel often span multiple countries. According to Victor Fung, chairman of Li and Fung, a Hong Kong–based intermediary that primarily sources apparel from low-wage countries such as China for importers in developed countries, a typical order for ten thousand garments from a European retailer might involve buying yarn from a Korean manufacturer. The yarn is then woven and dyed in Taiwan and the garments made in five different factories in Thailand. Production would also depend in part on effective sourcing of other components that are typically made by Japanese companies such as YKK in

Chinese factories. Hence, even for this relatively simple product, the tasks—from demand generation in Europe to manufacturing in at least four countries (Korea, China, Taiwan, and Thailand)—need to be coordinated across multiple countries.

Growth in outsourcing production tasks to lower-wage countries is not confined to manufacturing. Kennedy and Lewis (2002), who trace the growth in information-technology-enabled services (ITES) from countries such as India, report that Indian exports of ITES are projected to grow from $264 million in 2000 to $4 billion in 2005. They maintain that growth in outsourcing such services to developing countries can be traced to economic liberalization, the spread of English, the "digitization" of business processes, liberalization of the telecommunications sector, and skill shortages in categories such as software development. They observe that firms that outsourced ITES to developing countries, in addition to reducing costs by 50 to 60 percent, also enjoyed improved service levels and better "time matching" with clients in developing countries. Medical audiotape transmitted at the end of the day from the United States, for example, could be transcribed in a few hours in India and sent back to the United States by the start of the next business day.

Looking at historical data and projecting forward suggests that supply chains will become increasingly global over the next few years. The rapid pace of globalization will have considerable social implications as well. For example, the loss of manufacturing jobs in developed countries like the United States will have implications for labor and labor groups, such as unions, that might be expected to use their political clout to oppose such a trend. Consider Figure 12.3, which suggests the effect of U.S. imports from China on other exporters of radios. Japan, Malaysia, Korea, and Taiwan seem to have their share of imports reduced by the shift in manufacturing of radios to China. Similar repercussions can also be expected in smaller developing countries, such as Bangladesh, Sri Lanka, and Vietnam, from the concentration of labor-intensive manufacturing in China. The pace of concentration in China is expected to hasten in the next five to ten years when textiles and apparel (which have been historically largely immune to such concentration due to quotas on Chinese exports) have their import quotas phased out in 2005. In many of these countries, the balance of trade depends

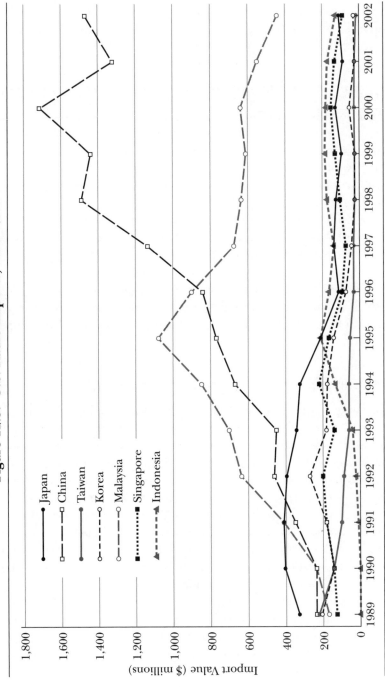

Figure 12.3. U.S. Radio Imports, 1989–2001

Source: Adapted from U.S. International Trade Commission data, 2002.

substantially on exports of labor-intensive products, such as apparel, even though the countries account for a small percentage of world trade in these categories.

Supply Chain Management: A Primer on Concepts

In this section, we define supply chain management and trace the current attention it receives from senior management to three phenomena that occurred in operations management in the last few decades of the twentieth century. We subsequently identify and briefly describe several concepts that are central to effective supply chain management.[3]

Supply chain management is the management of inter- and intrafirm flows of materials and information so as to reduce operating cost and ensure the quality and availability of products or services delivered to intended customers. Although practiced in one form or another for quite a few centuries, supply chain management has gained senior management attention and a place in the operations management nomenclature only within the past few decades.

The Genesis of Supply Chain Management

The current attention accorded supply chain management can be traced to three phenomena that substantially influenced managers' and academics' views on operations management: the changing role of logistics in operations; recognition of the value that can be derived from better operational coordination, specifically with respect to the impact of manufacturing resource planning (MRP) and enterprise resource planning (ERP) systems; and acknowledgment of the weaknesses in information and material flow across firm boundaries in supply chains. We review how the evolution of each of these phenomena contributed to the current senior management focus on supply chain management.

Logistics managers have traditionally been concerned with such topics as the location and operation of warehouses and efficient routing of trucks. In most companies, logistics was assigned a tactical role of executing (possibly at minimum cost) a strategy chosen without much attention to logistics issues. Notwithstanding their tactical roles, logistics employees, being the primary interface with suppliers and customers on a day-to-day basis, represented the operational face of the firm to customers. Over time (particularly during the 1980s and early 1990s), companies came to realize that logistics could and often needed to have a strategic role (Bowersox and others, 1989). In part, this acknowledgment was driven by the recognition that logistics, being the operational face, had to be able to execute the strategic initiative. Companies also realized that logistics capabilities could be a source of competitive advantage, a recognition that was more or less concurrent with a similar recognition of operational capabilities leading to competitive advantage (see Wheelright and Hayes, 1985, for a discussion of the stages of operations strategy). Shapiro and Heskett (1985) trace changes over time in management's view of the role of logistics.

Top management's current elevated attention to supply chain management can also be traced in part to the field of operational coordination. Many of the companies that implemented MRP systems during the 1970s and 1980s realized tremendous benefits.[4] These systems facilitated better information exchange and thereby improved decision making within manufacturing, leading in many cases to improved factory productivity. ERP systems installed during the late 1980s and 1990s expanded the footprint associated with MRP systems by integrating other functions with manufacturing functions. Some companies attributed significant productivity improvements to the deployment of ERP systems. Although their locus is within the enterprises (and not across different firms in a supply chain), MRP and ERP signaled to managers the benefits that stood to be realized from sharing information across different operating units and improving decision making in operations.

Persistent weaknesses observed in information and material flows in their supply chains constitute the third driver of top management's heightened interest in supply chain management. Most companies recognized, for example, that they rarely shared demand data or forecasts with suppliers. A manufacturer without access to its distributors' or retailers' sales data made decisions about what and when to produce based on the orders received. The inefficiencies (such as excessive inventory, low capacity and labor utilization, and poor service levels to customers) that attended such arms-length relationships were glaringly manifested in the "beer game," in which the participants simulate a supply chain for beers.[5] Inevitably, the beer game illustrates the bullwhip effect, whereby small changes in downstream demand (for example, end consumer demand) occasion significant fluctuations in orders and production decisions upstream in the supply chain. Participants often experience in the simulation very much what managers experience in their own supply chains. "Barilla SpA," "Campbell Soup: A Leader in Continuous Replenishment of Products," and other case studies about companies that have experimented with streamlining information and material flows across firm boundaries, illuminate similar issues in supply chains (see Hammond, 1994a; McKenney and Clark, 1994).

Central Concepts for Effective Supply Chain Management

We identify and examine four concepts considered to be central to effective supply chain management.

Data and Information Sharing

Poor coordination that led to inefficiencies in material and information flows in their supply chains could often be traced to the inability to share data and information. Dedicated information systems such as electronic data interchange and more general information infrastructures such as the Internet began to be used to share point-of-sale (POS) data, inventory levels, and forecasts. Sharing such information reduced uncertainty about supply chain requirements, which helped to reduce supply mismatches and attendant costs. Its benefits notwithstanding, observations suggest that information sharing might need to be augmented with changes in decision rights or at least supply chain focus.

Participants, for example, in the beer game simulation, come to realize that the bullwhip effect is caused in part by one firm's inability to observe demand and inventory at other firms in the supply chain. Participants upstream in the supply chain, such as those in the role of the factory, are often surprised to learn that consumer demand for beer was essentially flat during the entire simulation. In the absence of retail POS data, they were often forced to try to discern patterns in consumer sales data from the orders placed by downstream firms, a task rendered difficult by virtue of orders being a function of a firm's perception of consumer demand. Watson and Zheng (2002) show how a manager's perceiving the strength of demand signals to be greater than actual leads her to overreact to such signals and cause unnecessary fluctuations in order sizes.

Many who participate in the beer game argue that performance could be improved if all firms in the supply chain were given access to retail POS data. Simulations of the beer game where such data transfer was permitted have offered limited improvement in supply chain performance. In simulations conducted with M.B.A. students at Harvard Business School, average system costs decreased by 26 percent when all participants in the supply chain were able to view POS data. Although enormously helpful, POS data are not sufficient for supply chain efficiency because upstream firms are still expected to meet downstream firms' orders, which are often poorly correlated with consumer demand (which is tracked by POS data). Thus, order-focused approaches, despite information sharing, still leave supply chains vulnerable to miscoordination and supply mismatches (Watson and Zheng, 2003).

POS data transfer has consequently been augmented by other initiatives that either transfer decision rights or promote collaboration within the supply chain. Initiatives that transfer data and decision rights, such as vendor managed inventory (VMI), shift decision rights on retail inventory levels from retailers (such as Wal-Mart) to manufacturers or vendors (such as Procter and Gamble), which are subsequently responsible for managing their retailers' as well as their own inventory levels.[6] Case studies that describe the concept and implementation of VMI and similar initiatives include "Barilla SpA" and "Campbell Soup: A Leader in Continuous Replenishment of Products." Collaborative planning, forecasting, and replenishment initiatives (CPFR) encourage the firms in a supply chain to collaborate on forecasting and inventory planning. Although pilot implementations of CPFR involving limited stockkeeping units (SKUs) and stores have yielded impressive results, we are not aware of any such programs that scaled up well (that is, were able to handle large volumes of trade).

Lead Time Reduction (Quick and Accurate Response)

Managers also realized that especially for products with short life cycles and unpredictable demand, such as fashion apparel and personal computers, reducing lead times could add significantly to the gains achieved by emphasizing forecasting and inventory planning. Research had shown demand forecasts to be far more accurate if they were based on even limited early sales data. Moreover, companies that had reduced lead times, such as Zara and World in apparel and Dell in personal computers, had achieved higher profits and lower inventory levels than their competitors had (see Pich and Van der Heyden, 2002; Raman, Fisher, and McClelland, 2001; Dell and Magretta, 1998). Increasing product variety was yet another driver of lead time reduction as markdowns and stockout costs had risen substantially in many product categories as a result. Department store markdowns, for example, had risen steadily from 8 percent of sales in 1970 to more than 35 percent of sales in 2002 (National Retail Federation, 2002).

Accurate Response proposed that companies couple lead time reduction to improved inventory planning to more fully exploit the benefits of shorter lead times (see Fisher, Hammond, Obermeyer, and Raman, 1997, for a discussion of these concepts). Taking into account that levels of demand uncertainty and, hence, inventory risk varied widely across products, Accurate Response suggested that companies could benefit by tracking demand uncertainty carefully and using reactive capacity (their ability to react to demand signals) only for the portion of demand that carried very high inventory risk. Accurate Response also demonstrated that lead time was often a function of a supply chain's inventory decision. In the leather footwear industry, for example, the substantial portion of lead time that is typically used to procure leather can be reduced substantially by intelligently holding inventory in the supply chain.

Superior Decision Making and Information Technology

Effective decision-making methodologies embedded in information technology also supported heightened interest in supply chain management. Much work has been done since World War II in the academic areas of operations research and management and computer science to improve operational decision making. Optimization techniques developed in these fields have been variously applied to improving the mix of products produced in oil refineries, ensuring more accurate forecasts, developing superior worker and machine schedules, and more effectively routing trucks. Embedded over time in suitable software, these methodologies have occasioned dramatic improvements in operational performance (see Raman and Singh, 1998, for a discussion of such technologies and their applications in business).

Progress in embedding these optimization approaches in commercially usable software was accelerated by plummeting prices of computers, memory, and communications infrastructure. Finally, relatively cheap and abundant venture capital that became available during the mid- to late 1990s made it easier to set up firms that specialized in such software.

Incentive Alignment and Contracts

Companies that sought to improve supply chain performance through collaboration, lead time reduction, and superior decision making and information technology frequently discovered that the initiatives they had undertaken were difficult to implement because key decision makers and even firms in the supply chain were not rewarded suitably for participating. In the Barilla SpA case, for example, salespeople and distributors whose incentives were not aligned with it resisted adoption of the just-in-time development program. Distributors believed that, transferring replenishment decision rights to Barilla's logistics department would reduce both their control over purchase quantities and their ability to profit from forward buying during the company's frequent price promotions.

Over time, many supply chain managers have realized that they need to attend explicitly to incentive alignment and contracts while implementing supply chain initiatives. However, supply chain practitioners consider a true nature of collaboration within a chain to be very beneficial for the overall management of the chain. This collaboration, for example, allows firms to make requests of each other that may not be covered by contracts but provide mutual benefits at least in the long term. Recognizing the value of such sensibilities, some managers explicitly incorporate their development and maintenance in their management strategy.

What Is Different About Global Supply Chain Management?

The description of fundamental concepts in supply chain management begs the question as to what is different about global supply chain management. Does something change fundamentally when a supply chain spans multiple countries? Or as some of our colleagues have asked periodically, are we simply changing parameters in existing supply chain models?

We argue in this section that global supply chain management exhibits unique characteristics that differentiate it substantially from non–global supply chain management. We emphasize that this uniqueness reflects largely differences in contract enforceability, factor costs, tacit knowledge, infrastructure, cultural factors, and the applicability of heuristics that supply chain managers have developed over time. Moreover, managers must be cognizant of potential exchange rate fluctuations across the different parts of a supply chain that spans multiple countries. Finally, we consider the argument that longer lead times differentiate global from non–global supply chains. Because they have been examined in the academic literature, we begin by examining the roles of lead time and currency fluctuation.

Lead Times

Some authors have opined that lead time should correlate with transportation time and thus be shorter for domestic than for more distant oversees suppliers (for example, see Hammond, 1990). In fact, shorter lead times have been offered as one of the ways in which U.S.-based manufacturers can be competitive with manufacturers in low-wage countries. It was for precisely this reason that the Quick Response program was promoted aggressively by U.S. manufacturers and even parts of the U.S. government (see U.S. Congress, 1987). The logic that leads us to conclude that domestic suppliers will de facto have shorter lead times is flawed, however, insofar as it takes transportation time to be the primary driver of response time. Our interactions with numerous supply chains have revealed response times to be driven in large part by time to procure raw material and capacity and supply chains' daily capacities, neither of which affords domestic suppliers an advantage (Hammond and Raman, 1994b). To the contrary, domestic suppliers, owing to lower production capacities, frequently have longer response times than overseas suppliers in low-wage countries.[7] Differences in response times between domestic and overseas suppliers (and, hence, between nonglobal and global supply chains) thus being ambiguous, we do not believe lead time to fundamentally differentiate global supply chains.

Currency Fluctuation and Taxation

The academic literature in supply chain management has also examined the impact of currency fluctuation on global sourcing. Exchange rate fluctuations create transaction exposure risk if there is a delay between price agreement or determination and payment, or operational or business risk exposure for long-term relationships if exchange rate fluctuations change the value of foreign products relative to domestic products (Austin, 1990). The supply chain management literature includes both static optimization models of the trade-off between costs and exchange risks and models for dynamic optimization given multiple decision epochs (Gutierrez and Kouvelis 1995; Dixit, 1989a, 1989b; Kogut and Kulatilake, 1994; Huchzermeier and Cohen, 1996; Kouvelis, 1999). The research suggests the value of a network of supply (or by extension market) opportunities and multisupplier sourcing strategies for hedging exchange rate fluctuations, but cautions that switching costs between suppliers or transaction costs for changing amounts sourced implies some insensitivity to small changes in exchange rates.

One possible solution for transaction exposure risk is the use of financial hedging mechanisms such as futures, whereby a firm agrees to buy or sell a particular currency at a specific price at a future date. Austin (1990) emphasizes that the operational flexibility of these mechanisms might be limited by contract sizes, for example, which would render the precise value of the transaction unredeemable, or the prefixed dates for redeeming futures or fixed coverage period of such contracts, which make it difficult to match redemption dates with transaction dates. Transaction payments that are delayed for any reason also reduce the efficacy of these mechanisms. Austin (1990) points out that these contracts might not exist for certain countries, or the infrastructure to accommodate the demand for these contracts might be poor.

Countries' taxation rates and policies can pose challenges to optimizing material flows through the supply chain. Different taxation rates and policies might suggest a specific cash flow strategy for the profit centers of a supply chain located in different host countries. Such a cash flow strategy would be facilitated by centrally determined transfer prices, which would also govern the flow of materials through the supply chain. The transfer price that supports a material flow adequate to ensure the availability of product might be at odds with that required to reduce the cost of the material flow paid out in taxes.

Contract Enforcement and Compliance Issues

The legal infrastructure in less developed countries can be weaker or simply different from that in developed countries with implications for the enforceability of contracts. An executive at a spice importer, for example, unable to get an exporter to abide by the forward contract once spot market prices for a particular spice exceeded the price specified and determining that it would be extremely time-consuming to take the exporter to court given the delays in the exporting country's legal system, deemed the contract unenforceable.

Unenforceability of contracts is a cause for concern to most managers who source from overseas suppliers. Consider the apparel industry, in which purchasing contracts are written six to twelve months before merchandise is received. A supplier that signs a contract with an importer committing to deliver product on a specific date at a given price might subsequently accept orders from other customers (that might, for example, offer to pay higher prices) and delay or cancel the shipment it agreed to make to the first importer. Companies also have difficulty enforcing agreements relating to intellectual, design, and brand-related property rights. Consider the experience of New Balance athletic shoes (Kahn, 2002). New Balance outsourced to a Chinese manufacturer that produced more than New Balance's order and then sold the balance, with the New Balance brand signature, at discounts in the same market that New Balance was targeting.

U.S. companies tend to be surprised that certain contracts are easier to enforce overseas. In the United States, for example, manufacturers are often prohibited from engaging in resale price maintenance, that is, specifying to retailers the price to be charged for particular products. This can, as multiple authors have argued, complicate supply chain coordination (see, for example, Narayanan, Raman, and Singh, forthcoming). However, such resale price maintenance can often be legal in other countries.

Global supply chains face compliance issues of another sort when, for example, a supplier acts legally in its country of operation but violates accepted ethical norms in the importer's country. Consider the problem of child labor. Companies such as Nike need to be concerned, if they manufacture in supplier factories that employ children, about the potential damage that can be done to their image and brand even though the use of child labor might be legal and even morally acceptable in the country in which the supplier is located (Spar and Burns, 2000; Rosenzweig, 1994). Consumers often hold companies responsible not only for communicating the importance of not using, but also for enforcing agreements to not use, child labor.

To do business in developing countries, supply chains need to find creative ways to enforce relationships and contracts. Contracts are enforced in developing countries, albeit often in ways that are different from those employed in the developed world. One approach we have seen used quite often is to rely on relationships in lieu of relying on only legal mechanisms to enforce agreements. Narayanan and Raman (2000) argue that relationship-based mechanisms differ from purely legal contracts in that they rely on repeated interactions to align incentives in the supply chain. The incentive to preserve and enhance reputation for fair play, according to the authors, is a powerful vehicle for incentive alignment in relationship-based supply chains. Consider the case described earlier of the supplier that reneged on a forward contract to deliver product at a set price on a specific date. A supplier that had repeated long-term interactions with the importer would be wary of pursuing short-term gain at the expense of jeopardizing its reputation. (The use of relationships to enforce contracts is illustrated later in this chapter.)

Factor Cost Differences

Factor costs (the costs of factors such as labor and capital that are inputs to the supply chain) can vary substantially across a supply chain. Differences in labor costs in different parts of a supply chain are usually well understood. In fact, they are often one of the primary drivers of a supply chain's becoming global. Operating managers, however, seldom recognize differences in capital costs across a supply chain. Yet capital costs can vary substantially across different parts of a supply chain. Raman (1995) found that apparel exporters in India face extremely high working capital costs, often exceeding 3 percent per month (or a compounded annual rate in excess of 36 percent). The high cost of working capital made these exporters reluctant to carry fabric inventory, and this, he argues, inhibited their ability to respond quickly to customer orders.

Capital costs can be expected to differ across country boundaries. Difficulty enforcing contracts in courts causes lenders to charge higher rates. Moreover, in many developing countries in which the highly regulated and often state-owned banking sector is the primary source of working capital for many exporters, the rates charged for loans often do not reflect market rates.

In some extreme cases, working capital simply is not available. Examples are periods of macroeconomic crisis in a country or region. During the Asian financial crisis in 1997–1998, many exporters in countries such as Thailand were unable to obtain loans to finance inventory, forcing Hong Kong intermediaries such as Li and Fung to assume the role of banks and provide vital working capital to the supply chain (Moore and Ihlman, 1998).

Tacit Knowledge in Operations

Managers in global supply chains are often surprised by how commonly used terms and concepts are misinterpreted in parts of the supply chain that do not possess the knowledge to interpret them appropriately. One U.S. apparel importer that contracted with an Asian supplier for black garments unfortunately neglected to specify that the supplier use black thread to stitch the garments. The importer emphasized that it would not have been necessary to specify the appropriate thread had the supplier been aware of consumer tastes and requirements in the United States. Similarly, in studying the fashion skiwear supply chain (see the "Sport Obermeyer Ltd." case study in Hammond and Raman, 1994, for a description), we were surprised to learn during visits to factories in China that workers in the factories had no concept of skiing and no idea how these products would be used. Not surprisingly, these workers needed highly detailed and explicit instructions for each production step. Managers who outsource to physically and often culturally distant countries often fail to account for the lack of shared tacit knowledge in their supply chains.

Infrastructure

One characteristic of developing countries is that infrastructure along some dimension is in a significant stage of development. Austin (1990) identifies two types of infrastructure: physical and informational. Physical infrastructure includes stocks of roads, transportation modes, and telecommunications and other utilities. Informational infrastructure involves sources of information about, for example, domestic supply and demand, prices, availability of resources, and government regulations. Insufficient investment in physical infrastructure incurs some of the same consequences as high capital costs, together with some additional operational consequences: that execution will require extra attention in the face of poor physical infrastructure, which increases operating costs. One difference between low stock of infrastructure and high capital costs is that infrastructure is usually sharable. This means that investment in infrastructure can serve the needs of a firm and often, for a low marginal cost, be made available to the host country for rent or other kinds of concessions. Deficiencies in informational infrastructure increase the risk of poor coordination and planning (as in the beer game), but due to usually consequent under investment in physical infrastructure or high capital costs, the fixes are even more challenging than in developed countries. Again, informational infrastructure is sharable and firm investment, although costly, might yield high and multifaceted returns.

Cultural Factors

Given the widespread reference to them, we would be remiss in not discussing the role of cultural factors and cultural differences when discussing the complexity associated with global supply chains. Cultural factors are often referred to in common parlance and even in academic writing, yet we have found the definition of the term to be elusive. Observed Austin (1990), "Culture is communication's companion; all key relationships and interactions are culturally shaped" (p. 347). Cultural considerations and their implications for operating portions of supply chains in other countries or sets of countries are varied and not necessarily straightforward. Navigating these considerations increases the challenge of managing relationships so as to effect timely and appropriate material and information flow within the chain.

Culture determines relationship protocol for organization and decision making; norms for personnel management in terms of selection and modes and outcomes of motivation; attitudes toward time and environment that affect planning and scheduling; and rules of communication for generating clarity and emphasis and for establishing and maintaining relationships. With respect to relationship protocol, for example, developing country cultures tend to be more accepting of hierarchical structures than of more equal distributions of power. Norms for decision making and execution might also differ: efficient decision making for a U.S. manager that involves bypassing a superior might not be considered appropriate behavior by an Italian counterpart. Gender roles remain a sticky issue in many countries, males still being expected to fill positions of power. Incentives might motivate different kinds of behavior in different cultures: a higher wage rate, for example, might result in less work because of a culture's preference for leisure over wealth. Many jokes have been told in which the punch line is based on a particular group's different appreciation for time or deadlines or destiny and its manipulation. Culture as it accompanies communication determines not only language and even, within a language, manners of speech, but also interpretation and color ranging from emphasis to subtlety and nuance.

Culture in tandem with communication can also be the means by which deficiencies in a country's socioeconomic framework are met. A legal infrastructure's inability to enforce contracts might be mitigated, by example, by cultural adaptations that help to enforce agreements or provide the perception or inspire faith that the agreements are binding. Consider the following Mexican minister's explanation of why an American sales executive failed to close a deal in Mexico:

> I like the American's equipment and it makes sense to deal with North Americans who are near us and whose price is right. But I could never be friends with this man. He is not my kind of human being and we have nothing in common. He is not *simpático*. If I can't be friends and he is not *simpatico,* I cannot depend on him to treat me right. . . . If we could be friends, he would feel obligated to me and this obligation would give me some control. Without control, how do I know he will deliver what he says he will at the price he quotes? [Hall, 1960, p. 95].

Heuristics and Benchmarks

Heuristics are decision rules that managers use in specific decision-making contexts. For example, production managers often schedule in their factories the task with the earliest due date. Similarly, managers use benchmarks, such as labor utilization, to evaluate the performance of part of their operations or compare performance among different parts.

However, heuristics and benchmarks are context sensitive, so what might be an appropriate benchmark or heuristic in one context might be totally inappropriate in another. For example, factory managers in labor-intensive industries such as apparel and footwear manufacturing have traditionally paid close attention to direct labor productivity, a focus that was justified because even at ten dollars an hour, direct labor was the biggest cost component in their factories. A focus on direct labor is often inappropriate, however, when production is moved to low-wage countries in which direct labor can cost roughly a dollar a day. The eighty-fold reduction in hourly labor cost (from ten dollars an hour to one dollar a day) renders inappropriate heuristics and benchmarks that have been developed in higher-wage contexts.

It is easy to point out here that heuristics should match the supply chain environment. What is probably more crucial to point out is that institutional norms, experience, and even common sense can lead a firm to underestimate how badly its own heuristics will perform within the new global environment. Given many uncertainties about operating in a global environment, managers often find it difficult to determine when parameters have changed sufficiently for new heuristics to be warranted, devised, and implemented. The cultural considerations of working in a global environment are especially tricky to navigate. Observations of successful global operations suggest that some culturally based adaptation is necessary as even our discussion of intermediaries suggests. Our argument here is that managers need to attend to these heuristics because contexts often differ substantially in different parts of global supply chains. Heuristics that perform well in one part often perform poorly elsewhere.

Managerial Implications

This section discusses the role of supply chain intermediaries; the discussion is needed for two reasons. One is that supply chain intermediaries often play a vital role in coordinating and controlling global supply chains. Yet their contributions are often not understood by other supply chain firms that then attempt to replace the intermediaries. Then we argue that observing processes and performance at intermediaries that have coordinated operations in supply chains that span multiple countries can yield valuable lessons on the management of global supply chains. We draw specifically on the experiences of two supply chain intermediaries that have been described in considerable detail by other authors: Massimo Menichetti, an intermediary in the textile supply chain based in Prato, Italy, and Li and Fung, a Hong Kong–based intermediary that primarily sources apparel from low-wage countries such as China for importers in developed countries such as the United States (Loveman and O'Connell, 1995; Magretta, 1998). Neither Menichetti nor Li and Fung actually owns factories, retail stores, or brands, but both play vital roles in coordinating their supply chains.

Menichetti's operations in the Prato supply chain revolved around the charismatic personality and individual attributes of the late Massimo Menichetti. There is no evidence that the leader was able to imbue a firm with his character and passion. Li and Fung, in contrast, is an organization. The company employs thousands, and a million people worldwide work in Li and Fung–controlled factories. Profits rose from HK$225 million in 1995 to HK$782 million in 2001, sales from roughly HK$9 billion to HK$33 billion over the same period (here, 1 U.S. dollar equals 7.8 Hong Kong dollars). Return on equity (ROE) exceeded 30 percent from 1995 to 2000; its ROE was greater than 60 percent in 1999. Operating cash flow, moreover, was positive during these years despite rapid growth in sales. Highlights of the company's financial performance during the period 1995 to 2001 are presented in Table 12.1. We analyze how these intermediaries make it easier for a global supply chain to enforce contracts, share tacit knowledge, and exploit factor market imperfections.

Enforcing Contracts and Engendering Trust in the Supply Chain

Menichetti was, and Li and Fung is, instrumental in enforcing contracts in their respective supply chains. Apparel importers in developed countries in North America and western Europe often place orders for apparel months in advance of scheduled delivery. In the absence of an intermediary such as Li and Fung, it is easy and

Table 12.1. Li and Fung's Financial Performance

	Sales (millions of HK$)	Profit (millions of HK$)	Return on Equity (%)
1995	9,213	225	35.3
1996	12,514	300	43.4
1997	13,346	375	39.5
1998	14,313	455	43.7
1999	16,298	575	60.2
2000	24,991	870	47.8
2001	33,029	782	27.3

Source: Adapted from Standard & Poor's Global Vantage.

tempting for a supplier offered a better price to renege on a previously accepted offer from an importer. Not only are legal contracts preventing such behavior difficult to enforce in many developing countries, but exporters in developing countries worry that importers, unable to sell it, might reject merchandise they had received on the basis of frivolous quality considerations.

Importers and exporters alike realize that their current contracts with an enterprise on the scale of and Li and Fung are not likely to be their last. Suppliers are unlikely to renege on and importers to exploit contractual commitments for fear of jeopardizing future contracts with the company. Intermediaries such as Li and Fung and Menichetti, by converting episodic relationships to repeated interactions gain the leverage to enforce interfirm agreements. Li and Fung effectively serves as an informal performance rating and contract enforcement mechanism in its supply chain and provides opportunities for suppliers and exporters to preserve and enhance their reputations over time.

Sharing Tacit Knowledge in the Supply Chain

Menichetti described the sharing of tacit knowledge in a supply chain in the context of his development of samples and patterns:

> A weaver comes to me with a sample. The colors are nice, the finish good and it looks as though it would sell next season. I go with it to one of my customers in New York. They say it is beautiful, we like it, but we cannot pay $5/meter; we can buy it for four. So what I do is go back to the same firm. [After a few iterations of the process], if he or she does not want the business, I will do two things: go with this yarn to another customer who might buy it at $4.50 or find another vendor to make the present sample cheaper [Jaikumar, 1986, p. 6].

Knowledge (often tacit) of different firms' requirements and capabilities enabled Menichetti to simplify transactions and reduce the number of times a particular design had to go back and forth from supplier to importers. Menichetti was prepared, for example, to provide feedback on a design's quality and compliance with customer's requirements and to pass judgment on a supplier's production capabilities and a customer's willingness and ability to pay. Moreover, Menichetti's knowledge and his willingness to use that knowledge only appropriately was apparent to the suppliers and customers in the supply chain with which he interacted.

Leveraging Market Imperfections to Reduce Factor Cost

Menichetti enabled and Li and Fung continues to enable their respective supply chains to obtain lower-cost capital and reduce labor costs concurrently. Li and Fung, for example, often manufactures in countries such as China in which labor costs are quite low (often as low as a dollar a day). But because they often face extremely high capital costs (as for working capital), many of these factories are reluctant or unable to carry inventory levels that are optimal for the entire supply chain. An intermediary such as Li and Fung that can arrange suitable financing and even carry inventory of needed materials is extremely valuable. Not surprisingly, Li and Fung is located in Hong Kong, which has excellent banking and legal infrastructures that help to keep capital costs low. When the recent financial crisis in parts of Asia made it difficult for apparel factories in countries (such as Thailand and Indonesia) to obtain capital loans to finance inventory, Li and Fung became the supply chain's banker and arranged financing for these suppliers.

Conclusion

We have examined the drivers of global trade volume and offered evidence that supply chains for a range of products and services are becoming increasingly global. We reviewed data for global trade in many product categories, paying explicit attention to China's exports, and discussed the potential implications of China's dominance. We argued that the increasing globalization of supply chains makes it imperative that managers adopt a more global perspective in managing supply chains.

We subsequently reviewed the central concepts in supply chain management and examined whether and how they are altered in the context of global supply chains. We analyzed the roles of contract enforceability, tacit knowledge, and factor market imperfections and the impacts of longer transportation times and currency rate fluctuations. Finally, we explored briefly steps taken by intermediaries such as Li and Fung and Menichetti to address these issues in their respective supply chains.

CHAPTER 13

Globalization of Retailing

David E. Bell
Rajiv Lal
Walter J. Salmon

Gielens and Dekimpe (2001) conclude that retailers are more likely to be successful at expanding internationally if they are first to enter the foreign market, with substantial scale, using no partners or acquired assets, and at the same time offering a store format that is at the same time new to the host market and familiar to the parent firm. These conclusions were based on an exhaustive study of 160 foreign entries by Europe's top seventy-five food retailers in western Europe and a variety of transition economies in eastern Europe. The success of the entry decisions was measured by long-run sales performance of a retail firm's foreign operations.

The findings in Gielens and Dekimpe (2001) seem to prescribe that retailers should enter markets where they are able to be the first to enter the foreign market and they should do it using no partners and acquired assets. They should also achieve substantial scale and introduce a format that is new to the foreign market and yet familiar to the global retailer to be successful. In this way, Gielens and Dekimpe's study provides answers to two questions: What is the criterion for selecting the market when expanding internationally? and What does it take to succeed in a foreign market?

In this chapter, we focus on the top three global retailers—Carrefour, Wal-Mart, and Ahold—and investigate if the conclusions that Gielens and Dekimpe (2001) reached can help us understand these companies' strategies for entering foreign markets. We have collected data from multiple sources, including extensive field interviews in Latin America, to consider the validity of these prescriptions.

Carrefour

Carrefour is the second largest retailer in the world after Wal-Mart.[1] It operates hypermarkets, supermarkets, and hard discount stores in thirty countries across Europe, Latin America, and Asia. With a compounded annual growth rate of 24 percent since 1996, its sales were $69 billion in 2001 despite the fact that Carrefour has no stores in the United States, United Kingdom, and Germany.

Carrefour opened its first store (with seven thousand square feet) in the basement of the Fournier department store in Annecy, France, in the summer of 1960. In 1963, it opened its first hypermarket outside Paris. The store was unique in its size (twenty-seven thousand square feet and parking for 450 cars); consumers could meet all their shopping needs under one roof. The store provided self-service groceries at discounted prices but also offered clothing, sporting equipment, auto accessories, and consumer electronics.

French consumers were excited about the Carrefour proposition, and the company grew rapidly. Carrefour invented the hypermarket concept in 1963. Between 1965 and 1971, sales growth exceeded 50 percent per year, with nonfood items accounting for more than 40 percent of sales. Its stores average 108,000 square feet, are usually located outside towns in commercial areas where land is cheap, and are easily accessible by highways. The company also prefers simple facility construction that allows it to achieve a total investment per square meter of selling space of about one-third that of traditional supermarkets.

The success of the hypermarket concept can be attributed to convenience and price. Almost any product a consumer can think of buying more than once a year can be bought at a Carrefour store. Price is another key to Carrefour's consumer acceptance. Carrefour always maintains a sharp focus on its pricing. It is always vigilant of competitive prices and surveys prices on the most important items across all stores within a five-minute drive of the target store. Prices are then set to match or be lower than competitive prices. Carrefour's prices average 5 to 10 percent under those of retailers in traditional outlets. Gross margins on food and nonfood differ somewhat, but on average, gross margins of 15 percent translated to 4.5 percent operating margins after SG&A in 1998.

As competitors tried to copy the concept, Carrefour sought to differentiate itself by purchasing locally and selling private labels. Purchasing locally was a key strategy as it pleased the local authorities and met the needs of the local consumers. Buying locally also allowed Carrefour to execute its strategy of positioning itself as a leader in every fresh product department (butchery, bakery, delicatessen, and others). Private labels offered value-for-money to consumers as Carrefour offered private labels of equal technical quality as compared to national brands at a price that was often 15 to 30 percent lower than the national brands.

Another reason for Carrefour's success is its decentralized organizational structure, which allows it to continue to focus on local needs. The head office in Paris deals with the long-term strategy and policy and financial and technical matters, and provides advice when requested. It also provides intellectual capital in terms of information and experience and is responsible for capital investments and new store locations.

Store managers are responsible for the store's profit and have a great degree of freedom in formulating forecasts. The process starts at the department level in each store and includes both sales and margins estimates. Before the estimates are sent to headquarters, the store manager has a chance to revise them if necessary. In the end, the store manager has the final word on the forecasts. Store managers are judged on profits and their ability to meet forecasts. Comparisons are also made with other stores and departments in the region to benefit from best practices. Almost all promotions are from within the organization, with significant emphasis on on-the-job training. A prospective store manager moves through all the departments of the store, and managers that were appointed to a new store are on-site at the beginning of the construction.

With this level of decentralization, support services like information technology and logistics are treated as vendors. Over time, this led to an underinvestment and caused Carrefour a competitive disadvantage of 2 percent of sales in operations and SG&A.

While Carrefour flourished in the local markets, it took a toll on the small mom-and-pop traditional grocery store in France. A large number of these disappeared (80,000 out of 203,000) between 1961 and 1971. These small shopkeepers had significant political influence and sought government intervention to slow the march of hypermarkets. In the end, the French National Assembly passed a law that taxed retail stores to provide for the pensions of the small shopkeepers, and zoning laws made it difficult to find space for hypermarkets.

International Expansion

With limits to growth in France, Carrefour expanded into Belgium in 1969, barely six years after opening its first store. In the next few years, it expanded into Spain and brought the hypermarket concept to Latin America in 1975. In expanding to Latin America, Carrefour adopted the concept of self-funding and provided starting capital for only one store and a half. It opened its second store only after it was able to generate enough funds from the operations of the first store. This discipline forced Carrefour to experiment with the first store until it was successful in the local market. Between 1975 and 1985, Carrefour opened only ten stores, using capital available from operating stores. Growth accelerated in 1985, and by 2001 Carrefour had seventy-seven hypermarkets in Brazil, twenty-two in Argentina, five in Colombia, and five in Chile.

During the late 1980s, the Brazilian economy experienced severe inflationary pressures, and the local Carrefour management responded to this challenge, producing great financial results for the company. The decentralized structure paid off handsomely. The key to their strategy was to negotiate longer terms of payments to the vendors and to increase throughput. Discounts available from suppliers were plowed back to lower prices and increase sales volumes. Today, with the acquisition of Norte and merger with Promodes, Carrefour has multiple formats in the region (hypermarkets, supermarkets and discount stores) and a total of 222 hypermarkets and supermarkets in Brazil and 150 in Argentina.

Carrefour has maintained its strategy of decentralization as it has expanded internationally. The store manager continues to have profit and loss responsibility for the store. Store managers and department heads have decision-making authority over nearly all aspects of the store. The store manager is responsible for the layout, space allocation to the various departments, and the store environment. Together with the department head, the store manager decides on the product mix and ensures consistency of positioning across departments. The department head has full responsibility over purchasing, promotion, pricing, and motivating and training assistants. Department heads decide what they wanted to buy and from whom. They buy centrally through Carrefour only when the benefits of central purchasing outweigh the benefits of buying locally. This implies that the assortment can vary by store and the vendor would have to sell the product at the local level to ensure distribution in a region or a nation.

Carrefour's headquarters in Paris negotiate with only fifteen to twenty vendors on a worldwide basis. These negotiations typically include discussions of expansion into other countries and projects and discussions that can be initiated without compromising the pricing negotiations at the national or regional level. Groups of stores from all over the world are typically represented at these discussions through one of their store managers. Paris continues to provide the lead on central services such as accounting, finance, logistics, and information technology.

Carrefour's Experiences

Currently, with the merger with Promodes, Carrefour faces the significant challenge of integrating two management structures: a completely decentralized and autonomous structure in the hypermarket division and the more centralized structure practiced by Promodes in the supermarket division. This merger also provided Carrefour the opportunity to benefit from economies of scale without having to open more hypermarkets than can be sustained in the local market.

Today, Carrefour is among the most successful operators in Latin America. It has a market share of 13 percent in Brazil and 32 percent in Argentina. Latin America accounts for as much as 12 percent of its sales and 2 percent of profits.

Carrefour's experience in Latin America lends credence to the conclusions described in the literature that better performance is expected when entering early, using no partners, and offering a format that is at the same time new to the host market and familiar to the parent company. With respect to the prescription of entering with substantial scale, Carrefour preferred to take the time to learn about the environment and discover the right formula before scaling up. The Brazilian market is heterogeneous, and good locations are hard to come by. It was only in 1999 that Carrefour opened its first distribution center because logistics in Brazil was new for the company. Thus, Carrefour seems to have traded off the benefits of size, in terms of buying power, distribution and logistics costs, and marketing costs, for getting the format right. Moreover, since the international expansion started fairly early, six years after opening the first hypermarket in France, and Carrefour was privately held until 1970, there did not seem to be as much pressure on the sales and profit contributions from international operations to the growth plans of the company.

Carrefour is now present in thirty countries and with three different formats. Its mode of entry into Asia has been similar to that in Latin America. In Asia, Carrefour is present in Malaysia, Singapore, Indonesia, Thailand, Taiwan, Japan, South Korea, and China, and the region contributes $5 billion to total company sales. In some of these countries, although Carrefour was the first foreign retailer to enter these markets, the mode of entry has been through joint ventures because it was obliged to do so due to government regulations. However, it seeks to have a majority ownership in these ventures to take control of the day-to-day management of the stores. Thus, it is seen that Carrefour's mode of entry remains to be greenfield except when constrained due to local market regulations (see Table 13.1 for Carrefour's history of global expansion).

Carrefour's strategy in these markets continues to focus on local needs, with a strong emphasis on prices. In Mexico, Carrefour has worked hard on the atmosphere in the stores, using colorful decor to give it a look and feel of a market. It has focused its efforts on fresh products, some of which, like tortillas, tacos, and fruit juices, are made in front of the customer. In Taiwan, 70 percent of the products in stores are Taiwanese, 20 percent Asian, and the remaining 10 percent from the United States or Europe. In Korea,

Table 13.1. Carrefour's History of Global Expansion

Country	Date of Entry	Number of Hypermarkets	Sales (billions of dollars)	Net Sales	EBITDA/ Net Sales	EBIT (billions of dollars)
Europe		499	72.00	22.1	5.80%	0.74
France	1960	214	43.10	34.3	7.40	1.9
Belgium	1969	57	5.11			
Spain	1973	113	11.10			
Portugal	1992	5	0.88			
Italy	1993	37	6.40			
Greece	1999	11	1.40			
Czech/ Slovakia	1997	11	0.30			
Turkey	1993	10	0.44			
Poland	1997	9	0.66			
Latin America		124	10.10	8.4	4.30	0.053
Mexico	1994	19	0.79			
Brazil	1975	74	4.30			
Argentina	1975	22	4.60			
Columbia	1998	5	0.23			
Chile	1998	4	0.14			
Asia		108	5.10	4.6	6.90	0.134
Taiwan	1989	26	1.46			
Korea	1996	22	1.24			
China	1995	27	1.34			
Thailand	1996	15	0.35			
Malaysia	1994	6	0.24			
Indonesia	1998	8	0.20			
Worldwide				69.5	6.50	2.8

Source: Compiled from Carrefour company records.

Carrefour offers home delivery and installation of appliances as well as after-sales service. In Thailand, adapting to the local market has meant that 95 percent of the products are bought locally and products are displayed by product line rather than by brand, as is often the case elsewhere.

In summary, Carrefour's experience is consistent with the prescription that it is better to be the first to enter the foreign market and the mode of entry should be through greenfield operations. However, in some foreign markets, the entrant may not have a choice with respect to mode of entry due to regulations in the local market and is forced to pursue a joint venture. Moreover, the prescription for scaling up fast is challenged because Carrefour waited to get the retail formula right before increasing the size of its operations. In addition, the more recent expansion in operation has been achieved through merger with Promodes and with Dia, the discount stores in the portfolio; economies of scale in procurement and distribution are being accomplished by expanding the number of formats in the portfolio rather than through sheer growth in the number of hypermarkets, the format that was new to Latin America yet most familiar to Carrefour.

Wal-Mart

Today Wal-Mart is the world's largest retailer, with sales of $218 billion and a cash flow of $10 billion in 2002. Wal-Mart operates several formats, including the traditional discount store, supercenters, and Sam's Clubs. The traditional discount store was a 100,000 square foot store in a small town or suburb built over twenty acres of land with lots of parking space. The store was organized into thirty-six departments and carried eighty thousand stock-keeping units (SKUs), including housewares, hardware, electronics, home furnishings, small appliances, automotive accessories, garden accessories, sporting goods, toys, pet foods, cameras and camera supplies, health and beauty aids, pharmaceuticals, jewelry, fabrics, stationery, books, and shoes. In 1992, Wal-Mart opened its first supercenter by adding a sixty thousand square foot grocery store to its traditional discount store.

History and Corporate Strategy

Sam Walton opened his first Ben Franklin franchise store in 1945 in Newport, Arkansas. After being turned down for opening stores in small towns, Sam and his brother Bud opened their first Wal-Mart Discount Store in 1962 in Rogers, Arkansas. Wal-Mart offered a simple value proposition: a large number of product categories at discount prices and supported by friendly service. By 1970, Wal-Mart had grown a chain of thirty stores in rural Arkansas, Missouri, and Oklahoma. It went public in 1972 when it needed to build a warehouse at a cost of $5 million.

Wal-Mart focused on two things as it continued to expand in the United States. Stores were located in small towns and rural areas with populations of fewer than twenty-five thousand. Walton was convinced that if he offered prices that were as good as or better than stores in the city, consumers would prefer to shop in their towns. The second element of Wal-Mart's expansion strategy was described by David Glass, the CEO at that time, as "pushing from inside out. We never jump and backfill."[2] By the mid-1980s, Wal-Mart did not face any competition in a third of its markets, but by 1993, K-mart and Target were direct competitors in 55 percent of the markets.

Walton had one overriding philosophy for his business: deliver good value to customers and keep prices below those of all competitors. He also kept trip expenses below 1 percent; this meant that executives, including himself, would share hotel rooms and walk rather than take taxis on buying trips.

Walton considered his relationship with the employees to be the most important reason for Wal-Mart's success. He believed that if you wanted "associates" to take care of the customers, you had to make sure that you were taking care of the employees. By 1998, Wal-Mart employed 910,000 people. Walton empowered his employees and rewarded them through recognition and profit-sharing plans, with the result that they were deeply committed to the company and its success. Managers, supervisors, and store personnel with more than one year of employment were offered incentive plans and bonuses based on store profitability. Walton's management style is often described as "management by walking and flying around." Like all regional vice presidents and buyers, he spent more than 50 percent of his time visiting stores. Wal-Mart had a very centralized organizational structure and weekly meetings were always held in the headquarters. Weekly meetings, held every Friday, were used to discuss store and category sales performance at every location. Management, associates, friends, and relatives participated in an informal motivation session on Saturday morning. Decisions made over the weekend were implemented throughout the organization on Monday morning. Wal-Mart was considered to be one of the best one hundred companies to work for despite the fact that the company was not unionized and 30 percent of the staff worked overtime.

Another key to Wal-Mart's success is its use of information technology in merchandising and distribution and logistics. It uses a satellite system to communicate and transmit point-of-sale (POS) data through the store, supplier, and distribution network. A typical distribution center has an area of 1 million square feet, operates twenty-four hours a day by a staff of 750 employees, and serves 150 stores within a radius of two hundred miles. Wal-Mart supplies 80 percent of a store's needs through its distribution system, which uses a cross-docking system to reduce handling and inventory costs. A typical store receives deliveries almost every day, as one truck could resupply many stores on a single trip. Wal-Mart trucks pick up supplies from vendors on their way back, running at 60 percent of capacity on the backhaul. In 1993, Wal-Mart had a 1.1 percent advantage over its direct competitors due to its efficient distribution systems.

Wal-Mart's merchandise plans were developed centrally using data on SKU movements in the store and comparable information from its other stores in the market. Wal-Mart's promotional strategy of "every-day-low prices" offered customers well-known brands at prices lower than those at competing stores. Wal-Mart offered few promotions. It offered thirteen circulars annually compared to fifty to one hundred advertised circulars used by competitors to build store traffic at an estimated savings of more than 0.5 percent of sales.

Finally, vendor relationships were also a unique aspect of Wal-Mart's business model. As Wal-Mart developed its relationships with vendors such as Procter and Gamble, these relationships transformed into partnerships. Using electronic data interchange (EDI), vendors interacted with Wal-Mart electronically. They used EDI for receiving orders, forecasting, planning, replenishment, and shipping applications. Many key suppliers were given captainship of their categories and were responsible for vendor-managed inventory to replenish stocks and help deliver sales and profitability targets for the category as a whole. Wal-Mart spent 1.5 percent of sales on its information systems, significantly higher than many of its competitors did.

Wal-Mart's International Expansion

In 1991, thirty years after opening its first store in Rogers, Arkansas, Wal-Mart made its first entry into markets outside the United States. Wal-Mart entered Mexico when there were no other formidable international competitors. It started its international operations in Mexico by forming a partnership with CIFRA, the most successful Mexican retailer, which had sales of more than $5 billion in 1997. This expansion was viewed favorably by several analysts because of the promise of the North American Free Trade Agreement and the familiarity and demand for U.S. products, as many middle-class consumers had friends and relatives living in the United States. Although sales were down in 1993, Wal-Mart continued its international expansion by buying 122 Woolco stores in Canada, which it quickly converted into the Wal-Mart format. Despite initial doubts, the entry into Canada has been a smashing success by all accounts. Local competitors doubted Wal-Mart's ability to buy locally, run a hub-and-spoke distribution system in a country that is three thousand miles long and one hundred miles deep from the U.S. border, operate the Wal-Mart format in Woolco stores that were on two levels, and motivate service personnel to accept the Wal-Mart cheer.

Wal-Mart entered Latin America in 1992 when it opened its first store in Buenos Aires, Argentina. After the third store in Buenos Aires, Wal-Mart started opening stores in smaller cities in the interior of Argentina. In 1995, Wal-Mart entered Brazil through a joint venture and subsequent acquisition of Lojas Americanas. Latin America was the first region where cultural habits were different than in the United States, and local competitors included several well-established international players, such as Carrefour.

Wal-Mart entered these markets through the discount store format but also opened a few warehouse membership clubs. Wal-Mart's experience in Latin America has been quite a contrast to that in Mexico and Canada. CSFB estimates Wal-Mart sales in Argentina and Brazil for the year 2002 to be about $300 million and $500 million, respectively. These are small compared to the corresponding numbers for Carrefour of $4.6 billion and $4.3 billion. Wal-Mart's less-than-spectacular performance in Argentina has led to four overhauls of its top management in four years. Most of these problems are attributed to Wal-Mart's desire to make its model successful in Latin America without making too many adjustments. Don Bland, president and CEO of Argentina, was reported to be saying that "following our blueprint too closely wasn't a good idea."

Many believed Wal-Mart was arrogant in its approach to Latin America because it was slow to adapt to local tastes, and many irrelevant items in the merchandise offered reinforced this perception. Wal-Mart did not even respect the local differences inside the same city between low-income and high-income areas. It maintained the same type of assortments and pricing without distinctions. Even the store layout was considered too distant from local tastes and needs. It is believed that most of these problems were due to the centralized nature of decision making in company headquarters in Bentonville, Arkansas, an important component of Wal-Mart's formula for success to date. Most of the store layout decisions, assortments decisions, buying decisions, and pricing decisions seemed to be made at headquarters, with little scope for adaptation to the local markets in Latin America. Wal-Mart seemed to be relying more on its traditional formula for success, purchasing power, every-day-low pricing, customer service, state-of-the-art information systems, and sophisticated logistics and distribution systems.

In contrast to Canada and Mexico, Wal-Mart seemed to have met its match in Latin America in a fierce competitor. Carrefour, which had been in Latin America much longer and used decentralization as the bedrock of its success, was able to respond to Wal-Mart in a timely and effective manner. With respect to Wal-Mart's price advantages in other markets, Carrefour's prices were competitive and were often perceived as lower than those of Wal-Mart. Similarly, the every-day-low pricing strategy of Wal-Mart seemed to be misplaced in this market. Wal-Mart never really advertised or explained its message in Argentina. Given the promise that "nobody beats Carrefour at lower prices" and the fact that Carrefour had been delivering this message long before Wal-Mart entered these markets, the meaning of Wal-Mart's every-day-low pricing was lost on the customer. Last but not least, consumer attitudes toward shopping are significantly different from those in the United States and Canada. In developed markets, shopping is considered a chore, and therefore the every-day-low pricing is a great value proposition. In Latin America, shopping is perceived to be a social event: consumers tend to meet regularly and discuss and make recommendations to their friends and family. Price discounts contribute to this social experience. Every-day-low pricing therefore may not have the same appeal as in the developed countries.

Wal-Mart seems to be learning by doing and avoided making many of its earlier mistakes when it opened its store in La Plata, fifty miles southeast of Buenos Aires, in 1997. The aisles were wider than in the first few Buenos Aires stores, and the floor was made of scuff-resistant tile, not carpet. Metal displays for fish gave way to ceramic tile reminiscent of traditional Argentine fish markets. Wooden wine shelves with overhanging arbors replaced metal racks, a change that bolstered wine sales by 20 percent in other stores. Tailoring its La Plata store to the local tastes meant glazing doughnuts with dulce de leche, a local caramel confection. Clothing racks held more articles in medium sizes and fewer in large sizes. The chain even adopted some French touches by offering big supplies of croissants in the bakery department and tripe in the meat aisle. "Let's call it a tropicalized Wal-Mart way," said Cristian Corsi, an Argentine Wal-Mart district manager. With a Carrefour store just down the street in La Plata, Wal-Mart is able to keep a close eye on its competitor.

Despite all these changes, Wal-Mart had only 1.8 percent market share in Brazil in 2000, a distant sixth behind the leaders, Carrefour and a local chain Pao de Acucar, each with a 13.0 percent share. In Argentina, Wal-Mart has a share of 13.3 percent compared with 49.0 percent for Carrefour in sales through hypermarkets.

Since its expansion into Latin America, Wal-Mart has entered the United Kingdom through acquiring Asda and entered Germany by acquiring twenty-one Wertkauf and seventy-four Interspar stores. The Asda operation is believed to be doing much better than the German venture, where Wal-Mart has run into some difficulties as its pricing policies seem to have been adversely affected by the local German regulations (see Table 13.2 for Wal-Mart's history of global expansion).

Lessons Learned

The experiences of both Carrefour in Latin America and Wal-Mart in Mexico and Canada seem to confirm that international retail expansion is more likely to succeed if the retailer is the first to enter the foreign market. However, is it best to enter an international market through greenfield operations and not through a local partner, as Gielens and Dekimpe (2001) prescribed? While Carrefour's experience in Latin America may support this point of view, Wal-Mart's experience does not. To the contrary, its success in Canada and Mexico suggests otherwise. With respect to scale, it seems that greenfield operations scale up slowly, consistent with

Table 13.2. Wal-Mart's History of Global Expansion

Country	Date of Entry	Sales	Number of Supercenters
United States	1962		636
Canada	1994	5,673	
Germany	1998	2,458	95
United Kingdom	1999	15,300	229
Mexico	1991	9,448	62
Brazil	1995	439	14
Argentina	1995	300	13
China	1996	737	6
Korea	1998	347	5
International sales (millions)		35,485	

Source: Compiled from Wal-Mart company records.

market needs, while scale comes with a joint venture or an acquisition. Both companies have introduced formats that are new to the foreign market but familiar to the entrant.

What lessons can we draw from Carrefour and Wal-Mart's experiences? It seems that Gielens and Dekimpe's prescriptions (2001) are incomplete. They are incomplete to the extent that retailers do not always have the luxury of entering a foreign market first. Moreover, by definition, only one firm can enter a foreign market first. Hence, a central question that remains unanswered by the study is how an organization can succeed if it is not the first to enter a foreign market. These recommendations are also misplaced to the extent that retailers do not have a choice of entering first or second in a foreign market. When retailers decide to go international, they have two major decisions: which markets to enter and how to succeed in those markets. Gielens and Dekimpe suggest that firms should enter those markets where it is possible to be the first to do so, develop greenfield operations, operate at a sufficient scale, and transport a format that is known to the entrant and new to the market.

Our interpretation of the data (see Tables 13.1 and 13.2) leads us to a different set of conclusions. First, market attractiveness should be evaluated not in terms of the ability to enter first into the market but, instead, whether the market is in a state of early economic development for food retailers, as in Latin America in the 1970s or Asia in the 1990s, or well developed as in the case of Europe, Canada, and, to a lesser extent, Mexico. Markets are characterized as early in their economic development if the retail trade is not well organized, most of the retail trade is conducted by mom-and-pop shops, and there are few, if any, retail chains. One way of measuring the state of economic development may be through the market share of wholesalers as they play a key role in supplying the unorganized retail shops. The second criterion for evaluating markets should be the need for customization. If the customers in the foreign market are very different from the entrant's domestic market, the need for customization in terms of assortment, merchandising, pricing, service, and retail environment will be significant. This is the environment that both Carrefour and Wal-Mart faced in Latin America. However, Wal-Mart's need for customization was less salient in markets like Canada and Mexico.

The experiences of Wal-Mart and Carrefour suggest the following answer to the second issue: how to succeed in a foreign market. If a firm enters a developing market and the need for customization is high, the entrant is more likely to succeed through greenfield operations scaled up at a pace that is consistent with the economic development of the local market. This pace of expansion also provides the entrant enough opportunity to learn about the local market and develop the right format. If the need for customization in such a market is not as salient, the case can easily be made for scaling up faster to benefit from economies of size in the form of buying power, distribution, and logistics costs, as well as marketing costs. However, if the market is economically developed, as in the case of Canada and Mexico, it seems that the mode of entry is likely to be through acquisitions. This is because there are more likely to be entrenched competitors in a developed market and a potential entrant is less likely to find good store locations at an attractive price. Hence, greenfield operations may not be an option. Furthermore, in these markets, if the local operator is unable to compete with a foreign entrant, it is easier to find candidates for joint venture or acquisition at a reasonable price. Hence, it can be argued that if a firm is entering an economically developed market where the need for customization is not great, it should look for an acquisition that would give it a large footprint and all the benefits of economies of scale in a short amount of time. Not having the benefits of economies of scale will make it exceedingly difficult to compete with well-entrenched incumbents. In contrast, if the need for customization is high, there may be merits to a joint venture or an acquisition where the footprint or the scale of operations may or may not be of sufficient scale. This argument is driven by the need for and the amount of time it takes to learn about the local environment and adjust to working with a partner in a market that is significantly different from the entrant's domestic market. Thus, we present recommendations for how to succeed in Figure 13.1 below.

Wal-Mart's experiences in Canada, Mexico, Latin America, the United Kingdom, and Germany fit our recommendations well. Wal-Mart entered these markets when the retail market was well developed (although it was the first foreign retailer to enter Canada and Mexico) through joint ventures or acquisitions. Moreover, the joint

Figure 13.1. Entry Strategies Suggested by Carrefour and Wal-Mart's Experiences

| | Need for Customization | |
	High	Low
Developing Retail Market	Greenfield operations/scale up slowly	Greenfield operations can be scaled up fast
Developed Retail Market	Joint venture or acquisition (small or large operator)	Acquisition (preferably a large operator)

ventures or acquisitions in Canada, Mexico, and the United Kingdom have been much bigger in scale as compared to those in Latin America and Germany, where the need for customization can be argued to be significantly higher. In contrast, Carrefour expanded globally by entering foreign markets at an early phase in their economic development and chose to start with greenfield operations unless constrained by local regulations.

In summary, it seems that the real choice is whether to enter a foreign market, with the decisions about mode, scale, and timing of entry dictated by the state of economic development in the foreign market. With respect to the prescription that successful entrants offer a format that they are familiar with but is new to the foreign market, both Carrefour and Wal-Mart introduced familiar formats that were new to the foreign market.

This analysis has suggested that it is unclear that companies have real choices with respect to decisions regarding mode of entry, scale, and entering a market early or late. To the extent that companies are willing to learn and adapt and can do so at a low cost, they are more likely to succeed in markets that are at an early stage of economic development. But the key question for many retailers is whether they can succeed when entering a foreign market that is sufficiently mature and, if so, how they can do so. Since most retailers export the existing format to a new market when expanding internationally, the question can be rephrased as, Which format or strategy is more transportable to a new market?

Carrefour's strategy of decentralization and adaptation to the local market is its key strength and therefore is transportable. However, the magnitude of its success in a particular market will be dictated by the nature of the existing competition in the well-developed market. In Brazil alone, despite its early entry, it shares the lead in market share with a strong Brazilian competitor, Pao de Acucur. In contrast, Carrefour has achieved an enviable 49 percent market share in Argentina because there are no dominant local competitors. Hence, Carrefour's retailing concept is most transportable to markets with a high need for customization that are in an early phase of economic development. It is hard to imagine the possibility of developing markets that would not need significant customization.

Wal-Mart, in contrast, has tried to export its concept built around economic efficiency with limited success to date. Its goal is to be the lowest-cost operator in the market by leveraging its strategy based on every-day-low pricing, effective use of information, and efficient distribution and logistics. While many industry experts believe that Wal-Mart's difficulties lie in its lack of desire to adapt and continue with centralized control of its operation from its U.S. headquarters, its experience in Latin America presents a different perspective. In expanding to a new market, the goal of a retail model based on economic efficiency is to replicate the customer experience at a given price point in a different economic, cultural, and social environment. The challenge for Wal-Mart is to determine whether the sources of economic efficiency gained through better use of information technology, efficient distribution and logistics, and every-day low prices can continue to deliver a unique value proposition in the new environment. Transporting information technology often seems easier than it is. In order to use the information technology in Brazil, Wal-Mart needed to accomplish two goals: capture the information that is relevant to the local market and make good use of the decision rules developed at its U.S. headquarters. Given the lack of presence of people in Wal-Mart who speak both English and Portuguese and are familiar with both the U.S. and Brazilian environments, it has taken Wal-Mart a long time to modify the systems to capture information specific to the local market. Furthermore, it has taken even longer for managers in Brazil and the United States to understand and use the decision-making tools that were developed in the United States and have to be customized for the foreign market. Thus, transporting information systems into a new economic, social, and legal infrastructure often takes longer than expected, and whether they are successful is never apparent until they are actually in the market. The same is true of distribution and logistics.

Clearly, the challenges of setting up efficient systems without an efficient scale of operations in Brazil are enormous for Wal-Mart. These challenges are complicated by the need to adapt to the local market. To the extent that Wal-Mart tried to figure a way to implement its strategy successfully in Brazil, it was not able to focus on the needs of the local consumers, who perceived the resulting assortments and merchandising as more American than Brazilian. Companies transporting retail models based on economic efficiency therefore often find themselves losing significant amounts of money and generating bad press in the initial phases of their entry into a new market. It is often difficult to forecast the success rate of these adventures. Wal-Mart's Canadian competitors expected that Wal-Mart would fail in its entry into Canada because it was not expected to customize its offerings sufficiently, but Wal-Mart's operations in Canada are anything but a failure. All elements of its strategy, use of better information systems, efficient distribution and logistics, every-day-low prices, and better in-store service have been key to its success in Canada and Mexico. Hence, one might conclude that Wal-Mart's retail concept based on achieving economic efficiency and therefore staking a claim to be the lowest-cost operator is more transportable to markets that do not have as much need for customization and are further along in economic development. Their short-term success is likely to vary depending on the need for customization. In markets requiring significant customization due to the unique taste and preferences of the local population, it is likely to lose money in the short run; economic success in the short run is more ensured in markets with less need to customize. Wal-Mart's successes in Mexico, Canada, and the United Kingdom compared to its difficulties in Latin America and Germany, where the need to customize may be higher, again lend support to our hypothesis.

In summary, the Carrefour model is more likely to succeed in developing markets, and Wal-Mart is more likely to succeed in developed markets, although it may not be profitable in the short run in markets with a high need for customization. Hence, the choice of foreign markets to enter is likely to be dictated by the format exported by the global retailer. Now we turn to our third observation. How does Ahold's global expansion relate to our conclusions from Carrefour and Wal-Mart?

Royal Ahold NV

The most distinguishing characteristic of Ahold's strategy to its international expansion is its sole reliance on joint venture and acquisitions.[3] Whereas Carrefour and Wal-Mart enter new foreign markets by exporting the familiar hypermarket and discount stores concepts that were new to the foreign market, Ahold has expanded by joint venturing and acquiring a large number of companies in different parts of the world without focusing on a single format. In this way, it provides a direct contrast to Carrefour and Wal-Mart in that it does not follow the recommendations of Gielens and Dekimpe (2001).

Royal Ahold NV started with humble beginnings in 1887 when Albert Heijn took over his father's grocery store in Zandam, Netherlands. The 130-square-foot store sold many things, including groceries, wooden shoes, liquor, dredging nets, and tar. The operation grew to twenty-three stores within ten years. Private label products emerged as early as 1911 when Heijn started baking cookies in the kitchen of an old mansion that were sold under the Albert Heijn name. In 1948, the company was listed on the Amsterdam Stock Exchange, and the store count had risen to 65 by 1951 with the purchase of the Van Amerongen grocery chain. In 1955, Albert Heijn opened its first self-service supermarket in Rotterdam, and the popular format expanded quickly to a chain of 100 supermarkets by 1955. One hundred years since its inception, Albert Heijn stores were the leading grocery store chain in the Netherlands, with a market share of 27.7 percent and a network of over 560 stores.

Ahold started its international expansion as early as 1977 when it acquired the BI-LO chain of stores in the eastern United States. Four years later, it made its second acquisition in the United States, with the purchase of Giant Food stores. The third acquisition in the United States was that of First National Supermarkets in 1988. Ahold made a clear distinction between two types of market opportunities in its international expansion: mature and growth opportunities. Mature markets were defined as those with high supermarket concentration and low growth in purchase power, and growth markets as those with low supermarket concentration and high growth in purchase power.

With respect to mature markets, Ahold believed that many U.S. food retailers would be good acquisition opportunities because they were not big enough to benefit from economies of scale in distribution and logistics, information systems, marketing, and manufacture of private label. Ahold's strategy was to leave the consumer interface unchanged and improve the back end to provide for more efficient operations. Hence, it identified regional chains with good management talent as good candidates for acquisition. In the late 1980s and 1990s, many family-owned U.S. chains were struggling with issues of family succession and the minimum scale of operations required to remain competitive in a fast-changing retail landscape increasingly dominated by Wal-Mart. Many of these chains wanted to continue their legacy and were proud of the management they selected to run their operations and the relationships they had built within their communities. These chains had a good fit with the acquisition goals of Ahold. Stores with strong management talent, a strong position in their local market, and potential synergies with Ahold's existing holdings became the focus of their international expansion strategy.

As of 2002, Royal Ahold NV also owned Stop & Shop, Tops Markets, Giant Food, and Bruno's supermarkets and had established a strong presence on the eastern seaboard of the United States. Total sales from U.S. retail operations were $23 billion in 2001.

Supermarket penetration and growth in purchasing power were very different in the growth markets of Asia, Latin America, and eastern Europe. While supermarket penetration in the United States was around 80 percent, many parts of Asia had a supermarket penetration of less than 1 percent. "Half of the people around the world have never seen a decent supermarket in their lives," observed Cees van der Hoeven, CEO of Royal Ahold. Growth in purchasing power was expected to be no more than 2 to 3 percent in the United States and almost stagnant in Europe. In contrast, markets in Asia were expected to grow at a rate of 6 to 8 percent, markets in Latin America at a rate of 3 to 4 percent, and eastern Europe at 4 to 6 percent a year. Recognizing the difficulties in entering these markets from an operational and strategic viewpoint, Ahold decided to pursue these markets as joint ventures with local partners. Ahold needed a local partner not only to gain a good understanding of local consumers but also to procure good locations and good management talent in these markets that were often not the most cooperative with foreign entrants.

Partners in these developing countries often had plenty of capital and manpower but lacked supermarket expertise. Joint ventures in Asia and Latin America brought together the local knowledge of real estate and local business practices with Ahold's functional expertise. Ahold used a structured market analysis to identify potential partners. Beginning with the board identifying a region of interest, a report was prepared for each country in the region on growth potential, political stability and risk, economic currency stability and risk, concentration of population centers, and retail infrastructure. Ultimately, the most critical factor in assessing potential partners was management skill and culture. Ahold was prepared to wait as long as it took to find the right partners.

Ahold's expansion in southern and eastern Europe has been through joint ventures in Portugal, Poland, and Spain and through a fully owned subsidiary in the Czech Republic. Ahold has also expanded into Latin America, again through joint ventures and operations. Argentina, Brazil, Chile, and Guatemala contributed $4.7 billion euros toward the worldwide sales of 66 billion euros in 2001. Ahold's expansion plans in Asia have been no different. Its operations in China, Indonesia, Malaysia, Singapore, and Thailand are also based on joint ventures but with a distinct strategy of rolling out the Tops and BI-LO formats that are adapted to the local country needs (see Table 13.3 for Ahold's sales and international expansion).

To some extent, Ahold's strategy can be seen as the result of the environment created by the entry of large global retailers in a particular foreign market. In many foreign markets, as in Argentina, the entry of a large global retailer like Wal-Mart or Carrefour creates a more difficult environment for the local retail chains.

Table 13.3. Ahold's History of Global Expansion

Country	Date of Entry	Sales (billions of dollars)	Number of Outlets	EBIT
Europe		21.80		0.87
Netherlands	1897	9.80	2,300	
Belgium				
Spain	1996	2.00	623	
Portugal	1996	1.60	200	
Poland	1996	0.55	146	
Czech	1996	0.80	200	
Northern Europe	1999	7.00	3,000	
United States	1977	23.2	1,313	1.28
Central Ameria	1999	1.40	260	
Latin America		4.90		0.203
Brazil	1996	2.00	110	
Argentina	1996	2.10	235	
Chile	1998	0.80	96	
Asia		0.40	104	−0.018
China (closed in 1999)	1996			
Thailand	1996	0.29	41	
Malaysia	1996	0.09	39	
Indonesia		0.03	21	

These local chains, like Disco in Argentina, face a more uncertain future because they have neither the scale nor the expertise of a global retailer, and they sometimes lack the financial wherewithal to compete effectively against giants like Carrefour and Wal-Mart. The chains therefore look for partners that can infuse capital to strengthen and modernize their stores and operations to compete effectively in an increasingly competitive environment. Ahold looks for such opportunities, and its success depends mainly on the price it pays for acquiring such assets and the quality of local management. Given that Ahold does not intend to change any aspect of the operation that concerns the consumer and offers expertise in the back office, it can implement this strategy without being wedded to a specific format. Thus, the key to Ahold's success lies in timing the market: the ability to make the right acquisition at the right price.

Another interesting fact that seems to jump out is that while Carrefour always seems to enter the market early, Wal-Mart enters when it has sufficiently developed, and Ahold seems to enter last. This causes us to wonder whether there is freedom in choosing the markets to enter for these firms. One interpretation of the facts might be that since Carrefour began operations as early as 1963 and the regulatory environment in France became less conducive to growth as early as 1970, Carrefour was forced to look for markets outside France if it were to grow further. Many markets at that time were in the early phase of economic development, and since Carrefour's strategy is to adapt the hypermarket concept to the local environment with the help of decentralized decision making, it has been successful in its international expansion. Wal-Mart saw huge opportunities in the domestic market and therefore did not see a need to grow internationally until 1995. Its sales reached $82 billion, significantly higher than Carrefour's sales of $69 billion today, before it ventured outside its domestic market. Hence, it can be concluded that food retailers in the United States look for international growth much later than European retailers do and therefore are likely to enter an international market later in its development cycle as compared to the European retailers. Compounded with the pattern that most U.S. retailers expanding internationally seem to be exporting a format based on economic efficiency as compared to the European retailers, which are adapting their formats to offer a compelling value proposition based on adapting the format to local tastes, it seems that even the pattern of entry in various international markets and mode of entry and the subsequent decisions can be explained by country of origin with the propensity toward economic efficiency in the U.S. formats.

This observation might also explain the difficulty U.S. retailers have had in succeeding internationally. For retailers expanding late in the economic development of the market and only after exploring the limits to growth in a big market like the United States, the pressure on delivering sales and profitability results from international operations is likely to be more severe for U.S. retailers. This pressure results in a desire to show good performance in the short run, and if the dominant retail format exported by U.S. retailers is based on economic efficiency, U.S. retailers are likely to stick to their knitting before concluding the need for local adaptation to make the international venture successful.

Conclusion

If it is safe to believe that American retailers are likely to export formats based on economic efficiency and are likely to enter a foreign market late in its development cycle after exhausting the opportunities for growth available in the huge domestic market. If they are late in entering a foreign market, they are most likely to succeed in markets where the need for customization of the format is not extensive and the mode of entry is through a joint venture or an acquisition. They may also be successful in developed markets where the need for customization is significant, but it is likely to take much longer as the costs of adjusting the format in these circumstances can be expensive and hence are likely to be unprofitable in the short run. If it is safe to believe that European retailers are more likely to export retail formats that add value by catering to the needs and tastes of the local market, they are likely to enter foreign markets that are developing and are likely to scale up profitably, keeping pace with the economic development of the market place. It is indeed surprising that country of origin can shed so much light on the global expansion of Carrefour, Wal-Mart, and Royal Ahold.

PART 7

Setting the Global Agenda

The 1990s was a period of unprecedented growth for multinational corporations. The fall of the Berlin Wall and its aftermath released hundreds of millions of consumers from behind the iron curtain into the free market system. American multinationals in particular were quick to establish beachheads in the newly emerging economies, leveraging the United States's vast pool of capital to pick off the best local partners, acquire the best local firms, and exploit first-mover advantages. Consumers in these markets eagerly snapped up the formerly forbidden fruit of Western brands. There was no time, and perhaps no need, to adapt products or marketing approaches to local needs. And most certainly, there was little interest in figuring out how to penetrate further down the socioeconomic spectrum in these emerging economies; the key was to gain a foothold with the existing product line at the top end of each market. Finally, in the case of technology products, the full focus of research and development had to be on designing the next-generation product. There were no resources to customize the existing generation to fit local needs more closely.

During this period, the emphasis in multinational corporations was on centralized marketing of standard products worldwide. Many companies reduced the power of their country general managers or dispensed with them altogether in favor of regional structures or global strategic business units. Country subsidiaries, formerly independent and run by politically well-connected local managers, were often cut back to nothing more than sales and distribution offices. Not all multinationals made these mistakes; Nestlé

313

of Switzerland stayed the course, maintaining its longstanding decentralized approach. But many multinationals lost their humility and their local sensitivity during this period.

As the 1990s progressed, criticisms of globalization gained strength. Although trade barriers were falling, as a result of agreements such as the North Atlantic Free Trade Association, smaller developing economies seemed to be losing ground while richer countries appeared to be becoming ever wealthier. Although low-cost workforces in emerging economies were manufacturing sneakers for virtual corporations like Nike, these economies were said to be capturing precious little of the value added. For example, the *maquiladora* system, which permitted American companies to have their products assembled by low-cost Mexican labor, gave Mexico a huge increase in high-tech exports, but the value added was only 2.7 percent. After ten years of hearing about the virtues of trickle-down globalization but seeing no results, Third World political leaders such as Mahathir Mohammed of Malaysia, supported by international nongovernment organizations, began to protest. The Asian financial crisis of the late 1990s highlighted the fragile foundation on which the uncertain prosperity of the developing world was being built. The worldwide economic recession at the start of twenty-first century, the debt overhang confronting many emerging economies, and corporate scandals in the United States and elsewhere fueled further debate over the benefits of globalization.

Many multinationals got the message, reaching out again to local business partners for advice on how to adapt marketing programs to respond to local tastes and preferences in order to penetrate further into local country markets. Others acquired and relaunched local brands after improving product quality. More authority was again delegated to local managers. Increasing emphasis was placed on being a good local citizen through the use of local raw materials, employment of local managers, and even sponsorship of local soccer teams. Paradoxically, the future of global marketing appeared to be in being more local than global. Douglas Daft, chief executive of Coca Cola Company, captured the mood swing in March 2000, pronouncing that the company's approach was henceforth, "Think local, act local."

In Chapter Fourteen, Daniel Litvin examines the flawed policies of four multinationals, two historical examples and two (Shell and Nike) from modern times, in managing political and governmental relations. Whether because world headquarters was disinterested in local problems or because their local managers were unable or unwilling to communicate the seriousness of the situations that were brewing, these organizations all suffered long-term reputational and business consequences as a result of not responding adequately or promptly. Litvin questions whether corporate social responsibility initiatives, launched by Nike and Shell in the wake of these public relations disasters, are sufficiently robust and linked to management reward systems.

V. Kasturi Rangan and Arthur McCaffrey conclude the book in Chapter Fifteen by noting that the 3 billion people in the world who have to survive on less than two dollars a day know little of the globalization of markets and are far from participating in the "convergent commonality" that was the focus of Levitt's 1983 article. These authors go beyond the obvious suggestions to multinationals of strategic philanthropy and marketing stripped-down basic products in smaller packages to be more affordable. Instead, they offer a three-part ethic of engagement covering sustainable development, principled investment, and market construction to guide multinationals in their approach to the world's poor.

It remains to be seen in the twenty-first century how many multinationals will embrace broader responsibilities beyond merely increasing short-term shareholder value. Given their size and power relative to the size of most of the world's country economies, their leaders should respond to these challenges.

CHAPTER 14

The Empire Strikes Flak
Powerful Companies and Political Backlash
Daniel Litvin

Giants really do stalk the world, and most of creation trembles.
KIRKPATRICK SALE

In current debates about globalization, the image of Western-based multinational companies as politically powerful, controlling giants has become embedded in the public imagination. Large companies are often assumed to be clever, if not cunning, in their ability to manipulate governments and societies to serve their own commercial ends. This is believed to be particularly true when they operate in developing countries where their profits may dwarf the size of local economies.

This chapter tests this assumption by briefly examining a handful of examples of highly powerful, or at least publicly controversial, multinationals: two from past centuries (the English East India Company and the British South Africa Company) and two from the present (Royal Dutch/Shell and Nike). It focuses on these companies' attempts to anticipate, and to manage to their advantage, the social and political context in which they have operated in poorer parts of the world.

The chapter finds that these companies have in fact struggled to a surprising degree, given their size and resources, to manage such political pressures. In this sense, they appear more like clumsy, partially sighted giants than all-powerful ones.

The evidence also suggests that both in past centuries and currently, the Western opponents of such large companies (or anti-globalization activists, to use a modern phrase) have often tended to focus their attention on issues that appear important from a Western perspective rather than on the concerns that are most important to local people. Those scrutinizing the companies from the West, in other words, would appear to be partially sighted too.

The four examples, as well as the overall findings, are drawn from "Empires of Profit: Commerce, Conquest and Corporate" (Litvin, 2003), a more in-depth examination of the political record of and activism surrounding Western multinationals in poor countries. "Empires of Profit" looks at a larger sample of powerful companies through history and analyzes each in more detail than is provided here. Among the other companies it examines, for example, are United Fruit, the American banana multinational whose political machinations in Central America in the early twentieth century helped give rise to the term *banana republic,* and the various large American energy firms that ran Saudi Arabia's oil industry from the 1930s to the 1970s. In this sense, this chapter provides a snapshot of the themes and material of this broader work.

Before moving on to the examples, a few further points of context may be helpful. How, for example, does this chapter fit into the general discussion in this book about Levitt's article? Clearly, the subject matter is somewhat different: the focus here is the management of political pressures by big companies rather their marketing strategies. Nonetheless, a general criticism that has often been made against Levitt's article in recent years—that he overstated the case for standardized global products and management processes—parallels neatly the evidence on political pressures presented here. Just as companies have found that to thrive commercially they must be sensitive both to global and local dynamics and to local variations in consumer preferences, so the complexity and variability of the social and political contexts in which they operate across the world mean that any global, standardized management response to these political pressures is bound to be too crude for the task at hand.

One of the reasons the companies examined here have behaved like clumsy giants is indeed partly because of the sheer complexity of the pressures they have faced. Even managers with a high degree of political skill and cunning might have found the situations described difficult to deal with. But another reason is management failure—the repeated failure of the corporate headquarters, for example, to understand and control what managers in poor countries do and the repeated use of simplistic management techniques.

An interesting question is whether the set of management tactics that today goes under the name of corporate social responsibility is an example of such an overly simplistic response. The examples of Shell and Nike certainly suggest this is the case. This question is explored as well in the last section of this chapter on management lessons.

Finally, it should be emphasized that the overall aim of the chapter, as of "Empires of Profit," is not to draw a moral judgment about the multinationals examined, that is, not to conclude whether overall they were good or bad for the societies in which they invested. It is rather to sketch as objectively as possible their social and political interactions to see if any patterns can be detected through history.

Of course, there are vast differences between the historical periods. The companies of the imperial era, in particular, were far more willing than modern firms to use naked force to overcome local resistance to their activities. However, some striking patterns through time are apparent: the way in which the companies have repeatedly fumbled their political interactions and also the recurring Western bias of many of their critics. It is these patterns that will be highlighted in the following sections.

The English East India Company

One of the earliest, and certainly among the most extraordinary, multinational companies the world has ever seen, the English East India Company began life in 1600 as a small trading concern. Run from offices in Leadenhall Street in the City of London, it evolved over time into a major territorial power. By the mid-nineteenth century, it was in charge of government of the entire Indian subcontinent and numerous other colonies besides. This shift was reflected in the composition of the company's revenues over time. For the first century and a half of the company's existence, these came primarily from trading a broad range of commodities, including tea, cotton, silks, and spices, between Asia, England, and elsewhere. From the 1750s onward, however, taxation of the Indian population became an increasing proportion of its revenues, and the administration of India swallowed up much its expenses.

The reason that the company evolved in this way from a trader to a governing power was partly political turmoil in the region in which it was operating, a situation with parallels to that experienced by foreign investors in the more unstable developing countries today (even if their response is typically rather different). In the case of the East India Company, it was the decline during the eighteenth century of the Mughal empire, which once ruled much of the Indian subcontinent, and the fragmentation of this imperial state into a series of smaller principalities and kingdoms, often warring with each other, that helped draw the company into local political disputes. Already an influential economic presence in the region, the company was seen by some Indian rulers as an ally and by others as an enemy, and hence it became embroiled in local military conflicts. Conquering territory by territory and over the space of a century, it thus ended up acquiring ownership of India.

Perhaps inevitably, the company eventually became unpopular among many Indians as a governing power. Local anger erupted in the Great Indian Rebellion of 1857–1858, which began when Indians serving in the company's own army mutinied. The revolt was quashed. But shortly after, the British government decided to take over the job of ruling India from the East India Company, thus effectively nationalizing the centuries-old corporation. The rebellion had raised serious doubts in the minds of British politicians as to whether such a private sector entity could be trusted to continue the delicate task of colonial rule.

That is a potted overview of the company's long and fascinating history. Its story also contains some early examples of anticorporate activism. Indeed, centuries before the emergence of the modern antiglobalization movement in the West, there was pressure from activists in Britain over the East India Company's behavior in India. But as with (it will be argued) the Western pressure surrounding many modern companies, the British critics of East India Company adopted a Western-centric perspective, disconnected from what are likely to have been the concerns of Indians.

One of most popular complaints in Britain against the company, for example, concerned the behavior of its managers who had enriched themselves through corruption in India (and embezzlement and private trade among these expatriates in India was indeed legion). What appeared particularly to annoy many British people, however, was the way in which these nouveau riche company men (who became known as nabobs, a corruption of *nawab,* the Indian word for Mughal governor) came back to England, some of them buying up country estates and even parliamentary seats. The effect of their corruption on the Indian people seems to have been less of an issue.

Admittedly, at a later stage in Britain, there was more explicit public pressure on the company to behave "ethically" in India. But interestingly, it was this that actually helped provoke Indians' anger. The period in question was the early nineteenth century, when the company was encouraged by the British government and others at home more actively to impose British values in India. Previously, the company's managers had been content simply to trade with Indians or at least to take taxes from them, without significant cultural imposition. Christianity, the English language, British legal principles: all now as a result began to be inculcated by the British in India with greater vigor. This was one of the reasons (albeit not the only one) for the Indian rebellion against the company's rule in 1857—that is, "ethical" reforms that the British had assumed Indians would welcome gratefully were seen by them as riding roughshod over their culture and traditions.

The East India Company certainly developed over time into a hugely powerful force in India. So in what way can it be said to have fumbled its political interactions? The answer is, the stark sense that its invasion in India was in part a management accident. In general, the instructions issued by the company's directors in London to its officers on the ground were that they should engage only in peaceful trade. Yet these instructions were often ignored by local managers, men such as Robert Clive (or Clive of India), who had a stronger appetite for war and political maneuvering than for commerce—and who found themselves in their element in unstable, post–Mughal India. The long time lag in communication between London and India made it difficult for directors to prevent such independent-minded behavior: wars and territorial acquisition were often reported back to them as faits accomplis.

The process of the company's invasion of India was thus largely that of local officers becoming embroiled in fights with Indian princes (Clive's battle with Siraj-ud-daula, the Indian ruler of Bengal, at Plassey in 1757 was only the first and most famous of these local conflicts). And it occurred not so much because it was willed by the corporate headquarters, but because the headquarters failed to understand and control the local situation.

Perhaps predictably, the invasion proved unsatisfactory from a commercial perspective (as well as being ethically dubious). The wars themselves cost the company money, as did administering the new territories, and the tax revenues the company was able to raise from the local population in the new domains often turned out to be less than had been anticipated. Partly as a result, the company came close to bankruptcy at various points after 1750. The political clumsiness of this particular giant cost it dearly.

The British South Africa Company

This London-based multinational conquered swathes of overseas territory for the British empire. Dating from 1880s, it was run by Cecil Rhodes, the megalomaniac tycoon who also had a role in the early history of De Beers, the company that still today dominates the world trade in diamonds. The British South Africa Company was Rhodes's vehicle for acquiring supplies of another precious mineral: gold. It was believed at the time that the lands of the Matabele and Shona people (the region covering present-day Zimbabwe) sat on large reserves of gold. Rhodes triumphed in a race against commercial interests allied with various other imperial powers (all part of Europe's so-called scramble for Africa), to secure control of these lands from the native population.

He achieved this in the typical style of the times: either by bribing local chieftains (among them was Lobengula, the once-feared king of the Matabele) to give his company access to the minerals under their land or, if local rulers proved eventually to be uncooperative, as did Lobengula, to wage wars against them and invade their territory. (Lobengula met his end in 1893, committing suicide following the defeat of his warriors by the company's army.) In such conflicts, it helped that Rhodes's soldiers had Maxim machine guns, while the Africans attempting to defend themselves were often armed merely with spears.

At a later stage—in a parallel with the experience of the East India Company following its conquest of India—there was a local rebellion against the British South Africa Company's rule. In 1896, both the Matabele and Shona people took up arms and tried to evict the company (together with the European settlers it had brought with it) from their lands. As with the Great Indian Rebellion, however, the revolt was eventually quashed and British rule reasserted.

The story of Rhodes's company also contains an illustration of early Western anticorporate activism focusing on issues disconnected from the reality on the ground. There were certainly various British-based groups critical or suspicious of the British South Africa Company; among them was the Aborigines Protection Society, devoted to upholding the welfare of the native races. But the key issues, in the view of most such campaigners, were combating slavery, preventing the spread of alcoholism among Africans, and introducing Christianity. The sheer brutality of Rhodes's treatment of the Matabele and Shona appears to have sparked comparatively limited attention.

In fact, Rhodes was often able to respond to Western "ethical" pressures, and sometimes even turn them to his advantage, without compromising his freedom of maneuver in Africa. The British South Africa Company's charter, for example, committed the company to combat the slave trade and prevent the sale of "intoxicating liquor to the natives." The latter commitment was certainly no problem for the company given that drunken Africans would be less productive as mine laborers. To win support from the British public, the company also sent an official representative to a major antislavery conference in Brussels in 1889–1890, where it supported tougher regulation. In London in 1889, meanwhile, Rhodes had tried to advance his claim over Nyasaland (present-day Malawi), another territory over which he had ambitions, by offering to help clear Arab slave traders from the region.

In terms of the management lapse illustrated by the story of the British South Africa Company, it should have been relatively apparent to Rhodes and his managers that they were little liked by the Matabele and Shona, yet they notably failed to anticipate the rebellion of 1896. There were ample reasons for discontent among the Africans: not only had much of the their best land and cattle been appropriated by white settlers; they had also became subject to a widely despised "hut tax" under the company's rule, as well as to the rough justice of the company's police.

Admittedly, given the complex and shifting nature of African tribal society, keeping track of local sentiment would never have been an easy task for the company. But Rhodes and his managers not only made little effort in this respect; they were deluded about local sentiment, convincing themselves the Africans were pleased to have them there because of the economic stability the company brought and because, at least as they saw it, tyrants like Lobengula were no longer in charge. The following excerpt from a letter sent by one of the settlers to his mother shortly before the rebellion erupted illustrates the degree of ignorance among the British about the political context in which they were operating: "There was a rumour of a possible rising among some of the tribes . . . but that was of course all moon-shine. . . . The natives are happy, comfortable and prosperous and the future must be magnificent" (Thomas, 1996, p. 306).

A month later, the natives were spearing and slaughtering many of the whites and their families. Although the revolt was eventually quashed, this was not without cost to the company, as well as loss of life on both sides. A powerful multinational, in short, had once again shown itself to be politically blinkered, with disastrous consequences.

Two Modern Multinationals

An examination of two modern multinationals, Nike and Shell, whose operations in developing countries have provided the focus of some of the loudest protests by the antiglobalization movement in recent years, reveals interestingly similar patterns to the two case studies from history, as well as the inevitable differences given the centuries that have elapsed.

Nike

Nike has attracted major criticism in the West over the past decade regarding alleged labor abuses in its supply chain, particularly in the contract export factories in Asia from which it buys many of its sneakers and apparel. In the 1990s, Western unions and human rights activists accused these factories, and Nike by implication, of numerous ethical lapses, including employing children, paying low wages, and using harsh physical punishments against misbehaving workers. In certain cases, these criticisms were founded. And in terms of low wages, it was true that for a pair of Nike shoes retailing in the West for, say, $120, employees in a poor Asian counties might receive just $2 a day, a gap that certainly appeared stark in the eyes of many liberal-minded Westerners.

In this sense, Nike became a symbol for Western activists of everything that in their eyes was wrong with Western consumer culture: the exploitation of workers, for example, overconsumption of material goods, and a reliance on branding and advertising rather than the intrinsic value of products. Importantly, however, as in centuries past, the Western activists were still often focusing on different issues from those most important to local people.

True, instances of physical punishment and exploitation of children were clearly important to the victims concerned and ought to be considered inexcusable in any part of the world, rich or poor. But missing from the accounts of many of the Western activists was an understanding of the broader social and economic context for workers in developing countries—the fact, for example, that the growth of jobs in export factories in Asia, such as those that sell shoes to Nike, has assisted many families to lift themselves out of poverty and that the wages paid, however low by Western standards, are often considered attractive locally.

Factory work has also assisted the empowerment of women in many tradition-bound Asian societies, a point little noted by Western activists. The Asian export factories are similar in this sense to the sweatshops of industrial revolution Britain. But however grim the working conditions in countries such as Bangladesh, these factories are providing the first opportunity for women to gain paid employment outside their homes, and hence the control of their husbands, a trend that the women themselves often view favorably.

The British academic Naila Kabeer (2000) has done some interesting research on this issue.

In a similar vein, there are examples of Western boycotts against goods made by child labor that actually harm the interests of children. The threat of one such boycott by the United States in the 1990s, for example, led to the firing of some fifty thousand children from export garment factories in Bangladesh as local factory owners sought to uphold foreign demand for their goods. Research showed that many of these children went on to more hazardous jobs, including scavenging for waste, breaking bricks, and street hawking (Clean Clothes Campaign, 1998). Poverty had originally driven these children into the labor market, and little had been done to fix this underlying problem.

Nike's story reveals as well another example of corporate management struggling to manage the complex political context of their business and, at least at first, walking half-blind into problems that should have been possible to predict. When the criticism regarding alleged labor abuses in its contract factories first arose in the 1990s, Nike appears to have been poorly informed itself about the actual conditions on these factories. It was paying its Asian contractors to make shoes and apparel without monitoring in much detail how they treated their workers. Given the interest of Western unions in stemming the loss of jobs to Asia and also the interest of Western activists in targeting high-profile companies such as Nike, the company's managers ought arguably to have foreseen that public attention soon would be directed toward precisely the issue of working conditions in its supply chain.

Later in the 1990s, as a result of all the public pressure, Nike focused considerable attention on upholding labor standards among its suppliers, much more so indeed than most other Western multinationals. As well as issuing a code of conduct, for example, it hired a small army of labor monitors to check that factories are treating workers fairly. It signed numerous external initiatives promoting corporate social responsibility (CSR) such as the United Nation's Global Compact. It also became an enthusiast for stakeholder dialogue. This a popular tactic among firms wanting to prove their CSR credentials and is premised on the idea that by consulting with activists, unions, and other groups, companies can develop a broad public consensus in their favor.

Interestingly, however, while public criticism of Nike has diminished to a degree, damaging attacks on the company's reputation, and hence brand, have continued sporadically. One of the problems is that the CSR tactics that Nike initially adopted may have been too simplistic for the complex task at hand. A number of times since 2000, for example, the company has been taken by surprise by revelations in the media or from nongovernmental organizations (NGOs) and other groups of continuing abuses in some of its factories, including the discovery of more child workers, for example, and complaints of harassment by women employees. Nike's own team of labor monitors had failed to detect these abuses.

Nike's global supply chain, like that of many other modern multinationals, is large and complex, comprising not just many suppliers but many suppliers of each these suppliers, and so on. Even if Nike labor monitors paid daily visits to all of these factories, this would not guarantee their compliance with its code of conduct (harassment of employees, for example, can be particularly difficult to detect by such outsiders). Nike's labor monitoring system thus may need to become more elaborate and sophisticated to succeed in this respect. Also, however much stakeholder dialogue the company conducts, its high-profile brand and reliance on low-cost labor from the developing world are likely to attract Western unions and activists eager to unearth further examples of alleged exploitation.

These are some of the complexities of the social and political pressures faced by modern multinationals that will be touched on again in the next sections. For now, however, it is enough to note that Nike's management, in spite of its recent efforts, continues to face challenges aplenty in this area.

Shell in Nigeria

As one of the world's biggest oil companies, Royal Dutch/Shell, the Anglo-Dutch multinational, has attracted public attention on a number of social and environmental issues in a variety of different countries. In the mid-1990s, its operations in Nigeria, where it is the largest foreign investor in the country's oil industry, became a particular rallying point for the antiglobalization movement, just as did Nike's labor practices around the same period. This is why Shell's Nigerian activities provide the focus of this final case study.

Complaints had been rumbling among campaign groups for some time about the company's environmental record and alleged complicity in human rights abuses in the Niger Delta, the region of Nigeria where the oil reserves are concentrated. These exploded into an international controversy in 1995 when the Nigerian government (then run by the dictator Sani Abacha) executed Ken Saro Wiwa, an anti-Shell activist and representative of the Ogoni people, one of the numerous ethnic groups living in the delta. Shell was accused, fairly or unfairly, of being guilty by association. In Western countries, campaigners produced posters of its logo dripping with blood.

Whatever the rights and wrongs of Shell's actions during this period (and although not all the criticisms against it were merited, it clearly had not exerted as much pressure as it might have done to dissuade the Nigerian government from executing Saro-Wiwa), the relationship between Western criticisms against the company and the concerns of local people was not simple either. For while the Western campaign groups focused on the alleged environmental and human rights outrages, what was driving local anger at least as much was an issue that surfaced relatively little in the Western media and Western political debates: the question of how Nigeria's oil revenues should be distributed between different ethnic groups and different parts of the country.

The ethnic groups living in the Delta had long complained—with some justification, given their crushing poverty—that they received few economic benefits from the oil pumped from under their land. Nigeria's federal government had long distributed the oil revenues down lines of political patronage, which saw little trickling back to these local communities.

It was not until the emergence on the political scene of Ken Saro-Wiwa, however, that these local grievances gained international attention. And one of the reasons was that Saro-Wiwa, an astute and media-savvy political operator, understood that the way to gain the attention of Western audiences and NGOs was to emphasize the environmental, human rights, and anticorporate grievances of the Delta communities—issues, in other words, that resonated with the suspicions of many Westerners as to the behavior and impact of their powerful corporations. In this way, a complex political dispute over distribution of oil revenues within Nigeria became portrayed in the Western media as a rather simpler story of a rapacious multinational abusing Nigeria's environment and people.

The point being made here, it should be emphasized, is not that environmental and human rights issues were unimportant to delta communities, but rather that they occupied a less central role in their litany of complaints than the narrative of most Western activists suggested.

A further indication of this is that in recent years, while the environmental and human rights situation in the Niger Delta has in many respects improved (Shell, for example, has improved its pollution controls, and the Nigerian government has evolved from a dictatorship to a democracy of sorts), there have been regular outbreaks of local violence, anger, and civil unrest driven, as before, by disagreements over the distribution of oil revenues. The delta region remains both mired in poverty and highly volatile politically. Yet in contrast to 1995, with the Western NGOs now paying less attention to Nigeria, these local problem have gained relatively little Western media coverage. As through the centuries, Western compassion and local concerns have proved to be somewhat disconnected from each other.

Also fitting the historical pattern are the problems encountered by Shell's managers in attempting to deal with the political and ethical pressures in Nigeria. The picture here once again is of a company not so much cunningly controlling and manipulating its political environment in its favor but rather colliding with a series of unexpected obstacles.

Like Nike, for example, Shell was taken by surprise by the fierceness of the global campaign against it in the 1990s. And as with Nike, it can be argued that Shell's managers ought to have foreseen that a storm was brewing. The decades of neglect experienced by the Delta communities at the hands of Nigeria's federal government, for example, meant that an upsurge of local anger was inevitable at some point. One of the problems may have been that Shell's management in Nigeria had become too focused on keeping on good terms with the federal government, for this was where the main political threat to its operations laid in the past: in the 1970s, the government had nationalized various Western oil assets. But whatever the cause, Shell's local management clearly paid too little attention in advance to the brewing discontent in the Delta, at a cost to their company's global reputation.

Now, partly as a result of the 1995 controversy, Shell has committed itself loudly, like other high-profile multinationals, to the doctrine and practices of corporate social responsibility. As well as bolstering its environmental performance, Shell's Nigerian subsidiary undertakes much more stakeholder dialogue with local communities than before and has tripled its annual spending on local welfare projects, such as schools and small business ventures, to over $60 million. It has also exerted pressure on the Nigerian government to raise the proportion of oil revenues that flow back to the Delta region, and partly as a result the proportion was raised to 13 percent (the figure was 3 percent previously).

Interestingly, however, and again in parallel with Nike's experience, Shell's CSR efforts in Nigeria have so far failed to protect the company from continuing political problems. While attention from Western NGOs has died down, the situation in the Delta region remains politically volatile. In March 2003, for example, fighting between ethnic groups and government troops forced Shell and other Western firms to shut down much of their Nigerian oil production. One of the problems is that the Nigerian state system is riddled with corruption and has itself failed to deliver basic public services in the Delta region, such as decent education and health care system. In such a situation, however much Shell spends of its own money on local welfare projects, this is unlikely on its own to make much of a dent on local poverty, and hence on local tensions.

The increase in state oil revenues now starting to flow to the Delta may help in this respect over the long term. But Shell's tactic of applying pressure on the federal government to assist the oil-producing region in this way also poses a fresh set of risks for the company. It will require Shell managers to walk a political tightrope in the coming years: any increase in political activism on their part, however discrete, could potentially be perceived by some Nigerians as a return to neocolonialist meddling. True, Shell ought arguably to have applied more pressure than it did on Sani Abacha back in

1995. But if it is seen to become too involved politically now, it risks a backlash from politicians at the federal level anxious not to see any further reduction in their slice of the oil cake. Maybe Shell will succeed in walking this tightrope. But it certainly requires a delicacy of political touch that has often been absent from the sample of multinationals examined in this chapter.

Management Lessons

Would an examination of a different sample of firms through history have led to different conclusions? Without doubt, many large firms have managed their political interactions much better than those examined here, and certainly not all Western activists have failed to appreciate fully the local perspective, as did many of those described here.

Even so, the firms in this sample were some of the most powerful or publicly controversial multinationals of their era, widely perceived as epicenters of power and political savvy. The finding that they often fumbled their political interactions would suggest that the general reputation of large multinationals for being cunning operators at least needs to be called into question. Similarly, the fact that these multinationals were among the companies most heavily scrutinized by Western activists in their era suggests that a discrepancy between Western and local perspectives is probably a general pattern of anticorporate campaigns. The other multinationals examined in "Empires of Profit" fit these findings.

While the main aim of this chapter has been to highlight the patterns through history rather than to draw specific management lessons for companies, some basic conclusions in this respect are unavoidable. Even given the inherent complexity and unpredictability of many political pressures, for example, it is clear that the companies examined here would have been able to predict at least some of the problems they faced had they developed a more sophisticated system of social and political intelligence and risk assessment. It is also clear that such an understanding ought to have informed their overall business strategy and processes.

In the case of the East India Company, for example, a better understanding on the part of the London headquarters as to the political pressures faced by managers in India would have high-lighted the need for much tougher controls on these local managers' behavior. In the case of Nike, better intelligence early on regarding the labor conditions in its contract factories would have indicated the need for a tougher monitoring and control system so as to preempt potential criticisms. In the case of both Shell in Nigeria and the British South Africa Company, an earlier management awareness of the growing discontent of local people, and how this might become explosive if left to fester, would likely have made both companies more attentive to local needs.

In the cases examined in this chapter, in other words, better intelligence and a preemptive management response would have allowed financially costly or reputationally damaging situations to have been avoided, or at least the risk of such problems to have been reduced. Once the problems had actually arisen (whether violent rebellions in the case of the colonial—era companies or global NGO campaigns in the case of the modern companies), the management solutions available to the firms (whether military counterattacks or global public relations campaigns to rebut the criticism) were much more costly and often less than effective.

So the prescription from the evidence presented here is clear: multinationals need to develop a more sophisticated understanding of their social and political context and to use this genuinely to inform the way they do business. As a final point, it is worth exploring briefly why such an apparently obvious prescription is often difficult for firms to implement.

Part of the problem lies in the traditional structures and divisions of responsibility within many large firms. The departments charged with managing reputational and political issues in firms today, for example, are often the "public affairs," "corporate affairs" or "communications" divisions—in other words, the functions whose principal task within the company is seen to be that of public relations: promoting the company in the media and elsewhere externally and also rebutting unfair criticisms.

Such departments often lack the internal legitimacy to secure changes in corporate behavior that may be necessary to preempt public criticism or political backlash. Put another way, the unreasonable expectation from other corporate functions is that the standard public relations tactics of rebuttal or lobbying should be sufficient to fend off problems while the rest of the firm can continue with business as usual. Public affairs departments also traditionally operate in a reactive mode, responding to problems as they arise rather than focusing on analysis of likely future political trends and pressures.

Related to this, the strength of corporate culture can prove to be an obstacle too. While many companies find that a sense of purpose or mission is a prerequisite for commercial success, pride and insularity often accompanies strong cultures, and this can blind managers and employees to the external environment in which they are operating and to the differing perspectives of local people. (This was a particular problem faced by the management of the United Fruit Company, one of the other case studies in "Empires of Profit.")

Another related problem is the difficulty of constructing sound internal systems of communication and control between head office and local operations regarding political and social issues. Even internal reporting and control systems on financial performance remain imperfect in many large companies today, and complex local political situations cannot be summarized and communicated to headquarters in the same standardized way as, say, data on quarterly profits. The East India Company's system of internal control on political issues was clearly seriously flawed. But in many modern firms too, headquarters finds it difficult to guarantee that local managers are implementing all the global corporate policies on, say, the environment or labor standards or avoidance of bribery. Such internal assurance is necessary to reduce the risk that potential critics will find grounds to attack the company.

All of this also helps to explain the limitations of the corporate social responsibility tactics enthusiastically adopted by many modern organizations. Without doubt, CSR can be genuinely useful for companies, as well beneficial for the wider world—if it induces among managers a greater sensitivity to social and reputational issues. But within firms, responsibility for CSR tends to be handed to the public affairs or an equivalent department. Hence, the focus of much CSR work tends to be on producing well-meaning sustainability reports rather than on the more challenging task of ensuring that corporate policies are implemented globally, even though this is crucial for protecting the corporate reputation.

Furthermore, a common assumption that underlies the CSR efforts of many firms—that through consultation, they will be able to balance the interests of their numerous stakeholders—belies the often conflicting nature of the pressures they face. As the examples in this chapter have indicated, responding to the demands of Western activists may lead to a different set of actions from those that would be needed to keep on the right side of local people or of host governments in developing countries.

The management challenges that multinationals in this area face, in short, are unlikely to be solved overnight. The political clumsiness of corporate giants, a pattern that began with the East India Company, can thus be expected to repeat itself well into the future.

CHAPTER 15

Globalization and the Poor

V. Kasturi Rangan
Arthur McCaffrey

When Ted Levitt (1983) extolled the virtues of global marketing twenty years ago, he was bewitched by the commercial capability of new technology to "equalize" trade, communication, transport, and travel, all of which he predicted would drive the world toward a "converging commonality." Twenty years later, his populist sentiments and optimism have not been realized. The experience of globalization has been divergent for billions of the world's population, where the masses in developing countries share little in common with the elite beneficiaries of global trade in advanced Western industrial societies. Such differences are thrown into sharp relief when we attempt to evaluate the impact of globalization on world poverty and assess both its reality and its potential for transforming the lives of the global poor.

We have chosen to represent these divergent differences and contrasts using our pyramid of poverty shown in Figure 15.1. According to the latest World Bank poverty statistics (World Bank, 2003a, 2003b), the poor are at the bottom of the global socioeconomic pyramid. Nearly 3 billion people are forced to survive on less than $2 a day.[1] They constitute almost half the planet's population living in developing countries, mostly in Asia (two-thirds of world's poor) and sub-Saharan Africa (one-quarter of world poor).

The World Bank indexes use a measure of income poverty, but poverty is more than just lack of income, and one could also approach it from other perspectives, such as "wealth poverty" (Tufano,

Figure 15.1. Global Income Pyramid

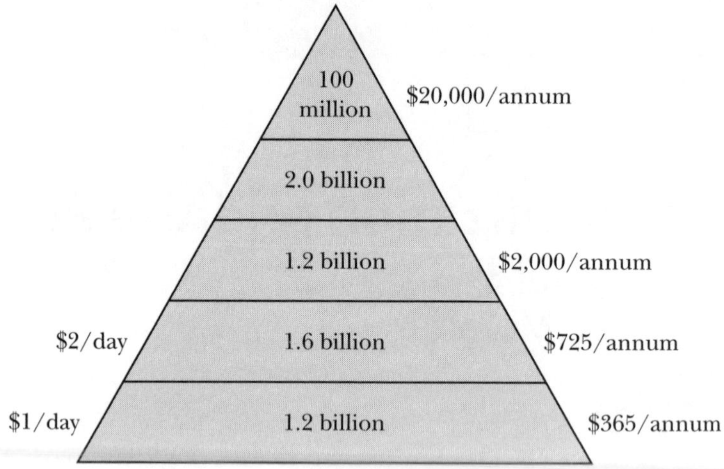

Source: Compiled from World Bank data, 2000.

2002) or "capability poverty" (Sen, 1999). However defined, global poverty manifests itself in rather universal patterns of distress, similar for the poor in both rich, industrialized nations and in developing ones: lower levels of life expectancy; higher infant mortality; inadequate food, water, sanitation, housing, and education; limited or no employment opportunities; lack of access to capital, assets, productive resources, or social services; and deprivation of basic capabilities (Meier, 1984; Sen, 1999; Tufano, 2002; World Bank, 2000b, 2001a; Bennet, 2003).

Global Consumers: Changing Choices versus Changing Lives?

The impetus toward globalization of trade and commerce that Levitt foresaw in 1983 has gathered momentum since the end of the cold war toward a worldwide liberalization of markets in the name of free market capitalism. Globalization has become synonymous with a liberalization of trade, which is intended to allow the free movement of goods across borders unhindered by tariff and trade barriers. The resultant extent of modern globalization activity can be assessed by aggregate economic measures such as stock of foreign direct investment (FDI) as a percentage of gross domestic product (GDP), size of net capital outflows, exports as a percentage of GDP, and so on. The major thrust for globalization of trade has come from the private sector side, so that the most visible face of globalization has been the kind of market-driven, profit-driven private investment that is most talked about in the press and literature. Companies seeking growth and profit for their shareholders have brought their products and services to global markets in a search for greener pastures. The initiatives of the private sector, especially in the retail and consumer goods category (for example, cars, consumer electronics, apparel, fast food franchises, and entertainment), have stimulated explosive growth in worldwide trade in the past fifteen years, estimated to be about $6.3 trillion in 2001.

Yet one gains an entirely different perspective on the impact of globalization depending on whether one is looking down from the top or up from the bottom of the pyramid. The life challenges facing either constituency are entirely different. The international flow of consumer goods and services that characterizes so much of the globalization movement serves primarily the top 2 billion customers in our global income pyramid (Figure 15.1). For these consumers, globalization means changing consumer choices and lifestyle preferences over a wider array of products and services. They live in a world of consumption, transacting products and services in the marketplace of exchange. They calculate the utility of a purchase and are willing to pay a cost to obtain that good because the perceived benefits exceed costs. The products of liberalized trade increase their range of consumption options, and such increased variety and choice may contribute to a perception that globalization has increased the quality of an already affluent life, although the Society for International Development (SID; Liamzon, Rogers, and Clugston, 1996) and the World Health Organization ("Developing World Afflicted by Diseases of Affluence," 2002) might disagree.

This kind of globalization is not relevant to the people at the bottom of the pyramid, who have been classified as the "excluded class" (Liamzon, Rogers, and Clugston, 1996) or the "poverty market" (Rangan, 2002). These 2.8 billion poor live in a completely different world, where the daily challenge is changing their lives of poverty. They do not transact in a world of exchange, and they are not consumers of retail items such as running shoes, electronic equipment, automobiles, soft drinks, or fast food. They cannot afford the kind of goods and services that globalization provides to the consumers at the top of the pyramid and often would not know how and where to acquire such products. It is not worry over product or lifestyle choice that consumes them but rather access to the necessities of life. They need basic products and services like food, clothing, shelter, and health care, and also some education, vocational training, or resources like land ownership (De Soto, 2002) and agricultural inputs, or a loan to initiate a microbusiness. Those living in poverty are likely to include subsistence farmers attempting to eke out a living in rural Kenya, or casual construction laborers living in the slums of Mumbai, or young women, barely earning living wages, sewing garments in the "export processing zones" of the Philippines (Klein, 1999).

Globalization, Poverty, and "Freedom"

These nearly 3 billion poor are hardly global in their outlook, tastes, and consumption patterns, but despite their lives of misery and poverty, their needs and desires are no less real. So how does their socioeconomic development take place? Who looks after the poor? Who invests in them? If they are a missing factor on the demand side of globalization, are they still targets or beneficiaries of investment and intervention on the supply side? Has the globalization of trade and investment helped or hindered their economic development—and not only that, also their political, social and cultural development? And, ultimately, has globalization made them free?

Such is globalization's reach that it has now become fashionable in the West to rate or rank the percentage of countries that are "free" in a conservative economic sense. Indexes of "economic freedom" or rankings of a country's economic status have been attempted by, among others, the World Freedom Foundation ("The Prosperity League," 2002), the Heritage Foundation (O'Driscoll, Holmes, and Kirkpatrick, 2001), and the World Bank (2002c). The World Freedom Foundation report, for example, characterized about forty of the world's economies as free under a strict definition of the term and also identified another forty countries as having begun the process of opening their economies to advance gradually to a free market goal.

But there is obviously more to freedom than simply economic liberalization. The most optimistic champions of globalization were hopeful that it would be a force for the promotion of economic democracy and might thus contribute (even indirectly) to the development of human rights in poor countries. But what are rights for? In a recent conference, Ignatieff (2003) cites Sen (1999) to argue that the purpose of human rights is to emancipate human agents to be free. Sen's conception of development as freedom is premised on the exercise of fundamental rights by the poor and marginalized, including their rights to development and governance. Therefore, we need to ask not only whether globalization has created economic freedom for developing nations, but also if it has contributed to these more fundamental aspects of global emancipation. At a programmatic level at least, the World Bank has recognized these wider challenges of development and investment in poor countries. A World Bank directive in May 1966 put poverty reduction at the center of their country assistance strategies, while the World Bank president, noting that the number of global poor had increased between the late 1980s and the early 1990s, stated that the key development challenge today is "inclusion," that is, promoting equitable access to economic and social benefits of development, regardless of nationality, race, or gender (World Bank, 1997).

The Multidimensional Nature of Globalization and Poverty, and the Responsibility of Investors

The answers to the questions we raised above about the global poor are complicated, since the phenomena under study are multidimensional. Poverty, for instance, is not only income poverty but also lack of control over resources and assets (both financial and nonfinancial), lack of access to services, illiteracy, poor health, and the systemic context of poverty that includes incompetent or corrupt governance (World Bank, 1999). Likewise, there are many faces of globalization—political, social and cultural, as well as economic (Hoffmann, 2002)—and a dialogue about the impact of globalization on poverty reduction needs to make it clear which aspects one is talking about. Furthermore, when it comes to investing in poverty reduction, while developing countries are the targets or recipients of a great deal of both private investment and public agency intervention in the form of direct aid, loans, FDI, or infrastructure development projects, the record of both kinds of investment over the past several decades does not make it clear that either sector has the best interests of the poor end customer at heart.

True, many economic measures of the impact and effects of globalization tell success stories. But these are only a part of a larger narrative about the mixed blessings of globalization. The public debate over globalization has recently witnessed sharp criticism of the globalization process and its effects from both within and outside the field. We will discuss in more detail several recent critiques by Stiglitz (2002), Caufield (1996), and Hoffmann (2002) of the overemphasis on the benefits of economic globalization that ignore many more negative side effects (social, cultural, and political), while, in addition, there is a whole antiglobalization movement (Klein, 2002) that has sprung up in the past decade to oppose the spread of free market liberalism.

We have listened to this debate from the perspective of the poor at the bottom of the pyramid. In the rest of this chapter, we take a closer look at some of the contributions and responsibilities of the private and public sectors in regard to poverty relief, particularly since they tend to invest in different kinds of outcomes and have varying degrees of involvement, direct or indirect, with the reduction of poverty. One of the messages of this chapter that we would like to communicate to the corporate sector is the need to balance a company's profit aspirations on behalf of shareholders with a more enlightened style of investment that does not leave local stakeholders (including the poor) behind. We begin our assessment of the debate by asking: In the big business of globalization, who looks after the poor?

Who Looks After the Poor?

We have noted the World Bank's identification of income poverty. Might there perhaps also be an "investment poverty" that prevents adequate funds from getting to poor countries? The simple answer is no, if the measure is sheer dollar amount of investment, which was running in the $200 to $300 billion range annually for public and private monies invested in developing countries between 1997 and 2000 (World Bank, 2000b, 2001b, 2002c, 2003a). The more complicated answer is, yes; perhaps there is investment poverty if we are concerned not about dollar quantity but about the quality and effectiveness of that investment and about the positive contribution it makes to poverty relief. When we examined the empirical evidence (Rangan and McCaffrey, 2003) in order to answer our question, "Who looks after the poor?" we found ourselves confronting a paradox: while the bulk of the world's population resides at the lower levels of the pyramid and does not benefit (as consumers) from the commercial effects of globalization like their counterparts at the top, they are still the targets of an international flood of public and private investment and intervention that pours into developing countries. So what is wrong with this picture? Are these billions of dollars in aid and investment money well spent? Is it helping to reduce poverty?

As Table 15.1 shows, in the thirty years from 1970 to 2000, there was a nineteen-fold increase in total investment and aid (public and private) to developing countries, from $13.8 billion in 1970 to $261 billion in 2000. To be sure, the 1980s (the lost decade for the poor) saw a sharp decline in new money to developing countries, with a halving of net resource inflows between 1981 and 1987 (as a share of world FDI, total aid to developing countries fell from one-third in 1968 to one-fifth in 1988, with the lion's share of investment going to Latin America and Asia; World Bank, 1991). But the upward trend was recovered in 1991 ($85 billion net), never fell below $200 billion for the rest of the decade, and surged to a peak of total investment of $338 billion in 1997.

In conclusion, the gross cumulative amount of private and public investment and intervention funding going to developing countries over the past thirty years is in the trillions of dollars (getting close to $2 trillion in the past ten years alone). Given that sheer quantity of cash flow, has it made a dent in global poverty? To answer that, we turn to an examination of the profile and trends of poverty in developing countries for the same time period.

Profile of Global Poverty, 1970–2000

In the 1970s, the number of world poor was about 700 to 800 million—around 20 percent of a world population of about 4 billion. By 1980, developing countries contained about 80 percent of the

Table 15.1. Private and Public Investment, Aid, and Resource Flows to Developing Countries, 1970–2000 (billions of dollars)

	1970	1980	1981	1988	1989	1990[a]	1991	1993	1994	1995	1996	1997	1998	1999	2000
Total public[b]	5.3	29.8		51.0	34.0	49.0	70.0	51.7	48.6	53	63.6	39.1	50.6	45.7	35.3
Foreign direct investment	2.5	8.6	46.0[c]	17.0[c]	24.0	22.0	35.9	65.1	80.1	95.5	88.8	163.4	170.9	185.4	166.7
Other private	6.0	36.9	53.0		8.0	6.0		92.6		61.8					
Total private[d]	8.5	45.5			32.0	28.0		157.6	158.8	184.2	150.6	299.0	267.7	219.9	225.8
Total aid to developing countries[e]	13.8	75.3	100.0[c]	66.0	66.0	77.0	85.0[c]	209.4	207.4	237.2	214.2	338.0	318.3	265.5	261.1

[a]The World Bank started publishing these data systematically in 1990 in its annual *Global Economic Prospects* report.
[b]Includes official development assistance.
[c]Net.
[d]Includes FDI and portfolio.
[e]Total public and private aid.

Sources: Compiled from various World Bank publications, including *World Development Report*, *World Development Indicators*, and *Global Economic Prospects*.

world's population and about 32 percent of the global poor, which had now risen to 1.4 billion. By the end of the twentieth century, the number of global poor had reached about 2.8 billion (living at less than a dollar a day), getting close to 50 percent of the world population in 2000 (with developing countries containing 40 percent of that population).

In conclusion, from being around 20 percent of world population in 1975 to constituting close to 50 percent today, the poor are always with us. Despite the trillions of dollars gushing in investment and aid to developing countries over the same period, hardly a dent has been made in the problem (apart from some recent limited regional successes that do not seem to generalize readily to other poor regions of the world).

If globalization was supposed to liberate developing nations and bring them into the global marketplace and confer new freedoms on the economically destitute, it has not happened. The hard numbers suggest that the economic miracle of globalization has not happened for too many people and that limited successes that have been claimed have occurred under very qualified conditions that are region and economy specific.

We spend the rest of this chapter analyzing some of the reasons that the investment clout of rich nations has not substantially helped poor ones. Despite the sheer number of arrows that have been shot, why have so many failed to hit the target? We want to understand why it is not the quantity but the quality of aid and investment that seems to be at issue. It is not the theory of globalization that seems to have failed to realize Levitt's promise but rather the manner in which it has been practiced. Since 1989, global liberalization of trade and markets has mostly meant that rich countries by and large have stayed rich, poor countries have by and large have stayed poor, and a minority of lucky entrepreneurs have amassed personal wealth while the global gaps between the rich and the poor have by and large increased.

We therefore need to address two questions: How did this come about? and What can we do about it? To answer the first, we consider a range of interdisciplinary literature in economics, international development, political science, as well as the social activist, antiglobalization literature, to appreciate critiques of globalization and its effects from inside and outside the phenomenon. To answer the second requires addressing the complex, multidimensional nature of both globalization and global poverty. It is not an easy task. We address one important piece of this puzzle—the customer perspective—using our particular expertise in marketing. We offer a simple (but, we hope, not simplistic) marketing perspective and strategy to guide businesses and international investors in their dealings with poor countries. We will argue that investment capital lacks a process for aiding the poor and will sketch out a model of engagement based on our own recent research.

Globalization and Its Discontents

A wealth of private and public funds has been invested in developing countries in the name of globalization, but has hardly made a dent in the problem when viewed from the perspective of the poor at the bottom of the pyramid. We begin our critical diagnosis of where the problems might lie by clarifying some of the structural constraints that limit the effectiveness of development aid. We then go look at institutional issues by reviewing criticisms of the process and practice of globalization by Rodrik (1999, 2002), Stiglitz (2002), and Caufield (1996), who lay the blame squarely at the door of the primary players in the development game: the World Bank and the International Monetary Fund (IMF). We conclude our brief critique of globalization and its discontents by considering arguments from the antiglobalization camp by Klein (1999, 2002) and others.

Globalization is not a monolithic, homogeneous phenomenon, but rather is multifaceted in its process and impacts, affecting different countries in different ways. Its benefits also come with costs. On purely economic or fiscal terms, becoming a member of the globalization club has a price, since governments of second- or third-tier economies have had to deregulate, or liberalize, their economies to make them attractive to foreign capital investment, technology, and expertise. As Harvard economist Dani Rodrik (1999, 2002) has pointed out, here again we see different faces of globalization at work. In countries with more controlled economies, like China, India, and Vietnam, which have adapted globalization on their own terms and are playing by their own rules, trade liberalization has brought benefits. However, other regions, like Latin America and especially Russia and other countries that tried to liberalize too quickly and open up their domestic markets too readily to globalization on the promoters' terms, suffered the consequences of collapsed economies, fiscal crises, and increased disparities in wealth and income among their citizens, exacerbating poverty levels. As Rodrik notes, IMF loan terms are usually good for the lenders but not for the recipients.

The IMF and the World Bank are targets of critiques by Stiglitz and Caufield, who give insiders' looks at the institutional dynamics and ideologies that hinder the effectiveness of IMF and World Bank aid programs. In his best-selling book on globalization, *Globalization and Its Discontents* (2002), former World Bank chief economist and Nobel laureate Joseph Stiglitz believes that the kind of top-down economic globalization promoted by public agencies like the IMF and World Bank is just another form of failed trickle-down approaches to economic development that were popular after World War II (Rostow, 1965, 1971). Then as now, the much vaunted widespread dispersion of prosperity predicted by top-down economic planning has failed to materialize. Stiglitz says that the poor have fared badly under globalization, citing World Bank statistics to show that during the booming global trade years of the 1990s, the number of the global poor living on less than two dollars a day increased. If we define globalization broadly as the freer movement of money, goods, services, and people across borders, then Stiglitz thinks that 1990s-style globalization has put many developing countries through a decade of financial and economic turmoil (Hilsenrath, 2002).

Like Rodrik, Stiglitz believes that the market liberalization promoted by globalization has been problematic for underdeveloped nations, which, Stiglitz thinks (Hilsenrath, 2002), have been pushed by an aggressive IMF (and its shareholders) to liberalize their economies and open their markets too quickly; instead of receiving much-needed economic stimulus, poor countries instead got fiscal austerity (the sister of "liberating" liberalization). He argues that the pressures for quick privatization by the IMF have led to negative consequences for the distribution of wealth in society, leading, for example, to the widening gap between the haves and have-nots, between urban dwellers and the rural poor. According to Stiglitz, such globalization pressures distracted developing countries from focusing on the creation of social safety nets to protect their citizens from the economic volatility and unemployment that initially result from freer trade and capital markets. Stiglitz lambastes the IMF for not balancing economic efficiency with social justice, so that the benefits of trade liberalization will truly be global. IMF investment and intervention policies have proven to be counterproductive: by forcing government officials to choose between fiscal balance and their social contract with their citizens, IMF policies have undermined the legitimacy of governments and the very process of market liberalization that it was trying to promote (Eichengreen, 2002).

Finally, Stiglitz comments on the necessary interdependent relations between market institutions, good governance, and progressive development, a point that we endorse in our own research (Rangan and McCaffrey, 2003) and that the World Bank (2002a) has recently championed. Stiglitz stresses that the promoters of globalization ignore the necessary regulatory prerequisites and supporting infrastructure that must be in place before mature, competitive markets can develop in poor countries, such as sophisticated public administration and good corporate governance, not to mention the hard task of building institutions (we return to this critical issue later in the chapter).

Caufield's institutional critique of globalization (1996) takes on the IMF's sister institution, the World Bank. As we have seen in our study of the empirical evidence, the World Bank has a great impact on the lives of the global poor as a major player in global financing through its funding of massive infrastructure projects in developing countries and its significant influence on local governments' fiscal and economic policies. Caufield's particular targets are the infrastructure projects funded by the World Bank in developing countries—what she calls the devastating effects of "bank-financed development disasters" (p. xii). One example is the Upper Indravati Valley in the Singrauli region of India, home to a huge dam, five coal-fired power plants, and twelve massive open-pit coal mines. The World Bank has been a major funder of the Singrauli region for over twenty years. According to Caufield, the human and environmental fallout from such projects has been devastating: three hundred thousand people displaced from their homes several times; gross pollution of soil, water, and air; disruption of traditional livelihoods; and creation of social dislocation and slums.

Caufield notes that the resettlement effects of large infrastructure works are particularly acute in heavily populated countries like India, where it is estimated that since independence, 11 million people have been forced from their homes by large dams and another 4 million people have been displaced by mines, industrial development, and wildlife sanctuaries. Lacking a proper resettlement plan, millions of Indians have been added to the poverty rolls.[2] Caufield thinks that the amount of taxpayers' dollars wasted in ill-conceived global megaprojects is mind-boggling, and she is concerned with the World Bank's role in financing such projects, all in the name of improving the lot of the poor (a professed goal of the bank since the 1960s).

Caufield blames the poor investment results on many of the working assumptions underlying the World Bank's investment philosophy, which she thinks is too simplistic (for example, that there is a single global crisis, underdevelopment, whose remedy is development). Preoccupied with physical infrastructure projects, the World Bank's experts were often blind to the human, ecological, social, and economic casualties of the vast schemes it promoted. The World Bank has long been a major player and instigator of globalization through its massive international investment schemes, but Caufield concludes that its professed war on poverty has made victims out of its alleged customers. Its large-scale experiments in poverty reduction have, over many years, "cost many billions of dollars and millions of disrupted human lives, and required the sacrifice of vast areas of productive forests, soils, rivers, and coastlines" (Caufield, 1996, p. 338). After examining the World Bank's record, she concludes regretfully that fifty years of "development" have profited neither the poorest people nor the poorest countries. Instead, they have paid dearly for the disproportionately small benefits received.

So who has benefited from all these billions of dollars of investment? In the supply chain of World Bank financing-lending-debt, there are many other groups holding their hands out long before any relief reaches the poor at the bottom of the pyramid. The long list of middlemen includes the national and international bureaucracies with which the World Bank does business; heads of government (often autocratic) in developing nations for whom the World Bank represents the lender of first and last resort; a wide assortment of middlemen in rich countries, including contractors, exporters, and consultants; and multinational corporations and international banks doing business in target countries. As our marketing argument at the end of this chapter goes, among all these vested interests, there is no one to represent the interests of the poor client residing at the end of the long chain of so-called relief.

Caufield judges the World Bank's practice of "development" to be monopolistic, formulaic, foreign dominated, arrogant—and failed. And given that ultimately the World Bank is spending money given by ordinary taxpayers in donor countries, the World Bank style of global investment has been "largely a matter of poor people in rich countries giving money to rich people in poor countries" (Caufield, 1996, p. 338).

The Antiglobalization Movement

The critiques by Stiglitz and Caufield come from insiders who are not necessarily against the concept of globalization and growth per se but rather its manner of implementation by the major public funding agencies. The activists in the antiglobalization camp, in contrast, have targeted private corporations investing in developing countries. For example, social activist and writer Naomi Klein (1999, 2002) has leveled scathing criticism at Levitt's (1983) characterization of global corporations:

> Levitt's "global" corporations were, of course, American corporations and the "homogenized" image they promoted were the images of America; blond, blue-eyed kids eating Kellogg's cereal on Japanese TV; the Marlboro Man bringing U.S. cattle country to African villages; and Coke and McDonald's selling the entire world on the taste of the U.S.A. As globalization ceased to be a somewhat kooky dream and became a reality, these cowboy-marketing antics began to step on a few toes. The twentieth century's familiar bogeyman—"American cultural imperialism"—has, in more recent years, incited cries of "cultural Chernobyl" in France, prompted the creation of a "slow-food movement" in Italy and led to the burning of chicken outside the first KFC outlet in India [1999, p. 116].

It is not globalization itself that Klein questions but rather the exploitation of the resources in Third World countries by the global brands—Nike, McDonald's, Shell, Reebok, and Gap among them. She documents in detail her visits to Asian sweatshops producing Nike sneakers, Gap jeans, and London Fog jackets, where thousands of workers, mainly young women, work far below living wages. For example, the living wage in China in 1998 was about eighty-seven cents an hour (compared to the U.S. average of about fifteen dollars an hour). Yet according to Klein (1999), the big global brands paid their workers an average of thirteen cents an hour. Klein is just as critical in accusing Shell of exploiting the Ogoni people in the Niger delta, in connivance with the military rulers of Nigeria. Shell has the drilling rights to the rich deposits of oil in the Niger delta, which is situated at the heart of Ogoni lands, whose people have had little power in the Nigerian political system. According to Klein, $250 billion worth of manufactured products were exported by the export processing zones in Asia, and about $30 billion worth of oil was exported from Nigeria. Much of this has gone to fatten the pockets of the corporations and their sponsors and not the core resource owner, the locals, who made the value-added possible, according to Klein. She identifies this economic exploitation as the root cause for the resentment and organized activism against global brands.

Views like Klein's have started to coalesce into a number of formal, organized forms of opposition to globalization. Those that received most media attention were the protesters in Seattle against the World Trade Organization (WTO), in Washington against the IMF and the World Bank, in Davos and New York against the World Economic Forum, in Genoa against the Group of 7, and most recently in Prague—all sites where street activists successfully disrupted meetings of the architects and planners of globalization programs (Klein, 2002; "Rising Credibility for NGOs," 2002; "World Social Forum," 2002).

However, the major international nongovernmental organization in the antiglobalization camp, the World Social Forum 2003 (WSF), has had less sensationalist but no less important annual meetings, starting in Porto Alegre, Brazil, in January 2001. The WSF explicitly stands in opposition to the World Economic Forum (WEF), held annually in Davos, Switzerland, for the past thirty years. The WEF has played a strategic role in formulating the thinking that promotes and advocates neoliberal policies the world over.

Its organizational base is a Swiss foundation that functions as a UN consulting body and is funded by more than a thousand multinational corporations. The WSF is intended to highlight civil society's ability to mobilize against the forces of economic globalization, a force epitomized by WEF/Davos, which represents the place where the theory of world domination by capital, within the parameters of neoliberalism, is constructed and steadily put into practice. WSF seeks to provide an alternative international framework for all those opposed to globalization and dedicated to building alternatives for thinking and organizing together in favor of human development and for surmounting market domination of countries and international relations.

Public response to the WSF has been positive. The *Financial Times* ("Rising Credibility for NGOs," 2002) reported the results of an Edelman public opinion poll at the time the WSF meetings were being held in parallel with the 2002 annual meeting of the WEF in New York. The poll found that the popularity and credibility of nongovernmental organizations (NGOs) represented at the WSF had risen on both sides of the Atlantic: "NGOs had now become the fifth estate of government and the true credible force on issues related to the environment and social justice" (p. 7). According to Edelman, many of the NGO organizations protesting at WEF 2002 enjoyed greater public trust than the big names of capitalism at the WEF. Some NGOs were now "superbrands" with worldwide reputations—Amnesty International, World Wildlife Fund, Greenpeace, Oxfam (all represented at WSF 2002)—that topped the public trust ratings, well ahead of corporate brands.

What emerges from these diverse antiglobalization perspectives is a strikingly convergent viewpoint: economic globalization is far too removed and abstract to be useful to the poor, who are, curiously enough, presumed to be the beneficiaries of much of the economic activity. While the theory of globalization may be attractive, its record of implementation is full of contradictions, failed promises, inequities, and resentments. The multilateral financial and developmental institutions work on the basis of economic models of poverty alleviation that may be flawed not only from a market creation perspective but also from a lack of sensitivity to their social, cultural, and political ramifications. The very mixed record of the practice of globalization to date indicates that all

interests—private corporations, public agencies, domestic governments—are implicated in the flawed conception, poor execution,
and bad management of intervention and investment programs in
poor, developing countries. So what is a poor corporation to do?

Putting a New Face on Globalization

While it is easy to blame the multilateral institutions and the country governments for the sorry state of affairs with respect to globalization and its impact on the poor, lurking prominently in the
background are the global corporations that are just as culpable.
These private investors are the ones who bring in the machinery,
the know-how, the technology, the capital, and the risk management that go with large-scale projects aimed at economic development. What should their role be in contributing to a solution
for redressing poverty? In our own research on this problem (Rangan and McCaffrey, 2003), we have used case studies of the actions
of multinational American companies in developing countries in
order to develop an agenda of practices for corporations to adopt
in the face of the challenges of globalization and poverty that we
are dealing with here.

We will draw on that research to construct the final arguments
of this chapter as we put all the data and all the arguments we have
considered up to now into perspective and offer some positive prescriptions for conducting business in poor countries from a cus-
tomer-centered marketing stance. First, having studied the data
and listened to all the critiques, can we find a balanced perspective from which to evaluate the consequences of globalization for
the alleviation of world poverty? Fortunately, in a prescient article
in *Foreign Affairs* (2002), Stanley Hoffmann (2002), a Harvard professor of government and international relations, provides a comprehensive framework for analyzing the practice of globalization
from the perspective of international relations, nation building,
and world governance to assess the geopolitical effects of a decade's worth of global trade.

Hoffmann identifies three forms of globalization—economic,
cultural, and political—each carrying its own baggage and problems. We have extrapolated Hoffmann's main points about the similarities and differences in these three faces of globalization.[3] Each

face of globalization shows the tensions and problems associated with it, and Hoffmann's sober and cogent analysis shows us the global context and realities in which a study of modern poverty must take place. We think it is fair to say that most of the chapters in this book deal with only one of the facets of Hoffmann's model, economic globalization, and we agree with Hoffmann that the tensions of globalization become exacerbated when one single-mindedly pursues only the economic version of it, ignoring the consequences for the other two kinds. What is needed is a balanced, integrated version of all three.

Within the Hoffmann perspective, the globalization-antiglobalization antagonism might be said to represent two different monologues, each trying to talk to the other about a different face of globalization. The tension in the debate over economic globalization arises from the perennial conflict between market efficiency and global equity and fairness, but now on a much larger scale than ever before. The counterreaction to the spread of economic globalization has spawned a global clash between different ideologies and conceptions of markets in relation to poverty alleviation. This has pitted the WEF (champions of private interests and private good) against the WSF (champions of public interests and the public good). Within the context of our analyses, the WEF appears to be only addressing the top half of our pyramid of poverty in Figure 15.1 with priorities of markets, trade, and profitability, while the WSF is addressing the bottom half of the pyramid, as advocates on behalf of people, habitats, and ecologies.

We summarize here Hoffmann's points that are most pertinent to our argument. First, globalization is uneven and inequitable in its effects and impacts; its reach remains limited because it excludes the poor. It is hyped mostly by privileged actors who have the most to gain from furthering its agenda. Second, the effects of economic globalization and liberalization of trade are hard to control, and so become unwieldy as a poverty alleviation strategy. Despite the emergence of international NGOs and nongovernmental institutional networks with an agenda of human rights and justice and fairness in the operation of world markets, such organizations are usually powerless to control the unfettered flow of capital around the world. This roving global capital exploits indigenous resources, damaging both human and natural habitats (which in turn provokes antiglobalization protests). In the din of such a multitude of stakeholders, it is not clear that the voice of the poor is heard. From the perspective of an international relations expert, Hoffmann reaches a similar pessimistic conclusion: the alleged benefits of globalization do not reach the bottom of the pyramid of poverty.

What Is a Corporation to Do?

So what is a poor, maligned corporation to do? What are the prospects for nations, citizens, and multinational corporations? Should they continue to pursue economic globalization in the name of national or vested interests, and the consequences be damned? Or should they continue to practice economic globalization, but in a different way, with a different set of ethics and with a different political and cultural nuance? The remainder of this chapter argues on behalf of the latter, preaching a message of corporate collectivism and global equity, based on norms of principled investment in developing countries. We draw some connected strands and themes from the analyses by Hoffmann and others and weave them into a blueprint for action, which we call an ethic of engagement. Our proposed ethic is based on three interrelated dimensions of the problem of globalization and poverty relief that we have identified in our research (Rangan and McCaffrey 2003): sustainable development, normative standards of conduct in global commerce, and a paradigm of market construction to guide intervention and investment in developing countries. The pivot on which we build this conceptual framework is the poor client, who is most affected by the impact of global intervention and investment.

We focus on the role of the corporate sector in contributing to the alleviation of poverty, but we do not mean to imply that the major responsibility for economic development and poverty relief rests with the corporate sector. We all know that the situation is vastly more complex and the reasons for enduring poverty are complicated, with many actors and institutions bearing a responsibility. It is just that the corporate sector has a significant role to play in bringing the appropriate investments to enable economic development in poor countries. Yet much of the corporate sector may not yet have grasped the full implications of that role for the conduct of their business practice, and corporate capital seems to lack a marketing process to help make their investments work harder for the poor. In the arguments that follow, we hope to convince private corporations that there are productive ways to leverage their collective clout in the service of a more just and equitable practice of globalization.

An Ethic of Engagement

We will now respond to our earlier question, What is a corporation to do? by offering a hopeful alternative that will allow corporations to engage in a more enlightened form of globalization. We offer an ethic of engagement that has three parts: an ecological doctrine of sustainable development, an entrepreneurial doctrine of principled investment based on shared norms and standards of global trade and investment, and a new development doctrine of market construction to replace the traditional but maladapted notion of market operation. In Hoffmann's language, we hope that this ethic will help put a new face on globalization—one that will be more hospitable to and respectful of the poor clients at the bottom of the pyramid. It should also provide encouragement to companies that take their corporate social responsibility seriously by allowing them to share responsibilities for global business practices and to leverage their collective clout on behalf of investment and intervention policies and practices that favor the poor more than heretofore. We mentioned at the start of this chapter that the World Bank (1997) stated that the key development challenge today is inclusion, promoting equitable access to the economic and social benefits of development. It is our fervent hope that the following recipe for an inclusive model of globalization, based on a truly interdisciplinary foundation for collective action, will defuse and transform the antagonism between pro- and antiglobalization forces.

Sustainable Development

We need a new conception of enlightened self-interest among corporations and investors based on the fragility of the planet and its limited nonrenewable resources. That conception can be derived from the scientific research of renowned sociobiologist E. O. Wilson (2002) and his warnings about ecological economics, the shrinking ecological footprint, and the exhaustion of the planet's resources. Wilson's lesson is clear: we can no longer afford to conduct business as usual, or there soon will not be any resources left to conduct business at all. It is in every multinational corporation's best interests to stop the practice of exploiting the planet's finite supply of resources. Businesses need to change their focus from maximization of profit to environmental sustainability. Rangan (2002) and Liamzon, Rogers, and Clugston (1996) have similarly urged that the goal of economic globalization not be an obsessive quest for economic growth at all costs, which results in the excessive exploitation of people and resources. According to the Society for International Development, if business wants to practice environmental sustainability, the best way to do that is to promote economic development for poorer countries, which nurtures sustainable livelihoods that are more ecofriendly. Providing jobs to alleviate poverty that are not qualitatively different from wasteful jobs in consumer societies means only that we are exporting the problems of a Western consumer society to poorer nations.

The Normative Consensus and Principled Investment

The idea of a normative consensus on international business practices reflects a recent, very powerful cooperative movement by actors and agencies in both the private and public sectors to develop a universal set of norms and standards for global investments that respect people and their habitats (Khagram, Riker, and Sikkink, 2002). The good news is that this is not just some project dreamed up by an altruistic few, but is the outcome of a worldwide cumulative process that is gathering momentum in uniting a variety of special interests into a collective entrepreneurial force that we have referred to in our own research (Rangan and McCaffrey, 2003) as the normative consensus (NC). The NC is a truly public-private partnership that cuts across sector boundaries, comprising private corporations, and domestic and international NGOs, united in a common effort to conduct business according to norms and rules of global commerce, investment, and intervention. The NC movement represents a momentum toward a global pressure to conform, to conduct international business according to common standards.

Harvard professor Sanjeev Khagram (2002) has recorded the rapid growth of this movement and argues that norms of business conduct are becoming increasingly consequential in international relations and international organizations. Effective transnational advocacy networks have been built on broad intercultural agreement around common perceptions of justice and injustice across cultural boundaries in three central issue areas: human rights, the environment, and women's rights. He writes, "NGOs amplify, interpret, and legitimate local claims by appealing to international norms. Networks use the international arena as a stage or mirror to hold state and international organization behavior up to a global judgment about appropriateness" (2002, p. 16).

These advocacy networks are now being rapidly joined by governments, investors, corporations, aid agencies, and local NGOs in developing countries, so that it is now possible to identify a critical mass of actors from the public and private sectors converging on a common set of norms and principles to guide intervention and investment practices in poor, developing countries. The motives range from self-interest to salvation of the planet to humanitarian concerns for the poor, but regardless, the NC movement is building up steam, and more and more players are getting on board. The good news for the individual CEO or corporation that is genuinely concerned with balancing shareholder and stakeholder interests is that they do not have to go it alone and risk letting their good intentions destroy their competitive edge. They now have an institutional platform (or choice of platforms) that lets them join like-minded companies in a new kind of corporate collectivism. If they join the NC movement, they will become known on the global scene by the company that they keep—and that in itself will provide a new kind of competitive edge. Companies that are known as proenvironment and pro–human rights will increasingly find themselves welcomed by "green" investors and countries and supported by NGOs.

The NC movement represents a force for good for global poverty because its heterogeneous mix of coalitions shares a common agenda of trying to include rather than exclude local interests (human and ecological) in their transglobal interventions and investments. The NC is, by definition, an ethic of global engagement.

A New Paradigm of Market Construction on Behalf of Poor Clients

The third component of our ethic of engagement is also about more inclusion of poor customers of the kind advocated by the NC proponents. The private sector shares a responsibility in broadening its view of customers. It cannot be the narrow immediate customer of its products or technology, nor can it stop with the government or political institution that has the legal rights to award it concessions or contracts. The private sector has to bring its influence to bear on broader questions: Who is the customer? Who are the project's stakeholders? and What value does the project bring to the poor? This is the only way to reconcile the economic, social, political, and cultural conflicts of globalization that Hoffman described.

Global corporations need to develop customer sensitivity for overseas investments. This must entail an attempt to calculate a calculus of value and value reconciliation for a complex array of stakeholder interests. First, it means constructing a market engagement process that brings the voice and interests of poor customers to be included and represented at the table of policy planning and debate. Table 15.2 illustrates such a process. The right-hand side of that table details our proposed new marketing architecture of market construction, built around a heuristic of interest representation, voice, and advocacy (based on our research program at Harvard Business School on a marketing approach to poverty; Rangan and McCaffrey, 2003). We hope this paradigm will allow both the marketing profession and their corporate partners to tackle the problem of global poverty more meaningfully and effectively. The poor at the bottom of the pyramid do not have a voice, their interests are often very poorly represented, and they have little power in a society's value reconciliation process. The model of the market construction process in Table 15.2 is a more proactive attempt to specify the necessary preconditions for a fair and equitable representation of the interests of the poor end client in the economic development process.

Table 15.2. A Market Construction Paradigm

	Market Operation	Market Construction
Functional processes	Exchange paradigm Selling and promotion	Interest representation Voice and advocacy
Aim	Change choices	Change lives (macro)
Outcomes	Change behavior (micro)	Reconciliation of values and interests
Business role	Represent vested interests	Represent unrepresented customer interests Surrogate voice Serve clients Intermediator Sell client/customers to organizations (public, private)
Vision		Lay foundation for prototype markets

Source: Rangan & McCaffrey, 2003.

Our market construction model operates under a completely different set of assumptions from the operations model illustrated on the left-hand side of Table 15.2. It basically turns this traditional marketing paradigm on its head by manipulating the company or corporate institution rather than the customer. Typical marketing sells the organization to the customer, whereas our new paradigm seeks to sell the customer to the organization, using voice and advocacy to promote and represent the unrepresented interests of the poor. Business has traditionally concerned itself with the exchange paradigm on the left side of Table 15.2. There, knowledgeable customers are able to sort through the choices created for them, evaluate their consequences for their welfare, and then select the one that meets their private interests. In a sense, then, the "vested interests" of the corporate world and the "private interests" of the customers meet in a level playing field called "market," and in the long run, customers always win; businesses that cannot demonstrate sustained value will be extinguished by the dispassionate hand of the market. Successful businesses are the ones that can find a win-win for themselves and their customers. Customers are at least coequals in the exchange world in a way that poor customers never are in a developing world. But this paradigm of market operation in mature markets is completely inappropriate in poor countries where markets are often nonexistent or fledgling and immature. Yet it is still the standard paradigm that globalizing businesses and investors operate by in developing countries, with the counterproductive consequences we have examined in this chapter.

There are serious misconceptions in the marketing field about the different dynamics and very different assumptions that underlie market construction as opposed to market operation. Our alternative paradigm is intended to address and rectify these fallacious assumptions about the role of marketing institutions in developing countries, and we hope it will permit a more appropriate and effective applicability of marketing skills and expertise to the intractable problem of global poverty.[4]

Conclusion

We conclude by reiterating the suggestion of Garten (2002) that multinational corporations need to develop a "foreign policy" for overseas investment—but with a difference. Typically, U.S. foreign policy represents America's interests to the world. We propose to turn this conception on its head by recommending a corporate foreign policy that represents local interests to the investors, planners, and policymakers. By so doing, we can promote a customer-driven conception of globalization that would contribute to the operation of a more equitable global market—something that even the most die-hard antiglobalist would find hard to resist.

We believe that both of the new initiatives that we have identified here—the normative consensus movement and our market construction paradigm—provide the private and public sectors with common organizing principles for guiding globalization initiatives that will ensure the proper representation of the interests of the poor in developing countries. If business were to adopt these models for investment in poor countries as a marker for best practices, it would ensure that the end customer or poor client was the enduring pivot of all intervention and investment programs and that bottom-up planning was an integral part of all policy and investment planning. We could thus move closer toward our ideal of valid, authentic, and effective representation of the interests of the poor, always.

We began this chapter with an examination of the empirical evidence concerning the dubious compatibility of globalization and poverty relief. The conclusion from that evidence is that it is not the quantity of aid and investment in developing countries that matters so much as the quality and manner of its execution and implementation. In that spirit of enlightenment, let us move away from the antagonism that has characterized the globalization debate for the past twenty years and impeded alleviation of global poverty. We offer the powerful corporate world our ethic of engagement as a means of moving away from destructive, wasteful competition toward a corporate collectivism and cooperation, to enhance what Garten (2002) calls the "overall welfare of society" and Cahill (2002) calls the global "common good."

Notes and References

Introduction

References

Klein, N. *No Logo.* New York: Picador, 2000.
Levitt, T. "The Globalization of Markets." *Harvard Business Review,* May-June 1983, pp. 92–102.
Lorenz, C. "The Overselling of World Brands." *Financial Times,* July 19, 1984, p. 26.
McLuhan, M. *The Gutenberg Galaxy.* Toronto: University of Toronto Press, 1962.
Servan-Schreiber, J. J. *The American Challenge.* London: Hamish Hamilton, 1967.

Chapter One

Notes

1. We are employing the vocabulary of T. Kuhn in *The Structure of Scientific Revolutions,* 2nd ed. (Chicago: University of Chicago Press, 1970), pp. 23–51.
2. T. Levitt, "World War II Manpower Mobilization and Utilization in a Local Labor Market" (unpublished doctoral dissertation, Ohio State University, 1951).
3. T. Levitt, "The Dilemma of Antitrust Aims: Comment," *American Economic Review* 42 (1952): 893–895; T. Levitt, "Investment, Depression, and the Assurance of Prosperity," *Journal of Finance* 9 (1954): 235–251; T. Levitt, "Labor Force Stability and Armed Forces Expansion: A Comment," *American Economic Review* 44 (1954): 637–644; T. Levitt, "The Lonely Crowd and the Economic Man," *Quarterly Journal of Economics* 70 (1956): 95–116. S. M. Livingston and T. Levitt, "Competition and Retail Gasoline Prices," *Review of Economics and Statistics* 41 (May): 119–132.
4. T. Levitt, "Marketing Success Through the Differentiation of Anything," *Harvard Business Review* 58(Jan.-Feb. 1980): 83.

5. T. Levitt, "The Globalization of Markets," *Harvard Business Review* 61:3 (1983): 92–103.

6. See, for example, A. P. Felton, "Making the Marketing Concept Work," *Harvard Business Review* 37 (1959): 55–65; C. P. McNamara, "The Present Status of the Marketing Concept," *Journal of Marketing* 36: 50–57; A. K. Kohli and B. J. Jaworski, "Market Orientation: The Construct, Research Propositions, and Managerial Implications," *Journal of Marketing* 54 (1990): 1–18; P. Kotler, *Marketing Management*, 9th ed. (Upper Saddle River, N.J.: Prentice Hall, 1997): 19–27. The literature on "the marketing concept" is endless. It has been located as far in the past as 1776, when Adam Smith observed in *The Wealth of Nations* that the point of production was consumption. More common is to look to the General Electric Annual Report of 1952, which declared that "the marketing man" should be "introduce[d] . . . at the beginning rather than at the end of the production cycle and [should] integrate marketing into each phase of the business." R. M. Hill, "Theodore Levitt's Refinement of the Marketing Concept," in A. R. Andreasen and D. M. Gardner (eds.), *Diffusing Marketing Theory and Research: The Contributions of Bauer, Green, Kotler, and Levitt* (Chicago: American Marketing Association Proceedings Series, 1979), pp. 98–99.

7. For a critique of the view that there has been a migration from the production concept to the sales concept to the marketing concept, see R. A. Fullerton, "How Modern Is Modern Marketing? Marketing's Evolution and the Myth of the 'Production Era?'" *Journal of Marketing* 52 (1988): 108–125.

8. R. S. Tedlow, *Giants of Enterprise: Seven Business Innovators and the Empires They Built* (New York: HarperBusiness, 2001), pp. 231–232.

9. Levitt has a remarkable gift for making brief statements that bring readers up short and make them think. One example is the first line in his classic "Marketing Myopia": "Every major industry was once a growth industry." "Marketing Myopia," *Harvard Business Review* (July-Aug. 1960): 45. Neither has Levitt been averse to the shocking or outrageous declaration—for example, "Every sustained wave of technological progress and economic development everywhere has been fueled by greed, profiteering, special privileges and megalomania." "Yes, Throw Money at Problems," *New York Times*, Apr. 28, 1978, p. 27.

10. T. Levitt, conversations with coauthor R. S. Tedlow.

11. C. M. Christensen, *The Innovator's Dilemma: When New Technologies Cause Great Firms to Fail* (Boston: Harvard Business School Press, 1997).

12. E. S. Carpenter and M. McLuhan (eds.), *Explorations in Communication: An Anthology* (Boston: Beacon Press, 1960), p. xi, quoted in *Oxford English Dictionary*, 2d ed., s.v. "global."

13. "Nuclear Test-Ban Treaty." *Encyclopaedia Britannica Online.* 2002. [http://www.search.eb.com/bol/topic?eu=57860&sctn=1&pm=1]. This was followed by the Nuclear Non-Proliferation Treaty, which was signed by sixty-two countries in 1968: "Non-Proliferation of Nuclear Weapons, Treaty on the." *Encyclopaedia Britannica Online.* 2002. [http://lib.harvard.edu:2790/bol/topic?eu=57471&sctn=1&pm=1].

14. "Millions Join Earth Day Observances Across the Nation: Activity Ranges from Oratory to Legislation," *New York Times,* Apr. 23 1970, p. 1.

15. G. Jones, *The Evolution of International Business: An Introduction* (London: Routledge, 1996), p. 251.

16. J.-J. Servan-Schreiber, *The American Challenge* (New York: Atheneum, 1969). Originally published in French as *Le Défi Américain* (Paris: Denoël, 1967).

17. R. J. Barnet and R. E. Muller, *Global Reach: The Power of the Multinational Corporations* (New York: Simon & Schuster, 1974).

18. "Excerpts from President's Speech to National Association of Evangelicals," *New York Times,* Mar. 9, 1983.

19. United Nations, Department of International Economic and Social Affairs, *Statistical Office, 1983/84 Statistical Yearbook,* 34th ed. (New York: United Nations, 1986), pp. 6, 62–68.

20. For a recent discussion, see D. L. Spar, *Ruling the Waves: Cycles of Discovery, Chaos and Wealth from the Compass to the Internet* (New York: Harcourt, 2001).

21. R. D. Buzzell and others, *Marketing: A Contemporary Analysis,* 2nd ed. (New York: McGraw-Hill, 1972), p. 641.

22. H. C. Livesay, *American Made: Men Who Shaped the American Economy* (New York: Little, Brown, 1979), p. 281.

23. R. D. Buzzell and J.-L. LeCocq, "Polaroid France (S.A.)," in S. H. Star and others, *Problems in Marketing,* 5th ed. (New York: McGraw-Hill, 1977), pp. 191–213. See also R. S. Tedlow, "Advertising and Public Relations," in G. Porter (ed.), *Encyclopedia of American Economic History: Studies of the Principal Movements and Ideas* (New York: Scribner's, 1980) pp. 685, 677–695.

24. "Japan's Record Vehicle Output," *New York Times,* Jan. 27, 1981.

25. See, for example, "The Heat's on Levitt," *Marketing and Media Decisions* (Dec. 1984): 116–117, and "Is Global Marketing a Wise or Doable Strategy?" *Marketing and Media Decisions* (Jan. 1995): 47–55.

26. By the word *heuristic,* we mean a tool for understanding the world. For example, almost everyone agrees that a great deal of trade takes place in the world and that by many measures, the amount of trade has increased substantially over the past several decades. The question is how to interpret that fact. What does it mean? Globalization can be thought of as a tool for interpreting the fact of increased trade.

27. This is the title of a recent essay by three prominent economists: M. D. Bordo, B. Eichengreen, and D. A. Irwin, "Is Globalization Today Really Different Than Globalization a Hundred Years Ago?" in S. Collins and Robert L. Brookings (eds.), *Trade Policy Forum* (Washington, D.C.: Brookings Institution, 1999). Also see K. H. O'Rourke and J. G. Williamson, *Globalization and History: The Evolution of a Nineteenth-Century Atlantic Economy* (Cambridge, Mass.: MIT Press, 1999), and H. James, *The End of Globalization: Lessons from the Great Depression* (Cambridge, Mass.: Harvard University Press, 2001).

28. F. Braudel, *Civilization and Capitalism, 15th-18th Century,* 3 vols. (New York: HarperCollins, 1985).

29. An authoritative overview is J. Frankel, "Globalization of the Economy," in J. S. Nye and J. D. Donahue (eds.), *Governance in a Globalizing World* (Washington, D.C.: Brookings Institution Press, 2000). This enormous literature is also summarized effectively for managers by P. Ghemawat in his "Economic Evidence on the Globalization of Markets," Harvard Business School Note 701–015, 2000.

30. K. Ohmae, "Managing in a Borderless World," *Harvard Business Review* (May-June 1989).

31. As an aside, it is interesting to contemplate the demand for blue jeans and other consumer products in the context of the effectiveness of advertising. There was no advertising for such products designed specifically for communist countries, and yet the demand for them was intense. For a noteworthy essay on advertising in the communist world, see P. Hanson, *Advertising and Socialism: The Nature and Extent of Consumer Advertising in the Soviet Union, Poland, Hungary, and Yugoslavia* (Old Tappan, N.J.: Macmillan, 1974).

32. P. Ghemawat, "Distance Still Matters: The Hard Reality of Global Expansion," *Harvard Business Review* (Sept. 2001).

33. J. A. Quelch and C. A. Bartlett (eds.), *Global Marketing Management* (Reading, Mass.: Addison-Wesley, 1999), p. 2.

34. Levitt, "Globalization of Markets," p. 99. On the homogenizing influence of technology, see also pp. 93, 97, 99, and 102.

35. Levitt, "Globalization of Markets," p. 2.

36. Levitt, "Globalization of Markets," p. 92.

37. See, for example, P. J. Katzenstein, "Regionalism in World Politics," unpublished manuscript, Nov. 2001; The Group of Lisbon, *Limits to Competition* (Cambridge, Mass.: MIT Press, 1995); and P. Hirst and G. Thompson, *Globalization in Question,* 2nd ed. (London: Polity, 1999).

38. R. Gilpin, *The Challenge of Global Capitalism: The World Economy in the 21st Century* (Princeton, N.J.: Princeton University Press, 2000).

39. On regionalism, see R. Z. Lawrence, *Regionalism, Multilateralism, and Deeper Integration* (Washington, D.C.: Brookings, 1996).

40. P. J. Katzenstein, "Asian Regionalism in Comparative Perspective," in P. J. Katzenstein (ed.), *Network Power: Japan and Asia* (Ithaca, N.Y.: Cornell University Press, 1997); and Katzenstein, "United Germany in an Integrating Europe," in P. J. Katzenstein (ed.), *Tamed Power: Germany in Europe* (Ithaca, N.Y.: Cornell University Press, 1997).
41. J. A. Quelch and E. J. Hoff, "Customizing Global Marketing," *Harvard Business Review* 64:3 (May-June 1986): 59–68.
42. This was clear by the late 1980s as well. An insightful analysis of nine successful and eight failed cases of marketing standardization can be found in K. Kashani, "Beware the Pitfalls of Global Marketing," *Harvard Business Review* 67 (Sept.-Oct. 1989).
43. V. Forrester, *L'Horreur Economique* (Paris: Fayard, 1996).
44. A. Roy, "Power Politics: The Reincarnation of Rumpelstiltskin," in A. Roy (ed.), *Power Politics* (Boston: South End Press, 2001), pp. 35–86. The novel that made her literary reputation and won her the Booker Prize is *The God of Small Things* (New York: Random House, 1997).
45. R. Abdelal and L. Alfaro, "Malaysia: Capital and Control," Harvard Business School case 702–040, 2001.
46. Levitt, "Globalization of Markets," p. 101.
47. R. Abdelal, *National Purpose in the World Economy* (Ithaca, N.Y.: Cornell University Press, 2001).
48. F. Fukuyama, *The End of History and the Last Man* (New York: Free Press, 1992).

Chapter Two

References

Levitt, T. "Marketing Myopia," *Harvard Business Review* (July-Aug. 1960): 45.
Levitt, T. *Innovation in Marketing*. New York: McGraw-Hill, 1962.
Levitt, T. "Marketing Success Through the Differentiation of Anything," *Harvard Business Review* (Jan.-Feb. 1980).
Levitt, T. "The Globalization of Markets," *Harvard Business Review* (May-June 1983).
Levitt, T. *The Marketing Imagination*. New York: Free Press, 1983.

Chapter Three

References

Asahi Shinbum. Jan. 5, 2003.
Central Council for Financial Services Information. "Kinyuu Shisan no Jyoukyou [State of holding of financial assets]." 2003. [http://www.save info.or.jp/down/hist/histmenu.html].

Council of Japanese Stock Exchanges. *Share Ownership Survey.* Tokyo: Council of Japanese Stock Exchanges, 2003.

Economic and Social Research Institute, Cabinet Office. "Survey of Consumer Trends." 2003. [http://www.esri.cao.go.jp/jp/stat/shouhi/0203fukyuritsu.xls].

Gourman, J. *The Gourman Report: A Rating of Graduate and Professional Programs in American and International Universities.* New York: Princeton Review, 1997.

"International Public Offerings." *Investment Dealers' Digest,* Jan. 10, 2000, p. 35.

"International Public Offerings." *Investment Dealers' Digest,* Jan. 8, 2001, p. 59.

Japan Electronics and Information Technology Industries Association. "Domestic Shipments of Major Consumer Electronic Equipment." 2003. [http://www.jeita.or.jp/english/stat/shipment/2001/index.htm].

Kikuchi, M., Nagayoshi, H., and Fujita, K. Japan Strategy Memo. 2002.

Levitt, T. "The Globalization of Markets." *Harvard Business Review* (May-June 1983).

Ministry of Education, Culture, Sports, Science and Technology. "Worldwide Nobel Prize Winners." [http://wwwwp.mext.go.jp/kag2002/index-58.html#ssA.3.20].

Ministry of Education, Culture, Sports, Science and Technology, *White Paper, Science and Technology, 2002.*

Ministry of Economy, Trade and Industry. *Service-Sangyo no Genjo* [Current report of service industry]. Tokyo: METI, 2002.

Okabe, K., Kose, N., and Nishimura, K. *College Students Who Cannot Calculate Fractions* [Bunsu ga Dekinai Daigakusei]. Tokyo: Toyo Keizai Shinpousha, 1999.

Organization of Economic Cooperation and Development. "Knowledge and Skills for Life: First Results from PISA 2000." [http://www1.oecd.org/publications/e-book/9601141E.PDF].

"The 100 Top Brands." *Business Week,* Aug. 2001. [http://www.businessweek.com/pdfs/2001/0132-toprank.pdf].

Porter, M. E. *Competitive Advantage of Nations.* New York: Free Press, 1990.

Porter, M. E., and others. *The Global Competitiveness Report 2001–2002: World Economic Forum.* New York: Oxford University Press, 2002.

Porter, M. E. Takeuchi, H., and Sakakibara, M. *Can Japan Compete?* Cambridge, Mass.: Perseus Publishing, 2000.

Works Institute of Recruit "*Syusyoku Sibousaki* [Preferred companies to work ranking]." [http://www.works-i.com/pdf/univ_jikeiretsu.xls].

World Economic Forum. *The Global Competitiveness Report, 2001–2002.* 2003. [www.weforum.org].

Yano Research Institute. *Import Market and Brand 2002.* Tokyo: Yano Research Institute, 2002.

Chapter Four

Notes

1. T. Levitt, "The Globalization of Markets," *Harvard Business Review* (May 1983).
2. See, for example, G. S. Becker, *Accounting for Tastes* (Cambridge, Mass.: Harvard University Press, 1996); A. Damasio, *The Feeling of What Happens* (San Diego: Harcourt, 1999); T. D. Wilson, *Strangers to Ourselves: Discovering the Adaptive Unconscious* (Cambridge, Mass.: Belknap Press, 2002).
3. This stylized example is based on data from a field study supervised by the first author and realized by Harvard Business School students Nikita Agrawal, Ada Lien, and Daniela Nedialkova.
4. See, for example, M. H. Bond, *Beyond the Chinese Face* (New York: Oxford University Press, 1994).
5. Damasio, *The Feeling of What Happens.*
6. J. LeDoux, *The Emotional Brain* (New York: Touchstone, 1996).
7. For a review, see G. Zaltman, *How Customers Think: Essential Insights into the Mind of the Market* (Boston: Harvard Business School Press, 2003).
8. M. Mark and C. S. Pearson, *The Hero and the Outlaw: Building Extraordinary Brands Through the Power of Archetypes* (New York: McGraw-Hill, 2001).
9. D. E. Brown, *Human Universals* (New York: McGraw-Hill, 1991).
10. Damasio, *The Feeling of What Happens*; J. LeDoux, *Synaptic Self* (New York: Viking, 2002); Wilson, *Strangers to Ourselves.*
11. D. L. Schacter, *The Seven Sins of Memory* (Boston: Houghton Mifflin, 2001).
12. We do not mean to say that each consumption act should require high involvement. What we mean is that successful products will produce a confirmation or an enhancement of the self.
13. M. Csikszentmihalyi, *Flow: The Psychology of Optimal Experience* (New York: HarperCollins, 1990); E. J. Langer, *The Psychology of Control* (Thousand Oaks, Calif.: Sage, 1983); B. Schmitt, *Experiential Marketing: How to Get Customers to Sense, Feel, Think, Act, Relate to Your Company and Brands* (New York: Free Press, 1999); T. Scitovsky, *The Joyless Economy: The Psychology of Human Satisfaction* (New York: Oxford University Press, 1992).

Chapter Five

Notes

1. See R. E. Vernon, "International Investment and International Trade in the Product Cycle," *Quarterly Journal of Economics* 80 (1966): 190–207.

2. See J. M. Stoppard and L. T. Wells Jr., *Managing the Multinational Enterprise* (New York: Basic Books, 1972).
3. For cases and readings that reflect the concerns of the time, see S. M. Davis, *Managing and Organizing Multinational Corporations* (New York: Pergamon Press, 1979).
4. See C. K. Prahalad and Y. L. Doz, *The Multinational Mission: Balancing Local Demands and Global Vision* (New York: Free Press, 1987); and Y. L. Doz and C. K. Prahalad, "Headquarters Influence and Strategic Control in MNCs," *Sloan Management Review* 22, (1981): 55–72.
5. See W. G. Egelhoff, *Organizing the Multinational Enterprise: An Information Processing Perspective* (New York: Ballinger, 1988).
6. See J. I. Martinez and J. C. Jarillo, "The Evolution of Research on Coordination Mechanisms in Multinational Corporations," *Journal of International Business Studies* 22 (1989): 429–444; A. K. Gupta and V. Govindarajan, "Knowledge Flows and the Structure of Control Within Multinational Corporations," *Academy of Management Review* 16 (1991): 768–792; and N. Nohria and S. Ghoshal, *The Differentiated Network: Organizing Multinational Corporations for Value Creation* (San Francisco: Jossey-Bass. 1997).
7. See B. Kogut, "Designing Global Strategies: Comparative and Competitive Value-Added Chains," *Sloan Management Review* 26 (1985): 15–28; and B. Kogut, "Designing Global Strategies: Profiting from Operational Flexibility," *Sloan Management Review* 26 (1985): 27–38.
8. See M. E. Porter, *Competition in Global Industries* (Boston: Harvard Business School Press, 1986); Prahalad and Doz, *The Multinational Mission*; and S. Ghoshal, "Global Strategy: An Organizing Framework," *Strategic Management Journal* 8 (1987): 425–440.
9. See C. A. Bartlett and S. Ghoshal, "Managing Across Borders: New Strategic Challenges," *Sloan Management Review* 27 (1987): 7–17; and C. A. Bartlett and S. Ghoshal, "Managing Across Borders: New Organizational Responses," *Sloan Management Review* 27 (1987): 43–53.
10. See G. Hedlund, "The Hypermodern MNC: A Heterarchy?" *Human Resource Management* 25 (1986): 9–35.
11. See Prahalad and Doz, *The Multinational Mission*.
12. See C. A. Bartlett and S. Ghoshal, *Managing Across Borders: The Transnational Solution* (Boston: Harvard Business School Press, 1989).
13. See Nohria and Ghoshal, *The Differentiated Network*.
14. See Bartlett and Ghoshal, *Managing Across Borders*.
15. For an in-depth look at BP on this issue, see S. E. Prokesch, "Unleashing the Power of Learning: An Interview with British Petroleum's John Browne," *Harvard Business Review* 79 (1997): 107; and M. T. Hansen and B. Von Oetinger, "Introducing T-Shaped Managers:

Knowledge Management's Next Generation," *Harvard Business Review* 75 (2001): 146–163.

16. See B. Kogut and U. Zander, "Knowledge of the Firm, Combinative Capabilities, and the Replication of Technology," *Organization Science* 3 (1992): 383–397; C. Hill, "Diversification and Economic Performance: Bringing Structure and Corporate Management Back into the Picture," in R. Rumelt, D. Schendel, and D. Teece (eds.), *Fundamental Issues in Strategy* (Boston: Harvard Business School Press, 1994); and J. Nahapiet and S. Ghoshal, "Social Capital, Intellectual Capital and the Organizational Advantage," *Academy of Management Review* 23 (1998): 242–266.

17. Personal interview, July 2002.

18. See P. R. Lawrence and N. Nohria, *Driven: How Human Nature Shapes Our Choices* (San Francisco: Jossey-Bass, 2001).

19. This section draws on M. Hansen, "Turning the Lone Star into a Real Team Player," *Financial Times*, Aug. 8, 2002; and M. Hansen, B. Lovas, and L. Mors, "Barriers to Knowledge Sharing in Organizations: A Four-Factor Perspective," Harvard Business School working paper, 2002.

20. See, for example, M. B. Brewer, "Ingroup Bias in the Minimal Intergroup Situation: A Cognitive Motivational Analysis," *Psychological Bulletin* 86 (1979): 307–324; and H. Tajfel and J. C. Turner, "The Social Identity Theory of Intergroup Behavior," in S. Worchel and W. G. Austin (eds.), *Psychology of Intergroup Relations,* 2nd ed. (Chicago: Nelson Hall, 1986).

21. See P. J. Oakes, S. A. Haslam, B. Morrison, and D. Grace, "Becoming an In-Group: Reexamining the Impact of Familiarity on Perceptions of Group Homogeneity," *Social Psychology Quarterly* 58 (1995): 52–61; and D. A. Wilder, "Reduction of Intergroup Discrimination Through Individuation of the Out-Group," *Journal of Personality and Social Psychology 36* (1978): 1361–1374.

22. See R. H. Hayes and K. B. Clark, *Exploring the Sources of Productivity Differences at the Factory Level* (New York: Wiley, 1985); and R. Katz and T. J. Allen, "Investigating the Not Invented Here (NIH) Syndrome: A Look at the Performance, Tenure, and Communication Patterns of Fifty R&D Project groups," in M. L. Tushman and W. L. Moore (eds.), *Readings in the Management of Innovation,* 2nd ed. (New York: Ballinger/HarperCollins, 1988).

23. See also S. Ghoshal and L. Gratton, "Integrating the Enterprise," *Sloan Management Review* 44 (2002): 31.

24. See M. T. Hansen, "The Search-Transfer Problem: The Role of Weak Ties in Sharing Knowledge Across Organization Subunits," *Administrative Science Quarterly* 44 (1999): 82–111.

25. For more details on knowledge management in management consulting companies, see M. T. Hansen, N. Nohria, and T. Tierney, T.

"What's Your Strategy for Managing Knowledge?" *Harvard Business Review* 77:2 (1999): 106–117.

26. See S. Milgram, "The Small World Problem," *Psychology Today* 2 (1967): 60–67; and D. Watts, *Small Worlds* (Princeton, N.J.: Princeton University Press, 1999).

27. See A. K. Gupta and V. Govindarajan, "Knowledge Flows Within Multinational Corporations," *Strategic Management Journal* 21 (2000): 473–496.

28. See W. Tsai, "Social Structure of 'Competition' Within a Multiunit Organization: Coordination, Competition, and Intraorganizational Knowledge Sharing," *Organization Science* 13 (2002): 179–190.

29. For a detailed description of these changes at Morgan Stanley, see "Morgan Stanley: Becoming a One-Firm Firm," Harvard Business School teaching case no. 9–400–043, 2000, and "The Firmwide 360-Degree Performance Evaluation Process at Morgan Stanley," Harvard Business School teaching case no. 9–498–053, 1998.

30. See U. Zander and B. Kogut, "Knowledge and the Speed of Transfer and Imitation of Organizational Capabilities: An Empirical Test," *Organization Science* 6 (1995): 76–92.

31. See M. Haas, unpublished dissertation, Harvard Business School, 2002.

32. See Hansen, "The Search-Transfer Problem."

33. Hansen, "The Search-Transfer Problem."

34. This grouping is based on a factor analysis of the sixteen items listed in Table 5.1. The correlations are higher among the items within a category than among items across categories.

35. This section draws on Hansen and Von Oetinger, "Introducing T-Shaped Managers."

36. Hansen and Von Oetinger, "Introducing T-Shaped Managers."

37. See R. H. Coase, "The Nature of the Firm," *Econometrica* 4 (1937): 386–405.

38. See R. E. Caves, *Multinational Enterprise and Economic Analysis* (Cambridge: Cambridge University Press, 1982).

39. See C. Barnard, *The Functions of the Executive* (Cambridge, Mass.: Harvard University Press, 1939).

Chapter Six

Notes

1. For an illustration of the difference that this might make, see the "Convergence Dynamics" section indicating that global pricing might reduce rather than increase the equilibrium degree of global product standardization.

2. The one respect in which STAR seems not to have changed its initial strategy was that it continued to be a portal for diffusing content across Asia. But while its strategy continues to involve standardization in this sense, it was less standardized than the strategy pursued early on, which involved and in fact focused on standardization of content. This primary dimension of attempted standardization was clearly overturned later, as described later in the text.
3. Author's interview with STAR TV CEO James Murdoch and COO Bruce Churchill, May 1, 2001.
4. Estimates of News Corporation's total investment were reported in Lippman (2002). Estimates of the present value of the total investment as of early 2002 are based on a discount rate of 12.5 percent and the author's interviews with current and format STAR TV executives regarding the time pattern of investment.
5. Author's interviews with analysts and former STAR employees.
6. In addition, the notion that the delay was an optimally flexible response to an uncertain environment was undercut by the large amount that News Corporation paid for STAR. This presumably reduced the attractiveness of engaging in experimentation or on-line learning by initially retaining the business model that STAR had started with and changing it only as changes clearly became necessary relative to a situation in which the upfront commitment was relatively small.
7. A more complete analysis of these data would also have to control for variations in barriers to imports, but that falls outside the scope of this chapter.
8. For a recent survey of some of the economics of two-sided markets, see Evans (2002).
9. At least one kind of international homogeneity could easily be dealt with by aggregating similar countries into clusters. Intranational heterogeneity would require an analytic shift to individual segments. Some analysis along the latter lines is sketched in the next section, which looks at the impact of demand dynamics on globalization.
10. The generalization to price-elastic demand is nontrivial and typically requires strong symmetry assumptions to yield closed-form expressions (Anderson and de Palma, 2000). In the context here, it seems more important to allow for strategic asymmetry between the globally standardized producer and locally customized producers rather than allocate complexity so as to focus on price elasticity.
11. Mass customization suggests a possible caveat to this conclusion. Note, however, the limits that have been observed to date in successful implementation of such strategies.
12. Caves, Porter, and Spence (1980) informally reach similar conclusions.

13. There were probably some reductions in programming costs, adjusted for quality, as well.

14. Just in case this second possibility seems rather improbable, it is worth mentioning that data from the past few decades have indicated greater geographical dispersion rather than concentration of production in most categories of products around the world (Knetter and Slaughter, 1999) and led to a rejection of product life cycle theory by its original proponent, the late Raymond Vernon, principally on the grounds that it no longer makes much sense to talk of lead countries (see Vernon, 1966, 1979). Also note that at least some microeconomists find it natural to assume that globalization is making consumers more rather than less picky (Anderson and de Palma, 2000), that is, increasing t_i.

15. In spring 2001, Murdoch's initial attempts to acquire General Motors's interest in DirectTV to fill out the U.S. gap in News Corporation's global satellite TV holdings were challenged by Senator John McCain, then chairman of the Senate Commerce Committee, on the grounds that it could result in "a consolidation of power the likes of which this country has not seen since William Randolph Hearst" (Harding and McGregor, 2001, p. 1).

16. Rupert Murdoch, quoted in the *Los Angeles Times,* Feb. 13, 1994, p. D:1.

17. For some evidence in the context of the Taiwanese market, see Chen (2001).

18. This discussion of the positive spillovers from *Kaun Banega Crorepati?* to the rest of STAR's lineup is based on research by Bharat Anand.

19. Author's interview with STAR TV CEO James Murdoch and COO Bruce Churchill, May 1, 2001.

20. Krever (1998).

References

Anderson, J. E., and Marcouiller, D. "Trade, Insecurity, and Home Bias: An Empirical Investigation." National Bureau of Economic Research Working Paper, no. 7000, 1999.

Anderson, S. P., and de Palma, A. "From Local to Global Competition." *European Economic Review,* 2000, *44*(3), 423–448.

Appadurai, A. "Disjuncture and Difference in the Global Cultural Economy." *Theory, Culture and Society,* 1990, *7*(2–3), 295–310.

Arnold, D., Birkinshaw, J., and Toulan, O. "Implementing Global Account Management in Multinational Corporations." Unpublished manuscript, Marketing Science Institute Report, 2000.

Batra, R., and others. "Effects of Brand Local and Nonlocal Origin on Consumer Attitudes in Developing Countries." *Journal of Consumer Psychology,* 2000, *9*(2), 83–95.

Biltereyst, D. "Language and Culture as Ultimate Barriers? An Analysis of the Circulation, Consumption and Popularity of Fiction in Small European Countries." *European Journal of Communication,* 1992, 7(4), 517–540.

Boddewyn, J. J., Soehl, R., and Picard, J. "Standardization in International Marketing: Is Ted Levitt in Fact Right?" *Business Horizons,* 1986, *29*(6), 69.

Buzzell, R. D. "Can You Standardize Multinational Marketing?" *Harvard Business Review,* 1968, *46,* 102–113.

Caves, R. E., Porter, M. E., and Spence, A. M. *Competition in the Open Economy: A Model Applied to Canada.* Cambridge, Mass.: Harvard University Press, 1980.

Chen, P.-H. "Transnational Cable Channels in the Taiwan Market: A Study of Domestication through Programming Strategies." Unpublished manuscript, Graduate Institute of Mass Communication, National Taiwan Normal University, 2001.

Chmielewski-Falkenheim, B. J. "Asymmetries Reconfigured: South American Television Flows in the 1990s." *Canadian Journal of Communication,* 2000, 25(2), 285–306.

Cowen, T. *Creative Destruction: How Globalization Is Changing the World's Cultures.* Princeton, N.J.: Princeton University Press, 2002.

Djankov, S., McLiesh, C., Nenova, T., and Shleifer, A. "Who Owns the Media?" National Bureau of Economic Research Working Paper, no. W8288, 2001.

Douglas, S. P., and Wind, Y. "The Myth of Globalization." *Columbia Journal of World Business,* 1987, *22*(4), 19–29.

Evans, D. S. "The Antitrust Economics of Two-Sided Markets." Unpublished manuscript, SSRN Electronic Paper Collection, 332022, 2002.

Gabler, N. "The World Still Watches America." *New York Times,* Jan. 9, 2003, p. A27.

Ghemawat, P. *Commitment: The Dynamic of Strategy.* New York: Free Press, 1991.

Ghemawat, P. "Star TV in 1993." Harvard Business School Case, no. 9–701–012, 2000a.

Ghemawat, P. "Star TV in 2000." Harvard Business School Case, no. 9–701–031, 2000b.

Ghemawat, P. "Distance Still Matters: The Hard Reality of Global Expansion." *Harvard Business Review,* 2001, *79*(8), 137–147.

Ghemawat, P. "Arbitrage: The Forgotten Strategy." *Harvard Business Review,* 2003a, *81*(11), 76–84.

Ghemawat, P. "Semiglobalization and International Business Strategy." *Journal of International Business Studies,* 2003b, *34*(2), 138–152.

Ghemawat, P., and Mallick, R. "The Industry-Level Structure of International Trade Networks: A Gravity-Based Approach." Unpublished manuscript, 2003.

Ghemawat, P., and Spence, A. M. "Modeling Global Competition." In M. E. Porter (ed.), *Competition in Global Industries.* Boston, Mass.: Harvard Business School Press, 1986.

Hannerz, U. "Cosmopolitans and Locals in World Culture." *Theory, Culture and Society,* 1990, 7(2–3), 237–251.

Harding, J., and McGregor, D. "Senator Warns Murdoch over U.S. Satellite Plans." *Financial Times,* May 10, 2001, p. 1.

Johansson, J. K. *Global Marketing: Foreign Entry, Local Marketing, and Global Management.* Chicago: Irwin, 1997.

Kanso, A. "International Advertising Strategies: Global Commitment to Local Vision." *Journal of Advertising Research,* 1992, *32*(1), 10–13.

Kapferer, J.-N. *Strategic Brand Management: Creating and Sustaining Brand Equity Long Term.* (2nd ed.) Dover, N.H.: Kogen Page, 1997.

Kapferer, J.-N. "Is There Really No Hope for Local Brands?" Paper presented at the Marketing Science Institute's conference on Global Branding, Milan, Italy, June 20–21, 2000.

Klein, N. *No Logo: No Space, No Choice, No Jobs.* London: Flamingo, 2000.

Knetter, M. M., and Slaughter, M. J. "Measuring Product-Market Integration." National Bureau of Economic Research Working Paper, no. 6969, 1999.

Krever, R. "Not Shaken, Not Stirred: Murdoch, Multinationals and Tax." Australian Broadcasting Company, Mar. 22, 1998. [http://www.abc.net.au/rn/talks/bbing/stories/s10609.htm].

Levitt, T. "The Globalization of Markets." *Harvard Business Review,* 1983, *61*(3), 92–102.

Lippman, J. "Star TV Records First Profit on Progress in India and China—Results Mark Turning Point in Asian TV Market." *Wall Street Journal Europe,* Apr. 11, 2002, p. A8.

Montgomery, D. B., Yip, G. S., and Villalonga, B. "Demand for and Use of Global Account Management." Marketing Science Institute Report, no. 99–115, 1999.

Morwind, K., and Schroiff, H.-W. "Global Branding: Changes and Risks for a Transnational Company." Paper presented at the Marketing Science Institute's conference on Global Branding, Milan, Italy, June 20–21, 2000.

"Murdoch Bets on Channels' Star Potential." *Financial Times,* Aug. 3, 1993, pp. 20.

"Murdoch's Twinkler; Indian Television." *Economist,* July 26, 2003, p. 63.

Narayandas, D., Quelch, J. A., and Swartz, G. "Prepare Your Company for Global Pricing." *MIT Sloan Management Review,* 2000, *42*(1), 61–70.

Pedder, S. "Survey of Television: Think Local." *Economist,* Apr. 13, 2002, p. 12.

Pine, B. J., II. *Mass Customization: The New Frontier in Business Competition.* Boston: Harvard Business School Press, 1992.

Quelch, J. A. "Global Marketing Guru Interview by Randall Rothenberg." *Strategy and Business,* 2000, third quarter, pp. 93–100.

Rousslang, D. J., and To, T. "Domestic Trade and Transportation Costs as Barriers to International Trade." *Canadian Journal of Economics,* 1993, *26*(1), 208–221.

Shapiro, C. "The Theory of Business Strategy." *Rand Journal of Economics,* 1989, *20*(1), 125–137.

Steenkamp, J.-B., Batra, R., and Alden, D. L. "How Perceived Brand Globalness Creates Brand Value." Unpublished manuscript, Michigan Business School, 2000.

Sutton, J. *Sunk Costs and Market Structure: Price Competition, Advertising, and the Evolution of Concentration.* Cambridge, Mass.: MIT Press, 1991.

Sutton, J. *Technology and Market Structure: Theory and History.* Cambridge, Mass.: MIT Press, 1998.

Terpstra, V. *American Marketing in the Common Market.* New York: Praeger, 1967.

Vernon, R. "International Investment and International Trade in the Product Cycle." *Quarterly Journal of Economics,* 1966, *80*(2), 190–207.

Vernon, R. "The Product Cycle Hypothesis in a New International Environment." *Oxford Bulletin of Economics and Statistics,* 1979, *41*(4), 255–267.

Waterman, D., and Rogers, E. M. "The Economics of Television Program Production and Trade in Far East Asia." *Journal of Communication,* 1994, *44*(3), 89–111.

Yip, G. "Global Strategy in the Twenty-First Century." In S. Crainer and D. Dearlove (eds.), *The Financial Times Handbook of Management.* London: Pitman Publishing, 2001.

Chapter Eight

References

Levitt, T. "The Globalization of Markets." *Harvard Business Review,* May-June 1983, pp. 92–102.

Tomkins, R. "As Hostility Towards America Grows, Will the World Lose Its Appetite for Coca-Cola, McDonald's and Nike?" *Financial Times,* Mar. 19, 2003, p. 19.

Chapter Nine

References

Anderson, B. *Imagined Communities: Reflections on the Origin and Spread of Nationalism.* New York: Verso, 1983.

Bartlett, C. A., and Ghoshal, S. *Managing Across Borders.* (2nd ed.) Boston: Harvard Business School Press, 1998.

Hannerz, U. *Cultural Complexity: Studies in the Social Organization of Meaning.* New York: Columbia University Press, 1992.

Holt, D. B., Quelch, J., and Taylor, E. "Make the Most of Your Global Brand." Harvard Business School, working paper, 2003.

Johansson, J. K., and Ronkainen, I. A. "The Esteem of Global Brands." McDonough School of Business, Georgetown University, working paper, 2003.

Klein, N. *No Logo: Taking Aim at the Brand Bullies.* New York: Picador, 2000.

Levitt, T. "The Globalization of Markets," *Harvard Business Review,* 1983, *61*(3).

Quelch, J., and Hoff, E. J. "Customizing Global Marketing." *Harvard Business Review,* 1986, *64*(3), 59–68.

Steenkamp, J.E.M., Batra, R., and Alden, D. L. "How Perceived Brand Globalness Creates Brand Value" *Journal of International Business Studies,* 2003, *34,* 53–65.

Chapter Ten

Notes

1. J. Quelch, "The Return of the Global Brand," *Harvard Business Review,* 2003, *81*(8), 22–23.
2. Quelch, "The Return of the Global Brand."
3. *PR Week,* Feb. 14, 2003.
4. B. B. Gardner and S. J. Levy, "The Product and the Brand," *Harvard Business Review,* Mar.–Apr. 1955.

Chapter Eleven

Notes

1. Cf. Kanso and Nelson (2002) and the references cited there.
2. This growth rate calculation was based on WPP's estimates of the size of the worldwide marketing communications expenditures presented each year in its annual report.

3. It bears noting that the gross incomes and ranking shown in Table 11.1 differ from those reported by AA for two reasons. First, in contrast to generally accepted accounting principles (GAAP), AA calculates a parent firm's gross income by weighting the gross incomes of subsidiary organizations according to the percentage of equity owned by the parent. Under GAAP, the parent company reports the income of a subsidiary only when ownership exceeds 50 percent of the subsidiary's equity. Second, AA does not include in gross income revenues derived from several non-advertising-related services, including public relations and research. See Endicott (2002) for further details.

4. Agency size is sometimes gauged by the magnitude of clients' "billings," which include outlays for media space and time, charges for production advertising and promotional material, and the like. Estimates of billings are notoriously suspect as a measure of agency output or scale inasmuch as to varying degrees, they represent "capitalized billings," calculated by capitalizing an agency's gross income at some rate, such as the reciprocal of the commission rate on media expenditures used to compensate a "full-service" agency. Over time, capitalized billings have departed from true billings as agencies have expanded and unbundled the mix of services they offer and as clients have come to rely more on fee-based and less on commission-based compensation methods. Cf. Cardona (2002a).

5. Also see Sheth and Sisodia (2002).

References

American Association of Advertising Agencies. *A Practical Solution to Client-Agency Account Conflicts.* New York: American Association of Advertising Agencies, July 1979.

Anholt, S. "Updating the International Advertising Model." *Admap,* 2000, no. 407, 18–21.

Bailey, E. E., and Friedlander, A. F. "Market Structure and Multiproduct Industries." *Journal of Economic Literature,* 1982, *20,* 1024–1048.

Berndt, E. R. *The Practice of Econometrics.* Reading, Mass.: Addison-Wesley, 1991.

Bower, J. L., and Ellingson Hout, S. "WPP—Integrating Icons to Leverage Knowledge." Harvard Business School Case, no. 9-396-249, Nov. 14, 2001.

Cardona, M. M. "Billings Lose Agency Value." *Advertising Age,* July 22, 2002a, p. 6.

Cardona, M. M. "Ad Holding Company Model Defended at Conference." 2002b. *AdAge.Com.* [http://adage.com/news.cms?newsId=36625].

Caves, R. E., and Porter, M. E. "From Entry Barriers to Mobility Barriers: Conjectural Decisions and Contrived Deterrence to New Competition." *Quarterly Journal of Economics*, 1977, *91*, 241–261.

Doft, D. B., Ammon, A. M., and Gawrelski, K. "The Evolution of Advertising 2003." Equity Research, CIBC World Markets, New York, Nov. 14, 2002.

Elliot, S. "Advertising's Big Four: Its Their World Now." *New York Times*, Mar. 31, 2002, sec. 3:2, 10.

Endicott, R. C. "Fifty-Eighth Annual Advertising Agency Report." *Advertising Age*, Apr. 22, 2002, pp. 1, S1-S21.

Eviews4. *User's Guide*. Irvine, Calif.: Quantitative Micro Software, 2000.

Ezekiel, M., and Fox, K. A. *Methods of Correlation and Regression Analysis*. (3rd ed.) New York: Wiley, 1959.

Fallon, I. *The Brothers: The Saatchi & Saatchi Story*. Chicago: Contemporary Books, 1989.

Fine, L. R., and others. *Advertising and Marketing Services: Global Ad Primer*. New York: Global Securities Research and Economics Group, Merrill Lynch, Feb. 20, 2003.

Goldman, K. *Conflicting Accounts: The Creation and Rise of the Saatchi & Saatchi Advertising Empire*. New York: Simon & Schuster, 1997.

Horsky, S. "The Changing Architecture of Advertising Agencies." Arison School of Business, Herzliya, Israel, unpublished paper, July 2002.

Johnson, H. W., and Simon, J. L. "The Success of Mergers of Advertising Agencies." In J. L. Simon, *Issues in the Economics of Advertising*. Urbana: University of Illinois Press, 1970.

Johnson, R. *Marion Harper*. Chicago: Crain Books, 1982.

Kanso, A., and Nelson, R. A. "Advertising Localization Overshadows Standardization." *Journal of Advertising Research*, 2002, *42*, 79–89.

Khermouch, G., "Interpulic Group: Synergy—or Sinkhole?" *Business Week*, Apr. 21, 2003, pp. 76–77.

Kim, K. K. "Spreading the Net: The Consolidation Process of Large Transnational Advertising Agencies in the 1980s and Early 1990s." *International Journal of Advertising*, 1995, *14*(3), 1995, 195–217.

King III, C., Silk, A. J., and Kettelhohn, N. "Knowledge Spillovers and Growth in the Disagglomeration of U.S. Advertising Agency Industry." *Journal of Economics and Management Strategy*, 2003, *12*.

Lawrence, R. G. "Parents and Progeny." *Agency*, 2000, *10*, 10–11.

Levitt, T. "The Globalization of Markets." *Harvard Business Review*, 1983, *61*, 92–102.

MacDonald, G. M., and Slivinski, A. "The Simple Analytics of Competitive Equilibrium with Multiproduct Firms." *American Economic Review*, 1989, *77*, 941–953.

Mandese, J. "Consolidation or Consolation? Madison Avenue's Big Get Bigger." *ADMAP*, 2002, no. 430, p. 8.

Merron, J. "Putting Foreign Consumers on the Map: J. Walter Thompson's Struggle with General Motors' International Advertising Account in the 1920s." *Business History Review,* 1999, *73,* 465–502.

Paster, H. "Measuring the Size of an Advertising Agency." *American Association of Advertising Agencies Newsletter,* Sept. 1981, p. 2.

Paul, C. J. *Cost Structure and the Measurement of Economic Performance.* Norwell, Mass.: Kluwer, 1999.

Pindyck, R. S., and Rubinfield, D. L. *Microeconomics.* (3rd ed.) Upper Saddle River, N.J.: Prentice Hall, 1995.

Raynor, M. E., and Bower, J. L. "Lead from the Center: How to Manage Divisions Dynamically." *Harvard Business Review,* 2001, *79,* 93–100.

Schmalensee, R. L., Silk, A. J., and Bojanek, R. "The Impact of Scale and Media Mix on Advertising Agency Costs." *Journal of Business,* 1983, *56,* 453–475.

Schmidt, P. "A Note on the Estimation of Seemingly Unrelated Regressions Using Unequal Numbers of Observations." University of North Carolina, unpublished paper, 1975.

Sheth, J. N. "The Future of the Advertising Agency Business." Speech delivered at the Annual Meeting of the American Association of Advertising Agencies, Mar. 10, 1986.

Sheth, J. N., and Sisodia, R. *The Rule of Three.* New York: Free Press, 2002.

Silk, A. J., and Berndt, E. R. "Scale and Scope Effects on Advertising Agency Costs." *Marketing Science,* 1993, *12,* 53–72.

Silk, A. J., and Berndt, E. R. "Costs, Institutional Mobility Barriers, and Market Structure: Advertising Agencies as Multiproduct Firms." *Journal of Economics and Management Strategy,* 1995, *3,* 47–480.

Silk, A. J., and King III, C. "Changes in the Structure of U.S. Advertising Agency Industry." Harvard Business School, working paper, 2003.

Weinstein, A. K. "The International Expansion of U.S. Multinational Advertising Agencies." *M.S.U. Business Topics,* Summer 1974, pp. 29–35.

West, D. C. "From T-Square to T-Plan: The London Office of the J. Walter Thompson Advertising Agency." *Business History,* 1987, *29,* 199–217.

West, D. C. "Multinational Competition in the British Advertising Agency Business, 1936–1987." *Business History Review,* 1988, *62,* 467–501.

Wooldridge, J. *Econometric Analysis of Cross Section and Panel Data.* Cambridge, Mass.: MIT Press, 2002.

Chapter Twelve

Notes

1. We use the term *supply chain* to denote a set of firms (for example, suppliers, manufacturers, distributors, retailers, transporters) that interact to manufacture and deliver a product or service to a consumer.

2. Share of imports (as a percentage of units) is likely to be even higher given that shoes manufactured in China tend to be cheaper than those manufactured in countries such as Italy and Brazil, which also export substantial footwear to the United States.

3. Readers interested in understanding these concepts in greater depth are directed to Simchi-Levy, Kiminsky, and Simchi-Levi (2000) or a number of other texts for suitable reference lists.

4. In this chapter, we do not distinguish between MRP and MRP II systems. It is estimated that to date, U.S. companies have trained more than 1 million people to operate seventy thousand installed MRP systems.

5. The beer game is described in detail in Hammond (1994b).

6. They have also been termed ECR (efficient consumer response), CRP (continuous replenishment of products) and JITD (just-in-time delivery).

7. Domestic factories have more expensive labor that induces them to target higher-capacity utilization.

References

Austin, J. P. *Managing in Developing Countries.* New York: Free Press, 1990.

Bowersox, D. J., and others. *Leading Edge Logistics: Competence Positioning for the 1990s.* Oak Brook, Ill.: Council of Logistics Management, 1989.

Dell, M., and Magretta, J. "The Power of Virtual Integration: An Interview with Dell Computer's Michael Dell." *Harvard Business Review,* 1998, 76(2), 72–84.

Dixit, A. K. "Entry and Exit Decisions Under Uncertainty." *Journal of Political Economy,* 1989a, *973,* 620–638.

Dixit, A. K. "Hysteresis, Import Penetration and Exchange Rate Pass Through." *Quarterly Journal of Economics,* 1989b, *104,* 205–228.

Fisher, M., Hammond, J., Obermeyer, W., and Raman, A. "Configuring a Supply Chain to Reduce the Cost of Demand Uncertainty." *Production and Operations Management Journal,* 1997, *6,* 211–225.

Gutierrez, G. J., and Kouvelis, P. "A Robustness Approach to International Sourcing." *Annals of Operations Research,* 1995, *59,* 165–193.

Hall, E. T. "The Silent Language in Overseas Business." *Harvard Business Review,* 1960, *38,* 87–96.

Hammond, J. H. "Quick Response in the Apparel Industry." Harvard Business School Note, no. 690–038, 1990.

Hammond, J. H. "Barilla SpA (A)." Harvard Business School Case, no. 694–046, 1994a.

Hammond, J. H. "The Beer Game: Description of Exercise." Harvard Business School Case, no. 694–104, 1994b.

Hammond, J. H., and Raman, A. "Sport Obermeyer Ltd." Harvard Business School Case, no. 695–022, 1994.

Huchzermeier, A., and Cohen, M. A. "Valuing Operational Flexibility Under Exchange Rate Risk." *Operations Research,* 1996, *44*(1), 100–113.

Jaikumar, R. "Massimo Menichetti." Harvard Business School Case, no. 686–135, 1986.

Kahn, G. "Factory Fight: A Sneaker Maker Says China Partner Became Its Rival—New Balance, Other Brands Claim Suppliers Flood Market with Extra Goods—Setback from a Local Judge." *Wall Street Journal,* Dec. 19, 2002, p. A1.

Kennedy, R. E., and Lewis, L. H. "Exporting IT-Enabled Services from Developing Countries." Harvard Business School Case, no. 702–064, 2002.

Kogut, B., and Kulatilake, N. "Operating Flexibility, Global Manufacturing, and the Option Value of a Multinational Network." *Management Science,* 1994, *40*(1), 123–139.

Kouvelis, P. "Global Sourcing Strategies under Exchange Rate Uncertainty." In S. Tayur, R. Ganeshan, and M. Magazine (eds.), *Quantitative Models for Supply Chain Management.* Norwell, Mass.: Kluwer, 1999.

Loveman, G., and O'Connell, J. "Li & Fung (Trading) Ltd." Harvard Business School Case, no. 396–075, 1995.

Magretta, J. "Fast, Global, and Entrepreneurial: Supply Chain Management, Hong Kong Style: An Interview with Victor Fung" *Harvard Business Review,* 1998, *76*(5), 102–115.

McKenney, J. L., and Clark, T. H. "Campbell Soup Company: A Leader in Continuous Replenishment Innovations." Harvard Business School Case, no. 195–124, 1994.

Moore, J., and Ihlwan, M. "Cheaper Exports? Not So Fast." *Business Week,* Feb. 2, 1998, pp. 48–51.

Narayanan, V. G., and Raman, A. "Aligning Incentives for Supply Chain Efficiency." Harvard Business School Note, no. 600–110, 2000.

Narayanan, V. G., Raman, A., and Singh, J. "Agency Costs in a Supply Chain with Demand Uncertainty and Price Competition." *Management Science,* forthcoming.

National Retail Federation. *Financial and Operating Results of Retail Stores.* New York: Wiley, 2002.

Pich, M., and Van Der Heyden, L. "Marks and Spencer and Zara: Process Competition in the Textile Apparel Industry." INSEAD Case, no. 602–010–1. 2002.

Raman, A. "Apparel Exports and the Indian Economy." Harvard Business School Case, no. 696–065, 1995.

Raman, A., Fisher, M. L., and McClelland, A. S. "Supply Chain Management at World Co., Ltd." Harvard Business School Case, no. 601–072, 2001.

Raman, A., and Rao, B. P. "Tale of Two Electronic Components Distributors." Harvard Business School Case, no. 697–064, 1997.

Raman, A., and Singh, J. "i2 Technologies, Inc." Harvard Business School Case, no. 699–042, 1998.

Rosenzweig, P. M. "International Sourcing in Athletic Footwear: Nike and Reebok." Harvard Business School Case, no. 394–189, 1994.

Shapiro, R. D., and Heskett, J. L. Logistics Strategy. St. Paul, Minn.: West, 1985.

Simchi-Levi, D., Kaminsky, P., and Simchi-Levi, E. Designing and Managing the Supply Chain: Concepts, Strategies and Case Studies. New York: McGraw-Hill, 2000.

Spar, D., and Burns, J. "Hitting the Wall: Nike and International Labor Practices" Harvard Business School Case, no. 700–047, 2000.

U.S. Congress, Office of Technological Assessment. The U.S. Textile and Apparel Industry: A Revolution in Progress—Special Report. Washington, DC: U.S. Government Printing Office, Apr. 1987.

U.S. Department of Commerce, Bureau of the Census. Current Industrial Reports, 1997–2001. Washington, D.C.: U.S. Government Printing Office, 2001.

Watson, N., and Zheng, Y. "Adverse Effects of Over-reaction to Demand Changes and Improper Forecasting." Wharton School, University of Pennsylvania, working paper, 2002.

Watson, N., and Zheng, Y. "A Demand-focused Decentralization Scheme for Serial Supply Chains." Wharton School, University of Pennsylvania, working paper, 2003.

Wheelwright, S. C., and Hayes, R. H. "Competing Through Manufacturing." Harvard Business Review, 1985, 63(1), 99–109.

Yoffie, D. B., and Austin, J. K. "Textiles and the Multi-Fiber Arrangement." Harvard Business School Note, no. 383–164, 1983.

Chapter Thirteen

Notes

1. This section benefited from the research report, "Global Food Retailing Industry," by research assistant Mariano Garrasino for Professor Rajiv Lal.
2. Quoted in Harvard Business Review 70 (Mar.–Apr. 1992): 54.
3. Much information on the company is based on the HBS case, Royal Ahold NV, case number 9–598–055.

Reference

Gielens, K., and Dekimpe, M. G. "Do International Entry Decisions of Retail Chains Matter in the Long Run?" *International Journal of Research in Marketing,* 2001, *18,* 235–259.

Chapter Fourteen

References

Clean Clothes Campaign. "Unstitching the Child Labour Debate." 1998. [www.cleanclothes.org/publications/unst1.htm].
Kabeer, N. *The Power to Choose.* London: Verso, 2000.
Litvin, D. "Empires of Profit: Commerce, Conquest and Corporate." 2003.
Rhodes, T. A. *Rhodes: The Race for Africa.* London: BBC Books, 1996.
Sale, K. *New Internationalist,* 1993.

Chapter Fifteen

Notes

1. The World Bank uses purchasing power parity indexes (1985, 1993) to produce a definition of income poverty that sets poverty thresholds as persons living below one or two dollars (U.S.) per day (World Bank, 1999, 2001a, 2002a, 2003a, 2003b). By these measures, nearly 20 percent of the world's current population, approximately 1.2 billion people, lives in abject poverty below one dollar per day, with another 1.6 billion people living below two dollars per day.

2. Similar statistics have been compiled with respect to the large-scale displacement that is being caused by the construction of the massive Three Gorges dam in China (Qing, 1998), with its planned displacement of millions of people and the potential for devastating social, economic, and environmental havoc.

3. To complement Hoffmann's "3 Faces" analysis, we could also refer to the"3 Gaps" of globalization identified by Kanter (2002) as (1) between the promise of global integration and the current reality of divisiveness, (2) between macropolicies and micro-opportunities—(she criticizes macropolicies that produce structural adjustments that may create stability but not economic growth that reaches the poor), and (3) between men and women.

4. The market construction model of investment we are proposing here is probably most applicable to large infrastructure projects—(such as dams, power plants, national irrigation programs, major utilities, and road networks), which usually have a more massive impact on local

inhabitants, with disruption of lives and habitats. Multinational retailers like Coca Cola and Phillip Morris might reasonably argue that in their overseas business, they use a traditional market exchange process to sell products directly to customers able and willing to pay for them, so consequently our MC paradigm does not apply to their global business. We agree that that seems to be so, but behind every retail product is a long supply chain of sourcing of raw materials, production, and manufacturing (not to mention the postsale environmental effects of disposal of empty soda cans or the costly health consequences, both personal and social, of smoking). If we shift the focus away from the microbehaviors of retailing and selling of such products, and toward these more macroissues of global commerce, we believe our arguments on behalf of a market construction process of interest representation on behalf of poor clients are still valid.

References

Bennet, J. "Two Studies Find the Palestinian People Impoverished and the Economy in a Shambles." *New York Times,* Mar. 6, 2003, p. 12.

"Bono and Paul on Tour." *Wall Street Journal,* May 30, 2002.

Cahill, L. S. "Toward Global Ethics." *Theological Studies,* 2002, *63,* 324–344.

Caufield, C. *Masters of Illusion: The World Bank and the Poverty of Nations.* New York: Holt, 1996.

De Soto, H. *The Mystery of Capital.* New York: Carnegie Council on Ethics and International Affairs, 2002.

"Developing World Afflicted by Diseases of Affluence." *Financial Times,* Oct. 31, 2002.

Edwards, M., and Hulme, D. (eds.). *Beyond the Magic.*

Eichengreen, B. "The Globalization Wars." *Foreign Affairs,* 2002, *81*(4), 157–164, 2002.

Garten, J. "Globalism Without Tears: A New Social Compact for CEOs." *Strategy + Business,* 2002, no. 29, pp.37–45.

Hilsenrath, J. E. "Globalization Gets Mixed Report Card in US Universities." *Wall Street Journal,* Dec. 2, 2002, p. 1.

Hoffmann, S. "Clash of Globalizations." *Foreign Affairs,* 2002, *81*(4).

Ignatieff, M. "Governance and Development in a Dynamic Global Environment." Paper presented at the Ninth Annual Harvard International Development Conference, Harvard University, Apr. 4–5, 2003.

Kanter, R. "Filling the Gaps of Globalization." *HARBUS* [Harvard Business School student newspaper], Apr. 16, 2002.

Khagram, S. *Transnational Social Movements, Networks, and Norms.* Minneapolis: University of Minnesota Press, 2002.

Khagram, S., Riker, J. V., and Sikkink, K. (eds.). *Restructuring World Politics: Transnational Social Movements, Networks, and Norms.* Minneapolis: University of Minnesota Press, 2002.

Klein, N. *No Logo: Taking Aim at the Brand Bullies.* New York: Picador USA, 1999.

Klein, N. *Fences and Windows: Dispatches from the Front Lines of the Globalization Debate.* New York: Picador USA, 2002.

Levitt, T. "The Globalization of Markets." *Harvard Business Review,* May 1, 1983.

Liamzon, T., Rogers, T., and Clugston, R. (eds.). *Towards Sustainable Livelihoods.* "Report of 1994–95 SID PIED Workshops on Civil Society and Sustainable Livelihoods." Rome, Italy: Society for International Development, and Center for Respect of Life and Environment, 1996.

Meier, G. M. *Leading Issues in Economic Development.* New York: Oxford University Press, 1984.

O'Driscoll, G. P., Holmes, K. R., and Kirkpatrick, M. *2001 Index of Economic Freedom.* Washington, D.C.: Heritage Foundation, 2001.

"The Prosperity League—The Annual Economic Freedom of the World Report." *Economist,* June 22, 2002.

Qing, D. *The River Dragon Has Come! The Three Gorges Dam and the Fate of China's Yangtze River and Its People.* Armonk, N.Y.: M. E. Sharpe, 1998.

Rangan, V. K. "Comments on Prahalad." In *Reflections: The SOL Journal on Knowledge, Learning and Change.* Cambridge, Mass.: MIT Press, 2002.

Rangan, V. K., and McCaffrey, A. "Marketing's Role in Addressing the Global Poor." Working research report, Harvard Business School, 2003.

"Rising Credibility for NGOs." *Financial Times,* February 1, 2002, p. 7.

Rodrik, D. *The New Global Economy and Developing Countries: Making Openness Work.* Washington, D.C.: Overseas Development Council, 1999.

Rodrik, D. "Globalization for Whom? Time to Change the Rules and Focus on Poor Workers." *Harvard Magazine,* 2002, 104(6).

Rostow, W. W. "The Concept of a National Market and its Economic Growth Implications." In P. D. Bennett (ed.), *Marketing and Economic Development.* Chicago: American Marketing Association, 1965.

Rostow, W. W. *The Stages of Economic Growth.* Cambridge: Cambridge University Press, 1971.

Sen, A. *Development as Freedom.* New York: Knopf, 1999.

Stiglitz, J. E. *Globalization and Its Discontents.* New York: Norton, 2002.

Tufano, P. "Building Assets Among Low Income Families." Social Enterprise Seminar, Harvard Business School, Mar. 7, 2002.

Williamson, H. "Making a Commitment to Corporate Citizenship." *Financial Times,* Feb. 12, 2003.

Wilson, E. O. *The Future of Life.* New York: Knopf, 2002.

World Bank. *Global Economic Prospects and the Developing Countries.* Washington, D.C.: World Bank, 1991.

World Bank. *Global Economic Prospects and the Developing Countries.* Washington, D.C.: World Bank, 1992.

World Bank. *Global Economic Prospects and the Developing Countries.* Washington, D.C.: World Bank, 1993.

World Bank. *Poverty Reduction and the World Bank: Progress in Fiscal 1996 and 1997.* Washington, D.C.: World Bank, 1997.

World Bank. *Poverty reduction and the World Bank: Progress in Fiscal 1998.* Washington, D.C.: World Bank, 1999.

World Bank *Voices of the Poor.* PovertyNet, 2000a. [http://www.worldbank.org/poverty/voices/index.htm].

World Bank. *Global Economic Prospects and the Developing Countries.* Washington, D.C.: World Bank, 2000b.

World Bank. *World Development Report 2000/2001:Attacking Poverty.* New York: Oxford University Press, 2001a.

World Bank. *Global Economic Prospects and the Developing Countries.* Washington, D.C.: World Bank, 2001b.

World Bank. *World Development Indicators: 2001.* Washington, D.C.: World Bank, 2001c.

World Bank. *World Development Report 2002: Building Institutions for Markets.* New York: Oxford University Press, 2002a.

World Bank. *Globalization, Growth and Poverty.* Washington, D.C.: World Bank, 2002b.

World Bank. *Global Economic Prospects and the Developing Countries: Making Trade Work for the World's Poor.* Washington, D.C.: World Bank, 2002c.

World Bank. *Global Economic Prospects and the Developing Countries.* Washington, D.C.: World Bank, 2003a.

World Bank. *World Development Report 2003: Sustainable Development in a Dynamic World.* Washington, D.C.: World Bank, 2003b.

"World Social Forum." *Financial Times,* Feb. 5, 2002, p. 8.

World Social Forum. 2003c. [http://www.forumsocialmundial.org.br/home.asp].

"World's Most Respected Companies." *Financial Times,* Feb. 1, 2002, p. iv.

The Authors

John A. Quelch is senior associate dean and Lincoln Filene Professor of Business Administration at Harvard Business School. Between 1998 and 2001, he was dean of London Business School. Prior to 1998, he was the Sebastian S. Kresge Professor of Marketing and co-chair of the Marketing Area at Harvard Business School. Quelch's current research focuses on global marketing and branding issues in emerging, as well as developed, markets. He is the author and coauthor of sixteen books, including *Global Marketing Management* (1999), *Cases in Advertising and Promotion Management* (1996), and *The Marketing Challenge of Europe 1992* (1991). His most recent book is *Business Strategies for Muslim Countries* (2001). He has published numerous articles on marketing management and public policy issues in *Harvard Business Review, McKinsey Quarterly,* and *Sloan Management Review.* Quelch serves as a director of WPP Group plc, one of the world's largest marketing services companies. He previously served as a director of easyJet plc and Reebok International Ltd. He was educated at Exeter College, Oxford University (M.A.), the Wharton School of the University of Pennsylvania (M.B.A.), the Harvard School of Public Health (M.S.), and Harvard Business School (D.B.A.).

Rohit Deshpandé is Sebastian S. Kresge Professor of Marketing at Harvard Business School. He has a B.Sc. and M.M.S. from the University of Bombay, an M.B.A. from Northwestern University, and a Ph.D. from the University of Pittsburgh. His primary research interest concerns the impact of corporate culture on global marketing strategy. In a series of research papers, he has profiled high-performance, customer-centric companies in Europe, Japan, and the United States. He has published several technical articles and monographs and was cited in an American Marketing Association study as one of the most highly published full professors in the marketing field. His most recent books include *Developing a Market Orientation* (1999) and *Using Market Knowledge* (2001). He currently serves on the editorial boards of the leading marketing journals and on the Executive Directors Council of the Marketing Science Institute. He has also served as executive director of the Marketing Science Institute from 1997 to 1999.

Rawi Abdelal is an assistant professor at Harvard Business School in the Business, Government, and International Economy Unit. His primary expertise is international political economy, and he is a faculty associate of Harvard's Davis Center for Russian and Eurasian Studies and Weatherhead Center for International Affairs. Abdelal's first book, *National Purpose in the World Economy,* won the 2002 Shulman Prize. He is at work on a new book on the politics of financial globalization.

David J. Arnold is an independent consultant and educator who works with corporations and universities around the world. From 1996 to 2002, he was assistant professor of business administration at the Harvard Business School, acting as course head of the international marketing management course for the school's M.B.A. program. He is the author of *The Handbook of Brand Management* and *The Mirage of Global Markets.* He was educated at London and Harvard University.

David E. Bell is the George M. Moffett Professor of Agriculture and Business at Harvard Business School and chairs the school's Marketing Unit. Along with coauthor Walter J. Salmon, he has written two books on retailing, *Strategic Retail Management* and *Introduction to Retailing.*

Ernst R. Berndt is the Louis B. Seley Professor of Applied Economics at the MIT Sloan School of Management and serves as director of the Program on Technological Progress and Productivity Measurement at the National Bureau of Economic Research. He is an elected fellow of the Econometric Society. Berndt received a B.A. from Valparaiso University, M.S. and Ph.D. degrees from the University of Wisconsin, and an honorary doctorate from Uppsala University in Sweden. In 1989, he was named the most cited economist in the United States under the age of forty.

Pankaj Ghemawat is the Tiampo Professor of Business Administration at Harvard Business School and the head of the school's Strategy Unit. His current research focuses on globalization and strategy. His publications include *Commitment* (1991), *Games Businesses Play* (1997), and *Strategy and the Business Landscape* (1999), as well as several dozen articles and case studies. He serves as strategy departmental editor for *Management Science* and the *Journal of International Business Studies*.

Stephen A. Greyser is Richard P. Chapman Professor (Marketing/ Communications) Emeritus, Harvard Business School (HBS), specializing in branding, advertising and corporate communications, nonprofit management, and the business of sports. He has served as *Harvard Business Review* editorial board chairman and executive director of the Marketing Science Institute. He was elected a fellow of the American Academy of Advertising for career contributions to the field. He created the HBS corporate communications and business of sports courses. He is responsible for fifteen books and monographs, numerous journal articles, and over three hundred published HBS case studies. His most recent book is the coauthored *Revealing the Corporation: Perspectives on Identity, Image, Reputation, Corporate Branding, and Corporate-level Marketing* (2003).

Morten T. Hansen is an associate professor of business administration in the Organizational Behavior and General Management Units at the Harvard Business School. He received his B.A. from University of Oslo, Norway, his M.Sc. in accounting and finance from the London School of Economics, and his Ph.D. from the Graduate School of Business at Stanford University. Hansen worked for several years as a consultant at the Boston Consulting Group, first with the London office and then with the Stockholm office.

Douglas B. Holt is an assistant professor at the Harvard Business School, where he has recently developed a new course on branding, advertising, and culture. He holds a Ph.D. in marketing from the Kellogg School at Northwestern University, an M.B.A. from the University of Chicago, and an A.B. from Stanford University. He has worked in brand management at Clorox and Dole and previously held faculty appointments at Penn State and the University of Illinois. His research has been featured extensively in the *Journal of*

Consumer Research, and he has published two books: *Cultural Branding* and *The Cultural Activist Organization.*

Rajiv Lal is the Stanley Roth Sr. Professor of Retailing at Harvard Business School. His research is concerned with the dramatic changes affecting retail and the study of profitable ways for pursuing customer loyalty. His work has been nominated for such awards as best paper in marketing and management science, best paper published in marketing science and management science in 1985, and the John D. C. Little award for the best paper published in management science and marketing science in 1990. He was also awarded, with Jagmohan Raju and V. Srinivasan, the Frank Bass award for best dissertation paper.

Daniel Litvin is the director of Percept Risk and Strategy Ltd., a new, specialist advisory firm based in London that provides analysis to companies on issues of society and reputation. He is the author of *Empires of Profit: Commerce, Conquest and Corporate Responsibility* (2003). As a staff correspondent for the *Economist,* Litvin was joint winner of the Wincott Foundation Young Financial Journalist of the Year award in 1997. He has an M.Sc. from the London School of Economics and a B.A. from Oxford University.

Yu Liu is a doctoral student in the Marketing Program at Harvard Business School. She earned her M.B.A. from Yale University in 2002 and has had previous experience working for Procter and Gamble (China). She is interested in the extent to which social and psychological determinants of consumer behavior—attitudes, evaluations, emotions, motivations, and so on—occur unconsciously and automatically.

Arthur McCaffrey is a senior research associate in the department of marketing and the Social Enterprise Initiative at the Harvard Business School. He has collaborated with faculty in research on the interaction of business and society, including social policy and social marketing, globalization and poverty, law and ethics, nonprofit management, and corporate social responsibility. His publications include teaching cases, book chapters, and articles.

Nitin Nohria is the Richard P. Chapman Professor of Business Administration at the Harvard Business School. Nohria has written and edited twelve books, and his articles have appeared in *Harvard Business Review, Sloan Management Review,* and *Strategic Management Journal.* He received his Ph.D. from the Sloan School of Management, Massachusetts Institute of Technology, and a B.Tech. from the Indian Institute of Technology, Bombay.

Ananth Raman teaches in the M.B.A., executive, and doctoral programs at Harvard Business School and codirects a multiyear study of retail operations involving many retailers. He also teaches and chairs courses on supply chain management at a number of companies. His research and teaching focus on supply chain management and retail operations. Ideas from his research have been embedded in a number of commercial planning and forecasting systems.

V. Kasturi Rangan is the Malcolm P. McNair Professor of Marketing at the Harvard Business School. He has authored four books on business marketing and channel strategy. His research on those topics has appeared in various management journals in the field. In addition to his interest in business marketing, Rangan is actively involved in studying the role of marketing in the adoption of social ideas and economic development. He served as one of the founding cochairs of the Social Enterprise Initiative at Harvard, whose faculty study the challenges of nonprofit management. Rangan has a Ph.D. from Northwestern University.

Walter J. Salmon is the Stanley Roth Sr. Professor of Retailing, Emeritus, at the Harvard Business School. He earned his B.B.A. from the City College of New York and his M.B.A. and D.B.A. from Harvard Business School. His major fields are consumer marketing and retail distribution. His teaching assignments at Harvard Business School have included retailing, consumer marketing, the marketing course in the Advanced Management Program, the Program for Management Development, and First Year Marketing.

Nick Scheele is president and chief operating officer of Ford Motor Company and a member of the company's board of directors. Scheele has served in many senior management positions at Ford Motor Company, including group vice president, Ford North America; chairman, Ford of Europe; chairman and CEO of Jaguar

Cars Ltd.; and president, Ford of Mexico. He was awarded a knighthood by Queen Elizabeth in June 2001 and has been awarded the Order of St. Michael and St. George for services to British exports.

Hans-Willi Schroiff is vice president of market research/business intelligence at Henkel KgaA, Düsseldorf, Germany. He is also a member of the executive committee of the marketing science Institute (Boston) and teaches business administration at the Rheinisch-Westfälische Technische Hochschule in Aachen, Germany. He holds a Ph.D. from Aachen Technical University and was an assistant professor of psychology at Aachen University. His research focuses on transnational management of brands, knowledge, research, and innovation.

Alvin J. Silk is the Lincoln Filene Professor Emeritus at the Harvard Business School. His research is concerned with the economics of the advertising industry and includes econometric studies of scale and scope economies of agencies and holding companies, changes in the geographical distribution and concentration level of the U.S. advertising agency industry, and intermedia substitutability. Silk is director of the Marketing Research Network and coeditor of *Quantitative Marketing Research Abstracts Journal,* elements of the Social Science Research Network.

Martin Sorrell is chief executive of WPP Group plc, a post he has held since founding the company in 1986. An economics graduate of Cambridge University with an M.B.A. from Harvard Business School, Sorrell received an honorary doctorate in business administration from London Guildhall University in 2001. In 1997, he was appointed an ambassador for British business by the Foreign and Commonwealth Office and subsequently appointed to the Office's Panel 2000 aimed at rebranding Britain abroad. In 1999, he was appointed by the secretary of state for education and employment to serve on the Council for Excellence in Management and Leadership. In 2003, he was asked to serve on the Modern Apprenticeship Task Force, launched by the Department for Education and Skills.

Hirotaka Takeuchi is dean of Hitotsubashi University's Graduate School of International Corporate Strategy. He has authored many books, including *The Knowledge-Creating Company* (with Ikujiro Nonaka, 1995), which won the 1995 Best New Book of the Year Award for the business and management category by the Association of American Publishers. *Harvard Business Review, California Management Review, Journal of Retailing, Foreign Affairs,* among others, have published his articles, and he currently writes a column for *Weekly Toyo Keizai.* Takeuchi received his B.A. from International Christian University in Tokyo, Japan, and M.B.A. and Ph.D. from the University of California, Berkeley.

Earl L. Taylor is senior vice president of Research International/ USA. He currently heads Research International's U.S. business practices in the areas of branding and communications and consumer understanding. He is a frequent speaker at national and global market research and industry conferences and has conducted numerous workshops on these and related topics. He is coauthor of *The Masterbrand Mandate* (2000), which received the Atticus 2000 award as the best publication by an employee of WPP-owned companies worldwide. Taylor holds a B.A. from Rice University and a Ph.D. from Harvard University.

Richard S. Tedlow is the Class of 1949 Professor of Business Administration at Harvard Business School, where he specializes in business history. His most recent publications include *Giants of Enterprise* (2001) and *The Watson Dynasty* (2003). He is working on a book about Andy Grove of Intel.

Luc Wathieu is an associate professor at Harvard Business School. His research, published in leading journals such as *Management Science* and *Marketing Science,* provides basic insights into the formation of consumer behavior. His current work concerns the process by which firms enable consumers to gain greater control of their marketing environment. Wathieu's Ph.D. is from INSEAD, and he was on the Faculty of the Hong Kong University of Science and Technology prior to joining Harvard.

Noel Watson is an assistant professor of business administration in the Technology and Operations Management unit at the Harvard Business School. He received his Ph.D. from the Wharton School,

University of Pennsylvania. His principal areas of interest include supply chain management and retailing, specifically decision making and execution in inventory replenishment in supply chains and in store operations in retail stores.

Gerald Zaltman is the Joseph C. Wilson Professor of Business Administration Emeritus at Harvard Business School. He holds a Ph.D. from the Johns Hopkins University, an M.B.A from the University of Chicago, and an A.B. from Bates College. Zaltman has authored numerous books and has published widely in the major journals in marketing and the social sciences. He received the American Marketing Association's Richard D. Irwin Distinguished Marketing Educator Award in 1989, the Association for Consumer Research Distinguished Fellow Award in 1990, the Knowledge Utilization Society's Thomas J. Kiresuk Award for Excellence in Scientific Research in 1992, and the JAI Press Distinguished Scholar Award from the Society for Marketing Advances in 2000. Zaltman consults with diverse clients around the world.

Index